In this classic work, first published by Pantheon in 1948, Sir Herbert Read makes an analysis of the artistic activity in children, illustrated by many reproductions of children's drawings, and shows how these drawings can be used to determine the psychological disposition of the individual child. The methods of teaching and the school environment are discussed, and in the end the purpose of education is seen as the integration of the individual in a free society. Parents, educators, teachers of art, students of psychology, anyone interested in the psychology of children and adolescents, will find this book fascinating reading and an indispensable tool for their work with young people.

EDUCATION THROUGH ART

ABOUT THE AUTHOR

A distinguished poet and one of the finest prose stylists of our time, Sir Herbert Read was also a philosopher, a student of aesthetics, one of the foremost literary critics, and an authority on the history of art. In addition to *Education Through Art,* his most famous work, he has also written almost twenty books, among them *The Art of Sculpture, Art and Alienation, Art and Society, The Philosophy of Modern Art,* and *Anarchy and Order.*

PANTHEON BOOKS
A Division of Random House
New York
5/74   PRINTED IN THE USA

EDUCATION THROUGH ART

by

HERBERT READ

*I am simply calling attention to the
fact that fine art is the only teacher
except torture.*　　*Bernard Shaw*

PANTHEON BOOKS

A Division of Random House

NEW YORK

Published in the United States by Pantheon Books,
a division of Random House, Inc., New York, and
simultaneously in Canada by Random House of
Canada Limited, Toronto.

LC: A60-2803

ISBN: 0-394-49178-5 tr
ISBN: 0-394-70640-4 pbk

Manufactured in
the United States of America

PREFACE

The writing of this book was made possible by my appointment to a Leon Fellowship in the University of London for the years 1940–1 and 1941–2, and I wish in the first place to express my gratitude to the Chairman and members of the Committee who made the award. I owe a special debt to Professor Sir Fred Clarke, the Director of the Institute of Education and one of the members of the Committee, who has given me the benefit of his friendly advice through all the stages of my research. Without his encouragement and criticism my shortcomings would have been much more obvious.

The heads of schools and teachers of art who have given me their willing co-operation are too numerous to mention: I am particularly grateful to those who have supplied me with drawings to study and to illustrate. But certain teachers who have helped me by conducting experiments and making specific observations should be named. I am particularly indebted in this sense to Miss Beatrice M. Culham (Isleworth), Mrs. Curtis (Langford Grove School), Mrs. Durell (Bedales), Miss Gwendolyn M. Fry (Milham Ford, Oxford), Miss Mary Hoad (Hall School, Weybridge, and Sir William Perkins's School, Chertsey), Miss Ruth Scrivener (Bedales and Haberdashers' Aske's School), Miss Olive Sullivan (Warrington Secondary School and Manchester Municipal School of Art), Mr. Maurice Feild (The Downs School, Colwall), Mr. H. C. Whaite (the Institute of Education, University of London), and to Miss Audrey Martin, Miss Nan Youngman and other officers of the Society for Art in Education.

Dr. Samuel Lowy very kindly read through Chapter VI and made some valuable suggestions. Dr. Thomas Munro, of the Cleveland Museum of Art (Ohio, U.S.A.), supplied me with some very relevant American literature and Mr. F. V. Morley made various inquiries for me in New York.

Mr. Henry Morris, Director of Education for Cambridgeshire, was kind enough to have drawn specially for this book the plan of the Impington Village College illustrated on page 300; this practical demonstration of idealism in education is a rallying-point for all reformers who realize the importance of the environment and the functional structure of the school.

To the British Council I am indebted for permission to reproduce a number of photographs taken in connection with the very successful exhibitions of children's drawings which they have lately been sending abroad. I must also thank Miss M. A. Rickeard and her staff at the National Gallery for the excellent photographic work they have done for me.

Finally, I must thank Miss Leonie Cohn for her very efficient secretarial assistance.   H.R.

PREFACE TO THE SECOND EDITION

In this impression a number of misprints have been corrected; I am particularly grateful to Sergeant Ivor Morrish for a most useful list of errata. Two or three correspondents have pointed out the ambiguity of the word 'impressionist' when used to describe one of the types of children's drawings, and I have substituted (p. 143 ff.) the necessary neologism 'empathetic', the meaning of which I hope will be clear in the context. Other ambiguities of expression have been corrected, and I am again indebted to various correspondents, and particularly to Miss Irene Maguinness for a valuable critical commentary.

October, 1945   H.R.

PREFACE TO THE THIRD (REVISED) EDITION

It is thirteen years since this book first appeared. A book which I first thought of as an academic treatise has established itself as a manifesto for much needed educational reforms. I have often been urged to simplify the text, but I have found this impossible. I have, however, in this revised edition relegated some further technical matter to an appendix, and I have removed a few passages which seemed to interrupt the flow of the argument. The many contributions to the subject made since 1943 have been taken into account, and forty further titles have been added to the bibliography. Except for the addition of four new colour plates, for which the blocks have been kindly lent by the proprietors of the *Sunday Pictorial*, the illustrations remain the same—children's art is not subject to fashion and there was no need to change them.

I have through this book established many contacts with teachers and psychologists throughout the world, and I continue to be indebted to them for criticism and support.

December, 1956   H.R.

CONTENTS

CONTENTS

CONTENTS

CONTENTS

VIII. THE AESTHETIC BASIS OF DISCIPLINE AND MORALITY (*Continued*)

ILLUSTRATIONS

Abbreviations: B=boy. G=girl. E=elementary, junior or primary school. P=private or preparatory school. S=secondary school. These classifications do not correspond to the present grading of the schools, but to that prevailing when the drawings were made. The first figure after 'boy' or 'girl' gives the years and the following Roman figure the months of the child's age.

MONOCHROME PLATES
(at the end of the book)

1a B 3   *'Dollies'*   HOME
Abstract 'schema'. Direct representation of purely affective or 'haptic' realization of the object. See pp. 90, 133–5.

1b G 5   *'Snake round the World and a Boat'*   HOME
Abstract symbolic drawing, entirely spontaneous in origin. See p. 189.

2   B 4   *'Father Feeding the Birds'*   HOME
The 'schema' becomes more realistic, but is still an expression of the sensational affect. The birds are represented by an abstract symbol (wavy line).

3a B 4   *Portrait*   DUNHURST (P)
Early evidence of intelligent observation and organic feeling (there is some attempt to unite the figure with its environment). The child is described as 'remarkably observant and intelligent, but most uncommunicative'. Probably introvert thinking type.

3b G 4   *'With Love from Esther'*   DUNHURST (P)
By contrast with (a), a haptic, sensational drawing. Note: nose between the eyes, where it 'feels' to be, and cheeks realized as separate entities (round outlined blobs of red), white teeth, no torso. Title given by the child indicates desire to communicate. Described as 'very imaginative, sweet-tempered, with a definite will of her own'. Probably extravert feeling type.

4a G 5 VI *Figure*   ISLEWORTH (E)
Retention of affect-schema by child of backward intellectual development. Compare Plate 9a.

ILLUSTRATIONS

4b B 5 *Figure*   ISLEWORTH (E)

Disintegrate schema of a child of poor physique with marked want of co-ordination in speech deportment and general behaviour. Compare next illustration.

5a B 6 VI *'Teacher'*   ISLEWORTH (E)

A drawing by the same child as Plate 4*b* after eighteen months' progress. Lack of co-ordination still shown in patched colouring of dress (red and green).

5b G 5 *A first figure drawing*   DUNHURST (P)

Another drawing showing lack of co-ordination (e.g., disjointed arms). This child often dissociates colour from object in separate patches. Described as 'precocious, quick-witted, and full of "pretty" mannerisms'. Probably extravert thinking type.

6 G 5 *'Kitty in the Sun'*   L.C.C. (E)

Evidence of early imaginative activity. Kitty has a clearly articulated body, but the sun has limbs only, radiating from a face. Probably introvert feeling type.

7a G 5 *'Mother, Rain and a Flag'*   ISLEWORTH (E)

Another example of the retention of the schema in a child of retarded intellectual development (compare Plate 4*b*), but in this case there is more evidence of rhythmical pattern and of extraverted sensation (the mother is actually very stout; note also the ground line, which is not characteristic of the strict schema).

7b G 5 VI *'The Family'*   THE MARLBOROUGH SCHOOL (E)

Typical drawing of a robust child of normal intelligence, for comparison with Plates 4*a*, 5*b* and 7*a*. Individual characteristics (e.g. hair) are now differentiated; head and body are distinct entities but the greater sensational value of the head is indicated by its relatively greater size; note also that the cheeks are still a distinct feature.

8a B 5 *'Ladybird'*   HOME

The child has projected himself into the object, and is giving intuitive expression to its form and volume. It is the mode of apprehension and representation which in an older child is illustrated below.

8b G 15 *'The Cat'*   HIGHBURY HILL HIGH SCHOOL (S)

The volume and structural form of the animal are intuitively apprehended, and thrown out against the formal pattern of the carpet.

ILLUSTRATIONS

xiii

12*a* B 7

Bold, imaginative, excitable, often sensational. Extraverted sensation = empathetic. (br, g)

12*b* G 7

Sociable, rather superficial, conversational, great love of colour and dancing. Extraverted thinking=enumerative. (br, g, r, y)

12*c* G 7

Solemn, intelligent, but very reserved. Introverted sensation = expressionist. (br, g)

13*a* B 7

Backward through much absence, poor physique, quiet but friendly and co-operative, reliable. Extraverted thinking=enumerative. (br, g, r, y, bl)

13*b* B 7

Boisterous, sociable, generous, a natural leader, but impulsive. Extraverted feeling—decorative. (br, g, r, bl)

13*c* G 7

Self-conscious, timid. Introverted sensation=expressionist. (br, r, g, bl, y)

13*d* G 7

Twin sister to *c*, same disposition but less advanced, careful and polite, tends to lead but no real initiative. Introverted sensation = expressionist. (br, r, g, y)

14*a* G 7

Very poor physique; ? introvert. Introverted intuitive=structural form. (br, p, y, r, g)

14*b* B 7

Normal, uninteresting. Introverted intuitive = structural form. (r, g, y)

14*c* B 7

Affectionate, unsteady, sensitive. Introverted feeling=imaginative. (y, bk, g, bl, br)

15*a* G 7

Very poor physique, quiet, happy but not sociable. Introverted sensation = expressionist. (y, br, p, g)

15*b* G 7

All-round poor development, no initiative, over-careful mother. ? Introverted sensation=expressionistic form. (y, p, g, r)

15*c* G 7

Very poor nutrition, shy, sensitive. Introverted intuitive=structura form. (r, y, bk, bl, g, p)

16*a* G 7 *'A Garden Full of Flowers'* ⎫

16*b* B 7 VIII *The same subject* ⎭ ISLEWORTH (E)

An extreme contrast in modes of plastic expression. The girl (I.Q.101) produces a structural form of extreme rigidity, every detail balanced about the radial axes. The boy (I.Q. 112) produces a completely unbalanced distribution of details (our enumerative type). See p. 161 for a comparison of stories invented by the same children about the same time as these drawings were made. From this evidence it may be deduced that the girl is of the introverted intuitive type, the boy of the extraverted thinking type—a deduction confirmed by the teacher.

17–18 *Four Types of Animal Drawing by Children*

17*a* B 13+ *'The Cattle Show'* MILL HILL (S)

Extraverted attitude. The child is trying to record what his eye actually saw. He uses the 'imbricated' method of indicating perspective (building his objects up one behind the other) and thus achieves a certain sense of rhythmical pattern. Probably extravert sensation type (impressionist) with secondary intuitive tendency (rhythmical pattern).

17*b* B 13+ *'Cattle'* MILL HILL (S)

Introverted attitude. The child is trying to realize the contour and mass of each animal as a unique structure, a vital form. Comparable with bushman and neolithic art (*cf.* Hugo Obermaier and Herbert Kuhn, *Bushman Art* (Oxford, 1930), pls. 10–15). Probably introvert sensation type (expressionist) with secondary intuitive tendency (structural form).

18*a* B 13+ *'The Cattle Show'* MILL HILL (S)

Introverted attitude. The child tries to realize the animal as a moving object within an environment, thus showing an organic feeling for wholeness. Probably introverted feeling type (imaginative) with secondary thinking tendency (organic).

18*b* G 4 XI *'Tiger'* HOME

This drawing, by a much younger child, illustrates the wholly introvert, inorganic basis of the schema. Whatever image of a tiger the child may have, she pays no regard to it, but draws merely the tiger's stripes (blue on red) and thus creates an expressive symbol which corresponds not to her perceptual awareness or conceptual knowledge of the tiger, but to her feeling for the tiger's dominant features, its 'fearful symmetry'.

19a G 7 '*Daddy*' } ISLEWORTH (E)

19b B 14 '*War Wedding*' } LEICESTER (E)

These two drawings illustrate, at infant and adolescent stages, a type of unreflective and naïve expression which is characteristic of many children, and which persists into adult life. It is essentially the mode of expression of the extraverted feeling type, a superficial decorative style, which can develop into a talent for pretty embroidery, etc., but is not capable of the qualities necessary for art of any deeper significance.

20a B 6 III '*New York*' (crayon) HOME

An unusually early example of feeling for spatial depth and vertical 'perspective'. The child had been brought up in the country near London, and had never seen New York. It is an imaginative construction, and the child's work in general was of the introverted feeling type.

20b G 16 '*Home from the Sea*' (pen) LANGFORD GROVE (S)

The same mode of expression at a more advanced stage.

21a G 16+ '*Guernsey Harbour*' QUEEN'S COLLEGE, HARLEY STREET, LONDON (S)

A more sophisticated and decorative treatment of an architectural subject (done after the teacher's verbal description). Very bright colours.

21b B 16 '*Air Raid Shelter*' CRANBROOK (S)

The balanced symmetrical form probably imposed by the subject. Essentially an enumerative type of drawing based on an extraverted thinking attitude.

22–25 '*Mind-pictures*' MILHAM FORD, OXFORD (S)

26 B 7 '*Face*' DOWNS SCHOOL, COLWALL (S)

Object and drawing space completely fused—the object not conceived as a separate entity, with an environment. Introverted sensation type, with expressionist (haptic) mode of drawing. Compare Plate 37a by the same boy.

27a   G 13   *'Earache'*   DUNHURST (P)

Haptic over-emphasis of affected organ. The colouring is also expressionistic, the left half of the face being a sickly yellow, the right half an inflamed red.

27b   G 11   *'Two Heads'*   FRENSHAM HEIGHTS (S)

The expressionistic style of the introverted sensation type influenced by an intuitive awareness of structural form.

28a   B 10   *'Samson'*   ST JOHN'S JUNIOR,
                                           RED LION SQUARE, LONDON (E)

A perfect example of the expressionist style of the introverted sensation type. Note emphatic representation of the cheek. Reminiscent of the work of the French expressionist painter, Georges Rouault.

28b   B 10   *'Samson'*   ST JOHN'S JUNIOR,
                                           RED LION SQUARE, LONDON (E)

The same subject drawn by a boy of backward intellectual development. The same expressionist style. Samson is here carrying the Gates of Gaza on his shoulders, which is a more intelligent realization of the scene than that in *a*.

29a   G 12   *'The Flower Seller'*
                                     LADY MARGARET SCHOOL, LONDON

Introverted feeling type (imaginative mode of expression) with expressionist features due to subsidiary tendencies of introverted sensation attitude.

29b   G 12   *'Tom before he became a Water Baby'*
                               SIR WM. PERKINS'S SCHOOL, CHERTSEY (S)

Introverted sensation + introverted intuition = expressionist mode with structural form.

30a   B 8   *'Out for a Walk'*   LEICESTER (E)

Extraverted attitude (sensation) = empathetic type of drawing.

30b   G 7   *Self-portrait*   LEICESTER (E)

The same type. Compare Plate 50 for a more developed stage of the same style.

31   B 13+   *'The Princess and the Swans'*   MILL HILL (S)

The strong feeling for rhythm suggests the extraverted intuitive type.

ILLUSTRATIONS

32 G 14 *'The Babes in the Wood'*

SIR WM. PERKINS'S SCHOOL, CHERTSEY (S)

Treatment of a similar literary theme by a more introverted type (imaginative=expressionist).

33 G 11 *'The Witches'* HIGHBURY HILL (S)

Here the expressionist element tends to predominate over the imaginative. Probably introverted sensation type.

34 G 11+ *'Girl at Window'* HABERDASHERS' ASKE'S

SCHOOL, ACTON (S)

This drawing, with its extraordinary poetic atmosphere, is probably an expression of an integration of all the mental functions of an introverted attitude. Haptic expression is shown in the over-emphasized head and the undersized cat; imaginative expression in the association of images (girl, cat, tree and house); organic sensibility in the drawing of the tree and the fluttering of the curtains; structural form in the general balance and spatial coherence of the design. The colours show a restrained and harmonious control of purple, yellow, white and black.

35 G 14+ *'Wild Horses'* LANGFORD GROVE (S)

36 B 14 *'The Circus'* CHARTERHOUSE (S)

These two drawings show the persistence of the introverted attitude into the adolescent stage. The vigorous rendering of the action of the horses and the animation of the whole landscape suggest the introverted thinking type with an organic mode of expression; whereas the second drawing, with its more summary treatment of detail and its strong contrasts, is more expressionist in style and suggests the introverted sensation type.

37a B 7 *'Four Trees'* THE DOWNS SCHOOL, COLWALL (P)

37b B 9 *Landscape* CLIFTON COLLEGE (S)

These two drawings illustrate the contrast between an extraverted sensation of landscape (*a*) and an introverted intuition of a similar subject (*b*), the first resulting in an empathetic style of painting, the second in a strong emphasis on structural form.

38 B 12 *'Concert'* BEDALES (S)

Introverted sensation type=impressionist style.

39 B 14+ *'The Avenue'* MILL HILL (S)

Extravert sensation type=empathetic style. (The butcher's boy, whose blue-striped smock makes such an effective contrast to the black and white snow-scene, was the boy's own addition to the set subject.)

40 G 12 *'Bridling a Pony'*

THE HALL SCHOOL, WEYBRIDGE (S)

Extravert intuitive type=rhythmical pattern.

41 G 16 *'Trying on Wellington Boots'*

THE HALL SCHOOL, WEYBRIDGE (S)

This strongly emphasized rhythmical pattern suggests the extraverted intuitive type.

42 G 15 *'Snowballing'* THE HALL SCHOOL, WEYBRIDGE (S)

Similar rhythmical pattern, with colour more harmonized (subsidiary tendency to extraverted sensation).

43a B 14 *Landscape* CHARTERHOUSE (S)

Reduction of the subject to structural form. Suggests introverted intuition type. Everything is built up in the same vertical plane—the plane of the picture-surface—a characteristic of certain types of primitive art.

43b B 14 *'An Irish Valley'* CHARTERHOUSE (S)

By contrast, a landscape produced at the same school under the same conditions by a boy of the same age. Its expressionist style suggests an introverted sensation type.

44 B 14 *Landscape* (oil) THE DOWNS SCHOOL (S)

Painted directly from nature, but with unconscious emphasis, subordination and readjustment. Structural form imposed on organic (introverted intuitive + thinking type). The boy is now a musician.

45 G 16 *'The Beach'* ⎫ LANGFORD GROVE (S)

46 B 14 *'The Farm'* ⎬ BATH SCHOOL OF ART

Another landscape contrast (Pl. 45) is the decorative style characteristic of the extraverted feeling attitude; Pl. 46 shows structural form combined with organic style, which is the combination of attitudes (intuition + thought) which the academic tradition requires and which the average school of art tries to achieve.

47 G 13 *'Gypsies'* WARRINGTON SECONDARY SCHOOL

Decorative style (? extraverted feeling type).

48 G 13 *Family Group*

WARRINGTON SECONDARY SCHOOL

This extremely sensitive drawing suggests an integrated feeling + sensation type with extravert attitude (empathetic + decorative).

EDUCATION THROUGH ART

"I defy any teacher, of art or other subject, to read it and not be influenced by it. Mr. Read deals with cold facts, but with them he builds a glowing city of gold." —*Horn Book*

"Read's work is exhilarating for its scope and . . . for the care and sensitivity of its presentation." —*San Francisco Chronicle*

'*Snowballing*'   THE HALL SCHOOL, WEYBRIDGE(S)

ILLUSTRATIONS

FIGURES IN THE TEXT

ILLUSTRATIONS

Chapter One

THE PURPOSE OF EDUCATION

So musst du sein, dir kannst du nicht entfliehen,
so sagten schon Sibyllen, so Propheten;
und keine Zeit und Macht zerstueckelt
gepraegte Form, die lebend sich entwickelt.—Goethe

1. THE THESIS

The thesis which is to be put forward in this book is not original. It was very explicitly formulated by Plato many centuries ago, and I have no other ambition than to translate his view of the function of art in education into terms which are directly applicable to our present needs and conditions.

It is surely one of the curiosities of the history of philosophy that one of the most cherished notions of this great man has never been taken seriously by any of his followers, Schiller alone being an exception. Scholars have played with his thesis as with a toy: they have acknowledged its beauty, its logic, its completeness; but never for a moment have they considered its feasibility. They have treated Plato's most passionate ideal as an idle paradox, only to be understood in the context of a lost civilization.

The thesis is: that art should be the basis of education.

Stated so briefly it has admittedly an air of paradox. But a paradox may owe its apparent absurdity to an unfamiliar use of language, and my first care will be to give a general definition of the two terms here involved—art and education. I believe that Plato's reasonable thesis has been misunderstood, firstly because for centuries there has been no understanding of what he meant by art; and secondly because there has been an almost contemporaneous uncertainty about the purpose of education.

Of the nature of art I might conceivably persuade my readers that there can be no two opinions, for the definition I offer is objective. It implies no 'views', no transcendental elements whatsoever: it

1

brings art within the world of natural phenomena and makes it in certain essentials subject to the measurements upon which scientific laws are based. But it is not likely that I shall carry general agreement on the purpose I ascribe to education, for here there are at least two irreconcilable possibilities: one, that man should be educated to become what he is; the other, that he should be educated to become what he is not. The first view assumes that each individual is born with certain potentialities which have a positive value for that individual and that it is his proper destiny to develop these potentialities within the framework of a society liberal enough to allow for an infinite variation of types. The second view assumes that whatever idiosyncrasies the individual may possess at birth, it is the duty of the teacher to eradicate them unless they conform to a certain ideal of character determined by the traditions of the society of which the individual has involuntarily become a member.

2. TWO HYPOTHESES

Both theories are equally hypothetical, if only for the reason that the mind of the new-born child remains an incommunicable mystery, and long before the veil over this mystery can be lifted all kinds of environmental influences capable of distorting his original endowment have been at work. Certain instincts—the instinct to suckle, for example—are present from the moment of birth, and one school of psychologists maintains that the experience of birth itself leaves a permanent impress on the mind. The traumata of birth are variable, and there can be nothing uniform about their psychological effects— certainly nothing that can be described as necessarily good or evil. As for the neurotic trends which quickly develop in the infant and which give colour to the hypothesis of original sin—feelings of aggressiveness, of anxiety, of jealousy and fear—these are all certainly contingent; they are by-products of the processes of physical maturation and social adaptation, and can conceivably be controlled.

The educator, then, begins with an insoluble mystery—the mind of the new-born infant. Empirical evidence, whether anthropological, physiological or psychological, gives him no precise indication of its nature. We find the same impulses in primitive tribes and in modern society; some of these impulses seem to be constant throughout human history, some appear to come and go, or to be given a widely differing degree of significance at different times. How these impulses arise and how they develop; which comes first and which is most natural—we have only to ask such questions to discover the complete relativity of the moral world.[1]

The view that goodness is natural is based, however unconsciously, on the wider hypothesis of creative evolution. Good and evil are unknown to the animals, and we may if we like identify natural goodness with this natural state of innocence. But natural innocence is not a state we can recover, and remain men. At some point in the evolutionary process man acquired self-consciousness, and out of his relations with other self-conscious human beings were born those intuitive faculties to which we give the name 'moral conscience'. This moral conscience has been responsible for the development of those finer spiritual qualities in man which make up civilization, and our object as educators is not to eliminate those qualities, but to encourage their growth. At least one important psychologist (Trigant Burrow) believes that man's tragedy is that this sense of moral discrimination was allowed to disrupt the original societal consciousness that gave unity to the animal world and to primitive human communities. From this point of view the moral categories of 'good' and 'evil' are non-biological. Good may be identified, if we like, with tendencies that make for the organic unity of human associations, and evil with tendencies that destroy such unity. The primary facts, however, are not ethical at all, but merely animal; and for this reason the questions whether man was originally good or evil, or whether man is naturally good or evil, are nonsensical. The subman, like Nietzsche's superman, is *beyond* good and evil.

The hypothesis that man is naturally and inevitably evil is older than the hypothesis of creative evolution, and cannot logically include the evolutionary point of view. It implies that at some historical point there was an irrational catastrophe—a break in the evolutionary process. Man lost his animal innocence and became 'a horror to God and to himself and a creature ill-adapted to the universe'.[2] He can only enter a state of goodness or beatitude by serving his God in a prescribed way, and even then only through the intervention of

[1] Cf. F. C. Bartlett, *Psychology and Primitive Culture* (Cambridge, 1923), pp. 7–8: 'Students who have their eyes fixed upon the fundamental tendencies say that human nature never changes; those who concentrate upon the ways in which the tendencies are related to one another, and upon the ever-shifting play of external nature, assert that man moves endlessly towards the novel. Both views are, in fact, true.'

[2] *The Problem of Pain*, by C. S. Lewis (London, 1940), p. 57.

divine grace. This is the Christian doctrine of the Fall, and though it is not to be judged apart from the rest of Christian dogma, as a doctrine it has inevitably determined the practice of education during the Christian era. It led to the conception of education as a moral discipline, and in so far as Christians have contributed to the growth of the contrary conception of freedom in education, they have tended to ignore the doctrine of original sin in favour of the more optimistic outlook offered by the complementary doctrine of free will.

Rejecting the 'either/or' of good and evil in its entirety, we shall proceed on an hypothesis of *natural neutrality*. This hypothesis will be explained presently, but first let us glance at the educator's dilemma in its sociological aspects. Then the choice is seen to be between variety and uniformity: between a conception of society as a community of *persons* who seek equilibrium through mutual aid: and a conception of society as a collection of *people* required to conform as far as possible to one ideal. In the first case, education is directed towards encouraging the growth of a specialized cell in a multiform body: in the second case, education is directed towards the elimination of all eccentricities and the production of a uniform mass. The second aim involves a particular conception of the state and of the duties of its citizens—as, indeed, does the first aim. In modern terms the choice is between a totalitarian and a democratic theory of education. Though theoretically democracy may propose an ideal of 'the common man' to which all citizens should conform, and one in which all differences will be categorically eliminated, that is a conception of democracy which can only enter into an authoritarian mind. In democratic practice each individual has his birthright: he is not material to be poured into a mould and given a hall-mark.

The hypothesis of natural neutrality is the only hypothesis about human nature that can be linked logically with a libertarian conception of democracy and with a democratic conception of education. It is true that the libertarian state must, no less than the totalitarian state, have some ideal of citizenship towards which its educational system will tend. But that ideal is not, and could never be, an ideal of uniformity, nor of merely hierarchical classification. The essence of democracy lies in individualism, variety, and organic differentiation. The democratic state should be conceived as a vital organism, its limbs articulated, its functions determined and its forms proliferated by the natural mode of living.[3]

Cf. Erich Fromm, *The Fear of Freedom* (London, 1942), p. 9: 'Although there

3. A PRELIMINARY DEFINITION

Having made clear the choice I make between these necessary and fundamental assumptions, I can now give the first of the general definitions promised: it can best take the form of an answer to the question: *What is the purpose of education?*

An answer to this question is implied in a libertarian[4] conception of democracy. The purpose of education can then only be to develop, at the same time as the uniqueness, the social consciousness or reciprocity of the individual. As a result of the infinite permutations of heredity, the individual will inevitably be unique, and this uniqueness, because it is something not possessed by anyone else, will be of value to the community. It may be only a unique way of speaking or of smiling—but that contributes to life's variety. But it may be a unique way of seeing, of thinking, of inventing, of expressing mind or emotion—and in that case, one man's individuality may be of incalculable benefit to the whole of humanity. But uniqueness has no practical value in isolation. One of the most certain lessons of modern psychology and of recent historical experiences, is that education must be a process, not only of individuation, but also of *integration*, which is the reconciliation of individual uniqueness with social unity. From this point of view, the individual will be 'good' in the degree that his individuality is realized within the organic wholeness of the community. His touch of colour contributes, however imperceptibly, to the beauty of the landscape—his note is a necessary, though unnoticed, element in the universal harmony.

But, as many people will hasten to point out, this conception of organic wholeness implies potentialities of success or failure which differ in nothing but name from the old potentialities for good and

are certain needs, such as hunger, thirst, sex, which are common to man, those drives which make for the *differences* in men's characters, like love and hate, the lust for power and the yearning for submission, the enjoyment of sensuous pleasure and the fear of it, are all products of the social process. The most beautiful as well as the most ugly inclinations of man are not part of a fixed and biologically given human nature, but result from the social process which creates man. In other words, society has not only a suppressing function—although it has that too—but it has also a creative function.'

[4] It is possible that I ought to have given more emphasis to the distinction which exists, and which I believe to be fundamental, between a libertarian and an authoritarian conception of democracy, but I wish to exclude political discussions from this book and must refer the reader to two other books: *The Politics of the Unpolitical* (London, 1943) and *Anarchy and Order* (London, 1954).

evil. If an individual achieves social integration you will call him a good citizen; if he does not, you will call him bad. In this sense, if in no other, education must discriminate between good and evil inclinations, and therefore, in addition to its creative function, it must have a destructive or repressive function.

If the objection is in this manner posed abstractly, then it must be admitted. But it is really a question of social dynamics. To talk of encouraging in one direction and of repressing in another direction implies an exercise of power *from a centre*, and that is precisely the false authoritarian concept I am anxious to avoid. Evolution, history in the making, does not proceed from a fixed point. To describe the real nature of its activity some philosophers have used the word 'emergent' (Bergson used 'creative' with the same intention). But the point I wish to make is not quite covered by these terms. Freedom should not be conceived in a negative sense, as freedom *from* certain wants or restrictions. It is a state of being with positive characteristics, characteristics to be developed in all their self-sufficiency. My contention will be, that the development of these positive qualities inevitably eliminates their opposites. We avoid hate by loving: we avoid sadism and masochism by community of feeling and action. We shall not need to repress because we shall have made education a process which, in the old and literal sense of the word, *prevents* us in the ways of evil. The impulses which education will release precede and preclude the formation of those egoistic and anti-social impulses which are the present product of the social process.

Some such conception of education has been accepted by people of democratic faith for many years now, but like democracy itself, it is far from being consciously formulated or deliberately put into practice. It is not a specifically modern conception: in spite of the political limitations he placed on its application, Plato's theory of education assumes this principle of freedom. 'Avoid compulsion,' he says, 'and let your children's lessons take the form of play. This will also help you to see what they are naturally fitted for.'[5] But though there were earlier anticipations of many of its features, freedom as the guiding principle of education was first established by Rousseau. Rousseau did not by any means develop the theory to its democratic limits, and his writings even include a doctrine of sovereignty which

---

[5] *Republic*, VII, 536 (trans. Cornford). For an excellent account of Plato's conception of 'freedom through control' see W. J. McCallister, *The Growth of Freedom in Education*, ch. II.

was elaborated in a totalitarian direction by later philosophers.[6] After Rousseau came Pestalozzi, Froebel and Montessori, all of whom contributed to the growth of freedom in education; but it is not until modern times, as in the works of John Dewey and Edmond Holmes, that we get something like a theory of education fully integrated with a democratic conception of society.

Though it seems obvious that in a democratic society the purpose of education should be to foster individual growth, many problems arise when we begin to consider what methods we should adopt to this end. Growth itself is a process which has never been adequately defined. It is usually regarded as a process of gradual physical enlargement, of maturation, accompanied by a corresponding development of various mental faculties such as thought and understanding. We shall see that this is a wholly inadequate view of what is, in effect, a very complicated adjustment of the subjective feelings and emotions to the objective world, and that the quality of thought and understanding, and all the variations of personality and character, depend to a large extent on the success or precision of this adjustment. It will be my purpose to show that the most important function of education is concerned with this psychological 'orientation', and that for this reason the education of the aesthetic sensibility is of fundamental importance. It is a form of education of which only rudimentary traces are found in the educational systems of the past, and which appears only in a most haphazard and arbitrary fashion in the educational practice of the present day. It must be understood from the beginning that what I have in mind is not merely 'art education' as such, which should more properly be called visual or plastic education: the theory to be put forward embraces all modes of self-expression, literary and poetic (verbal) no less than musical or aural, and forms an integral approach to reality which should be called *aesthetic* education—the education of those senses upon which consciousness, and ultimately the intelligence and judgment of the human individual, are based. It is only in so far as these senses are brought into harmonious and habitual relationship with the external world that an integrated personality is built up. Without such integration we get, not only the psychologically unbalanced types familiar to the psychiatrist, but what is even more disastrous from the point of view of the general good, those arbitrary systems

---

[6] This development is clearly traced by Alfred Cobban in *The Crisis of Civilization* (London, 1941).

of thought, dogmatic or rationalistic in origin, which seek in despite of the natural facts to impose a logical or intellectual pattern on the world of organic life.

This adjustment of the senses to their objective environment is perhaps the most important function of aesthetic education, but there is another aspect which we shall have to consider, one which may profoundly modify our conclusions. The environment of the individual is not entirely objective: his experience is not only empirical. Within the individual are two 'interior courts' or existential states which can be externalized by the aid of the aesthetic faculties. One is somatic, and exists even in blind mutes: it is a store of imagery derived, not from external perception, but from muscular and nervous tensions which are internal in origin. In itself such 'haptic' (Gr. ἅπτειν, touch) sensibility is perhaps not important, but the neglect of this element as it appears in aesthetic expression has led to much misunderstanding of those deviations from photographic naturalism which are found in primitive and modern art.

But deeper and more significant than these proprioceptive states are those levels of the mental personality which are *subconscious*. More or less detached features of this level enter into the foreground of our awareness in the form of images. These images appear with apparent casualness during states of day-dreaming, hypnosis, or ordinary dreaming, and such imagery is a form of expression, a language, which can be 'educated'. It is one of the fundamental elements in all forms of artistic activity. We shall have to consider to what extent this imaginative activity as such should be encouraged by our methods of education.

4. SUMMARY

It is assumed, then, that the general purpose of education is to foster the growth of what is individual in each human being, at the same time harmonizing the individuality thus educed with the organic unity of the social group to which the individual belongs. It will be demonstrated in the pages which follow that in this process *aesthetic education* is fundamental. Such aesthetic education will have for its scope:

    (i) the preservation of the natural intensity of all modes of perception and sensation;

    (ii) the co-ordination of the various modes of perception and sensation with one another and in relation to the environment;

(iii) the expression of feeling in communicable form;

(iv) the expression in communicable form of modes of mental experience which would otherwise remain partially or wholly unconscious;

(v) the expression of thought in required form.

These various forms of expression will be explained and more clearly differentiated as we proceed, but the technique of aesthetic education has the following distinct aspects:

A.	Visual education	EYE =	⎫ Design
B.	Plastic education	TOUCH =	⎭
C.	Musical education	EAR =	Music ⎫ Eurhythmics
D.	Kinetic education	MUSCLES =	Dance ⎭
E.	Verbal education	SPEECH =	Poetry and Drama
F.	Constructive education	THOUGHT=	Craft

In practice it is difficult to separate visual and plastic experiences: they are both involved in any unified apprehension of the external world of space, and may be covered by the word Design. Dance and music have also a functional affinity, and, indeed, all these categories overlap in various degrees (dance with drama, for example, and design with craft). But it is feasible to regroup these techniques of aesthetic education so that they correspond to, and are an expression of, the four main functions into which our mental processes are traditionally divided:

I.	DESIGN ..	..	..	corresponding to	SENSATION
II.	MUSIC AND DANCE	..		,,	,, INTUITION
III.	POETRY AND DRAMA	..		,,	,, FEELING
IV.	CRAFT ..	..	..	,,	,, THOUGHT

This is a purely formal or descriptive classification, and its usefulness will only become obvious as we begin to accumulate facts and observations in the course of our inquiry.[7]

I shall begin with a definition of art, because I believe that to a false or inadequate use of this term all the misunderstanding of

---

[1] This classification, though arrived at independently, corresponds closely with one made by Edmond Holmes (*What Is and What Might Be*, London, 1911, pp. 164–9). Apparently elaborating John Dewey (*The School and Society*, Chicago, 1898, pp. 59–60), Holmes distinguishes six educable instincts:

Plato's theory of education is due; and if for centuries Plato has been misunderstood, I cannot hope, without some such preliminary clarification, that my own so much less graceful presentation of the same ideal will be accepted any more readily. This definition made, I shall proceed to an examination of the basic mental processes involved in art and education alike—perception and imagination. I realize that my treatment of such a subject as perception, or the related subject of consciousness, cannot appear to the scientist as anything but cursory and superficial. That is the inevitable indictment against anyone who, to establish 'values', intrudes into the world of 'facts'. My own point of departure is the aesthetic sensibility—a point of departure not very different from that of perception itself; and at no stage in my subsequent and perhaps more elaborate experience of the world do I find this element unessential. To establish its validity in the sphere of education, I find I must invade that field of experience which is labelled 'science', making use of the scientist's own instruments and terminology. But, to repeat an image I have used before, in order to keep my ground my excursions must be limited—in the nature of raids into occupied territory. If I ventured too far into the problems of perception and consciousness, I should lose my way, and perhaps my point of view. But I do assure the scientist who might happen to glance at these pages that I have the greatest respect for his methods and achievements, and that I am not out to conquer any of his territory or establish a rival power. To extend the metaphor a little farther, my proposals are federal. I

(1) the *communicative* instinct, the desire to talk and listen;
(2) the *dramatic* instinct, the desire to act.
These two instincts are related and grouped together as the SYMPATHETIC INSTINCTS.
(3) The *artistic* instinct, the desire to draw, paint and model;
(4) the *musical* instinct, the desire to dance and sing.
These two instincts are grouped together as the AESTHETIC INSTINCTS.
(5) The *inquisitive* instinct, the desire to know the why of things;
(6) the *constructive* instinct, the desire to make things.
These two instincts are grouped together as the SCIENTIFIC INSTINCTS.

This classification is again merely descriptive, but it already gives substantial importance to the aesthetic instincts. Further, it should be observed that aesthetic expression is by no means confined to what Holmes calls the artistic and musical instincts. The communicative and dramatic instincts can be expressed aesthetically in the art of poetry, and the connection between the artistic instinct and the constructive instinct, as both Dewey and Holmes recognize, is very close. It is the fifth instinct, which Holmes calls the inquisitive instinct, the desire to *know*, which stands out in sharp contrast to the rest, and which has received an overwhelming emphasis in the educational systems of the past.

10

believe that what is wrong with our educational system is precisely our habit of establishing separate territories and inviolable frontiers: and the system I propose in the following pages has for its only object the integration of all biologically useful faculties in a single organic activity. In the end I do not distinguish science and art, except as methods, and I believe that the opposition created between them in the past has been due to a limited view of both activities. Art is the representation, science the explanation—of the same reality.

Having established the relevance of aesthetics to the processes of perception and imagination, I shall then pass on to the less disputed ground of expression. Education is the fostering of growth, but apart from physical maturation, growth is only made apparent in expression—audible or visible signs and symbols. Education may therefore be defined as the cultivation of modes of expression—it is teaching children and adults how to make sounds, images, movements, tools and utensils. A man who can make such things well is a well educated man. If he can make good sounds, he is a good speaker, a good musician, a good poet; if he can make good images, he is a good painter or sculptor; if good movements, a good dancer or labourer; if good tools or utensils, a good craftsman. All faculties, of thought, logic, memory, sensibility and intellect, are involved in such processes, and no aspect of education is excluded in such processes. And they are all processes which involve art, for art is nothing but the good making of sounds, images, etc. The aim of education is therefore the creation of artists—of people efficient in the various modes of expression.

The establishing of this simple, and to some people obvious truth, will take us a long way into the jungle of psychology, and the reader might be grateful for a compass-reading of the direction I intend to take. There are at least three possibilities, and all have strong powers of attraction for me. I admire the inductive methods of Freud and his disciples: they are part of the empirical tradition of science for which I, like most Englishmen, have an innate preference. But these methods, however valuable as a description of mental processes, and as a healing therapy, have not been very successfully applied to the problems of expression. Here, in one direction, the aesthetician will tend to rely on the physiologists, particularly on Kretschmer and Pavlov, who have correlated modes of expression and somatic processes in the endocrine and nervous systems; and in another direction on the psychology of Jung, who has had far more success than Freud

in the interpretation of those super-individual or collective phenomena which take the form of myth and symbol, and are so much
involved in unconscious modes of expression. There is, however, still
another pull on the aesthetician venturing into the psychological field,
and I am not sure that it is not the strongest of all. This comes from
the Gestalt school and is strong precisely because it provides an
explanation where explanation is most needed—at the actual formative moment. It provides a principle of discrimination, and a basis
for mental evolution. It tries to solve the problem of why one form
should be preferred to another: the still more fundamental problem
of why form, as distinct from chaos, should exist at all. The application of Gestalt psychology to aesthetics has proceeded slowly, but no
firmer ground has ever been won, and the reader will see to what an
extent I rely on it in the pages which follow.[8]

Here let me add, that if a similar pointer-reading is needed for my
more metaphysical tendencies, then having no pretensions to originality in this direction, I should indicate the same sympathetic
attraction. At any rate, the William James Lectures delivered at
Harvard in 1934–5 by Wolfgang Koehler, one of the leaders of the
Gestalt school of psychology, and subsequently published as *The
Place of Value in a World of Facts* (London, 1940), seem to me to
express the kind of attitude towards the problems of philosophy and
science which, had I the training and knowledge, I might venture
to share and support. In particular, Koehler's doctrine of 'psycho-
physical isomorphism' removes for all time that tiresome bogey
dualism, and its equally tiresome companion, monism, spectres
which have for so long haunted philosophy with such disintegrating
effects. Koehler provides a theory of nature which satisfies the
aesthetician, who is so intimately concerned with the correspondences
between matter and mind.

The further development of my thesis, that art should be the basis
of education, takes us into the sphere of practical pedagogics, and
here again I have to offer my apologies to the experts. But education,
unfortunately for the educators, is a subject in which most people
can claim experience—if only the experience of the guinea-pig. We
have memories of our own schooldays, and have tested the adequacy
of what we then acquired in the post-graduate 'school of life'. Many

---

[8] A full and convincing application of Gestalt psychology to the study of art and
education is now given in *Art and Visual Perception: a psychology of the creative
eye*, by Rudolph Arnheim (Berkeley, California, 1954; London, 1956).

of us have become parents, and our love for our children has been the measure of our sense of the inadequacy of the existing system of education. These qualifications I can claim, and in addition a certain amount of teaching at the university stage. But all this leaves me very conscious of the far greater claims of those who, day-in, day-out, struggle with the raw material—with the multiple problems of the infant school and kindergarten, the day school and the boarding school; with problems of equipment and environment; with problems of economic security and professional integrity. I have seen enough of this agonizing reality to feel very humble in the presence of these brave men and women, and it would cause me acute distress if anything in the pages that follow were to be construed as talking down to them. I write from no priggish altitude, and if at any time any suggestion of condescension becomes falsely apparent, the reader who is a teacher has only to turn to the ninth chapter to see how vital a function is given to his or her calling, not only in the school, but also in the wider life of the community.

Chapter Two

THE DEFINITION OF ART

And the same is, of course, true of the appeal of a work of art: we are in contact with it by virtue of its structural qualities.—K. Koffka

1. A POINT OF DEPARTURE

Before we begin the discussion of our main problem, the value of art as an educative medium, I have undertaken to give the reader a definition of art. I am conscious of having done this already in a number of books, but it would be presumptuous to assume that my present readers are familiar with them. In any case, it is always possible to improve on the definition of a category like art, which is one of the most elusive concepts in the history of human thought. That it has been so elusive is explained by the fact that it has always been treated as a metaphysical concept, whereas it is fundamentally an organic and measurable phenomenon. Like breathing it has rhythmic elements; like speech, expressive elements; but 'like' does not in this case express an analogy: art is deeply involved in the actual process of perception, thought and bodily action. It is not so much a governing *principle* to be applied to life, as a governing *mechanism* which can only be ignored at our peril. My final contention will be, that without this mechanism, civilization loses its balance, and topples over into social and spiritual chaos.

I shall begin this definition at what may at first seem a distant point, situated within the realm of science rather than of art. But such a point of departure is essential to my purpose, which is to build up a conception of art as a part of the organic process of human evolution, and therefore as something quite distinct from the more or less arbitrary and ornamental activity which is all the function that biologists, psychologists and historians usually ascribe to it.

2. FORM

The question, what is art? is one which many wise men have tried

14

to answer, but never to everybody's satisfaction. Art is one of those things which, like air or soil, is everywhere about us, but which we rarely stop to consider. For art is not just something we find in museums and art galleries, or in old cities like Florence and Rome. Art, however we may define it, is present in everything we make to please our senses. We shall see presently that there is a kind of hierarchy in art, and that many qualities go to make a work of art of the highest type. But there is no genuine work of art which does not *primarily* appeal to our senses—our physical organs of perception—and when we ask: What is art? we are really asking what is the quality or peculiarity in a work of art that appeals to our senses. In the next chapter we shall find that according to one school of psychologists, an aesthetic element is present in perception itself.

Because the senses are so universal, so open to all kinds of impressions and so interwoven one with another, just because the mind is like an automatic telephone exchange with senses ringing up every second and asking to be connected in every direction—for that reason there is no simple answer to our question: What is art? But we can say, to begin with, that common to all works of art is something we call FORM. This is quite a simple short word, and it has a meaning familiar to everybody. If someone plays well, or runs well, or does anything well, we say that he or she is 'in good form'. And by this we mean, that they do what they undertake to do as well as possible. We mean that their bodies are in good trim, that they see and hear and act quickly and efficiently. If we use the same word about singing a song or playing a violin or acting in a play, then we are already using 'form' in connection with art.

We also use 'form' as a verb. We 'form' fours. We 'form' cricket clubs and football teams. We 'form' a society for nature study or for political agitation. In this sense the word 'form' means something like 'shape'; it means that we give shape to a number of people for a particular purpose. But we go further and say, for example, that ice 'forms' over a pond, or that dewdrops 'form' on the twig of a tree. Then 'form' does actually mean 'take shape'.

'Form' in our discussion of art has the same meaning. The form of a work of art is the shape it has taken. It does not matter whether it is a building, or a statue, or a picture, a poem or a sonata—all these things have taken on a particular or 'specialized' shape, and that hape is the form of the work of art.

I have said that the work of art 'takes on' its shape, but actually

15

the shape is given to it by a particular person, and that person we call an artist; and an artist, we must remember, is not only a man who paints pictures, but equally a man who makes music, or poetry, or furniture—even shoes and dresses. There are all kinds and degrees or artists, but they are all people who give shape to something.

If it is now clear what is meant by the form of a work of art, let us next ask: what is *good* form in art? For if we can say that one form is better than another, and that the work of art which pleases us best is the work of art with the best form, then we shall have explained the real meaning of art. The best works of art, we shall have said, are the works with the best form, and one form is better than another because it satisfies certain conditions.

What are these conditions? Generally, of course, they are the conditions which give our senses the most pleasure, and by that we mean the conditions which give pleasure, not only to one sense at a time, but also to two or more senses working together, and finally to that reservoir of all our senses which is our mind.

But this is where our difficulties begin. For what pleases one person does not necessarily please another. We even go so far as to say that one man's meat is another man's poison.

What we have to find, therefore, is some touchstone outside the individual peculiarities of human beings, and the only touchstone which exists is *nature*. And by nature we mean the whole organic process of life and movement which goes on in the universe, a process which includes man, but which is indifferent to his generic idiosyncrasies, his subjective reactions, and temperamental variations.

But nature is so immense and multiform that at first sight it would seem to be quite impossible to select any general or universal features which we could then take as the touchstone for the form of things we are to make. And actually, of course, artists have not usually sought for such a touchstone. They have *sensed* it: they have found it instinctively. But what I am now going to suggest is, that the elementary forms which men have instinctively given to their works of art are the same as the elementary forms which exist in nature.

What are these forms in nature? They are present in the vast interstellar spaces of the universe as well as in the most microscopic cells and molecules of matter. A scientist will make a model to show us, for example, the orderly arrangement of atoms inside a crystal of diamond. We then see that the atoms form a regular pattern, a pattern which the scientist himself will describe as 'beautiful'. Proof that this pattern is not invented by the scientist, but does actually exist, can be obtained by passing an X-Ray through, say, a crystal of kaliophilite (potassium aluminium silicate). The pattern of the atoms within the crystal is then translated by the X-Ray into a formal arrangement of light and shade which can be recorded on a photographic plate.

But to observe such patterns in nature we do not necessarily need the aid of a microscope. If we are to compare art and nature, we can simply begin with what the human eye sees in its daily activity, but ignoring, of course, all that has been formed by human hands. We must also put on one side what I will call the accidental forms of nature. Rocks thrown up in volcanic eruptions, trees blasted by lightning—these are not universal or absolute forms, and so do not for the moment concern us.

We are then left with such forms as all unimpeded growth assumes: the growth of crystals, the growth of vegetation, of shells and bones and flesh. All these processes of growth take on definite shapes and proportions, and if we can find general laws[1] which govern these shapes and proportions, then we shall have found in nature a touchstone of form which we can apply to works of art.

What we do find are certain mathematical or geometrical equations. Many centuries ago Plato and Pythagoras had already found in *number* the clue to the nature of the universe and to the mystery of beauty. Science and philosophy have undergone many transformations since that time, but the final result is the same, and goes to show that number, in the sense of mathematical law, is the basis of all the forms which matter assumes, whether organic or inorganic in kind. Moreover, we do not find a mathematical chaos, as might be the case if every form had its own mathematical equation: the truth is rather that the innumerable forms, of lifeless substance no less than of living things, obey a definite number of comparatively simple laws. That is to say, the growth of particular things into particular shapes is determined by forces acting in accordance with certain inevitable mathematical or mechanical laws.

The bee's cell might be taken as a simple example. Each cell in a honeycomb is a close approach to a perfect mathematical figure—or rather, to an uncompleted perfect mathematical figure, for one end is

[1] I am aware that the modern scientist does not use the word 'law' to describe these physical events, but the word has a significance for the general reader which does not involve any ambiguity.

left open. In the technical language of mathematics it is a hexagonal prism with one open or unfinished end, and one trihedral apex of a rhombic dodecahedron. And further, this form is not only the strongest possible structure for a mass of adjacent cells, but theoretically it is also the most economical, the one which requires the least possible amount of labour and wax. But it is no longer assumed that economy is the object of this minimal configuration: it is merely one of the characteristics of the given structure.

It is no wonder that ancient philosophers believed bees to be endowed with reason, but though there are naturalists who still speak as though the facts could only be explained by the bee's possession of a special instinct, we now know that actually the form of the cell is due to an automatic play of physical forces. 'The direct efforts of the bee or wasp may be supposed to be limited . . . to the making of little hemispherical cups, as thin as the nature of the material permits, and packing these little round cups as close as possible together. It is then conceivable, and indeed probable, that the symmetrical tensions of the semi-fluid films should suffice . . . to bring the whole system into equilibrium, that is to say, into the configuration which the comb actually assumes.'[2] If we remember the high degree of heat which is generated within the bee's hive, and the extreme thinness of the waxen walls, then it is possible to realize how the cells automatically assume a shape of mathematical regularity, that is to say, of minimal configuration. The process may be observed by blowing a mass of soap bubbles into a glass bowl, for the bubbles will tend to assume the shape of hexagonal cells as their surfaces come into contact and press against each other. A uniform flattening takes place with a tendency for the sides to meet at equal angles of 120°.

Many other tissues take on a mathematically regular form. The lens of a water-beetle's eye, for example, is exactly like a cross-section of a honeycomb, when seen under a microscope. A water-beetle is a sizable thing, but floating in the sea are millions of millions of microscopic animals and plants called radiolaria and diatoms. You would think that nature would be rather careless about the form of such countless objects, but there is nothing, perhaps, more 'beautiful' in nature than these regular but intricate forms—all, apparently, shaped

[2] D'Arcy Wentworth Thompson: *On Growth and Form* (new edn., Cambridge, 1942), pp. 542–3. I would like to pay a layman's tribute to this remarkable book, which should be regarded, not only as one of the classics of scientific literature, but as a work of fundamental importance for the understanding of all the problems of natural philosophy, not excluding the nature and scope of art.

by the same mathematical and mechanical laws that determine the forms of crystals and cells, snowflakes and beetles' eyes.

What I wish to stress at this point is that when we call such things 'beautiful', we are really admitting that certain mathematical proportions give rise to that emotion in us which we normally associate with works of art. What I am going to suggest presently is that when, without thinking, we use the same adjective to describe such apparently different things, we are not being careless or illogical, but are unconsciously identifying similar qualities.

But first let me remove a possible misunderstanding which our consideration of the bee's cell and of crystals might have led to—the notion that the beauty of natural forms is necessarily rectilinear and regular. That is far from being the case. There are other regular forms which are curvilinear, and there are a great many forms, perhaps the majority, which while obeying recognizable mathematical laws, are irregular and contorted. Of the first class, good examples are provided by the spiral conformations of many natural growths. Spirals are of more than one kind, but the logarithmic spiral is the one most commonly found in nature and most beautifully represented by certain shells. In their growth these shells—the pearly nautilus, for example, or the ammonite—obey absolutely uniform mathematical laws, due to a varying ratio in the rate of growth of the outer as compared with the inner surface of what would be, if the rates of growth were uniform, a tubular or conical shell. The same logarithmic spirals are to be found in plant growths, such as the florets of a sunflower, the scales of fir-cones, or the arrangement of leaves on the stems of most plants (phyllotaxis).

For an example of asymmetrical form in nature we might take any of the individual bones which make up a skeleton. There is every reason to believe that not only in its internal structure, but also in the actual form it assumes, the bone is a mathematical solution of a problem in strain and in stress. The bone grows, so to speak, exactly where there is most strain, and generally it conforms in its growth to the lines of tension and pressure to which it is submitted: an automatic effect of mechanical forces. The beauty which we recognize in modern cantilever bridges, where the form is a geometrical solution of a problem of strain and stress, of tension and pressure, must be due to the unconscious acceptance of the naturalness of a rational or mathematical structure: the bridge and the bone possess the same fitness, the same appropriateness.

19

We might venture the conclusion that there is not a form in nature which is not due to the operation of mechanical laws under the impulse of growth. The rate of growth, the basic material, the function or use may vary, but the laws of physics do not vary. 'The forces that bring about the sphere, the cylinder or the ellipsoid are the same yesterday and to-morrow. A snow-crystal is the same to-day as when the first snows fell' (D'Arcy Thompson). It is to these forces that we owe, not only the variety, but also what might be called the logic of form. And from the logic of form proceeds the emotion of beauty.[3]

3. NATURE AND ART

Let us now consider the forms of nature with the forms of art. I will leave out, of course, those art forms which are a deliberate imitation of natural forms—vessels in the shape of animals, dishes in the shape of leaves, etc. These are usually unintelligent facsimiles with no appreciation of the structure of what they imitate. The examples I shall take are of two kinds: they are either unconscious, that is to say, intuitive copies of the internal structure of natural forms; or they are due to the deliberate application of laws derived from the structure of natural forms.

Take the case of the humble jug. Jugs are of all shapes and sizes, but if we held a census of jugs, I think we should find that one form had predominated ever since pottery was invented: the pear-shaped or unduloid jug. Though it is pear-shaped I do not think this form is usually derived from the fruit. The form of the fruit itself is due to a basic law of physics. If you take a suitable liquid, a little denser than water and incapable of mixing with it, and pour a little into a glass of water, it spreads over the surface and gradually turns into a hanging drop, nearly hemispherical; but as more liquid is added the drop sinks, or rather grows downwards, still clinging to the surface film; and the balance of forces between gravity and surface-tension stretches out the drop until it assumes the pear-shaped or unduloid form, and finally breaks in two. But at the moment of greatest tension the drop assumes the pear shape; and this is a shape assumed, not only by the pear, but by many other objects in nature—the shells of

[3] In a more recent work (*Icon and Idea*, 1955) I have suggested that there are two principles with correspondingly distinct psychological processes: a principle of *vitality* derived from an intense awareness of animal forms; and a principle of *beauty* based on geometrical intuition. These two principles may be correlated with the subjective and objective aspects of art discussed in this chapter.

tiny molluscs, various seed-pods and cellular organisms. What I am suggesting is that when a coffee-pot or milk-jug assumes this shape, and we find it beautiful, it is because the potter, in shaping the pot, has instinctively given it the tense form of a liquid drop. Once having discovered this essential form, he can, of course, play variations on it: he can, for example, turn it upside down, elongate or depress it, though the limit of such variations is probably strict.

I now pass to a more complicated example. We find that many organisms—I am thinking particularly of plant growth—conform to a well-known numerical series—2:3, 3:5, 5:8, 8:13, 13:21, etc.—a series which has several curious mathematical properties. If arranged as fractions for instance, the denominator of each fraction is the numerator of the next; and each denominator is the sum of the preceding numerator and denominator. This series is closely connected with the Golden Section, that ideal proportion which is obtained by dividing a line in such a way that the shorter part is to the longer part as the longer part is to the whole. Now the presence of these proportions in plants can be explained as due to the simple operation of mechanical forces, just as the mathematical form of the bee's cell was explained. What is significant, for our present purpose, is that if we are sensitive to form we find the proportions represented by these figures especially pleasing, and a work of art which is based on them is, other things being equal, invariably pleasing. The steeple of St. Bride's in Fleet Street, or the tower of Saint-Sernin at Toulouse, are examples of the application, perhaps unconscious, of this principle: the intervals between each storey diminish as the structure of the tower rises in the same proportion as the intervals between the nodules in a shoot of bamboo or rush.

These are examples taken at random, and I confess that I have not had them measured by a mathematician and found correct. But the superficial similarity is at once apparent, and it would not be a difficult matter to find even more striking examples of the Golden Section in arthitecture.[4]

[4] That architecture is capable of taking over, not merely the proportions found in vegetable growth, but even its mechanical structure, was illustrated in the *Architectural Review* (January, 1937) by the Czech architect, Karel Honzik. The *Victoria Regia*, or South American water-lily, has a leaf about six feet wide which can support a large dog ar a small child on the water; the struts of this leaf, which serve the same purpose as the veining of an ordinary leaf, are enormously developed and correspond closely to the structural form evolved by engineers for a reinforced concrete roof-span. Indeed, Sir Joseph Paxton once, when explaining his plans for the Crystal Palace, held up a leaf of that water-lily and remarked:

But we must now leave the question of form, because form does not exhaust the properties of a work of art. There is also, to take the most nearly related property, *colour*.

4. COLOUR

Properly speaking, form cannot be perceived except as colour: you cannot separate what you see as form from what you see as colour, because colour is simply the reaction of the form of an object to the rays of light by means of which we perceive it. Colour is the superficial aspect of form. Nevertheless, colour has a very important part to play in art, because it has a very direct effect on our senses. The range of colours, indeed, might be placed in a series to correspond with the range of our emotions; red corresponding with anger, yellow with joy, blue with longing, and so on. There is probably a simple physiological explanation for this correspondence, the pleasure or discomfort being determined by the frequency with which the waves or rays of light strike the retina of the eye. That is the physiological aspect of colour, but colour has also its psychological aspects. Some people like or dislike colours because they associate them with their general likes or dislikes—they like green because they associate it with springtime, or blue because it reminds them of Italian skies; they dislike red because they associate it with danger, or mad bulls. These likes and dislikes perhaps have their source in the unconscious, and

'Nature was the engineer, providing the leaf with longitudinal and transverse girders and supports that I, borrowing from it, have adopted in this building.' And the architect Honzik, in the article I have mentioned, sums up the whole matter in these words: 'The cone, the pyramid, parallel lines, the plane and the globe are all "constants" in Nature's technique. Nature seeks an ideal state of equilibrium between these forces. The moment she begins to succeed she ceases to be formless; the result being an embodiment of the shapes characteristic of flowers, crystals and other organisms. We are told that everything on earth is changing, and so moving; but an equally universal law governs its movement: an urge to find a condition of harmony or rest; harmony, maturity or crystallization. The shape in which matter achieves a balance of strength is its perfection, a solution of its own particular problem in which there is no waste or superfluity. If we add to, or take something from, that perfection, the shape loses its equipoise, its characteristic appearance, and has to start in quest of both afresh. In the same way, human inventions arise from the will of man, and move towards the intrinsic perfection of a final form that can only be invalidated by the emergence of new conditions.'
  For a demonstration of the conscious application of mathematical laws in medieval architecture, see *The Gothic Cathedral*, by Otto von Simson (New York and London, 1956).

are, at any rate, part of the temperamental disposition of each individual. Such associative values have nothing to do with the aesthetic value of colour as such, though they may have a great deal to do with any particular individual's reaction to a particular work of art. In aesthetic experience we enter intuitively into the nature of the colour, appreciate its depth, or warmth, or tonality—that is to say, its objective qualities—and then proceed to identify these qualities with our emotions.[5]

In a work of art we are rarely concerned with a simple reaction to a single colour, though it has been demonstrated that the apprehension or appreciation of a single colour may be aesthetic. More generally we are concerned with several colours, and it is according to whether they make a harmony or a discord that we judge a visual work of art. But again there is probably a physical explanation, as there is in the case of music. Just as from a scale of notes you can, in accordance with certain laws of tonality, produce either harmony or discord of sound, so from the scale of the spectrum you can produce a similar harmony or discord of colour.

In considering the use of colour in the work of art we must remember two further facts: first, that the recording instrument, that is to say, the human eye and the nervous system with which it communicates, varies in efficiency from one individual to another, much in the way that the efficiency of radio receiving-sets varies. Secondly, in using colour to depict an object, that is to say, to give a pictorial imitation of an object, the artist will find that colour has certain visual properties which can be used to suggest space and therefore three-dimensional form— red, for example, seems to come out from the plane of the canvas, blue to sink into it. But these are technical niceties which we may leave aside in the present very general description of the properties of a work of art.

To resume: we have found two elements present in every plastic work of art: *form* which we have traced to the operation of universal laws of nature, and *colour* which is the superficial property of all concrete forms, and which serves to emphasize the physical nature and the texture of such forms. There are certain secondary properties which arise from the combination of two or more forms—from the way one form is related to another, or to several others—forms within

---

[5] Cf. Edward Bullough: 'The Perceptive Problem in the Aesthetic Appreciation of Single Colours' (*Brit. J. Psych.* II, 406 ff.) and 'The Perceptive Problem in the Appreciation of Simple Colour-combinations' (*Ibid.* III, 406 ff.).

forms, so to speak. *Balance, symmetry,* and *rhythm* are all properties of this kind, and their purpose is to suggest the static or dynamic, the passive or active condition of the related forms. *Composition* is the sum-total of all these secondary properties, including colour, and the purpose of composition is to organize all the physical elements which make up a work of art into a coherent pattern, pleasing to the senses. If the work of art involves an illusion of *space*, then all these properties must contribute to that illusion.

5. THE SUBJECTIVE ASPECT

So far we have been considering the work of art as though it were a natural phenomenon, an object focused by a sensitive instrument of uniform scientific precision. A good deal of aesthetics has proceeded on this assumption, and has resulted in a formalism far too limited to include within its scope the reality of art. It was Theodor Fechner, 'the father of modern aesthetics', who first broke away from this barren formalism by introducing the factor of association, and since his time (his principal work was published in 1867) much work has been done on what might be called the subjective aspects of art. For the work of art, however concrete and objective, is not constant or inevitable in its effect: it demands the co-operation of the spectator, and the energy which the spectator ' puts into' the work of art has been given the special name of 'empathy' (Einfühlung). Lipps, who gave currency to the term in aesthetics, defined empathy as 'the objectivated enjoyment of self', and it is often assumed that it means merely that the spectator projects into the work of art his own emotions or feelings. But this is not the proper meaning. By 'empathy' we mean a mode of aesthetic perception in which the spectator discovers elements of feeling in the work of art and identifies his own sentiments with these elements—e.g., he discovers spirituality, aspiration, etc., in the pointed arches and spires of a gothic cathedral, and can then contemplate those qualities in an objective or concrete form: no longer as vaguely apprehended subjective feelings, but as definite masses and colours.[6] But obviously such 'empathetic' perceptions

[6] The best definition of empathy I have ever discovered is given by Eduard Spranger in *Types of Men* (trans. Pigors, Halle, 1928), pp. 92–3: 'The expression used by Lipps, that empathy is objectivated enjoyment of self, is liable to be misunderstood. For one might think that this ego is the real ego in the sense of the really desiring, suffering and acting ego. But this putting oneself in another's place and empathic action is obviously something wholly different from the

will vary from individial to individual, according to emotional or psychological disposition. This is, indeed, the next important fact to recognize: namely, that the appreciation of art, no less than its creation, is coloured by all the variations of human temperament.

At first sight it would seem that in deserting the objective unity and form of the work of art, aesthetics merely flounders into a chaos of subjectivism, but many psychologists have worked on this problem (Binet, Dessoir, Bullough—we shall have occasion to mention some of their contributions to the subject in a later chapter) and as a result it has been possible to classify types of aesthetic perception, and to show that the varieties of art (or variations of *style*) correspond to these perceptive types.

It is far from my wish to deny the existence of a general factor in aesthetics. Both in the creation and the appreciation of the work of art there exists a state of aesthetic consciousness for which we can find physiological or even physical correlates. It is possible that the mental processes involved can be expressed in general terms,[7] just as, for example, the laws of organic growth can be expressed in general terms. But we are now concerned with a description of the species which are produced by a generic process, and we find that they can be

aesthetic attitude. In aesthetic contemplation we do not find in the particular object our real self but only "something psychical". The liveliness of a red is not our vivacity, but there is, in the specific object (for instance, in the perceived or imagined red) "something vivacious", and it is this which radiates back and gives our self the corresponding quality. One must not call these cognized feelings but, more accurately, feelings of empathy. Our soul, in the aesthetic state, apprehends in the object (besides the qualities which can be conceptually determined) psychical accompanying qualities, and when we live in these concretely our soul expands above the real sphere of its struggle with the external world to a free and floating imaginative self. Foreign selves too can be absorbed aesthetically. Then, however, the emphasis does not lie on the understanding or affirming of their individual existence and behaviour, but on a psychic empathy of our subjectivity which is expanded by the object and into it.'

A simpler definition is given by Martin Buber in *Die Rede, die Lehre, und das Lied* (Leipzig 1920), p. 34: 'Empathy means to glide with one's own feeling into the dynamic structure of an object, a pillar or a crystal or the branch of a tree, or even of an animal or a man, and as it were to trace it from within, understanding the formation and motoriality (Bewegtheit) of the object with perceptions of one's own muscles: it means to "transpose" oneself over there and in there.'

[7] Cf. H. J. Eysenck: 'The Experimental Study of the "Good Gestalt"—a New Approach'—*Psych. Review*, vol. 49 (1942), 344–64, where a 'law of aesthetic appreciation' is convincingly presented in the following terms: 'The pleasure derived from a percept as such is directly proportional to the decrease of energy capable of doing work in the total nervous system, as compared with the original state of the whole system.'

classified according to the psychological types through which the process operates.

We shall have a good deal to say about the psychology of types in a later chapter: at present the reader is asked to accept the statement that all the researches of modern physiology and psychology (including Kretschmer, Pavlov, Jaensch, Pfahler, Jung and Sheldon, upon whom we shall mainly rely) have not departed materially from a basic classification corresponding to the traditional classification of temperaments, which in its turn corresponds with an equally traditional classification of mental activities. According to this traditional classification, there are four basic types of mental activity—thinking, feeling, sensation and intuition; and according to the balance and scope of these activities within a particular individual, that individual will belong to a corresponding psychological type.

It may be fully admitted that this result is determined by such factors as endocrine constitution, cortical motility, and other purely physiological factors. For the moment we are not concerned with the factors which determine individual variations, but only with the final product—the personality[8] of the individual.

Just as we may recognize four[9] types of personality corresponding

[8] It may be desirable at this point to introduce certain definitions which will be observed throughout this book. They are based on a survey of current usage made by W. A. Willemse, *Constitution-Types in Delinquency*, London, 1932, pp. 226–7. *Temperament* includes affectability, tempo and intensity of impulse, and is closely connected with the neuro-glandular system and the relations of the cortex to the sub-cortex. *Character* is a product of interactions between the individual impulses (instincts), temperament, and the sociological environment; it therefore includes primarily the sociological attitudes and sentiments, and especially the aim-aspect, purposiveness or direction of the manifestation of these attitudes and sentiments, with particular stress on ethical values. *Constitution* is defined by Kretschmer as 'The totality of individual qualities which depend on heredity'. *Personality* is the most inclusive term, and is used to indicate the total individual as he manifests himself in all social relations. Certain aspects of physique are included ('imposingness' or 'insignificance', etc.) but personality is mainly determined by the combination of temperament, character and *intellect*. Intellect seems to be the only new factor present in personality, and it is closely related to the cortex of the brain, where even Pavlov, for example, allows that a controlling centre may be situated.

[9] Some writers (E. Spranger and F. Müller) recognize six basic types, but these further elaborations do not affect our argument—the corresponding types of art could be correspondingly elaborated. Dr. Joan Evans, who has made the most direct study of psychological types in their relation to the visual arts (*Taste and Temperament*, London, 1939) confines herself to four basic types. Dr. W. H. Sheldon (*The Varieties of Temperament*, New York and London, 1942) distinguishes three psychosomatic types (viscerotonic, somatotonic, and cerebrotonic) with dynamic and static variables.

to the four modes of mental activity, and having four distinct modes of perception, so it is possible to recognize four distinct modes of aesthetic activity expressed in works of art. This result may also be reached by an empirical classification of the historical styles of art, and the unsystematic phraseology of the history of art does in fact include four distinct styles or types. There is the style known variously as realism or naturalism, which consists in making as exact an imitation as possible of the objective facts present in an act of perception; there is the style known variously as idealism, romanticism, superrealism, fantastic or imaginative art which, while making use of images of visual origin, constructs from these an independent reality. Thirdly, there is the style which we call expressionistic, and which is determined by the artist's desire to find a plastic correspondence for his immediate sensations, his temperamental reactions to a perception of experience. Finally, there is the style which strives to avoid all personal elements and invites an aesthetic response to the purely formal relationships of space, mass, colour, sound, etc. This style is sometimes called abstract, but 'constructive', 'absolute', or 'intuitional' would be more exact terms.

Though it is easy to make a theoretical classification of art into four main types corresponding to the four main types of personality, in reality all the types, whether of men or their artifacts, merge into one another. Realism may be tinged with idealism, idealism with expressionism, and all three types with constructivism. Extreme modes of representation, no less than extreme modes of apprehension, are rare, and though we should resist the temptation to construct a hierarchy of types, in art as in men, nevertheless it may be doubted whether those works of art which humanity has for centuries accepted as universal in their appeal, are ever of a pure type. Great works of art are complex and various in their appeal.

It is the considerable achievement of modern psychology and of modern art to have made the world conscious of these facts, and tolerant (intellectually, if not politically) of variety. Modern art has broken through the artificial boundaries and limitations which we owe to a biased view of the human personality. Modern psychology has correspondingly shown that the mind of man is complex; that it is a balance of forces—of various impulses or unconscious 'drives', and that the various psychological types into which human beings can be divided are determined by the predominance of one particular impulse or group of impulses. What I am saying, therefore, is simple enough and should always have been admitted: namely, that there is not one type of art to which all types of men should conform, but as many types of art as there are types of men; and that the categories into which we divide art should naturally correspond to the categories into which we divide men. This statement does not exclude the philosophical problem of *value*, to which I shall come presently; I am not suggesting that there is no possibility of making judgments about the various types of art, or of men. But from a scientific point of view, each type of art is the legitimate expression of a type of mental personality. From a scientific point of view, that is to say, realism and idealism, expressionism and constructivism are all natural phenomena, and the warring schools into which men divide themselves are merely the products of ignorance and prejudice. A true eclecticism can, and should, enjoy all the manifestations of the creative impulse in man.

6. THE FUNCTION OF IMAGINATION

It may be objected that in thus disintegrating the concept of art, we lose sight of its essential unity—of the qualities which, irrespective of type, differentiate the *artistic* expression of men from more habitual modes of communication. We have, it is true, suggested that all works of art conform in some degree to the structural laws which are characteristic of the physical universe, but it might with some justice be argued that all expression, and indeed all perception, is inherently artistic—tends, that is to say, to seek an aesthetically satisfying form or configuration. In this sense, what works best, in any activity, is what is most functionally organized—whatever combines the greatest economy of material with the maximum structural strength (the bee's honeycomb, for example, or the crow of a cock, the song of a nightingale, the 'action' of a racehorse). But this quality in art is, let me repeat, the objective aspect, and man in his originating activity can only slavishly follow the models provided by Nature. He is not, so far as that aspect of art is concerned, a creator, but merely an imitator. But art has its subjective aspect, and the question we are now asking is whether, in that subjective aspect, it amounts to more than a reflection of the idiosyncrasies of each individual temperament. Briefly, is there a subjective state of aesthetic consciousness which is necessary, in any type of personality, for the production no less than for the appreciation of a work of art?

At the end of a survey of 'Recent Work in Experimental Aesthetics' written twenty years ago,[10] Bullough remarked that 'we have reason to believe that there *is* a distinction which imparts to the aesthetic consciousness a character and significance of its own, irreducible to the value of other attitudes'. He then called on aesthetic theory and experiment to define and analyse this consciousness, to ascertain the conditions of its realization and the range and typical features of its occurrence. Although Bullough himself made an important contribution to the discussion (the concept of 'aesthetic distance') the scientific analysis of aesthetic consciousness has not advanced much beyond the level it reached with Wordsworth and Coleridge and their German contemporaries. Wordsworth's description of 'the heightened state of sensibility' in which poetic composition can take place, and Coleridge's definition of imagination as the power which 'reveals itself in the balance or reconcilement of opposite or discordant qualities: of sameness with difference; of the general with the concrete; the idea with the image; the individual with the representative; the sense of novelty and freshness with old and familiar objects; a more than usual state of emotion with more than usual order; judgment ever awake and steady self-possession with enthusiasm and feeling profound or vehement; and while it blends and harmonizes the natural and the artificial, still subordinates art to nature; the manner to the matter; and our admiration of the poet to our sympathy with the poetry . . .'—this description and this definition carry the discussion as far as, at any rate, is necesssary for our present purpose. For imagination is revealed as the common factor in all the subjective aspects of art, and as the factor that reconciles these diverse subjective aspects with the invariable laws of objective beauty, the more than usual state of emotion with more than usual order. The *mode* of its operation will be discussed in the next chapter.

We must admit, of course, that in a certain sense, order in itself appeals to the imagination, and it is even possible to maintain that the highest type of imagination is precisely the one which occupies itself with the creation of abstract proportions and harmonies. This is the kind of imagination which, as we have seen, expresses itself in music, in architecture, in industrial design, and in abstract or non-figurative painting. But however highly we estimate such art, we cannot pretend that it *exhausts* the powers of the imagination, nor even that it satisfies the normal need for aesthetic expression. There is about such art

[10] *Brit. J. Psych.*, XII (1921–2), 76–99.

a purity, a severity and a discipline which corresponds only to one side of our nature—to the conscious desire to imitate and unconsciously to emulate the structural perfection of the physical universe. But we are endowed with a mind that is not satisfied with such a circumscribed activity—a mind that desires to create and adventure beyond the given. We are endowed, that is to say, with a free will, and in virtue of this freedom we strive rather to avoid the fixed and regular features of the laws of nature, and to express instead a world of our own—a world which is a reflection of our feelings and emotions, of that complex of instincts and thoughts which we call the personality.

7. THE PLACE OF VALUE IN THE WORLD OF ART

There are, of course, many degrees of feeling and many modes of expressing those feelings, and we are compelled to seek some standard of value to enable us to distinguish between them. It will not do to say that the strongest or most direct way is necessarily the best way: that would put a high value on a merely animal cry of joy or sorrow, and lead to what we call crudity or sentimentality in art. Obviously, if we are to distinguish an art of expression from expression itself, everything will depend on the elaboration or the refinement of these elemental responses.

We might begin by assuming that the artist himself *feels* so strongly and puts so much of this feeling into his work of art, that the work of art becomes as it were infectious, and communicates what the artist felt to anyone who looks at it. Such, indeed, is the basis of that kind of art already mentioned which has quite logically been called *expressionist art*. The artist strives to express his feelings rather than to record his observations. Indeed, it has been shown by experiments with the congenitally blind, that even people who have never had any *visual* images can nevertheless give plastic expression to their bodily sensations; it has been shown, too, that the expression of these nonvisual sensations accounts for certain qualities even in the art of normally sighted people, qualities of distortion and significant emphasis which have usually been regarded as arbitrary mannerisms of the artist. But these expressive qualities in art, though they may account for the deviations from the formal perfection of physical laws which our sensibility may seem to require, do not explain the appeal which art makes, not only to our sensations, but to the higher synthetic faculties of mind and imagination.

We have seen that the imaginative appeal of art is a very subtle process, taking place below the level of our normal conscious life, and I do not think any philosopher or critic would venture to explain it fully. If we look at a portrait by Raphael, or a landscape by Breughel or Constable, it is natural enough to assume that what appeals to us in such pictures is the sum total of what we see with our eyes and understand on the basis of everyday experience—the exact representation of the personality of a man or the details and atmosphere of an out-of-door scene. We appreciate the cleverness of the artist and if we are simple-minded we think that the art is in the cleverness, and that all paintings ought to be more or less like paintings by Raphael and Breughel.

We can look further around and we discover in other times and countries that the works of art made by men are very different from the works of art made by Raphael or Breughel. We discover that the Ancient Egyptians and Assyrians carved monstrous animals like the sphinx and the griffin; that the Indians cast bronze statues of goddesses with four or even six arms, and that when the Chinese paint a landscape they leave out nearly all the details and seem satisfied with a cloud, a mountain peak and perhaps one solitary tree. We find that the Greeks had one form of art, and the Celtic tribes in the North of Europe quite another; that when Africa and America and the South Seas were discovered, in each new continent a new and strange kind of art was found. In short, if we put together all the art of the world, the kind of art we associate with Raphael or Breughel or Constable is seen to be a minority. It is merely one kind of art, and it is confined to a few countries in one corner of the world. So we must not be too snobbish about it and imagine that it is the only kind of art, or necessarily the best kind. We must look at all types of art, and only then shall we be in a position to understand how art appeals to the imagination.

We have seen that the form of a work of art appeals directly to the senses; it is possible to explain that appeal in terms of physics and physiology, and since these sciences are universal, we might expect, and we do find, that the formal properties of art do not vary from country to country, or age to age. There are, of course, many different applications of the laws of nature, and the forms of art are as various as the forms of life; but the underlying principles of form and structure are the same. The remaining properties of art, those which are not formal, have no inevitable basis: they are rather fancies,

31

conjured up by the imagination. It is possible that imagination, too, has laws under which it operates—that the fantasies which seem so arbitrary when they come to us in the state of dreaming, and which are instigated by the pathological complexes which psycho-analysis reveals, have their own dramatic unities and tendencies to formal organization. We shall in a later chapter offer evidence which points in this direction. We speak commonly of 'calling up' images and the metaphor suggests that there is a hidden depth from which the images emerge—a well from which they rise up like genii in the Arabian Nights. And such we know to be the actual truth. These images, when we are not conscious of them, are stored more or less deeply in the mind, and when they are completely submerged we say that they are in the unconscious, which is that part of the mind to which we normally only have direct access in states of hypnosis or during sleep. A great part of our life—as much as a third—is spent in this state of sleep, during which we live in another dimension of time and space, full of an active play of images.

There is little doubt that some of the attraction we find in works of art is due to the presence in the work of art of primordial images which have found their way from the unconscious levels of the mind. Both the artist in creating the work of art, and we who look at the work of art, are penetrating more or less deeply into the world of dreams. From that world the artist derives what he calls his 'inspiration'—his sudden perception of an image or a theme—and into that world and in the very act of perception, the spectator—the person enjoying a work of art—brings a new image. The psychology of what then happens is still obscure, but we know that it depends, to a considerable extent, on what we bring with us when we come into the presence of a work of art—on what psychologists call our *adaptation*.[11]

[11] It was Bullough who first pointed out, in the article already quoted (*Brit. J. Psych.*, XII, 92–99), the importance of the stage of adaptation which precedes the apprehension of the aesthetic object. 'There is a growing sense,' he then wrote, 'that here, if anywhere, we may find that bedrock upon which the whole superstructure of aesthetic experience—of appreciation as well as artistic production—ultimately rests.' He defines the phenomenon in the following way: 'In a general way, adaptation implies, positively, the attending to the various aspects presented by the object (either spontaneously or by an act of voluntary attention), and the opening of all the channels of reminiscence, associations, historical and technical knowledge, inferences, emotional resonances, organic sensations, etc., in so far as they may serve to impart an adequate meaning to the object and to lead to an adequate interpretation of it on the lines predetermined by the artist. Negatively, it involves the cutting out of all irrelevant trends of thought, extra-aesthetic points

8. SUMMARY

A preliminary definition of art must halt at this point. We have seen that two main principles are involved—a *principle of form*, derived, in my opinion, from the organic world, and the universal objective aspect of all works of art; and a *principle of origination* peculiar to the mind of man, and impelling him to create (and appreciate the creation of) symbols, phantasies, myths which take on a universally valid objective existence only in virtue of the principle of form. Form is a function of *perception*; origination is a function of *imagination*. These two mental activities exhaust, in their dialectical counterplay, all the psychic aspects of aesthetic experience. But art has other aspects—biological and social—and it is far from my intention to underestimate their importance. Indeed, the following chapters are nothing but an inquiry into these wider aspects of the aesthetic activity, and an insistence on its fundamental importance in all spheres of life. But that kind of phrase does not adequately represent the total nature of my claim, for I maintain that life itself, in its most secret and essential sources, is aesthetic—that it only *is* in virtue of the embodiment of energy in a form which is not merely material, but aesthetic. Such is the formative principle discernible in the evolution of the universe itself. It would seem that the more the physicist is able to reveal of the nature of the physical structure of the world, the more he relies on numerical harmonies which are aesthetically satisfying. Fundamentally, the aesthetician, no less than the physicist, is ready

of view, the selection of valuable associations and the suppression of useless or disturbing dispositions, especially of such as by their intensity or nature would lead to deviating associations, purely personal interests, or reminiscences splitting the interest in the object or destroying the unity of attention and appreciation.' In the course of his further description of aesthetic adaptation, Bullough recognizes its impersonal or rather non-personal character as its most important feature —its divorce from all directly practical needs and functions and from the personal relevance of the object. 'It is neither agreeable (as a personal affection), nor useful (as fulfilling a practical function), nor directly ethically valuable (as serving a socially sanctioned, remotely personal purpose). At the same time, our adaptation is not impersonal, in the sense of scientific impartiality or mere intellectual curiosity. It is rather a non-personal relation to the object: its significance does not affect me in my everyday experience, yet it does not lose touch with either the emotional sphere or a generally human interest; and though the experience has a certain unreality or, if you like, fictitiousness about it, yet it does not fail to obtain a full response of the personality to which it appeals.' This description of the aesthetic experience, which everyone will recognize as exact, has, it seems to me, been largely substantiated by the hypothesis of the unconscious, particularly in its collective or non-personal aspects. See Chapter VII.

to accept a view of the universe which finds that the cleavage between the aesthetic and the extra-aesthetic domain of experience, no less than that between the scientific and the extra-scientific, is the cleavage between the metrical and the non-metrical rather than that between the concrete and the transcendental.[12]

[12] Cf. A. S. Eddington: *The Nature of the Physical World* (Cambridge, 1928), p. 275.

Chapter Three

ON PERCEPTION AND IMAGINATION

*A whole essay might be written on the danger
of thinking without images.—Coleridge*

1. THE PROBLEM OF PERCEPTION

No subject in psychology has involved so much research as the act of perception. It is the basic act of our psyche or mind, and unless we are clear what is involved in the act, the whole of our psychology will be false.

We can say (though some philosophers have questioned even this) that two terms are involved: an object and a subject. The object may be a part of the furniture of the mind, as we shall see later, but in the simplest case it is separate and external. The subject is a sensitive human being—that is to say, a living organism, part of whose physical equipment are certain senses which can be directed on to this external object. We can see it, touch it, taste it, smell it or hear it.

We are mainly concerned in this study with the sense of sight, and we shall for the most part discuss the problem of perception in relation to this sense alone. We have, therefore, an object 'x' and we have a sensitive human being directing his attention to this object. 'x' is seen: a reflection of its outline, mass and colour passes through the lenses of the eyes and is registered as an 'image' by the brain.

What the brain apprehends in this act is the *appearance* of the object. We learn by experience that the object has other characteristics which are not immediately evident to the eye, but for the moment we are not concerned with this process of learning, nor with the apprehension of the whole content of the object. The act of perception has culminated in an awareness of the appearance of the object.

But that is not the whole story. We do not live in a vacuum which at any one moment contains an isolated object and a mind as im-

35

personal as a mirror. The object, for example, is probably one of many that enter into the field of vision—it has a *context*, as we say, and the act of perception therefore becomes in some measure an act of discrimination, even, some psychologists maintain, discrimination in favour of a particular ('good' or 'best possible') pattern. Further, the brain which receives the reflection of the object is a brain that has, during the whole of its conscious existence, received many such reflections, and these reflections have left their impressions, impressions which are capable of being revived, and as it were, re-experienced. For 'it pertains to the very being of a mind that it has the facility, in and through subsequent states, of "reproducing" or "recalling" the awareness which was the awareness of the content of a previous state and of utilizing this retained awareness in the life of the present and of the future'.[1]

The retained awareness of the object, therefore, finds itself among the traces of other retained awarenesses, and it tends, by its mere physical presence, to attract to itself those awarenesses which are relevant, i.e., which complete the required pattern. If we open the door to go out and we see rain, we are immediately aware of the existence of objects which protect us from the rain, an umbrella or a raincoat. We call such a process of linking a present act of perception with a revived act of perception *association*, and the faculty which enables us to revive the awareness of previous perceptions we call *memory*. We may note here, for it will perhaps concern us later, that all associations are not of the simple rain-umbrella type[2]: the therapeutic method known as psychoanalysis is built upon the fact that associations can be indirect—that is to say, the connections between an awareness and a revived awareness, or between two revived awarenesses, is often hidden from the conscious mind of the subject.

2. THE AESTHETIC FACTOR

We are still treating the subject as a passive reflector, but actually it is 'sensitive', and reacts to the reception of the content of the act of apprehending. The subject that responds is actually a psycho-physical organism, and its reaction is a motor reaction of nerves, glands and the whole metabolism of the body to the stimulus received

[1] G. Dawes Hicks: 'On the Nature of Images,' *Brit. J. Psych.* XV (1924–5) 129.

[2] I am ignoring the problem of how such associations arise and are fixated: problems of attention, learning, behaviour-patterns, conditioned reflexes, etc.

through the sense organs. This motor reaction we call *sensation*. But there is besides the response of the affective system. The response of the mind to any act of perception is not an isolated event: it is part of a serial development: it takes place within a complete orchestration of sense perceptions and sensations, and is controlled—given its place within the pattern—by what we call *feeling*. We could not possibly live that 'life of pure sensation' which Keats desired: it would be a chaos from which mind could not emerge. We have therefore evolved, not only the power of discrimination, which is essential for the apprehension of a particular object, but a power of reacting in our own interests to our awareness of the object. If I hear the whistle of a descending bomb, I register not only the pitch of the note: I have not only those physical sensations of fear which physiologists tell us are due to the injection of adrenalin into the blood stream: but I have also an instant *feeling* for the whole situation. Time and space become more than objects of perception: they are factors in self-preservation and I seek cover with instinctive speed and economy of action. I am, after all, not a passive mirror of events, but an organism with the desire to live, and this biological aim is involved in all my experience —that is to say, even in my acts of perception.

Such an action (taking cover in the presence of danger) would normally be called instinctive, but from our immediate point of view it deserves a closer scrutiny. It is instinctive in the sense that the *motive* of the action is to preserve life: but it has not only a motive, but also a *pattern*. My agility, in the circumstances, was not deliberate. A detached observer might have discovered in it speed, economy and grace. If it had been clumsy, it would have been ineffective: I should have stumbled and been killed. I am therefore tempted to call the pattern of this reaction *aesthetic*, and I find support for this view among psychologists. For example:

'Long before we are able to think about life in general, and about its larger problems, we are guided in the pursuit of ends that are not comprised within the cycle of a single perception. And this guidance is afforded, not by discernment, but by *feeling*. In the discernment of a perceived event our disposition is a positive factor no less real than the event itself. The feelings which attach to a dispositional readiness for response—either in a single perception, or in a series of perceptions, interrupted, perchance, by pauses of sleep and distraction—are *aesthetic*. It is the aesthetic feelings that mark the rhythm of life, and hold us to our course by a kind of weight and balance...

A disposition to feel the completeness of an experienced event as being right and fit constitutes what we have called the aesthetic factor in perception.'[3]

3. THE NATURE OF THE IMAGE

I shall have something to say about the pedagogical significance of this fact presently, but first let us complete our account of the act of perception. We have hitherto spoken of awareness, and that is perhaps the best term for the content of the act of apprehending. But there exists the word *image*, which we must come to terms with, because even if we could dispense with it when describing the act of perception, we shall need it when we come to deal with imagination.

Some psychologists[4] consider the percept itself as the most perfect kind of visual image, but it is more usual to regard the image as something divorced from the act of perception. I look up and see a bird on a branch: so long as I keep my eyes on the bird, my brain continues to register a percept. I close my eyes, but if I so desire, I can still see the bird in my mind's eye. What I still 'see' (i.e. retain), is an 'image' of the bird. It is less distinct than the percept, though I may be able, by concentration, to make it clearer and more detailed. I then dismiss the bird from my mind and the image disappears; but if some days later I am reminded of the bird, the image returns, though the less distinct the longer the interval.

Memory is the capacity to recall such images, in various degrees of vividness; and imagination, as I shall use the term, is the capacity to relate such images one to another—to make combinations of such images either in the process of thinking, or in the process of feeling. It will be seen, therefore, that as Professor Dawes Hicks has said, 'the process of imagining is, in truth, of one piece, so to speak, with the process of perceiving . . . the chief difference being that in imagination a relatively larger proportion of revived factors are involved.'[5] But it is important to remember that even these revived factors are still images in the strict sense of the word, the term 'images' being reserved, in Dawes Hicks's words, for such contents as in memory and imagination do appear to stand over against the cognizing mind as objects, and upon which the act of apprehension seems (to the con-

[3] R. M. Ogden: *Psychology and Education* (New York, 1926), pp. 131–2, 133.

[4] For example, F. Aveling, *Brit. J. Psych.*, XVIII, 18.

[5] *Brit. J. Psych.*, XV, 131.

scious subject in question) to be directed.', We have been warned by another psychologist that 'whenever an author thinks that an image is a faint copy of a sensation the rest of his remarks on the subject may be ignored'[6]; and here, indeed, we have the strongest motives for affirming that sense-stimulation is involved in the process of imagination, for 'in imagination, where objective imagery is present, there is, as in perception, a real object upon which the art of discriminating is directed, and this accounts for the objective character which the content apprehended seems to possess, although the number of the features of this object actually discriminated is considerably less than in perception . . .' (Dawes Hicks, *loc. cit.*, p. 132). It is not suggested that the image includes the sensation which it aroused when it first entered the brain as a percept; nor that the revival or recall of an image is *necessarily* accompanied by a sensation similar in kind or degree to the primary sensation. Nevertheless, the image is always, at the moment of its appearance, an objective phenomenon.

From the image in this its normal sense (the memory image) we must distinguish two, if not three, other types of image. The first of these is easily disposed of—the so-called *after-image*. If, for example, we stare at a red object for twenty seconds or so, and then transfer our gaze to a neutral background, we see that object reappear, but in its complementary colour, green. This is a purely physiological phenomenon, and of no significance for our immediate study.

But there exist certain images which are not directly connected with perception, and which may exercise an important role in our lives. Until a few years ago these images would have all been included under the term *hallucination,* a distinction being made between those which appear to an individual in his sleep (dreams) and those which, in exceptional cases, appear during a normal state of consciousness.

Dream images will not concern us until a later stage in our inquiry. But certain waking images, of the same type as dream images, must be carefully distinguished from ordinary memory images.

Apart from memory images and after-images, standard psychology only recognizes the images involved in hallucination, and hallucination it would explain as a lapse in complete consciousness accompanied by an uprush of images from the unconscious levels of the mind. If the hypothesis of the unconscious is not recognized, then the psychologist of this school will not admit anything more than *illusions* (i.e. false perceptions) of varying degrees of vividness. And

[6] Charles Fox, *Educational Psychology* (London, 1930), p. 363, note.

illusions can be very vivid, even in moments of acute awareness. In trench warfare, for example, anyone who has acted as a sentry has seen shapes materialize in the darkness and become the moving forms of enemies. But even in daylight, and in the course of normal experience, an imperfectly apprehended phenomenon—the passing shadow of a bird, the fluttering of a leaf, a flash of sunlight on some bright surface—will bring a totally different, but vivid image into the field of awareness. This merely means that our senses are momentarily deluded: once the attention is thoroughly aroused and discrimination takes place, the illusion disappears.

4. EIDETIC IMAGES

Distinct from the memory-image and the after-image, and having nothing in common with the hallucinatory image except its vividness, and apparently distinguished from the dream image by a more direct connection with acts of perception, is another kind of image which has been called eidetic. By those who claim to experience such images, they are said to differ little, if at all, in completeness and vividness, from the original percept. Unfortunately the eidetic disposition is mainly confined to young children, from whom reliable evidence is difficult to obtain. But since the hypothesis was first put forward by the Marburg school, some twenty years ago, it has gradually established itself in modern psychology, in spite of formidable opposition.[7]

Professor Jaensch, the originator of the term, defines eidetic images in the following way:

[7] Formidable, and even violent. Cf. C. Fox: *Educationa Psychology*, p. 81. 'The inability to discriminate between hallucinations and normal mental imagery and the mental confusion thereby entailed is responsible for a psychological abortion called the "eidetic image". To the Marburg school under the direction of Jaensch we owe the introduction of this monstrous confusion into child psychology. When the eyes are closed in a darkened room, and sometimes when they are open, hallucinatory visions are seen, brought about by pressure on the eyeballs, the slight stimulation due to lens adjustment, by changes in the convergence of the eyeball, etc. Under emotional tension as in delirium it is easier by slight stimulation to produce these hallucinations. Now the same sort of phenomena are evident sometimes when one stares at a dark surface in daylight. If then a child is induced to look at a picture against a dark background and the picture is soon withdrawn he may be the victim of such hallucination so that he "sees" the picture after withdrawal. It is said that 60 per cent of all children investigated, between the ages of ten to fifteen, produce these "eidetic images". I have been present at such investigations and have been convinced that the whole operation is due to strong suggestion by the influence of the experimenter and the surrounding conditions, and the observations are worthless.'

'Optical perceptual (or eidetic) images are phenomena that take up an intermediate position between sensations and images. Like ordinary physiological after-images, they are always *seen* in the literal sense. They have this property of necessity and under all conditions, and share it with sensations. In other respects they can also exhibit the properties of images (*Vorstellungen*). In those cases in which the imagination has little influence, they are merely modified after-images, deviating from the norm in a definite way, and when that influence is nearly, or completely zero, we can look upon them as slightly intensified after-images.'[8]

There is a very general agreement among psychologists that the imagery of young children is exceptionally vivid. The question to decide is whether such imagery is *sui generis*, or merely due to an ability to retain and recall memory-images of exceptional vividness. In the presence of such images, is the act of perception always renewed: does the eidetic individual actually *see* the image; or does he, as in ordinary memory-images, merely revive a sort of mental token or 'sign' of the content of a previous state of awareness? As the methods by which eidetic imagery can be discovered in children are admittedly difficult, let us turn first to the evidence provided by adults who claim to see eidetic images.

Such people are generally artists—visual artists like painters, but sometimes also poets and musicians. It may be that such eidetic individuals are more self-analytical than an eidetic person without creative gifts would be, but the theory has been put forward by Jaensch and others[9] that such persons are creative artists *because they are eidetic*: a fact which, if it could be proved, would have considerable significance for our studies. A certain amount of evidence of this fact, but without specific reference to eidetic imagery, has been collected by Dr. Rosamond Harding.[10] She quotes statements by the painters William Blake and W. Northcote, writers such as Charlotte

[8] *Eidetic Imagery* (London, 1930), pp. 2–3.

[9] Cf. O. Kroh: 'Eidetiker unter deutschen Dichtern,' *Ztschf. f. Psych.* 85 (1920), pp. 118–62. Kroh gives evidence for eidetic disposition in the following German writers: Otto Ludwig, Ludwig Tieck, E. T. A. Hoffmann, J. V. v. Scheffel and Goethe. I have not been able to consult Jaensch's own work on this aspect of the subject, viz.: *Ueber das Wesen der Kunst und die Kunst des Kindes*, by E. R. Jaensch (Augsburg); *Studien zur psychologischen Aesthetik und Kunstpsychologie*, edited by E. R. Jaensch (Langensalza, 1929).

[10] *An Anatomy of Inspiration*, Cambridge (Heffer), 1940, pp. 27–30. Cf. also J. E. Downey: *Creative Imagination* (London, 1929).

Brontë, Charles Dickens, Thackeray, Alphonse Daudet, Shelley, Coleridge, and one musician, Elgar. All these statements point to the presence and use of eidetic imagery, and are sometimes very specific. For example, Medwin in his *Life of Percy Bysshe Shelley*, relates that the poet 'could throw a veil over his eyes and find himself in a *camera obscura*, where all the features of a scene were reproduced in a form more pure and perfect than they had been originally presented to his external senses'. It should be recalled that Shelley suffered from hallucinations, which sometimes had a disastrous effect on his life. From a less romantic source, evidence may be quoted which shows the high value which the artist places upon such images when he can command them. In his *Anecdotes*[11] Hogarth relates how, at an early age, he grew dissatisfied with the practice of 'copying' or 'transcribing'. 'Drawing in an academy, though it should be after the life, will not make the student an artist; for as the eye is often taken from the original, to draw a bit at a time, it is possible he may know no more of what he has been copying, when his work is finished, than he did before it was begun. . . . More reasons, not necessary to enumerate, struck me as strong objections to this practice, and led me to wish that I could find the shorter path—fix forms and characters in my mind, and, instead of *copying* the lines, try to read the language, and, if possible, find the grammar of the art, by bringing into one focus the various observations I had made, and then trying by my power on the canvas, how far my plan enabled me to combine and apply them in practice—I therefore endeavoured to habituate myself to the exercise of a sort of technical memory; and by repeating in my own mind, the parts of which objects were composed, I could by degrees combine and put them down with my pencil. Thus, with all the drawbacks which resulted from the circumstances I have mentioned, I had one material advantage over my competitors, *viz.* the early habit I thus acquired of retaining in my mind's eye, without coldly copying it on the spot, whatever I intended to imitate.'

This language is perhaps not as precise as the psychologist could desire, but it does indicate that Hogarth acquired by training, the power of retaining very precise images. It might be objected that Hogarth's language indicates that these images were *memory* images, continually in need of refreshment by reference to the original objects: but unless we can subject such evidence to direct examination, it is

---

[11] *Anecdotes of William Hogarth Written by Himself, with Essays on his Life and Genius, etc.* (London, 1833), pp. 3–5.

difficult (and in this case impossible) to draw the line between precise memory images and eidetic images.

What is significant about his evidence is, that in the case of painters it comes from one type—that which Hogarth calls 'a natural designer', and which is nowadays called 'naturalistic'. An accurate reproduction of some scene or object can, of course, be made by careful and assiduous copying, and probably most people could be trained in such a laborious talent. But certain people do not need to be so laborious about the task: they retain a perfectly clear image of the scene or object in their minds, and need to refer to the original only rarely—in exceptional cases only once. We must conclude, therefore, that such people have an exceptional power of visualization, and if the hypothesis of the eidetic disposition is accepted, it is reasonable to suppose that such people possess it in some degree. What is not yet clear is whether 'good visualizers' in the popular sense of the phrase are always eidetic. It should also be noted that though he was a 'good visualizer', and almost pathologically eidetic, Shelley's poetry is anything but 'visual'; it is, indeed, highly abstract or conceptual.[12] It is true that when he uses images they are very precise and vivid,— 'The lake-reflected sun illume/The yellow bees in the ivy-bloom'— but they are subordinated to the flow of his conceptual thoughts, and the expression of these is poetic in virtue of verbal (i.e. aural or musical) rather than of any visual appeal. Poets can be classified as predominantly 'visual' or 'aural', and our appreciation of poetry tends to be divided by the same line.

The case of William Blake, which would deserve a separate study, is perhaps too exceptional to be pressed in this connection: it might be maintained that in his case eidetic images were the hallucinations of a very abnormal mind. But in what sense abnormal? Contemporary accounts suggest that in Blake's case the images, whatever their nature, could sometimes be evoked voluntarily. Gilchrist relates that 'the visionary faculty was so much under control that, at the wish of a friend, he could summon before his abstracted gaze, any of the familiar forms and faces he asked for. This was during the favourable and befitting hours of night; from nine or ten in the evening until one or two, perhaps three or four o'clock in the morning; Varley sitting by, "sometimes slumbering, sometimes waking". Varley would say,

---

[12] I have dealt more fully with the psychological significance of this feature of Shelley's poetry in 'In Defence of Shelley', *The True Voice of Feeling* (London, 1953), pp. 244–6, 284–5.

"Draw me Moses", or David; or would call for a likeness of Julius Caesar . . . or some other great historical personage. Blake would answer, "There he is", and paper and pencil being at hand, he would begin drawing, with the utmost alacrity and composure, as though he had a real sitter before him. . . Sometimes Blake had to wait for the vision's appearance; sometimes it would not come at all. At others, in the midst of his portrait, he would suddenly leave off, and in his ordinary quiet tones, and with the same matter-of-fact air another might say "It rains", would remark: "I can't go on—it is gone. I must wait till it returns"; or: "It has moved. The mouth is gone"; or: "He frowns; he is displeased with my portrait of him" . . .'[13]

Other accounts suggest that the visions were accompanied by more mental agitation. 'A friend of James Porter's who happened one day to call on Blake, found him contemplating some sketches of Sir William Wallace and King Edward I. Blake, who was in a state of almost breathless ecstasy, said: "I was sitting meditating, as I had often done, on the heroic actions . . . of the Scottish hero, when, like a flash of lightning, a noble form stood before me, which I instantly recognized as Sir William Wallace. Knowing that it was a spiritual appearance which might vanish as quickly as it came, I begged him to remain a few minutes. The hero smiled and I sketched him. Presently the phantom vanished, and Edward the First, who also remained long enough to be sketched, occupied his place".'[14]

But the most precise evidence of the eidetic nature of Blake's images is given in the following observation of Varley's—it relates to the famous drawing of the *Ghost of a Flea*, done in Varley's presence. 'I felt convinced by his mode of proceeding that he had a real image before him, for he left off, and began on another part of the paper to make a separate drawing of the mouth of the Flea, which the spirit having opened, he was prevented proceeding with the first sketch, till he had closed it'.[15]

It may be suggested that the visualizing abilities of Hogarth and Blake represent two very different mental processes. It should be noted, however, that though Hogarth's faculty was acquired by assiduous practice, Blake's was not entirely innate or personal to him,

[13] *Life of William Blake*, by Alexander Gilchrist. Everyman's Library (1942), pp. 262–6.

[14] *The Life of William Blake*, by Thomas Wright, 2 vols. (Olney, 1929. Vol. II, 63–4.)

[15] Quoted by Gilchrist, *op. cit.*, p. 266.

for he taught his wife to see the visions. In both cases the images were precise. Blake, on two occasions, summoned[16] King Saul in order to complete the drawing of an intricate helmet he was wearing. In both cases the images depended on a process of concentration. The fundamental difference is not so much in the nature of the images as such, but in their origin. Hogarth's images were always based on objective observation: Blake's were purely subjective in their origin. Hogarth's images were stored just below the surface of consciousness: Blake's images came from the depths of the unconscious. But I see no real reason for supposing that in both cases the images were not, as it were, *projected* and actually seen, and therefore, in the strict meaning of the word, eidetic.

The conclusion we have reached may be expressed in the words of Professor Spearman: 'From this and many other pieces of evidence, we seem obliged to conclude that hallucinations are essentially the same thing as images, only pushed to a fuller degree of sensuousness'.[17]

Long before the hypothesis of the eidetic image was put forward, Francis Galton carried out his famous inquiry into the function of mental imagery.[18] His conclusions have been subjected to a good deal of criticism by later psychologists, but since they form the basis of all subsequent discussion of imagery, and anticipate some of the most recent theories, they must be briefly referred to here. Galton found, by questioning 100 adult men (of whom 19 were Fellows of the Royal Society), that there is a very wide variation in the power of visualization, and that as a rule 'scientific men' as a class come at the lower end of the scale. He found that the power is higher in the female sex than in the male, and is somewhat, but not much, higher in public schoolboys than in men. 'After maturity is reached, the further advance of age does not seem to dim the faculty, but rather the reverse, judging from numerous statements to that effect; but advancing years are sometimes accompanied by a growing habit of hard abstract

[16] The visions seem to have been invoked by prayer. George Richmond relates that on one occasion, when calling at Fountain Court, where he found the Blakes at tea, he was in low spirits. 'For a fortnight,' he said, 'I have been deserted by the power of invention.' Blake, turning to his wife, said: 'It is just so with us, is it not, for weeks together when the visions forsake us? What do we do then, Kate?'

'We kneel down and pray, Mr. Blake.'

[17] *Creative Mind*, by C. Spearman (London and Cambridge, 1930), p. 139.

[18] *Inquiries into Human Faculty and its Development*, 1883. Second edition Everyman's Library), 1907.

thinking, and in these cases . . . the faculty undoubtedly becomes impaired. There is reason to believe that *it is very high in some young children, who seem to spend years of difficulty in distinguishing between the subjective and objective world.*' This statement which I have italicized, is a remarkable anticipation of the findings of the Marburg school, and it is a pity that Galton does not give any specific grounds for his belief. One further point is worth noting: Galton states that he has abundant evidence to prove that the visualizing faculty is a natural gift, 'and, like all natural gifts, has a tendency to be inherited'.

There can be no doubt that in his reference to the visualizing faculty in children, and to the visualizing faculty as a natural gift, Galton is referring to the same phenomenon as Jaensch—that is to say, to an eidetic image which is *seen* in the literal sense, and is always accompanied by sensation. Galton assumed, as indeed does Jaensch, that all powers of visualization, including memory-images, are based on this primary faculty, and are always in some degree a depreciation of its original vividness and totality. But to this point of view there is a strong opposition. Professor Fox, already quoted, states very categorically, that 'the total disparity between primary and secondary presentation is obvious to introspection, though the majority of psychologists seem unaware of the distinction', and he quotes in support the evidence of Dr. Wohlgemuth, who describes himself as a good visualizer: 'That these memory-images are faint reproductions of the sensations, i.e. weak sensations, sensations of low intensity, is decidedly not true in my case; they are an experience *sui generis*'. According to Professor Colvin[19]—a mental image is 'that activity of consciousness in which an object of sensation is experienced as not immediately present to the senses'. And to make the distinction quite clear, Professor Fox adds: 'Unless the experience carries with it the feeling that the primary object is absent and only the secondary present, the psychosis is not properly described as a mental image'.[20] The distinction is important from the educational point of view because our pedagogic methods will depend on whether we are dealing with what Professor Fox prefers to call a psychosis, and which even Galton, sometimes, seems to have regarded as an exceptional gift; or with a normal faculty present in all children and gradually lost.[21] In

[19] 'Nature of the Mental Image,' *Psych. Review.* Vol. XV (1908).

[20] *Op. cit.* pp. 79–80.

[21] It might be as well to point out here Galton's inconsistency on this point.

the first case it would be important to identify such eidetic children and give them special treatment; in the second case we would have to decide to what extent our educational methods should encourage or discourage the retention of the faculty.

To this important question it does not seem that psychology can yet give a definite answer. The extreme 'genetic' theory as put forward by Jaensch, is not very simple. He admits that *all* children have not got eidetic images (*loc. cit.* p. 122) but makes a distinction between manifest and latent eidetic images. According to this theory, perceptions and ordinary memory-images have an 'eidetic component', present in every one. In the course of the perceptual process, the latent eidetic images can 'develop' and thereby give concreteness to the percept. Jaensch claims complete empirical proof for this theory —he says, indeed, that 'we are not dealing with theoretical questions here at all; they are purely questions of *fact*, and I can only ask my opponents over and again to test these *facts* for themselves. They have been verified by us and by others so often, from such diverse points of view, that I am quite content to take up a waiting attitude towards their attacks'. He proceeds to give a final summary of his conclusions:

'In our own investigations we followed the progress of many young individuals through a number of years and noted the changes that took place. In this way we came to the conclusion that the perceptions pass through a building-up process. That this is so, has also been sufficiently proved by the older empiricism, *e.g.* in its observations of people who were born blind and received sight later, and of people who were operated upon and had to learn to see and to

I have already quoted his view that the visualizing faculty is a natural gift, present in *some* young children, with a tendency to be inherited. This would seem to support the psychotic point of view, bringing eidetic images into line with hallucinations. But on a later page (*op. cit.*, pp. 176–7), generally neglected because it does not occur in the chapter on 'Mental Imagery', Galton writes: 'The visualizing tendency is much more common among sane people than is generally suspected. In early life, it seems to be a hard lesson to an imaginative child to distinguish between the real and visionary world. If the fantasies are habitually laughed at and otherwise discouraged, the child soon acquires the power of distinguishing them; any incongruity or non-conformity is quickly noted, the visions are found out and discredited, and are no further attended to. In this way *the natural tendency to see them* is blunted by repression.' Galton has substituted the word 'visions' for 'images', but from the context it seems obvious that he had the one phenomenon in mind—he cannot have thought that the child, already charged with the difficulty of distinguishing between his percepts and his memory-images, had the additional burden of distinguishing between memory-images and visions. It seems clear, therefore, that Galton would have welcomed Jaensch's integral and developmental conception of mental imagery.

localize. The development of perceptions passes through several phases. In each phase the perceptual world is as yet incomplete, and is related to the final form as a rich, completed drawing is to the original sketch. At each stage preceding the final completion, the contents of perception offer certain sketches and outlines, which can make even a weak eidetic disposition active. This disposition will then fill in the details with its products, however far removed these may be from manifest eidetic phenomena. Detailed experimental investigations have shown us that all eidetic elements are easily fitted into the external world, and from the point of view of the observer, become part of it, if they find "points of contact" in the above-mentioned sense (where, for instance, the data of perceptions to some extent already include the contents of eidetic phenomena, so that they do not arise out of nothing, but fill in a given frame, as a painting arises out of the preliminary sketch).'

We see, therefore, why Jaensch gives the eidetic image an intermediate place between the after-image and the memory-image. It tends to resemble the after-image in its physiological characteristics —that is to say, it is an object of visual sensation, but it shares with the memory-image a capacity to be recalled by peripheral or associative images, and is often, if not generally, an intensification or clarification of a given memory-image.

It is this characteristic which gives the eidetic image its genetic function. 'Its true function is performed only in the earlier years of mental development, when by preserving and elaborating sensory data it enhances the meaning of the stimulus situation for the child and enables him to perfect his adaptive responses.'[22]

5. EIDETIC IMAGERY AND EDUCATION

The pedagogical significance of eidetic imagery is obvious, and Jaensch has not been slow to make his claims in this direction. 'The value that is placed on pedagogical work', he writes, 'the emphasis that is given it, and the hopes that are centred in it, are always measured by the degree of *plasticity* or educability that the psychic organization is estimated to possess. It has always been correctly supposed that the higher psychic events can be influenced with ease, but the more elementary ones only with difficulty. But it was presup-

---

[22] 'Eidetic Imagery', by Gordon W. Allport. *Brit. J. Psych.*, XV (1924–5), 99–120.

posed that this "plastic" nature of the psychic only began above the perceptual sphere, which was almost always regarded as something absolutely rigid and merely physiologically determined. The new results about the structure of perception show the range within which human nature is "plastic" to be far wider than even the most optimistic were willing to admit. They show that even the perceptual sphere is plastic, although it has always been regarded as being the most rigid and least plastic part of the mind's inventory—as, indeed, it is. All this is not theory, but experimentally discovered fact.'[23]

This claim means that educational methods can be devised, and have been successfully carried out, which ensure 'that the eidetic phase and the whole mental structure accompanying it, in particular the perceptual structure peculiar to it', can be preserved longer than usual in children. These methods seem to consist of an extension of the familiar 'object lesson'; indeed, they are but an appreciation of the principles long ago enunciated by Rousseau: 'Keep the child dependent on things only', and 'Never show a child what he cannot see'—principles which, as Jaensch would admit, are already *to some extent* embodied in the *Arbeitsschule* of Germany and the similar American schools described by John and Evelyn Dewey.[24]

We are thus introduced to two very important and debatable questions:

1. The relevance of visual imagery to educational development, and, depending on our answer to this question:

2. The relative value of 'sensationalism' and 'intellectualism', not only in the scholastic sphere, but for humanity generally.

6. THE RELEVANCE OF IMAGERY TO THINKING

The smaller problem has so far received the most attention; indeed, the relevance of visual imagery to processes of thought has been one of the stock subjects for psychological investigation ever since Galton first raised the question, and much experimental work has been done on adults as well as on children. Up to the date of its

---

[23] *Op. cit.*, pp. 23–4.

[24] *Schools of To-morrow* (London, 1915). I emphasize the qualifying phrase 'to some extent' because there is a prevalent fallacy, which must be dealt with later, which confuses 'doing things' (constructive activity) with 'inventing things' (imaginative activity). Koehler's chimpanzees were constructive, and might with benefit have attended an *Arbeitsschule*; but even Koehler would not claim that they had creative imagination.

publication (July 1927), an adequate survey of the problem was made in a symposium contributed to the *British Journal of Psychology* by Professors T. H. Pear, F. Aveling, and F. C. Bartlett,[25] and from my own review of the literature of the subject written before and since that date, it seems that the 'considerations' then put forward by Professor Pear still represent the most positive findings of this research. Professor Pear made eleven propositions, namely:

(1) That the characteristics of visual imagery are extremely numerous and varied.

(2) That its development as a vehicle for thinking passes through different stages; that these stages ought to receive different names and ought not to be confused.

(3) That, while at some of these stages the visual image is disadvantageous for efficient abstract thinking, other ways of arriving at truth along visual routes may be uniquely efficient, and

(4) that this fact is more familiar to artists than to psychologists.

(5) That considering the patchy growth of recent psychology, it is quite credible if less creditable that workers should differ about the 'irrelevance' or 'discrepancy' of visual imagery.

(6) That to the results of some experiments investigating the usefulness of imagery in thought an unjustifiably wide significance has been attributed.

(7) That in considering the use of visual imagery the 'biological importance' of the situation in which it functions should not be neglected.

(8) That in many experiments, the situations were already 'half-abstracted', and so might discourage visual imagery even in a visualizer.

(9) That the apparent irrelevance of their imagery is sometimes experienced by visualizers themselves. Yet this irrelevance raises problems which require for their solution the concept of the unconscious.

(10) That the distinction between 'concrete' and 'abstract' imagery is not helpful.

(11) That the nature of visual imagery makes it difficult to record, that this hindrance may be minimized, with results which will be shown.

Professor Aveling's criticism of these propositions was mainly directed to the introspective methods by means of which they had

[25] Vol. XVIII, pp. 1–29.

been reached, and the conclusions he came to on the basis of his own objective methods were as follows: 'Thoughts may or may not be accompanied by sensorial elements (images), and they remain unimpaired while the imagery tends to become fragmentary, obscure, and even to drop out of consciousness altogether. Images, accordingly, are not relevant to thought in the sense of being necessary to it; though they may be relevant as associated with thoughts or illustrative of them. Further, the 'universal' tends to be present to consciousness as imageless substantive content; the 'individual', on the contrary, tends to be present as a concept in connection with sensorial contents (images). Finally, I concluded that the image best securing 'individual' thought is the direct image or percept. (*loc. cit.* pp. 19–20.)

Professor Bartlett's conclusion is not very different: 'It will be apparent . . . that I consider that most certainly the image is, in general, relevant to the process of thinking. I would in fact go further and say that in proportion as the *form* of thinking is to be given genuine material to work with, so more and more must images be utilized in our thinking process.

'But to say that images are relevant in general to the thinking process, is not to say that the latter is simply the utilization of the former. The device of images has its numerous defects which are the price of its peculiar excellencies. To take two of these only: the image and, in particular, the visual image, is apt to go farther in the direction of the individualization of situations than is biologically useful, and the principles of the combination of images have their own peculiarities, resulting in constructions which are relatively wild, jerky, and irregular compared with the somewhat orderly march of thought.' (*loc. cit.*, p. 27.)

Professor Bartlett would presumably allow us to identify the term 'imagination' as used by Coleridge and by literary critics generally with his 'principles of the combination of images'. There can, of course, be no question of the relevance of imagery to the process of imagination; but the point I wish to make in passing is that a modern psychologist is prepared to admit two distinct mental processes, possibly quite independent of each other—thinking and imagining. In the essay just referred to, Professor Bartlett distinguishes 'imaging' and 'thinking'[26] but it seems to me that the parallel mental activities

[26] 'Imaging' he defines as 'the reference to a concrete object or situation in the absence of peripherally aroused stimulation adequate to account for this refer-

51

are 'imagining' and 'thinking'. The distinction is important because in the *process* of imagining, the image may lose much of that 'individuality' or isolation which both Aveling and Bartlett regard as its limitation; and the relative wildness, jerkiness and irregularity of the imaginative process may not be any criterion of the value of the construction eventually arrived at—to resort to an image ourselves, it would be wrong to conclude that in its relatively wild, jerky and irregular flight the bee was not nevertheless fulfilling its function, which is to gather honey.

We shall return to the process of imagining presently, but first we must finish with the question of the relevance of imagery to thinking. We may take it as experimentally established that in the most abstract kind of thinking (that concerned with the relations of universals) imagery has no useful function, and may indeed impede the economy and efficiency of such thinking. But Galton's conclusion that a persistent indulgence in abstract thinking gradually leads to the atrophy of the visualizing faculty, still seems to hold good—and it therefore remains to ask what on balance is lost or gained in a general biological sense by such an uneven development of the mind.

Apart from such purely abstract thought, it is generally admitted that the visualizing faculty may have an ancillary function in the process of thinking—images are 'visual aids' to thought. As Galton put it: 'There can . . . be no doubt as to the utility of the visualizing faculty when it is duly subordinated to the higher intellectual operations. A visual image is the most perfect form of mental representation wherever the shape, position, and relations of objects in space are concerned. It is of importance in every handicraft and profession where design is required. Our bookish and wordy education tends to repress this valuable gift of nature. A faculty that is of importance in all technical and artistic occupations, that gives accuracy to our

---

ence. . . . "Image" is the name we give to the way in which the concrete object or situation which is then referred to appears to us, when it appears in some sensory (in so far as this discussion goes, in some visual) mode'. '*Thinking*' has three outstanding characteristics: (*a*) it is a capacity for dealing with situations at a distance, and hence involves the *use* of signs, of which visual images are one sort; (*b*) it is a capacity for responding to the qualitative and relational features of a situation in their *general* aspect, and hence involves the *formulation* of signs; and (*c*) in the great majority of cases it is a capacity for utilizing these general qualitative and relational features in reference to a special situation, often of a concrete nature, and having a problematic significance. In other words, thinking is not merely a reference to a past situation; it is a reference to a past situation in such a way, as to attempt to solve a present problem. (*loc cit*. p. 24.)

perceptions, and justness to our generalizations, is starved by lazy disuse, instead of being cultivated judiciously in such a way as will on the whole bring the best return.' And Galton then adds, which points to the direct relevance of this question to the subject of our inquiry: 'I believe that a serious study of the best method of developing and utilizing this faculty, without prejudice to the practice of abstract thought in symbols, is one of the many pressing desiderata in the yet unformed science of education.'[27]

This quotation from Galton has carried us rather too quickly into the heart of our problem: we should note first that the function of imagery in thinking is not merely illustrational. We do not always or necessarily think in abstract terms, and then translate these terms into concrete images for the sake of clarity. A good deal of thinking goes on in the form of imagining, and much of modern physics, for example, is stated in images, or at any rate images are offered as the only alternative to mathematical symbols. Between the mental reference to a symbol and an image there may be only a difference of degree: both are 'signs'. But the difference must then be one of sensorial concreteness. The mathematician may claim concreteness for the symbols $G_{\mu\nu}=\lambda g_{\mu\nu}$ as a representation of the law of gravitation; but the process of thinking in Newton's brain which discovered this law actually involved the much more sensorial concreteness of the falling apple. Either physics is a highly metaphorical science, or it is the result of processes of thinking which have involved imagery to a considerable extent. It is not enough to say that such processes have been 'accompanied by' or 'illustrated by' images: images were an integral part of the thinking. The laboratory experiments which tend to disprove the relevancy of imagery to thinking seem to me to take thought at a comparatively low level—the level of habitual conceptual thought. The higher in the scale of inventiveness or originality such thought rises, the more readily it seems to resort to imagery, excepting always the purely abstract consideration of 'universals'.[28]

[27] *Op. cit.*, pp. 113–4. I have dealt with this question at greater length in *Icon and Idea* (Cambridge, Mass., and London, 1955). The reader should consult Ernst Cassirer's *The Philosophy of Symbolic Forms* (3 vols., Yale University Press, 1953–7) for a full discussion of symbolic modes of thinking; also Susanne K. Langer, *Philosophy in a New Key* (2nd ed., New York and Oxford, 1951) and *Feeling and Form* (New York and London, 1953).

[28] Cf. Bertrand Russell, *The Analysis of Mind* (London, 1921), p. 212: 'Those who have a relatively direct vision of facts are often incapable of translating their visions into words, while those who possess the words have usually lost the vision. It is partly for this reason that the highest philosophical capacity is so rare: it

ON PERCEPTION AND IMAGINATION

7. THE GROWTH OF THE MIND

We have now reached a point at which we can begin to estimate the effect which teaching will have on the mental processes of the child. The growth of the mind is, of course, a process of learning,

requires a combination of vision with abstract words which is hard to achieve, and too quickly lost in the few who have, for a moment, achieved it.' The extent to which dream imagery comes in aid of waking conceptual thought is worth consideration. It is possible that one of the biological functions of the dream is to mediate between conscious thought in all its abstractness and an understanding which only becomes real to the extent that it becomes concrete in the unconscious.

This 'translatory' or 'mediatory' function of dreams may be illustrated by an experience of my own. I dreamt that I was in the air—presumably in an airship of some kind—and before me descended a large parachute which presently opened out and formed a suspended pavilion-like theatre. On to the platform came two figures—a youth and a girl—who began to enact a comedy. They were both dressed as parachutists, and I was absorbed, not so much by the comedy, but by the look of suffering on the faces of the actors, who seemed, in the midst of their playing, to be consumed with anxiety lest their parachute should fail to open if they stepped off the floating stage. I was puzzled by the manifest content of the dream, until during the following day I resumed the reading of a book on which I had been engaged the previous day. It was Kierkegaard's *Stages on Life's Way*, and there I found that I had marked the following passage: 'The more one suffers, the more, I believe, has one a sense for the comic. It is only by the deepest suffering that one acquires true authority in the use of the comic, an authority which by one word transforms as by magic the reasonable creature one calls man into a caricature' (Trans. by Walter Lowrie [Oxford, 1940], p. 231). My dream, therefore, was a translation into imagery of the purely abstract statement which my mind had registered during waking hours

This incident suggests the possibility that in dreams we seek or find images which are the visual or plastic equivalent of our abstract thoughts—at least, when such thoughts take the form, as in this case, of a paradox. The paradox had, of course, *struck* me: it may have seemed obviously true to me: nevertheless, it needed a certain amount of 'realization', which in the act of reading I had postponed. The thought had been 'registered' conceptually, but it had not been apprehended affectively. The mental tension thus created was released unconsciously in the form of a dream.

The riddle, which plays such an important role in primitive cultures, is essentially the same process. A series of symbolic images is more or less consciously elaborated to take the place of an abstraction. It may also be suggested that the fundamental part played by the dream in primitive cultures is in part due to the primitive man's inability to cope with abstractions. He depends on his dreams for an explanation of those natural phenomena and unusual events which his reason cannot explain. (Cf. *The Dream in Primitive Cultures*. By Jackson Steward Lincoln. London, 1935.)

This hypothesis does not necessarily conflict with the usually accepted theory of dream interpretation. The dream is still a wish-fulfilment: it is our conception of the 'wish' that needs revision. (Cf. *The Freudian Wish*. By Edwin B. Holt. London, 1915. A wish is defined as '*a course of action* which some mechanism of the body is *set* to carry out, whether it actually does so or not'. This definition is meant to preclude any merely hedonistic interpretation of the term.)

and one kind of 'education' takes place merely as the result of the impact of its environment on the child's sensibility. The word 'maturation' is perhaps better confined to those mental and physical changes which are the result of organic growth; but apart from any behaviour that may be due to inherited instincts, a child 'learns by experience'. But this innocent phrase disguises the infinite complexity of the process. Koffka, who has provided the best account of this process, differentiates four ways in which the mind grows.[29]

The first is concerned with purely motor phenomena. 'Movements and postures which appear at the beginning of life must be carried out with greater completeness; new movements must be built up and made more or less perfect. Beginning with the activities of grasping and locomotion, one attains in due course the ability to speak, to write, and to perform musically, gymnastically, in sport, in play, etc.'

The second way of development is in the field of sensory experience, and is one which immediately concerns us. The senses present the child with a multiplicity of phenomena, and these he must gradually organize into an intelligible pattern. We have seen that perception itself is a progress of integration, and that the child seems to possess a certain faculty for retaining sense-impressions in all their original vividness, so that he can assess and discriminate at leisure, when not immediately preoccupied with the motor stimuli aroused by the act of perception. But it is not merely a case of identifying and discriminating among the multiplicity of specific phenomena: these phenomena have to be related to one another, and a coherent view of the world built up.

The third way of development involves the co-ordination of the first two: that is to say, the child learns how to make its movements correspond to its will. As it builds up its world of integrated phenomena, so it moves about this world, behaves in it according to its pattern. A sensory component does, of course, enter into the movements described by Koffka as the first way of growth: we only learn to grasp things, or to move ourselves about *effectively*, by reacting to the sensory stimuli encountered in the course of the action. Koffka's point is that the sensory and motor processes are not independent, but interact in an integrated sensori-motor process. This can be proved experimentally by destroying specific sensory centres in the brain of an animal; but it is equally obvious without going to such extremes; for as Koffka himself remarks: 'a hen can run, and it can

[29] *The Growth of Mind*, 2nd ed. (London, 1928), pp. 160–251.

see black and yellow striped caterpillars, but the tendency to run away *when* it sees these caterpillars is acquired'.

The fourth type of development is also one which is obviously of pedagogical interest; Koffka calls it '*ideational behaviour*', and it is simply the ability to control our actions, not in relation to the phenomenal world actually present to the senses, but in relation to the ideals we have formed about the world. This really includes the whole field of purposive behaviour, intellectual and ethical, and education has had as its chief aim to teach the child how to discipline itself in this purposive way.

Perceptions resulting in images, sensations resulting in feelings—these are the elementary materials out of which we build our conception of the world and our behaviour in the world. The purpose of education is to assist the child in that process of learning and maturation, and the whole question is whether our educational methods are proper and adequate for that purpose. Obviously it would be possible to intervene too late in the process—the child would have acquired by its own efforts an accidental but fixed pattern or outlook, which it would be difficult to dislodge. Obviously, too, it would be possible to begin at the wrong end, and propose to the child standards of intellectual or ethical conduct for which he had not yet acquired the sensori-motor basis. That, according to the line of criticism which we shall adopt, is exactly what has happened.

8. THE LOGICAL BIAS

Let us begin with Jaensch's criticism:

'The doctrines and institutions of educational practice have always been dependent on current philosophies. This is true whether the men engaged in educational practice have sought counsel from philosophy herself, or whether their basic philosophic views and attitude have come to them along the countless and often untraceable channels of general culture, which is, as we know, always founded on some "*Weltanschauung*". Now, if we take a bird's eye view of the systems prevalent during the last centuries—leaving out of account a few smaller and less important counter-currents—we see that rationalistic systems of thought entirely predominate. The great philosophic systems, in which the conception of life that underlies the prevailing culture is always mirrored most faithfully, to a great extent see in some form of logic the deepest and finally directive discipline.

This conception appears in two substantially different forms. In the one, the thought process as conceived by the science of logic is regarded as giving to our whole method of acquiring knowledge, and, therefore, to our whole specifically human conception of the world, its deepest basis and final justification. At the same time, it lays down the forms that reality has to assume in order to become an object for knowledge. (Logic as a system of "innate ideas" or "rational truths", or even as "transcendental logic".) But the basic rationalistic hypothesis also appears in a second and more far-reaching form. Thought as conceived by the science of logic is not only regarded as laying down the forms and foundations for our methods of acquiring knowledge, and therefore for our conception of the world: Being, and the world, are themselves regarded as the products of such thought ("metaphysical logic" and "logical idealism").'[30]

The practical consequence of this rationalistic prejudice in the wider field of knowledge will be considered presently, but in pedagogy as a result of this prejudice educational practice necessarily took logic as its model. 'Since the beginning of logic in Aristotle, it has been bound up with grammar. Hence in the schools the ideal of the logician was often fused with that of the grammarian. This is not altered by the fact that logic was only rarely taught in the schools. The point is that it expressed a *tendency*, and it is that that we are here seeking to express in an extreme form. Where this tendency predominates, the subjects that are taught appear as a framework of logic filled with facts. Inner participation is not directed to the subject, but to the form of thought (formula, rule) which it expresses— the pedagogical ideal of the logician rests on the untrue assumption that productive logical thinking proceeds *because* of the laws of logic and also has its psychological basis in them, since it proceeds in *accordance* with them, and its *results* agree with them.'

Then Jaensch brings to bear on this state of pedagogy the results of his researches into eidetic imagery:

'The investigations into the structure of the personality of the child in the eidetic phase of development have shown . . . that *the closest parallel to the structure of personality of the child is not the mental structure of the logician, but that of the artist.* If we advocate that these facts should be recognized, we by no means wish to advocate or to start a culture of aestheticism, or a weakening of logical thinking. Productive logical thinking, even in the most exact

[30] *Op. cit.*, pp. 41–2.

sciences, is far more closely related to the type of mind of the artist and the child, than the ideal of the logician would lead us to suppose. That is shown in the loving attention to the matter in hand, in that close union of object and subject in children and artists, of which eidetic phenomena are merely a particularly evident expression. It is shown in the fusion of the person with the object, so that every lifeless system of signs ranged in between is felt to be a hindrance.[31] The grammatical structures of language are such a system of signs, unless concrete imagination infuses life into them. Only psychological research can discover how the thinking process takes place. Logic represents to us thoughts arranged in their inner order and deduces one from the other; but if we examine the autobiographies of successful scientists, we find that *productive thinking must have a close relation to artistic production. . . .*

'The "intellectualism" of the older system does not lie so much in the emphasis laid on certain subjects (*e.g.* the sciences in the university), as in the predominance of the logician's ideal, which permeates all subjects equally. A really fundamental change in this respect is not to be expected so much from new curricula or a readjustment of the relative importance of different subjects in the universities, as from the substitution for that misleading ideal of more correct conceptions about the psychology of thinking, particularly the thinking of the child.'[32]

Such is Jaensch's diagnosis of what is wrong with our educational system, and it is a criticism which has often been made on *a priori*

[31] This is fully confirmed by Piaget's researches. Cf. especially *The Language and Thought of the Child* (London, 1926), *passim*. E.g., p. 182: 'The child thinks and observes as he draws. His mind attaches itself to things, to the contents of a chain of thought rather than to its form—he contradicts himself rather than lose his hold on reality.' It may be useful to quote here Piaget's general description of the ego-centric nature of child thought. '(1) It is non-discursive, and goes from premises straight to conclusion in a single intuitive act, without any of the intervening steps of deduction. This happens even when thought is expressed verbally; whereas in the adult only invention has this intuitive character, exposition being deductive in different degrees. (2) It makes use of schemes of imagery, and (3) of schemes of analogy, both of which are extremely active in the conduct of thought and yet extremely elusive because incommunicable and arbitrary. These three features characterize the very common phenomenon called the syncretism of thought. This syncretism is generally marked by a fourth characteristic to which we have already drawn attention, *viz.*, a certain measure of belief and conviction, enabling the subject to dispense very easily with any attempt at demonstration.' (*Op. cit.* p. 127.) The nature of syncretistic perception, as further explained by Piaget, shows many points of contact with the hypothesis of eidetic imagery.

[32] *Op. cit.*, pp. 41–5. My italics.

grounds—it is the essential element in Rousseau's criticism, and has been repeated by many philosophers since his time—A. N. Whitehead is a notable contemporary example. But when it comes to suggesting the actual methods by which the necessary reform should be carried out, none of these philosophers or psychologists is very practical. Jaensch says frankly, that the basis of such a reform, which will be psychological, has yet to be built. But from the few indications of its structure which he gives, it is evident that the teaching of art would play a considerable part. He refers to the extraordinary successes of the painter, Erwin Heckmann, in the *deutsches Landerziehungsheim*, in Castle Ettersburg, in using and preserving the mental characteristics of the eidetic phases in children, and says that when these characteristics are thus kept alive, 'one finds an extraordinarily high percentage, in fact the majority of children, achieving results in drawing, painting and the plastic arts that are acknowledged to have artistic value by all who have seen them.'[33] That is not quite the point, of course. The purpose of a reform of the educational system is not to produce more works of art, but better persons and better societies. But as Jaensch himself observes, such artistic activity in children may be the beginning of the wider reform. 'Once the creative powers are freed in one direction, which, in this particular case, has been shown by our investigations to be wholly peculiar to the world of youth; once the shackles of school passivity are broken at one point, a kind of inner liberation, the awakening of a higher activity, generally sets in. Above all, to the eidetic sphere of development, as well as to the mentality of the artist, there belongs a peculiar structure of the mental powers, particularly of thinking; and the arousing and vivifying of these powers benefit all the subjects taught, even the most rigorously logical.'[34] This observation is being confirmed by the evidence that accumulates wherever there are schools that have given art activities an essential place in their curriculum.

9. EVIDENCE FROM GESTALT PSYCHOLOGY

Jaensch's observations have been confirmed by the Gestalt school of psychologists. This is not the place to examine the general assumptions of the Gestalt theory, but we must accept as valid, and relevant to our discussion, the emphasis which it gives to the interdependence

[33] *Ibid.*, p. 47.
[34] *Ibid.*, p. 48.

of the physical situation and the psychological (or biological) response. This is in itself a protest against a logical conception of knowledge or science: there are no 'facts' apart from the experiencing of them; 'the facts of a case' are not grasped by enumeration, but must be felt as a coherent pattern. In this sense, perception itself, as Koffka says, is artistic. 'Under the impact of a mosaic of stimulations which impinge on the retinas of the eyes, the nervous system of the organism produces processes of organization in such a way that the pattern produced is the best possible under the prevailing conditions. . . . Perception tends towards balance and symmetry; or differently expressed: balance and symmetry are perceptual characteristics of the visual world which will be realized whenever the external conditions allow it; when they do not, unbalance, lack of symmetry, will be experienced as a characteristic of objects or the whole field, together with a felt urge towards better balance.'[35]

If these facts are true—and the experiments of the Gestalt psychologists leave little doubt about the matter—then it is quite legitimate to call this factor of 'feeling' in perception and other mental processes *aesthetic*. 'A disposition to feel the completeness of an experienced event as being right and fit constitutes what we have called the aesthetic factor in perception.'[36]

Let us be quite clear what this means, for it is a suggestion with far-reaching consequences in educational methods. Professor Ogden, as a leading exponent of the Gestalt theory, is claiming that out of all possible patterns of behaviour, *one* is chosen by the individual as being peculiarly fit or appropriate. It *feels* right—'one feels at once the ease with which it is apprehended, and the appropriateness of the action that ensues'. Since this particular pattern of behaviour feels right, it tends to be repeated, and other modes of behaviour tend to become assimilated to it.

At the primitive level of perception, the process is one of 'differential sensitivity', and entirely unreflective. But the aesthetic criterion persists all through the process of learning—learning, that is to say, in the sense of acquiring skill in the doing of anything—walking, skating, weaving, painting, assembling an engine. 'Grace and skill go hand in hand; their achievement is never the result of combining acts

---

[35] 'Problems in the Psychology of Art,' *Art: a Bryn Mawr Symposium* (Bryn Mawr, 1940), pp. 260–1. Cf. also 'The Experimental Study of "Good Gestalt"— a New Approach,' by H. J. Eysenck, *loc. cit.*

[36] Ogden, *Psychology of Education*, p. 133. (See pp. 37–8 above for the context of this statement.)

which themselves are awkward and unskilful. In order to do anything gracefully and skilfully, one must first hit upon the "fortunate variation" in behaviour which is most suitable to the conditions.' (p. 137.)

The negative aspect of this truth has often been pointed out: a conscious analysis of what we are doing—throwing a ball to the wicket, for example—only results in breaking the unity of the action. It has been pointed out by Mukerji[37] that Indian weavers lose the skill and certainty of their weaving if they are made conscious of their actual movements. It is not merely a question of mnemonic aid. Facts which are difficult to memorize can be embodied in rhymes, and some people have the capacity for remembering seemingly endless series of figures which they fit to a rhythm. But such 'tricks' are only the conscious application of what is an unconscious principle of growth and adaptation. Balance and symmetry, proportion and rhythm, are basic factors in experience: indeed, they are the only elements by means of which experience can be organized into persisting patterns, and it is of their nature that they imply grace, economy and efficiency. What *works* right, *feels* right; and the result, for the individual, is that heightening of the senses which is aesthetic enjoyment.

10. FROM THEORY TO PRACTICE: PLATO

The educational implications of these facts are nothing short of revolutionary, and as we have seen, these implications are admitted by the psychologists themselves, even when, like Professor Ogden, they are also educationalists. If the child learns to organize its experience by means of aesthetic feeling, then obviously education should be designed to strengthen and develop such aesthetic feelings. But there is a vast difference between recognizing this fact, and putting it into practice. *How* vast that difference is, will perhaps be realized if we remember that this truth which has been so laboriously rediscovered by modern psychology was clearly demonstrated by Plato twenty-four centuries ago, and made the basis of his ideal educational system. Plato has been read and annotated, and has, indeed, been one of the dominant philosophical influences in the modern world. Yet so firmly have the opposed concepts of logical reasoning and intellectual science gripped the world, that not once, during the whole of this vast period of time, has a community ever

---

[37] Mukerji, *Caste and Outcast*. Quoted by A. C. Harwood, *The Way of A Child* (London, 1940), p. 10.

ventured to put Plato's educational ideals into practice. It is not until quite recent times, in the movement initiated by Emile Jacques Dalcroze, that some perception of their relevance has percolated into the educational systems of the modern world. But successful as the Dalcroze movement has been, there is no disposition on the part of educational authorities in Europe or America to make it the basis of the whole educational system. Physical 'jerks' have become a little less jerky, and may be accompanied by a forced mechanical rhythm beaten out of an old piano. But what Plato proposed, though very simple and very definite, was something much more fundamental. He said, as the modern psychologist says, that all grace of movement and harmony of living—the moral disposition of the soul itself—are determined by aesthetic feeling: by the recognition of rhythm and harmony. The same qualities, he said, 'enter largely into painting and all similar workmanship, into weaving and embroidery, into architecture, as well as the whole manufacture of utensils in general; nay, into the constitution of living bodies, and of all plants; for in all these things, gracefulness or ungracefulness finds place. And the absence of grace, and rhythm, and harmony, is closely allied to an evil style and an evil character: whereas their presence is allied to, and expressive of, the opposite character, which is brave and sober minded.'[38]

All this being plain fact, said Plato, we must necessarily attach supreme importance to that part of education which encourages the sense of rhythm and harmony—namely, musical education, 'because rhythm and harmony sink most deeply into the recesses of the soul, and take most powerful hold of it, bringing gracefulness in their train, and making a man graceful if he be rightly nurtured, but if not, the reverse'. Even when it comes to reasoning, added Plato, the aesthetic approach will have been the best, because it will have given a man that 'instinct of relationship' which is the key to truth.[39]

To attempt to answer the question *why* this simple and earnest doctrine of education was never adopted by any nation or community would demand a separate inquiry, and a very interesting one it would be. Nettleship, in his famous essay on 'The Theory of Education in Plato's *Republic*'[40] gives the following curious explanation:

'Few people, indeed, can seriously doubt that the character of im-

---

[38] *Republic*, III, 401.

[39] A fact recently reaffirmed by Professor G. H. Hardy in *A Mathematician's Apology* (Cambridge, 1940).

[40] In *Hellencia*, ed. Abbott, 1880, pp. 67–180.

aginative man is ultimately affected by what he habitually sees and hears; or again, that what one person apprehends as right or expedient, another person may apprehend as beautiful; or, once more, that devotion, similar in effect to that of the saint for the being whom he worships, may be felt by the man of science for the truth which he pursues. But when we have made a few general statements such as these, we are brought to a standstill by the intricacy of the subject and the limitations of our analysis. The fact remains irrefragable that to the vast majority of mankind, art and conduct, religion and science are very different things, with little or nothing in common; and that the attempt to fuse them generally results in sermonizing pictures, rose-water morality, and unctuous sciolism. And as, at most times and for most purposes, it is of more practical importance to realize proximate differences than fundamental unities, the world at large instinctively looks with suspicion upon those who, in trying to see through the ordinary distinctions of life, appear to be removing its ordinary landmarks.'

Written in 1880, this might be quoted as a masterly defence of Victorian compromise and complacency; but the irrefragable fact, if we take a longer and more realistic view, is that the vast majority have no understanding of the nature of art, and therefore cannot see the intimate connection which Plato saw so clearly between the form of art and the goodness and nobility of the soul. This blindness has, of course, an historical explanation in the history of European thought. Apart from the iconophobic and anti-vitalistic prejudices it inherited from the Semitic tradition; apart, too, from the antisensuous and therefore anti-aesthetic bias given to it by schizophrenic visionaries like St. Paul and St. Augustine, Christian morality, during the period of its formulation in the Middle Ages, was wholly under the influence of the logical intellectualism of the Aristotelian tradition. Such was the strength of this ethical dogmatism that when the Renaissance came with its widespread revival of aesthetic activity and with its revival of learning which included some measure of Platonism, there was still no real understanding of Plato's theory of education, nor the least question of introducing it as an alternative to the dogmatic teaching of the Church. It is true that in an isolated humanist like L. B. Alberti (1404–1472), one does find a reflection of the platonic ideal: the ideal expressed in his phrase: 'il bene e beate vivere', where 'bene' and 'beate' are indissolubly linked.[41] There are

[41] Cf. Woodward, *Education in the Age of the Renaissance* (Cambridge, 1924),

similar traces of the Platonic doctrine in Vittorino and Agricola, but in general, the Humanistic tradition in education, as represented by Erasmus and Elyot, is wholly on the side of the rationalistic or logical structure of learning. It is a grammarian's world. The arts are recognized only as recreations 'for the refreshing of wit'. Music, so highly prized by Plato, is the most suspect of the arts, only to be indulged in moderation, 'without wanton countenance and dissolute gesture'. If painting and sculpture are favoured more, it is because they can be more instructive as adjuncts to the teaching of history and strategy. There is absolutely no sign that any of these arts were appreciated by Erasmus or Elyot for aesthetic reasons; and that being so, it is difficult to see how these great scholars could have had the faintest glimmering of Plato's meaning, or any understanding of his theory of education. It is not until we come to the exact scholarship of Nettleship that Plato's real meaning begins to dawn on the scholastic world; and by then art has become something so debased that the theory can only be received with scepticism—as a paradox which may have been valid for the Greek world, but which is impossible in a world where it is of more practical importance to realize proximate differences than fundamental unities. 'The luxuriant development of the arts in modern times,' explains Nettleship, 'makes it difficult to apply to them conceptions formed at a time when they were modest and business-like appendages of religion, war or public amusement.' The arts of 1880 may be well described as 'luxuriant', and Nettleship was right in finding some difficulty in reconciling them with Plato's high regard for art: but he is surely wrong in assuming that the arts in Plato's conception were merely 'the most modest and business-like appendages of religion, war, or public amusement'. He has failed to appreciate the universality of the aesthetic principle in Plato's philosophy: the fact that it pervades, not only man-made things in so far as these are beautiful, but also living bodies and all plants, nature and the universe itself. It is because the harmony is all-pervading, the very principle of coherence in the universe, that this principle should be the basis of education, so that 'our young men, dwelling, as it were, in a healthful region, may drink in good from every quarter, whence any emanation from noble works may strike upon their eye or their ear, like a gale wafting health from salubrious lands, and win them imperceptibly from their earliest childhood

p. 57: 'With him (Alberti) the ultimate concepts of the moral life, of music, and of architecture were expressible in identical forms.'

64

into resemblance, love, and harmony with the true beauty of reason'.[42]

11. FROM THEORY TO PRACTICE: DALCROZE

It is extraordinary that we should have had to wait for a Swiss music master to rediscover the truths so eloquently proclaimed by Plato, but such is the fact. It seems to be a fact, too, that Dalcroze's ideals were a genuine rediscovery, arising directly out of his musical activities, and in no sense inspired by *a priori* notions derived from Plato. And yet it is in Plato's language, though with something less than his eloquence, that Dalcroze speaks; for example:

'The characteristics of rhythm are continuity and repetition. Every motor-manifestation, isolated in time, presents an exceptional and momentary emotional aspect, which is lost the moment it is repeated to form part of a continuous whole evolving at once in time and space. The two fundamental elements of rhythm, space and time, are inseparable. In certain of the arts, one or the other of these elements may be predominant; in music, and in the supreme art— life, they are indissoluble and of equal importance. Life, in effect, is itself a rhythm, that is a continuous succession of multiple units, forming an indivisible whole. Individuality may also be regarded as

[42] *Republic, loc. cit.* It is astonishing to find such a famous classical scholar as Sir Richard Livingstone, in his book on *The Future of Education* (Cambridge, 1941) deliberately avoiding the issue of Plato's theory. He quotes (pp. 23–4) from the same passage in the *Republic* (401 f.), but for Plato's *rhythm* and *harmony*, objective qualities in concrete things like paintings, textiles, architecture, plants, etc., he substitutes the typically 'grammatical' subjects of *literature* and *history*, and leads the reader to suppose that it is to these bookish subjects that Plato ascribes such an ennobling influence. The general tenor of Sir Richard Livingstone's book is one with which, as will be seen later, I have great sympathy, but this curious piece of false reasoning would seem almost dishonest were it not unfortunately but one more example of the systematic misrepresentation of Plato's theory of education which is traditional in English classical scholarship, and which is due fundamentally to an inability or unwillingness to accept Plato's theory of art.

It is sometimes suggested that Plato abandoned his early views on the place of art in education when he came to write his *Laws* late in his life, but it is precisely in this particular that there is no change. In Book II of the *Laws* he insists that our earliest education must come through the Muses and Apollo, and in a passage remarkable for its anticipation of our modern psychological approach to the question (653–4) he argues that only through the power to perceive and enjoy rhythm and melody is the means given us to inculcate 'a rightly disciplined state of pleasures and pains'—upon which, in turn, depends the true apprehension of good and evil.

More recently Plato's theory of art has been carefully and understandingly expounded by Professor Rupert C. Lodge (*Plato's Theory of Art*, London, 1953).

a rhythm, for the combination of its faculties, many of them con-flicting, constitute an entity. But every life and every work of art that conforms only to the idiosyncrasies of the individual is arrhythmic, for the rhythm of art and of life demands the fusion of all traits of character and temperament'.[43]

The difference between Plato and Dalcroze is fundamentally a difference in their conception of the scope of art. Plato would have agreed with Dalcroze that 'artistic feeling can only be developed with the co-operation of music, the only art inherently free from ratiocination'; but we have seen that artistic feeling is involved in the process of perception itself, which is free from ratiocination. Admirable, therefore, as eurhythmics is in the co-ordination of all bodily movement and expression, it can only be ancillary to those mental processes in which aesthetic feeling is involved, and to which we generally give the name of imagination. It is essential that the methods of eurhythmics should be supplemented by methods based on visual and tactile factors. What these methods amount to in detail we shall discuss in another chapter: here we will merely call them those plastic arts which, by evoking, defining and co-ordinating the mental imagery of the child, stimulate that creative use of imagery which generally goes under the name of *imagination*. I have already defined the sense in which we use the word 'imagination', and would only repeat here that the activity includes the productive use of sensory material that leads to scientific discovery no less than the similar use of such material that leads to the work of art—there being no essential difference in the processes, as has often been pointed out (e.g. by Galton, Poincaré, Whitehead, Jaensch, etc. See also Appendix A on page 70.)

12. AN OBJECTION ANSWERED

One preliminary objection must be met. It has been denied that there is any possibility of training the imagination in this sense. For example, Dr. P. B. Ballard, a well-known educationalist, says: 'I do not believe that imagination in the sense of calling up mental images can be trained at all. It is as natural a gift as physiological memory, and as incapable of alteration. We have it or have it not.'[44]

Dr. Ballard is basing himself too exclusively on his own exper-

[43] *Rhythm, Music and Education*, trans. H. F. Rubinstein (London, 1921), p. 238.
[44] Ballard, P. B., *The Changing School* (London, 1926), p. 174.

iences. He quotes the case of Galton's engineer ('I could mention instances within my own experience in which the visualizing faculty has been strengthened by practice; notably one of an eminent engineer, who had the power of recalling form with unusual precision, but not colour. A few weeks after he had replied to my question, he told me that my inquiries had induced him to practise his colour memory, and that he had become quite an adept at it, and that the newly acquired power was a source of much pleasure to him'), but dismisses the case as unconvincing. He then states that he himself has strenuously tried to strengthen his own weak powers of visualization, but wholly without success. But with due respect to Dr. Ballard, it should be pointed out that his case, equally with that of Galton's engineer, is irrelevant. It may be difficult—Hogarth's evidence, already quoted, is quite decisive as to the possibility—for an adult to increase his powers of visualization. But we were discussing children; and here it is a question, not so much of educing a faculty which has atrophied, or strengthening one which has become weak, as of *exercising* one which is natural, and, if we are to accept the hypothesis of the prevalence of the eidetic disposition in young children, one which has a supremely important biological function.

The prejudice which an educationalist like Dr. Ballard displays is, of course, derived from that logical tradition or *Weltanschauung* to which we have already referred. He can only conceive reality as a system of formal knowledge. He says, for example, that 'the main business of the mind is to think, and each mind in its own way. Different minds in thinking out a problem will, if they think validly, all arrive at the same conclusion; but they will all probably have travelled by different routes and through different mental scenery. The images are there to help thought. If they hinder it they had better be absent. The older one gets, and the more accustomed to abstract thinking, the greater is the tendency to drop superfluous imagery, and to think by means of words. And if efficiency is to be the criterion, bare verbal thinking seems to be considerably superior to thought accompanied by an abundance of vivid images'.[45] He goes on to regret that images will, nevertheless, keep creeping in. 'Images of words, at least, are always to be found. And it is when the mental impedimenta are reduced to this minimum that thinking becomes more rapid, more penetrating, and more rigidly logical.'[46]

[45] *Op. cit.*, p. 176.

[46] *Ibid.* Cf. Professor Fox, *op. cit.*, p. 86: 'Those (children) of the most fertile

13. THE WIDER ASPECT

It is not suggested that an integral mode of thought excludes logical thought in a tolerant world. But it is only too evident that a training directed exclusively to logical thought produces a type incapable of imaginative activity and sensuous enjoyment—we have only to remember Darwin's pathetic lament. And it is equally obvious that extreme eidetic types represented by certain artists are incapable of any mental activity which a logician would regard as coherent, intelligent, systematic or sound.

Both types will continue to exist and will contribute to the dialectical variations upon which the biological process seems to depend. But it should no longer be possible to direct the whole machinery of education to the exclusive production of one type—the logical.

Indeed, there is every reason to believe that the child is incapable of logical thought before about the age of fourteen,[47] and any attempt to force an early development of concepts is unnatural, and may be injurious.

The reality is a total organic experience, in which image and percept are not clearly differentiated, and to which anything in the nature of the abstract concept is foreign. Children, like savages, like animals, experience life directly, not at a mental distance. In due time they must lose this primal innocence, put childish things away. But what are they going to put in the place of the unified consciousness they have enjoyed? That is the fundamental question, and the only answer that modern civilization and its pedagogues can give is: a split consciousness, a world made up of discordant forces, a world of images divorced from reality, of concepts divorced from sensation, of logic divorced from life. At the best we can recover an integrated

imagery . . . were by no means those of the highest school intelligence. Other observers, too, have found that the correlations between vivid and clear visual and auditory imagery and school intelligence are low, or it may be negative. . . . As far as school studies are concerned vivid mental imagery may be detrimental or rather it bears no relation to the effectiveness of the mental processes which it accompanies.' Here the logical ideal is disguised as 'school intelligence', as measured, presumably, by examinations and intelligence tests.

[47] This generalization is based on Piaget (*The Language and Thought of the Child* and *Judgment and Reason in the Child*). But as Piaget remarks in the Preface to the first of these works, 'Child logic is a subject of infinite complexity, bristling with problems at every point—problems of functional and structural psychology, problems of logic and even of epistemology.' And Professor Claparède, in his Introduction to the same work, remarks: 'To the psychologist the mind of the child still gives an impression of appalling chaos.'

consciousness in our art, but even our art has been invaded by intellectual attitudes which destroy its organic vitality. The argument of this book is that the purpose of education, as of art, should be to preserve the organic wholeness of man and of his mental faculties, so that as he passes from childhood to manhood, from savagery to civilization, he nevertheless retains the unity of consciousness which is the only source of social harmony and individual happiness.

There is no difficulty at all in developing the mental imagery of the child, and we shall see in a later chapter with what rich results this is already being done. We shall see, too, that unless an exclusively logical ideal is imposed on education, there is no difficulty in prolonging the imaginative activity into adolescence and beyond.

What is now suggested, in opposition to the whole of the logico-rationalistic tradition, is that there exists a concrete visual mode of 'thinking', a mental process which reaches its highest efficiency in the creation of the work of art.

It is a mode of thinking which sustains that primary unity of perception and feeling found in the eidetic disposition. This primary unity develops into the unity of sensibility and reason (sensation and ideas) and is then the basis of all imaginative and practical activity.

In the wider sociological aspect, it is suggested that a way of life based on the knowledge of organic relationships (to use Plato's phrase) is a safer guide to conduct and a surer basis for social organization than those systems or ideologies which are the product of the logical mode of thinking, and which produce such perversions of natural development as those represented by the current doctrines of historical materialism, nationalism, totalitarianism—all of which, in one way or another, deny the fundamental truth that a law of growth is inherent in the universe and manifest in the natural man.

The aim of logical education may be described as the creation, in the individual, of an ability to integrate experience within a logical conception of the universe, a conception which includes dogmatic concepts of character and morality.

The aim of imaginative education has been adequately described by Plato: it is to give the individual a concrete sensuous awareness of the harmony and rhythm which enter into the constitution of all living bodies and plants, which is the formal basis of all works of art, to the end that the child, in its life and activities, shall partake of the same organic grace and beauty. By means of such education we make the child aware of that 'instinct of relationship' which, even before the advent of reason, will enable the child to distinguish the beautiful from the ugly, the good from the evil, the right pattern of behaviour from the wrong pattern, the noble person from the ignoble.

It will be already clear, therefore, that the claim I put forward for the place of art in the educational system is far-reaching. Indeed, the claim is no less than this: that art, widely conceived, should be the fundamental basis of education. For no other subject is capable of giving the child not only a consciousness in which image and concept, sensation and thought, are correlated and unified, but also, at the same time, an instinctive knowledge of the laws of the universe, and a habit or behaviour in harmony with nature.

APPENDIX A

EIDETIC IMAGERY IN CHILDREN

IN the article quoted on page 48 Dr. Allport makes a very objective but largely favourable examination of eidetic imagery. He objects to eidetic imagery being regarded as a transitional stage in the evolution of higher forms of imagery from lower, but it does not seem to me that Jaensch anywhere insists on such an evolutionary conception. I do not think he would question the account of the various types of imagery which Allport gives, and which it will be convenient to reproduce here.

'Memory images . . . are "well-structured" or esemplastic representations of previous experience in which the salient features are made prominent and irrelevant detail obscured or unrepresented. Blended with the visual picture are motor impulses and affective tendencies which give the image its significance as an agent in bringing about adaptive response. If memory-images were nothing more than copies of impressions our mental life would be an inextricable chaos of photographically accurate records. Such a state would not facilitate the organizing, fusing, abridging, and interchanging which enable the individual to vary his reaction; an image too closely bound to a specific previous situation would tend inevitably to stereotype his modes of response.

'The child, on the other hand, whose reactions are less predetermined by habit, and who requires not so much to vary his behaviour as to react appropriately to the concrete elements of a given situation, is benefited by an image which represents more literally the actual sensory details. A single fleeting presentation is not enough to enable the young child to derive the full "reactive significance" from the stimulus. He craves to be shown the same picture book again and again, and to be told the same story repeatedly, without the variation of so much as a word. It is only by virtue of such ceaseless repetition during this "sucking-in" period that the child can perfect his adaptive responses, and so make of them the material for his attitudes and habits of later life.

'The eidetic image seems to serve essentially the same purpose in the mental development of the child as does the repetition of a stimulus situation. It permits the concrete "sensory" aspects of the surrounding world to penetrate thoroughly into his mind. The young child delights in conjuring up his images: a parade of soldiers, a circus, a train journey, or even a trivial domestic scene may haunt him for days or weeks, furnishing him material of great interest for his play activities. It is sometimes only with difficulty that he is persuaded to distrust the reality of these vivid images. He reacts to them with the same degree of seriousness as to a genuine stimulus situation: he is terrified by his image of a wild animal; he is contented for hours with the companionship of his imaginary playmate; and he insists dogmatically upon the reality of his most fanciful visions. Such pseudo-sensory experience enables him to "study out" in his own way and in his own time the various possibilities for response contained within the stimulus situation. His reaction when the situation is first presented is often incomplete, the presence of adults, or the lack of time, preventing him from becoming thoroughly acquainted with its properties. A period of reflection is necessary, during which he may experiment in various ways with his image, varying his behaviour to conform sometimes to one and sometimes to another aspect of the situation, gradually gaining a comprehension of the full meaning of the whole, and building up the attitude which is to determine his future response to the same or to analogous situations.' (*Loc. cit.*, pp. 116–7.)

This account of the imaginative process in children agrees well enough with general psychological observations on the mental development of children such as those of Koffka, Buhler, Piaget and Susan Isaacs. From their various points of view they all testify to an early period in childhood during which the child is busy adjusting its inner world of imagery to the outer world. The process from this general psychological point of view is well described by Spearman:

'The explanation of the whole matter . . . seems to be that all cognitive growth—whether by eduction of relations or by that of correlates—consists in a progressive clarification; the mental content emerges out of a state of utter indistinguishability and ascends into ever increasing distinguishability. So soon as any item of mental content has become sufficiently clear and distinguishable, then and then only it admits of being abstracted; that is to say, it can be "intended" apart from its context. And when this happens, it can be thought of separately and given a name. This clarification may be likened to the ripening of a fruit; abstraction, to its consequent eventual falling from the stalk.'[1]

[1] *Abilities of Man* (London, 1927), p. 216. It might be as well to state here that I find nothing in Professor Spearman's principles of cognition which is essentially at variance with the point of view I am trying to present in this book. What he calls 'the eduction of correlates' seems to me to be a somewhat scholastic but essentially true description of the process of imagination, and I agree that 'the fault of assuming imagination to be a separate power does not lie in too high but too low

This carries us through the whole process of mental development, from perception to abstract thought; but even if we regard Jaensch's conclusions as hypotheses rather than as facts, they do seem to throw light on the process of progressive clarification. Spearman suggests no mechanism by means of which 'the state of utter indistinguishability' becomes increasingly distinguishable. Jaensch does. The function of the eidetic image is precisely to establish that concreteness in the object which permits it to be isolated, named and abstracted; and it is upon the gradual building-up of stable relations between concrete objects that abstract thought depends.

estimate of cognitive creativeness'. 'The popular view, that there exists an imagination as a creative faculty does not appear to assert too much, but rather too little; for *every* noetic process possesses, in addition to its function of discovering truth, that also of creating mental content. If there exists no special power of imagination in the creative sense, this is only because all our qualitative principles throughout all their manifestations constitute in this sense one general imaginative power.' (*The Nature of Intelligence*, pp. 338–9.) Professor Spearman's conception of intelligence will be discussed in a later chapter, but generally we may claim that in so far as the correlates educed take on a qualitative value, as pattern or structure, they obey aesthetic laws; and when it comes to giving the reader some conception of the final unity of the cognitive process, Professor Spearman is compelled to look up to Aeschylus and Beethoven. He has given a more extensive recognition to the aesthetic element in the higher cognitive processes in *Creative Mind* (1930).

Chapter Four

TEMPERAMENT AND EXPRESSION

The problem of the best methods of teaching or training and of the best choice of subjects is to be determined, not merely by a consideration of the general nature of the mind as such, but by a close and first-hand study of the needs and limitations of the particular individuals to be taught.—Cyril Burt

1. THE STUDY OF PSYCHOLOGICAL TYPES

It has already become clear, both from our definition of art and from our consideration of the function of imagery, that the process of education is crude and tyrannical if it is based on a simple conception of 'man' or 'human nature'. Human nature is infinitely various, and our first care must be not to break the shoots that will not bend in a required direction. Education, that is to say, must be based on an understanding of temperamental differences, and the claim now to be put forward is that the child's modes of plastic expression are the best key to the child's particular disposition.

In recent years, what is virtually a new science has grown up round the study of 'types'. It relies partly on physiological methods (more particularly on the chemical basis of metabolism established by the endocrinologists) and partly on psychoanalytical methods. Starting from widely separated points, both methods arrive at conclusions which show a considerable measure of agreement.

The tendency to divide human beings into distinct types is, of course, as old as philosophy itself. It is already evident in Hippocrates, the early Greek physician who taught that the human body is made up of the four elements—earth, water, fire and air—and that certain correspondences exist between these elements and bodily substances like blood, phlegm and bile. In the second century of our era, Claudius Galen elaborated a theory of temperaments which was

73

to last for ages and to become the basis of all kinds of popular and esoteric notions on the subject. Galen's classification was still four-fold, and the terms used to describe the temperaments or 'humours'—sanguine, phlegmatic, choleric and melancholic—passed into the vernacular of every subsequent civilization.

No attempt will be made here to review the vast literature of this subject; it has been done exhaustively by other writers,[1] and a particular study of psychological types in their relation to the visual arts has been made by Dr Joan Evans.[2] But I think it is necessary for our particular purpose to attempt a brief synthetic summary of the various schools of typology, because it is only in so far as our temperamental categories are firmly based on scientific facts that we can venture to make them the basis of our educational methods. I hope at least to show that we are dealing with physiological and psychological factors which are not merely variable, and classifiable, but which, once determined, can more readily be harmonized by the process of education.

2. OBJECTIVE AND SUBJECTIVE ATTITUDES

Schematically, the division of human beings into types begins with a simple antithesis, already present in the act of perception. We saw in the last chapter that perception is ambivalent—that is to say, it can be directed either to an object which is external to the perceiving organism, or to an object (image or sensation) which is internal. We must again ignore the solipsist argument based on the alleged impossibility of distinguishing between percept and object: it might modify the terminology of our exposition, but it would not affect our practical conclusions. We may then distinguish these opposite directions of perception as *objective* (thrown outwards) and *subjective* (thrown inwards), and on this difference of direction is based the fundamental distinction between types of human personality which has prevailed since Plato's time.

Before we pursue the elaboration of this distinction made by modern psychologists, it must be emphasized that these 'two contrary states of the human soul', as Blake called them, are both

[1] Cf. Gerhard Pfahler, *System der Typenlehre* (Leipzig, 1929). W. A. Willemse, *Constitution-Types in Delinquency* (London, 1932), gives a comprehensive survey of recent typological studies (especially in Chapter VIII).

[2] *Taste and Temperament* (London, 1939).

natural to any single person. It may be that the child begins by being wholly subjective, and only slowly and painfully acquires an objective outlook on the world; and it may be that some individuals succeed in altogether eliminating their subjective perceptions and feelings. But the socially integrated human being alternates between objective and subjective states of mind (or moments of attention), and it is only in so far as one or the other direction predominates in any one individual that such an individual can be described as an objective or subjective 'type'.

We shall ignore various dialectical terms which have from time to time been proposed, and which are in effect an emphasis on some special aspect of the objective-subjective classification. Such antitheses are: static and dynamic (Meumann), synthetic and analytic, practical and theoretical, Apollonian and Dionysian (Nietzsche), allocentric and autocentric (Burrow), tough and tender-minded (William James). What we must inquire into as a preliminary to our classification of types of aesthetic perception is first the physiological and then the psychological basis of the temperamental types.

3. THE PHYSIOLOGICAL BASIS

The physiological basis has been most thoroughly established by E. Kretschmer[3] and by W. H. Sheldon.[4] Though this work of psychophysical correlation has proved to be of increasing difficulty and complexity, Kretschmer's classification is now generally accepted. Though Kretschmer dismisses the old temperamental classifications as 'useless', his own, nevertheless, resolve into four main types, and it is perhaps to be regretted that Kretschmer did not follow Pavlov, for example, and make some attempt to give precision to the old terms. The 'depressive cycloid' temperament is certainly our old friend the melancholic humour, and the 'anaesthetic schizoid' is the phlegmatic. It must be admitted, however, that the sanguine and the choleric do not fit into Kretschmer's scheme so easily.

[3] *Physique and Character: An Investigation of the Nature of Constitution and of the Theory of Temperament.* Original German edition, 1921; English trans., London, 1925, second edition, 1936. See also (by the same author): *The Psychology of Men of Genius* (London, 1928) and *A Text Book of Medical Psychology* (Oxford, 1934).

[4] *The Varieties of Human Physique—an Introduction to Constitutional Psychology* (New York and London, fourth edition, 1940); *The Varieties of Temperament—a Psychology of Constitutional Differences* (New York and London, fourth edition, 1942).

Kretschmer's terminology is based on the psycho-pathological definition of types of insanity as either manic-depressive (cycloid or circular) or schizophrenic (dementia praecox). Kraepelin's 'masterly delineation', as it has been called, is now one of the accepted commonplaces of medical science, and Kretschmer's achievement has been to show that the bodily types which are so clearly defined in these extreme cases of insanity, have a quite general basis in normal psychological types. The insane types, that is to say, are but exaggerations of tendencies present in people who would be regarded as quite sane.

Other psychologists (for example, Trigant Burrow in *The Social Basis of Consciousness*) have shown the hypothetical nature of normality, but an hypothesis of normality is nevertheless useful, and Kretschmer has adopted the term 'syntonic', first introduced by Bleuler to indicate the purely hypothetical person whose moods are harmoniously balanced and free from the oscillations and reactions typical of the insane types.

It is now a matter of common knowledge that the physique of the individual is determined to an unknown, but certainly great extent by internal glandular secretions,[5] and Kretschmer's researches prove that in the process of determining the physique, these secretions also determine the temperament of the individual. In his own words: 'It is not a great step to the suggestion that the chief normal types of temperament, cyclothymes and schizothymes, are determined, with regard to their physical correlates, by similar parallel activity on the part of the secretions, by which we naturally do not mean merely the internal secretions in the narrow sense, but the whole chemistry of the blood, in so far as it is also conditioned to a very important degree, e.g. by the great intestinal glands, and ultimately by every tissue of the body. We shall therefore, instead of the one-sided parallel: brain and mind, put once and for all the other: soma and psyche —a way of looking at things which is being more and more adopted in clinical investigations.'[6]

[5] For an authoritative but not too technical survey of this subject, see *Endocrinology: the Glands and their Functions*, by R. G. Hoskins, Ph.D., M.D. (London, 1941).

[6] *Physique and Character*, p. 262. The somatic processes give rise to three well-defined constitution types: the pyknic, the athletic, and the asthenic or leptosome. There are, of course, mixed or intermediate types, and certain rare 'dysplastic' types of a quite exceptional nature (e.g. eunuchoids). Clinical evidence shows that the manic-depressive or cycloid disturbances occur in the pyknic types, whilst

TEMPERAMENT AND EXPRESSION

We cannot pursue the delineation of the types into all the detail given them by Kretschmer, but we must note first (because it will have a later significance) that the polar extremes within each main group are so extreme that we are virtually concerned with four separate temperaments, viz.:

1. hypomanic cycloid
2. depressive cycloid
3. hyperaesthetic schizoid
4. anaesthetic schizoid

Here, as briefly as possible, is a summary of Kretschmer's description of these four temperaments, drawn from various parts of his book:

1. *Hypomanic cycloid*: mercurial, energetic, hot-headed, quick-tempered, 'sees red', tactless, never nervous, sanguine, capacity for laughter, good mixer. Open to new influences, naive enjoyment of the good things of life. Lack of system; unconstructive.

2. *Depressive cycloid*: comfortable, warm-hearted, deep feeling, unassuming, non-moralizing ethical sense, pious but not bigoted, cautious, persevering, dependable.

Cycloids generally have a particularly well-orientated emotional life, alternating between cheerfulness and sadness in deep, smooth, rounded waves. No inhibitions, Sociable, friendly, realistic. A life in things themselves, a giving up of self to the external world, a capacity for living, feeling, suffering with one's surroundings.

3. *Hyperaesthetic schizoid*: timid, shy, with fine feelings, sensitive, nervous, excitable, fond of nature and books, helpless feeling of anxiety in new and unaccustomed situations.

4. *Anaesthetic schizoid*: pliable, clinging, honest, indifferent, dull-

schizophrenic disturbances are confined to the other types (leptosomes, etc.). It is on this somatic-psychic basis that the temperaments can be divided into two great constitutional groups, the cyclothymes and the schizothymes. Then, according to Kretschmer, 'inside the two main groups there is a further dual division, according as the cyclothymic temperament is habitually more on the gay or the sad side, and according as the schizothymic temperament tends towards the sensitive or the cold pole. An indefinite number of individual temperamental shades emerge from the psychaesthetic and diathetic proportions, e.g., from the manner in which, in the same type of temperament, the polar opponents displace one another, overlay one another, or relieve one another in alternation. Besides asking about the proportions of any given temperament, we must at the same time ask about its admixture, i.e., about the tone which the particular type of temperament which dominates has got from inherited ingredients of other types.' *Op. cit.* p. 265.

witted, silent, unfeeling towards outer world, cranky, fanatic.

Schizoids generally are on the surface either cuttingly brutal, sulky, sarcastic, or timidly retiring. Underneath, nothing but broken pieces, black rubbish heaps, yawning, emotional emptiness. Living with oneself. Unsociable, quiet, reserved, serious (humourless), eccentric, religious. No warm natural affection, but ecstasy or cynical coldness. Devotion to abstract ideals. Instead of a wavy affect-curve an abrupt, jagged one.

Such are the temperaments according to Kretschmer. It is important to realize that he nowhere assumes that they are constant in any one individual; on the contrary, within the main cycloid and schizoid groups, there are a considerable number of psychaesthetic variants and a considerable degree of psychomotility. Nevertheless, constitution and temperament are latent from the beginning—from earliest childhood there is a recognizable cycloid or a recognizable schizoid personality, and at puberty a typical manic-depressive or schizophrenic psychosis develops out of it. The individuals' career will depend on how he meets that psychosis, and it will at once be apparent to what an extent education *could* help him and guide him in the task.[7]

Apart from constitution and temperament which constitute he somatic psychic parallelism, Kretschmer distinguishes 'character' which he defines as the totality of all possibilities of affective and

---

[7] Pavlov has criticized Kretschmer's classification as 'mistaken' or 'inadequate' from a physiological point of view, but when he comes to distinguish the various types (whose existence he fully admits), he falls back on the traditional classification and even adopts the pre-scientific terms—choleric, phlegmatic, sanguine and melancholic. These four basic types are differentiated by Pavlov according to the degree of balance between the basic nervous processes of excitation and inhibition, and the relation of these processes to the strength or weakness, balance, lability or inertia of the nervous tissues (I. P. Pavlov: *Lectures on Conditioned Reflexes* (London, 1941), Vol. II, 177–8, Cf. also Y. P. Frolov: *Pavlov and his School* (London, 1937), pp. 201–10). In the end, Pavlov presents us with the same number of types and sub-types as Jung and Kretschmer: he does not refer to Jung, but his criticism of Kretschmer seems to amount to no more than an emphasis on the mechanism of the nervous system as opposed to the chemical functioning of the glandular system. The two processes are, of course, causally connected, and the point at issue is really the starting-point of the observer. It is much the same dilemma as that presented by the James-Lange theory (do we feel sorry because we cry; or do we cry because we feel sorry?). From our present point of view we can ignore these questions of priority in the factors leading to type formation, though it may be admitted that Pavlov's more dynamic or activist theory has a strong appeal to the educator. We can re-condition reflexes—it is part of the normal activity of teaching—but the metabolism of the glands is the business of the pathologist.

voluntary reaction in any given individual, as they come out in the course of his development, that is to say, what he inherits plus the following exogenous factors: bodily influences, psychic education, milieu and experience.[8] Under this heading he would include, not only those educational influences which are our immediate concern, but also those modifications (accelerations and retardations) of the psychic tempo which are due, not to chemical influences, but to inhibitions and the formation of complexes. These latter are, of course, the subject matter of psycho-analysis, and it is significant that psycho-analysis, too, has its theory of types which shows in its broad outlines a remarkable similarity to the psycho-physical classification made by Kretschmer.

Kretschmer has been criticized for an absence of sufficient data to substantiate his types, and (more seriously, by Sheldon) for his 'failure to grasp the idea of varying *components,* and his consequent effort to describe the variations of human morphology without the aid of structural *variables'.* Sheldon's own classification of types overcomes these failings, and presents us with a standardized description of sixty traits—'twenty in each of three correlated clusters—which collectively make up a scale for measuring what appear to be three primary components of temperament'. The following names are given to the three groups of traits:

'*Viscerotonia,* the first component, in its extreme manifestation is characterized by general relaxation, love of comfort, sociability, conviviality, gluttony for food, for people, and for affection. The viscerotonic extremes are people who "suck hard at the breast of mother earth" and love physical proximity with others. The motivational organization is dominated by the gut and by the function of anabolism. The personality seems to centre round the viscera. The digestive tract is king, and its welfare appears to define the primary purpose of life.

'*Somatotonia,* the second component, is roughly a predominance of muscular activity and of vigorous bodily assertiveness. The motivational organization seems dominated by the soma. These people have vigour and push. The executive department of their internal economy is strongly vested in their somatic muscular systems. Action and power define life's primary purpose.

'*Cerebrotonia,* the third component, is roughly a predominance of

---

[8] *Op. cit.,* p. 258. Cf. Willemse's definition, quoted p. 26 above. Cf. also Appendix B.

the element of restraint, inhibition, and of the desire for concealment. Cerebrotonic people shrink away from sociability as from too strong a light. They "repress" somatic and visceral expression, are hyper-attentional, and sedulously avoid attracting attention to themselves. Their behaviour seems dominated by the inhibitory and attentional functions of the cerebrum, and their motivational hierarchy appears to define an antithesis to both of the other extremes.'[9]

4. EIDETIC TYPES

But before proceeding to the psychoanalytical classification, we must glance for a moment at another psycho-physical classification which has direct relations with Kretschmer's, and comes, indeed, from the same university of Marburg. This is Jaensch's theory of types evolved from the eidetic investigations dealt with in the last chapter. Jaensch found that differences in image-perception corres-ponded to differences in types of mind, and that these in their turn were based on physiological differences. One type is distinguished by a heightened sensitivity of the optic sensorial nerves, and their nearest connections in the central organ. This is accompanied by an increase in the sensitivity of motor nerves to electrical and mech-anical stimulation. Outwardly the eyes are noticeably small, deep-set, comparatively lifeless, without lustre, with no 'soulful' expres-sion. 'Such eyes, as indeed the characteristic images of the type, point to a dissociation of functions and organic systems within the mental sphere, whilst the motor expressions remind one of an automaton or a machine.' 'In very pronounced cases there may also be present a peculiar, "pinched" facial expression, which probably also rests on hypersensitivity, and which, in its extreme form, is known to medical men as the "tetany face".' It is clear, according to Jaensch, that we are dealing with a normal youthful type, whose pathological form is the *tetanoid condition*, and to complete the materialistic analysis, he asserts that the normal type, like the pathological type, is susceptible to feeding with calcium, and that by this means the eidetic images of the individual can be increased or diminished.[10]

---

[9] *The Varieties of Temperament*, pp. 10–11. Sheldon's classification is more systematic than Kretschmer's, and he demonstrates that the relations between mental and physical characteristics lie deeper and are more complex than Kretschmer had pre-supposed. By taking the varieties of human physique as his index he arrives at a far subtler description of the quantitative relations between the constitutional and temperamental differences of human beings.

[10] *Eidetic Imagery*, pp. 30–1.

This type Jaensch calls the T-type.

The other type is similarly related to medical symptoms. The eyes tend to be large, lustrous and 'dreamily veiled', and pass imperceptibly into those protuberant eyes which are one of the most striking symptoms of Basedow's disease, better known in this country as Graves' disease. 'These scintillating eyes are the partial expression of a heightened sensibility of the vegetative nervous system, and in particular, of its quickened response to mental stimuli.' Among other characteristics of this type, Jaensch mentions a graceful build, a soft, satin or silky skin, with a low resistance to electrical currents. The thyroid gland is often slightly enlarged. Calcium has no effect on the type, which Jaensch designates as the B-type.

Jaensch stresses that when he is referring to the two types, he has in mind *normal physiological characteristics of a certain youthful stage of development*, which are in no way pathological. Pure types are admitted to be rare—especially in the case of the T-type—the great majority of people partaking of characteristics of both types. But a knowledge of the pure types enables us to separate the characteristics appertaining to the two types in each individual case of a mixed type.

This psycho-physiological division of types might seem merely to offer a parallel to Kretschmer's or Sheldon's divisions, but Jaensch relates his classification to the imaginative activity of individuals, and it is therefore very much our concern here. He finds that the eidetic images of the pure T-type resemble after-images, whilst those of the pure B-type resemble memory-images, though they are still optical phenomena, and literally *visible*. In fact, Jaensch contends, even in face of Allport's criticism,[11] that just as the physiological types shade off from the T extreme to the B extreme, with mixed types in between, so the imagery characteristic of the individuals so graded shades off from a predominance of after-images to a predominance of memory-images, with eidetic images as an intermediate and variable component.

Jaensch's next step is to relate his classification to the degree of integration which the individual establishes between his mental imagery and the external world. He nowhere (that I have discovered) goes so far as to say that the child originally possesses a complete unity of visual sensation, so that its mental processes evolve out of a state in which there is no distinction between image (always

[11] *Brit. J. Psych.*, XV (1924–5). See p. 70 above.

81

eidetic) and percept. But that is apparently the hypothesis he tends to work on. Younger children and primitive peoples belong to an earlier evolutionary type which Jaensch calls 'integrate'. More adult people have developed or adopted 'ready made' a high degree of distinction between perception and conception, and these types Jaensch calls 'disintegrate'.[12]

People who retain the eidetic disposition past childhood will tend to be 'integrate' rather than 'disintegrate', and this class will include all the mentally creative types, whether artists or scientists. 'Intuition', which is so characteristic of the integrate type, can perfectly well operate in mathematics and the exact sciences; indeed, it must if productive work is to be achieved. But the integrate type has got an inner relation to art, so that the difference between artistic and inartistic individuals also falls under the fundamental—and far wider—grouping into integrate and disintegrate types. *Art, too, is an attempt to revert from the disintegration induced by civilization to organic modes of being.*[13]

We shall have occasion to refer again to this definition of art which I have italicized, but we should note the possibility that art may be an activity of disintegrated types: it may be their attempt to escape from the limitations of their psycho-physiological type.

It should also be noted that Jaensch distinguishes a subform of the integrate type, which he calls the synaesthetic or S-type, 'a type with a particularly strong "autistic" mode of experience, which gives a picture of the world valid only for the individual himself'. It is to this type that the popular conception of the romantic artist may be related, especially those extreme type of romantic artist, who be-

---

[12] The relation between the B and T classification on the one hand and the integrate and disintegrate classification on the other hand is not made very clear by Jaensch. The integrate and disintegrate types are regarded as fundamental and the chief classes into which human beings can be divided are but special cases of these fundamental types—'the difference between youth and age, or male and female, or between northern and southern types as described by race biologists, are all special cases of the integrate and disintegrate fundamental types'. The B and T classification would seem to have reference only to the youthful stage of development; the integrate and disintegrate develop in later life on the basis of experience. The B and T classification is somatic; the integrate and disintegrate classification is more psychological, though in one place (p. 106) Jaensch claims that the difference between the two structures is 'no less than the difference between organic and inorganic types of process, one of the deepest and most radical distinctions that exist in the whole of reality'.

[13] *Op. cit.*, pp. 108–9.

come completely divorced from reality, and are to be identified with Kretschmer's hyperaesthetic schizoids.[14]

Jaensch summarizes the general significance of his investigations in the following manner: 'The question of *a priori* categories, which runs through the whole history of epistemological problems, is placed on a new basis; they make possible a more logically consistent development of empiricism; and they promote mutual tolerance, in epistemological systems, as well as in the whole communal life of man. . . .

'Our investigations show that, like the perceptual world, our world

---

[14] But what, in that case, are we to say to the conclusion arrived at by Erika von Siebold, quoted by Jaensch (*Op. cit.*, p. 115) to the effect that in the field of literature synaesthetic phenomena occur most often in French, least in English, and to a moderate degree in German literature? If the S-type is to be identified with the romantic artist, we would expect exactly the opposite conclusion.

Jaensch further observes that the S-type tends to introduce geometrical symbols for reality. This suggests a relationship with abstract geometrical types of art. In view of the fact that such types of art, as Worringer has shown (*Abstraktion und Einfuehlung*, Munich, 1907. Cf. also his *Form-probleme der Gothik*, Munich, 1912, and my introduction to the English translation, *Form in Gothic*, London, 1927) are characteristic of northern peoples, or peoples living in natural conditions of a harsh kind, it is interesting to observe that Jaensch attempts a correlation between integrate and disintegrate types and northern and southern types (*Op. cit.*, pp. 109–10). Unfortunately, Jaensch identifies integration with sun adaptation, which would seem to contradict the historical facts. But generally Jaensch's attempt to force racial distinctions, so characteristic of modern German scientists, contradicts the whole genetic theory of eidetics. For what is put forward as a general law of the individual's adaptation to reality cannot be correlated with such arbitrary categories as those of race. It is one thing to say that each individual's psychology is determined by his physiology—by the chemistry of his blood, the presence or absence of calcium or iodine in the soil he lives on, or even the proportion of sunlight he receives in his eyes. But the correlation of all these factors—apart altogether from psychic complexes induced by the individual's relation to the society he lives in—is always an individual problem, and cannot be subsumed under artificial categories like 'race', or 'nation' or even 'climate'. This is not to deny a general *average* of racial or national characteristics; but the extreme of the average is the universal. National differences are more likely to be the product of imposed conditions of an ideological kind, as Jaensch recognizes when he asserts (pp. 131–2) that the French system of education, 'which is designed on Cartesian lines of thought, is concerned above all with producing clear, easily impressed ideas, while less emphasis is laid on an objectivity that tries to follow the objective data of reality. In this way a form of experience is induced which favours the subjective component in the relation of "coherence" between subject and object, while objective reality has a smaller determining power in forming the outlook on the world.' Such a bias is not due to the proportion of sunlight in the light of France, for in this respect France can hardly differ from the country on the other side of the Rhine.

For the relation between Jaensch's and Kretschmer's types, see Jaensch, *op. cit.* p. 115.

of thought and knowledge is decisively determined by the structure of our consciousness. The kind of structure differs in the various fundamental types. The systems of knowledge of the different sciences are also based to a large extent on the different type of mind-structure operating in them. Different categories correspond to each. *Each structure of consciousness separates out different aspects of reality,* by reproducing certain categories of reality through the medium of categories of consciousness that are related to them. Those categories of reality, in which corresponding categories of consciousness are not present, remain unapproachable, and are apprehended through different structures. The danger of one-sidedness, subjectivity and error in the fundamental questions of knowledge, is chiefly due to the fact that every structure of consciousness claims unlimited validity; but in truth each makes very wide negative abstractions of reality. We can, therefore, only penetrate reality and approach the ideal of "pure experience" by successively taking up the standpoints of different mental structures. The typological basis of epistemology thus includes the principle of tolerance.'[15]

We shall see the significance of this conclusion for our own investigations towards the end of this chapter. Meanwhile, we must pass on to Jung's better-known psychological classification. But first let us note that Jaensch admits the subdivision of his integrate and disintegrate types according to whether the 'consciousness' of the individual is directed outward or inward. The two types thus become four types, and that they are quite distinct is shown by Jaensch's description of the outwardly and inwardly integrate types (p. 117); indeed, the inwardly integrate type is called 'the polar opposite of the outwardly integrate type'. It will be seen that by devious ways, and with another kind of evidence, we are back at the old fourfold classification.

5. JUNG'S PSYCHOLOGICAL TYPES

Jung takes the historical path. He reviews the main classifications made by his predecessors in the field, and his own classification is really an ordering of all the evidence, controlled by his own wide experience in psychiatry. His book, *Psychological Types, or the Psychology of Individuation,* is a rich survey of many aspects of culture, from the theological disputes of the ancient Church and the

[15] *Op cit.*, pp. 117–9.

problem of transubstantiation to Schiller's theory of naive and sentimental poetry and symbolism in Chinese philosophy. The historical distinctions between nominalism and realism, idealism and realism, naive and sentimental, Apollonian and Dionysian, rationalism and empiricism, are all shown to relate to the two directions of psychic mechanism which Jung calls extraversion and introversion, and to the combination of these mechanisms with one of the four basic psychological functions—thinking, feeling, sensation and intuition.[16] Notwithstanding the diversity of all these formulations, writes Jung, 'the common basis or fundamental idea shines constantly through: namely, in the one case an outward movement of interest toward the object, and in the other a movement of interest away from the object, toward the subject and his own psychological processes. . . .

'It is not easy to characterize this contrasting relationship to the object in a way that is lucid and intelligible; there is, in fact, a great danger of reaching paradoxical formulations which would create more confusion than clarity. Quite generally one would describe the introverted standpoint as one that under all circumstances sets the self and the subjective psychological processes above the object and the objective process, or at any rate, holds its ground against the object—the extraverted standpoint, on the other hand, sets the subject below the object, whereby the object receives the predominant value. The subject always has secondary importance; the subjective process appears at times merely as a disturbing or superfluous accessory to objective events. . . .

'These opposite attitudes are merely opposite mechanisms—a diastolic going out and seizing of the object, and a systolic concentration and release of energy from the object seized. Every human being possesses both mechanisms as an expression of his natural life-rhythm—that rhythm which Goethe, surely not by chance, characterized with the physiological concepts of cardiac activity. A rhythmical alternation of both forms of psychic activity may correspond with the normal course of life. But the complicated external conditions under which we live, as well as the presumably even more complex conditions of our own individual psychic disposition, frequently favour the one mechanism and restrict or hinder the other; whereby a predominance of one mechanism naturally arises. If this

---

[16] It is interesting to note that according to Jung the first psychologist to give 'a relatively appropriate character-sketch of the emotional types' was an English physician, Furneaux Jordan, in *Character as seen in Body and Parentage* (3rd edn., London, 1896). Cf. Jung, *op. cit.*, Chap. IV.

condition becomes in any way chronic, a *type* is produced, namely an habitual attitude, in which the one attitude permanently predominates; not, of course, that the other can ever be completely suppressed, inasmuch as it also is an integral factor in psychic activity. . . .

'More exact investigation of those individual psychologies which fall into either group at once yields great differences between individuals who, none the less, belong to the same group. . . . My experience has taught me that individuals can quite generally be differentiated, not only by the universal difference of extra- and introversion, but also according to individual basic psychological function. For in the same measure as outer circumstances and inner dispositions respectively promote a predominance of extraversion or introversion, they also favour the predominance of one definite basic function in the individuals.

'As basic functions, i.e., functions which are both genuinely as well as essentially differentiated from other functions, there exist *thinking, feeling, sensation* and *intuition*. If one of these functions habitually prevails, a corresponding type results. I therefore discriminate thinking, feeling, sensation and intuitive types. *Every one of these types can moreover be introverted or extraverted*, according to his relation to the object in the way described above.'[17]

Jung devotes a hundred pages to the detailed description of these eight types, but there is no need to recapitulate their characteristics here: it is sufficient to note for the moment that eight clearly differentiated types can be delineated. Their significance for our present investigation will be considered presently. Meanwhile, let us note, by way of transition to a purely aesthetic delineation of types, that Jung does deal in his book (Chap. VII) with one aesthetic classification, that made by Worringer, to which brief reference was made on page 83 above. Worringer's differentiation between abstraction and empathy ('feeling-into') is correlated with the introverted and extraverted attitudes, and we must refer to it briefly because it provides the link between the psychological types differentiated by Jaensch and Jung, and the functions of imagery dealt with in the previous chapter.

6. ABSTRACTION AND EMPATHY

I have dealt with this distinction in previous discussions on art,[18]

---

[17] *Op. cit.*, pp. 11–14.

[18] See especially *Art Now* (2nd edn., London, 1933), Chap. IV.

but it seems desirable to restate it very briefly in this present context, for Worringer originally formulated his theory long before the Marburg school began to publish their researches on eidetic imagery. What Worringer in effect suggested in his *Abstraktion und Einfuehlung* (written in 1906) and *Formprobleme der Gothik* (1912), is that two distinctive forms of art arise according as to whether man seeks to reproduce or to escape from his eidetic imagery. If man has a direct sensuous enjoyment of the world around him, he seeks to identify himself with the objects in that world, and *in the very act of perception*, he discovers in the object emotional qualities corresponding to his own psychic feelings. Worringer's formula is, then, *aesthetischer Genuss ist objektivierter Selbstgenuss*. That is to say, if the feeling we discover in the object is one which we enjoy and accept as part of the objective reality of our environment, then we shall feel ourselves in harmony with the object and call it beautiful. Empathy, therefore, is identical as a mechanism with Jung's extraversion; but it is extraversion directed towards a specific object, and conditioned by a readiness to accept this object.

Such a 'natural' adjustment to the outer world is characteristic of the tradition of Graeco-Roman art which after the Renaissance became the general tradition of western art, and it is possible, as we have already suggested, that such a tradition *originated* in the sunny and congenial geophysical atmosphere of the Mediterranean basin. It is equally possible that the opposite tradition, based on a diametrically opposed aesthetic attitude, originated in the uncongenial and harsh atmosphere of the sub-arctic belt which stretched from Eastern Siberia to Ireland, from where, as Strzygowski has shown, the first abstract art came. These two tendencies, the tendency towards empathy (Einfühlung) and the tendency towards abstraction, are definitely related by Worringer to the evolutionary development of the perceptual and conceptual processes. He depicts the primitive man, in whom the tendency to abstraction originates, as 'a creature who confronts the outer world as helplessly and incoherently as a dumb-founded animal, a creature who only receives shifting and unreliable *perceptual* images of the phenomenal world, and who will only, by slow stages of progressive and consolidated experience, remodel such perceptions into *conceptual* images, using these as guides for finding his way, step by step as it were, in the chaos of the phenomenal world'.[19]

[19] *Form in Gothic*, p. 15.

There is thus, at the beginning of the development, an absolute dualism between man and his surroundings, unmitigated by any congenial experience. Out of this dualism, this relationship of fear towards the outside world, 'there cannot but arise as the strongest mental and spiritual need, the urge to absolute values, which deliver man from the chaotic confusion of mental and visual impressions.' The religiosity of primitive man, with its absolute transcendent Deity to be propitiated at any cost, springs out of this need. So does his type of art, which seeks to symbolize the absolute in geometric forms. 'Artistic creation means for primitive man the avoidance of life and its arbitrariness, it means the intuitive establishment of a stable world beyond the world of appearances, in which the arbitrariness and mutability of the latter have been overcome. . . . His artistic will did not arise from the enjoyment of the direct sensuous perception of the object; instead, he created precisely in order to subdue the torment of perception, in order to obtain fixed conceptual images in the place of casual perceptual images.'[20]

[20] *Op. cit.*, p. 29. The dualistic attitude to the world is not, of course, confined to primitive man. It has found higher modes of expression in the East and in Oriental man Worringer distinguishes another stage of development with its distinctive religion and art. 'The art of the East, like that of primeval man, is strictly abstract and bound to the rigid, expressionless line and its correlate, the plane surface. But in the wealth of its forms and the congruity of its solutions, it far surpasses primitive art. The elementary creation has become a complicated artistic form: primitiveness has become culture and the higher, more matured quality of world-sensibility reveals itself in an unmistakable manner, in spite of the outward sameness of the medium of expression.' 'On contemplating Oriental man, this third great typical specimen of the development of mankind, there is forced upon us an entirely fresh standard of values in human development, which corrects our hasty European judgment. We are obliged to admit that our European culture is a culture of the mind and senses only, and that by the side of this culture of the mind and senses, which is associated with the fiction of progress, there exists another, nourished by deeper kinds of knowledge than that of intellect, nourished above all by that one most valuable kind derived from instinct; we have to admit that those intellectual types of knowledge are null and void and mere superficial sham. Oriental culture is once more built up on instinct and the cycle of development is complete.' 'The dualism of the Oriental is superior to knowledge. He is no longer confused and tormented by this dualism, but feels it as an exalted destiny and humbles himself silently and without desire before the great impenetrable secret of being. His fear has been chastened into worship, his resignation has become a religion.' (*Op. cit.*, pp. 35–7.) In spite of Worringer's differentiation of this third type, from our present point of view it is better to regard Oriental man as a further development of the same type as Primitive man, a view which is supported by an objective examination of the works of art characteristic of both types. There is no essential difference in the direction of what Jung would call the psychic mechanisms, and any differentiation according to basic psychological functions would include types other than Oriental art, though Oriental art might then well represent the introverted intuitive type.

The opposite tendency is typified by classical art, and for classical man the absolute dualism of man and the outer world ceases to exist, and consequently also the absolute transcendentalism of religion and art. 'Classical man no longer suffered from the torturing relativity and uncertainty of the world of appearance, from the torments of perception endured by primitive man. The regulating and adjusting activity of his mind had sufficiently controlled the arbitrariness of the phenomenal world to give free play to his enjoyment of life. The creative energies of his spirit, liberated from the immediate necessity of mental self-preservation, were freed for a more joyous, realistic activity, for art in our sense of the term, the sense in which art and science stand in absolute opposition.' To classical man 'artistic activity means fixing in visible form the ideal processes, whereby he accords his own sensibility to the living world around him; he no longer avoids the casualness of phenomena, but merely chastens them to an organically smooth orderliness: in other words, chastens them by means of the indwelling counterpoint of his own feeling for life of which he has become joyously aware'.[21] It is this transference of feeling, this objectified sense of one's enjoyment, which Worringer calls *Einfühlung* (Empathy).

It will be obvious that Worringer's classical man is identical with Jaensch's integrate type: for the distinguishing quality of both is that concept and percept complete each other. In religion God is not transcendent, but an idealization of the man; and in art, the work of art is not an abstraction from life, but a direct imitation of its sensuous perceptual appearance. Or as Jaensch puts it: Perception and feeling are indissolubly integrated in empathy.[22]

7. VISUAL AND HAPTIC TYPES

It might be asked what would happen if feeling were linked, not to perception, but to conception, and this is a question we shall

[21] *Op. cit.*, pp. 29–30.

[22] When Jaensch claims that 'the integrate mode of experience is the alphabet of art, and art rests on it' (*op. cit.*, p. 113) he is identifying art with classical art. He would presumably admit that there is a form of art valid for his disintegrate type, which is precisely the form of art described by Worringer as abstract, and that there is also a form of art valid for his synaesthetic type (egocentric art represented by certain types of superrealist painting). In so far as our ideal is the integrate type of man, so must our ideal be the classical type of art—but classical in the sense defined by Worringer, and not classical in the sense of the Academies, for whom art is decidedly 'an abstraction from life'.

answer presently. But the question has, to some extent, been answered by the consideration of the art of blind or weak-sighted children. The highly significant work of Viktor Loewenfeld will be examined more carefully in a later chapter, but here we should note that from his researches, two artistic types emerge which are of quite general application, and independent of the physiological facts of sight. These two types they call the *visual* and the *haptic*. The visual type is related to the empathic or integrate type. He 'starts from his environment' and builds up from his visual experiences a synthetic representation of his casual perceptions. The haptic type, on the other hand, is above all concerned with projecting his inner world into the picture, and in the case of the blind, it is entirely an inner world of tactile and visceral sensations. The haptic type attempts, therefore, to create a synthesis between his tactile perceptions of external reality, and his own subjective experiences. Interesting as this discovery is, as a differentiation between two manners of representing reality, it gains much wider significance in that Loewenfeld has been able to demonstrate that the two types of representation do not necessarily correspond to the degree of visual acuity. 'Extreme cases, which I found to be by no means rare, proved that, according to their mode of creative activity, some people with full sight must be classified with the non-visual blind, and, conversely, that many blind people have to be regarded as visual types.'[23] It seems to come to this: that apart from all question of blindness or visual acuity, the nature of the creative activity of the individual is still determined by those contrasted attitudes towards external reality so clearly delineated by Worringer.

8. TYPES OF AESTHETIC APPRECIATION

We have gradually approached the aim of this chapter—the differentiation of types of art according to psychological types of human beings, but before drawing our conclusions, there is one more important classification to note, and one which was made on purely aesthetic grounds. This is the classification made by Edward Bullough on the basis of experiments designed to show the differences existing in the perception of single colours, in so far as such perceptive differences condition differences of aesthetic effect—a funda-

[23] Loewenfeld, *The Nature of Creative Activity* (London, 1939), p. 90.

mental contribution to the subject whose importance has not been sufficiently recognized, especially abroad.[24]

The nature of the experiments is indicated by the title of the essay, but Bullough selected such an apparently barren field, first because the 'cognitive' value of colour is very low, and secondly because it possesses 'a peculiarly high suggestive power which is only rivalled by odour in diversity and precision'. A colour presents at once too few and too many indications to perception, and consequently 'any interpretation or meaning within the widest limits of fancy becomes possible'.

The attempt at the clarification of these responses revealed the existence among the individuals tested of what Bullough calls 'perceptive types'. These differences of type would appear to be the fundamental reason for the much debated differences of appreciation of colour. They would represent in fact, the ultimate point to which aesthetic analysis can penetrate in this direction. For the adherence to a special type seems to be a matter of general psychical constitution, the expression of the subject's personality, which not only makes itself felt in regard to colour-appreciation, but which determines his attitude to aesthetic objects as a whole, nay, which perhaps determines his attitude to things in general, and his experience in the widest sense. It is not necessary to describe Bullough's experiments in detail, but as a result of them he arrived at four groups of 'colour aspects' corresponding to different perceptive processes. These perceptive processes, in their turn, determine the divergencies of aesthetic colour-appreciation. To these four types Bullough gave the following names:

1. The objective type
2. The physiological type[25]
3. The associative type
4. The character type

[24] 'The "Perceptive Problem" in the Aesthetic Appreciation of Single Colours, *Brit. J. Psych.*, II (1906–8), pp. 406–463. A similar treatment of the problem in relation to music was later made by C. S. Myers and C. W. Valentine: 'A Study of the Individual Differences in Attitude towards Tones', *Brit. J. Psych.*, VII (1914), pp. 68–00. Cf. also C. S. Myers: 'Individual Differences in Listening to Music'. *Brit. J. Psych.*, XVIII (1922), pp. 52–71; and in relation to literature: June E. Downey, *Creative Imagination*, Chap. IX.

[25] This term proved to be 'too narrow' for the musical tests, and Bullough later agreed to the suggestion of Myers and Valentine that it should be re-named 'intra-subjective'. (*Brit. J. Psych.*, XII (1921–2), pp. 86–7.)

We must quote as briefly as possible his description of these four types.

1. *The 'objective' type*: 'Perhaps the most striking general peculiarity of this type is the constant tendency to a more *purely intellectual*, than emotional appreciation. This strong intellectual element . . . betrays itself, first in the obvious mental comparison involved in the attribute "pure", secondly in the marked inclination to analyse mixed colours into their components, and lastly in the somewhat dogmatic standardizing of the appreciation. The "objective" is, in a sense, by far the most critical of all attitudes, but also the least appreciative; but it is by no means the most sensitive. . . . In so far as such judgments do not involve the appreciation of the object in itself and in its unique individuality, but only in its relation and in complarison to the average type of that kind of object, they represent, I venture to think, the crudest form of aesthetic appreciation in general; they fail both objectively and subjectively in the peculiarly "autotelic", individualizing, isolating character of aesthetic appreciations and are generally expressive of the inability of the subject to place himself in any closer, more inward, and more personally interested relation to the object.'

2. *The 'physiological or intra-subjective' type*: 'Susceptibility to the "physiological" effects of colour is very likely the normal form of reaction to colour-impressions. . . . The criteria of this type are the stimulation and the temperature aspects of colour and very frequently its brightness. . . . The preferences are in the last resort decided by the general constitution of the individual, accordingly as he likes being stimulated or soothed, or prefers warmth or coolness.'

3. *The 'associative' type*: '. . . The name and the remarks previously made upon the associative aspect sufficiently explain the peculiarities of appreciation based upon association. . . . Unpleasant associated contents spoil the colour for the subject, as pleasant associations render the colour itself pleasant. . . . Only in cases of strictly personal associations did the subjects hesitate to allow any weight to the chance suggestions of the colours. . . . The "associative" type is most irregular, being at the mercy of associations. The *existence* of abstract predilections, however, is constant.'

4. *The 'character' type*: '. . . Absence of any abstract predilections for certain colours. The actual appreciations are catholic to such an extent, that it becomes practically impossible for an individual to single out any particular colour for special preference. A person of

this type may no doubt have certain leanings towards certain colours for definite purposes, but in the abstract there is usually a latent feeling that all colours may be beautiful, each in its own way and perfection, since each one represents an individuality so marked as to render any conscious comparison, such as is of necessity involved in preferences, a matter of practical impossibility . . . an unpleasant temperamental expression does not necessarily "spoil" the colour. . . . The whole process of the appreciations . . . shows the strange combination of *personal* elements (the "physiological" conditions from which the "character" is developed) with *impersonal* objective elements, as implied in the "exteriorization" and "objectivation" of these physiological features in the colour. This peculiar doubleness in the content of the temperament, with its strange correspondences and interpenetration of subjective states with the objective colour, the fact that—so to speak—the individual projects himself into the object and rediscovers himself in it, will help to explain the seemingly paradoxical statement that appreciations of this type are distinguished at the same time by a maximum of emphasis and by a minimum of *personal* feeling. . . . The unity of the attitude is guaranteed by the perfectly central position of the object within the subject's consciousness, and produces states of absorption and self-forgetfulness such as are never found in the frame of mind of other types.'[26]

[26] Bullough later drew attention ('Recent Work in Experimental Aesthetics', *Brit. J. Psych.*, XII (1921–2), pp. 76–99) to the remarkable parallelism, between his classification and the one arrived at independently by Binet. (A. Binet: *Etude expérimentale de l'intelligence*, Paris, 1903) on the basis of types of verbal description. Binet distinguishes four types: the *type descripteur* (content with a pure and bald description of the details of an object, without seeking to grasp their significance, much less their relation or the meaning of their collocation); the *type observateur* (which attempts to seize and gauge the expressive and significant features of an object); the *type d'érudit* (which does not attempt to describe the object at all, but to state knowledge about it); and finally the *type émotionnel* or *imaginatif* (which attempts to describe not so much the visible details of the object as its emotional meaning or its mood). Bullough correlates the two classifications as follows:

objective	= *descripteur*; *érudit*;
intra-subjective	= *observateur* plus *émotionnel*;
associative	= *observateur* plus *émotionnel* plus *érudit*;
character	= *émotionnel* plus *observateur*.

Binet's classification was tested by F. Müller in a series of experiments on the aesthetic appreciation of children (*Aesthetisches und ausser-aesthetisches Urteilen des Kindes bei Betrachtung von Bildwerken*, 1912) referred to with approval by Bullough (*loc. cit.*). Müller expands Binet's four types into six: (1) descriptive, (2) observing, (3) emotionally-descriptive, (4) emotionally-observing, (5) eruditely-descriptive, and (6) eruditely-observing. With Bullough's approval, he places both the *type descripteur* and the *type d'érudit* low in aesthetic valuation.

It is perhaps forcing the issue, but there seems to be another obvious parallelism between Bullough's four types and Jung's four basic psychic functions. The objective type obviously corresponds to the thinking type, the physiological to the sensation, the associative to the feeling and the character type to the intuitive type. Nor would there seem to be any difficulty in superimposing on Bullough's classification the further differentiation according to the *direction* of the psychic mechanism of the individual. Bullough, in his experiments, was naturally insisting on an extraverted attitude; but obviously in each case a situation governed by subjective factors would have been possible. This correlation is all the more remarkable in that Bullough's classification was made more than thirty years ago on empirical evidence which owed nothing to the kind of psychiatrical experience upon which Jung's classification was later based. It does not seem that Jung was ever aware of Bullough's work; at any rate he does not include it in his very general survey of the type-problem.

9. COMPENSATORY FACTORS

There are other classifications which we might have reviewed, but they either amount to alternative phraseology, or are earlier and more superficial aspects of the classifications made by later psychologists. Alois Riegl's distinction between geometric and naturalistic types of art, [27] for example, is the basis of Worringer's more detailed investigation. Heinrich Wölfflin's objective contrasts,[28] based on the analysis of works of art (linear v. painterly, surface v. depth, closed v. open form, manifoldness v. unity, etc.) have their origin in subjective factors which correspond to distinctive psychological types. The same is true of Max Dvořák's distinction between idealism and naturalism,[29] an historical analysis of great subtlety, with full awareness of the psychological implications.

The study of primitive art has given rise to similar antitheses: Max Verworn, for example, contrasts 'ideoplastic' and 'physio-

[27] *Stilfragen* (Berlin, 1893) and *Spaetroemische Kunstindustrie* (2nd ed., Munich, 1927).

[28] *Kunstgeschichtliche Grundbegriffe* (Munich, 1915). Many subsequent editions, Eng. trans., London, 1932.

[29] *Idealismus und Naturalismus in der gotischen Skulptur und Malerei* (Munich, 1918).

plastic' types of art,[30] and Herbert Kühn makes a more or less identical distinction between 'imaginative' and 'sensorial' types.[31]

Of all these classifications, Jung's provides the best working basis. It is the most finely and the most clearly articulated, and it has the advantage, not only of including, by easily established parallelism, most, if not all, of the other recent classifications, but also of starting from the traditional fourfold classification which, however unscientific in its descriptive formulation, is based on centuries of empirical observation. Nor does it necessarily contradict the physiological classifications of Kretschmer, Sheldon and Jaensch. Jung, indeed, insists that 'the contrast of types, as a universal psychological phenomenon, must in some way or other have its biological precursor'. He is the last man to underestimate the unconscious psychological adaptation which the infant, from the moment of birth, has to undergo under maternal influence. But this does not explain the undoubted fact that two children of the same mother may at a very early age develop into opposite types, without the smallest accompanying change in the attitude of the mother. The decisive factor must, therefore, be looked for in the original disposition of the child. And as for this, Jung concludes, 'in the last analysis it may well be that physiological causes, inaccessible to our knowledge, play a part'. In the last analysis, that is to say, those researches which demonstrate the interdependence of physique and character, are but an experimental confirmation of Jung's theories. And there is nothing in the findings of the psychopathological school which in any way detracts from the more purely psychological classification of types. Where a process is ambivalent or 'isomorphic', it is immaterial from which side it is investigated.

But it must be noted at this stage that Jung has introduced a further complication into his classification of types which goes beyond a psycho-physical parallelism. In addition to the *general attitude* distinguished by the direction of the individual's interest (outward or inward), and in addition to the bias or emphasis given to this general attitude by the relative predominance, in the individual, of one or other of the four basic psychic functions (thinking, feeling, sensation and intuition), there is also to be considered, in any particular type, certain compensatory factors which exist in the unconscious of that type. According to Jung, the conscious aspect of the

[30] *Ideoplastische Kunst* (Jena, 1914).

[31] *Die Kunst der Primitiven* (Munich, 1923).

individual's personality (his Persona) is balanced, in the unconscious, by a contra-sexual counterpart—that individual's Animus (the male counterpart in the case of a woman) or Anima (the female counterpart in the case of a man). We must postpone any detailed consideration of the pedagogical significance of this distinction to a later chapter, but it must be realized that whenever we speak of a particular type, say the extraverted thinking type, it is not to be assumed that anything more than a *predominance* of extraverted thinking is indicated. There will always be conflicting tendencies which, if not harmonized, may in particular cases lead to open conflict—that is to say, to mental confusion or a nervous collapse.[32]

10. TYPES OF AESTHETIC EXPRESSION

With such a warning proviso in mind, we may proceed to draw the conclusions which are warranted by the psychology of individuation in our particular sphere.

In general we may say, that since there exist these eight distinctive types of human psyche, we must expect from each a distinctive type of expression; and it follows that for each type its distinctive type of expression is valid. What we have to determine, before we go on to

[32] The following passage from Jung's book will make this point clear:
'In a general way, the compensating attitude of the unconscious finds expression in the process of psychic equilibrium. A normal extraverted attitude does not, of course, mean that the individual behaves invariably in accordance with the extraverted schema. Even in the same individual many psychological happenings may be observed, in which the mechanism of introversion is concerned. A habitus may be called extraverted only when the mechanism of extraversion predominates. In such a case the most highly differentiated function has a constantly extraverted application, while the inferior functions are found in the service of introversion, i.e. the more valued function, because the more conscious, is more completely subordinated to conscious control and purpose, whilst the less conscious, in other words, the partly unconscious inferior functions, are subjected to conscious free choice in a much smaller degree.

'The superior function is always the expression of the conscious personality, its aim, its will and its achievement, whilst the inferior functions belong to the things that happen to one. Not that they merely beget blunders, e.g. lapsus linguae or lapsus calami, but they may also breed half or three-quarter resolves, since the inferior functions also possess a slight degree of consciousness. ... On no account should we imagine that the unconscious lies permanently buried under so many underlying strata that it can only be uncovered, so to speak, by a laborious process of excavation. On the contrary, there is a constant influx of the unconscious into the conscious psychological process; at times this reaches such a pitch that the observer can decide only with difficulty which character-traits are to be ascribed to the conscious, and which to the unconscious personality.' *Op. cit.*, pp. 426–7.

a practical consideration of the place of art in the educational system, is whether each type possesses a distinctive mode of *aesthetic* expression; and a brief review of styles of art soon leads us to an affirmative answer. Admittedly this will still leave us with the problem of correlation—that is to say, the determination of the relative values of the various modes of aesthetic expression; but it will be found that Professor Bullough has provided us with a clue to the solution of this difficulty.

(A) *Modern Art*

It may be simpler to examine contemporary art first. Can this vast confusion of styles and movements be reduced to any order? I have already indicated in Chapter II that a general classification according to psychological types is possible, and I shall now attempt to give more precision to such a classification, making use of the terminology which has been evolved by artists and art-critics to express the distinctive schools of modern painting. These fall naturally into four groups:

1. *Realism*, naturalism, impressionism—terms which indicate an imitative attitude towards the external world of nature.

2. *Superrealism*, futurism—terms which indicate a reaction from the external world towards immaterial (spiritual) values.

3. Fauvism, *expressionism*—terms which indicate a desire to express the artist's personal sensations.

4. Cubism, *constructivism*, functionalism—terms which indicate a preoccupation with the inherent ('abstract') forms and qualities of the artist's materials.

I shall adopt the terms italicized as being the most exact and convenient to indicate the four groups. I cannot think of any type of modern art which does not fall within one or another of these groups.

As already suggested, these four groups may be equated with Jung's four function-types, as follows:

$$
\begin{array}{ll}
\text{realism} & = \text{thinking} \\
\text{superrealism} & = \text{feeling} \\
\text{expressionism} & = \text{sensation} \\
\text{constructivism} & = \text{intuition}
\end{array}
$$

Moreover, within each type of art it is possible to indicate objective (extraverted) and subjective (introverted) distinctions which correspond to Jung's general-attitude types.[33]

[33] Dr. Evans, in the work already referred to (*Taste and Temperament*), applies

TEMPERAMENT AND EXPRESSION

Realism, as an objective attitude in the artist, gives us that form of photographic naturalism sometimes called academic, and popularly regarded as the only aesthetic standard. It demands from the artist in general a subordination to the object: it is the object which controls his psychic activity, and his whole attention is devoted to the exact observation of the object. Secondary, unconscious factors in the artist's psyche may find expression in composition and colour.

Realism, as a subjective attitude, gives us what is generally included under the term impressionism.[34] The artist is still orientated towards the object, but the object is no longer a fixed phenomenon, a reality to be determined by thought as well as observation; it is an appearance to be seized immediately, in its momentary aspects as they are recorded by the artist's senses. Impressionism in this sense is the inner reflection of the external reality.

The contrasted attitudes are more difficult to indicate in superrealism because they have been much less clearly differentiated by modern art criticism. But nevertheless they exist, and are to be discerned, not only in the works of art themselves, but also in the inconsistencies of the theoretical background of the movement. Briefly, one type of superrealist artist is so completely introverted that he has no other desire but to express, through the direct automatism of his feelings, the latent images of his unconscious. He must compromise with reality to the extent of manipulating plastic materials: they will exist merely to record the nature of the obsessive images of his disintegrated personality. For this reason, this type of superrealist has no great regard for 'aesthetic' or 'artistic' values: the only value resides in the image itself. This image may be figurative (the typical dream imagery), or non-figurative, as in the style of art known as *tachisme* (Fautrier, Mathieu, Pollock).

The extraverted superrealist attempts to project his unconscious libido into external objects. This explains the considerable rôle of the 'objet trouvé' in the superrealist movement. We have to imagine the artist going about with a suppressed charge of feeling; in his wanderings he is 'struck' by an object—a stone or tree-stump or a chance

---

Jung's extraverted and introverted attitudes to both the appreciative and creative aspects of the visual arts, and further differentiates each attitide by a kinetic criterion (quick or slow).

[34] In the original sense of the word, invented (in 1847) to deride artists who painted their 'impressions'.

arrangement of incongruous objects which complete (to use the phraseology of the Gestalt school) the configuration and release the artist's suppressed feelings. Like the realist he projects himself empathetically into the form and features of the object, but not in order to exist as the object, or to get pleasure from *being* the object: on the contrary, he discharges into the object his own psychic individuality, so that the object exists for him, represents him by his oddness and unexpected isolation.

Expressionism, again, as an objective attitude, is most definitely conditioned by the object, as is obvious in the most simple type of expressionist art—the caricature of the individual. But generally, expressionist art of the extraverted type shows what Jung finds generally in the extraverted sensation type—'a pronounced sensuous hold on the object'. It reacts, not to the reality of the object, in the sense of its objective measurable quantities, nor to its superficial appearance, but to its sensational qualities. Rational and spiritual qualities are discarded, and the object as sensorially experienced, with pain or with pleasure, is reproduced with emphasis on the kind and degree of the sensation. It is the empathetic attitude.

In subjective expressionism, the artist's own sensations become the material for expression. This type of art is most perfectly represented by the haptic drawings and modelling of the congenitally blind, already referred to; but as Loewenfeld as so clearly demonstrated, the haptic type of expression is also found in people of normal sight. We cannot say that there is a definite school of contemporary art which is based on haptic sensibility, but particular artists normally grouped as expressionists certainly display such an introverted attitude (Heckel, Soutine, de Smet).

The contrasted attitudes are very clearly expressed in the intuitive type. In the extraverted type the intuitive apprehension of abstract proportions and relationships is objectified in so-called functional architecture, and in many types of industrial art (pottery, for example). Introverted, this attitude expresses itself in 'pure' or non-functional abstract paintings and carvings, where the artists' intuition is not directed to any external purpose beyond the expression, in the concrete elements of mass, outline, colour, and tone of his inward sense of harmonious relationships or proportions. But the distinction is not merely one between architecture and the other plastic arts; even within the art of painting, the movement known as cubism from the beginning showed two tendencies, which have been called objective and subjective.[35] Painters like Gleizes and Léger maintain, if not an objective relationship to the object, at any rate a rational mode of procedure which is not basically intuitive; whereas painters like Picasso and Braque, in their cubist period, worked on a purely intuitional basis. It is to be noted, incidentally, that it is this intuitive basis which distinguishes cubism, and constructive art generally, from decorative arrangements of colour and form which strictly speaking are a variety of introvert expressionism.

Just as we were warned by Jung that the psychological types were merely schematic, and are rarely represented in their purity by particular individuals, so we must emphasize that the corresponding types of art are rarely exhibited in their purity by particular artists. There are not only mixed types, and types which alternate or vary, but we find in art as in temperament those compensations due to the phenomena of consciousness. These may be expressed in the formal characteristics analysed by Wölfflin (open or closed form, for example), but they are most clearly displayed in the choice of subject-matter. An artist whose primary tendency is in the direction of extravert realism might express his unconscious in the choice of subjects with a symbolic value. Freud has demonstrated this possibility in the case of Leonardo da Vinci.[36]

(B) *The Art of the Past*

After this demonstration of the parallelism between psychological types and types of contemporary art, we need not spend much time in showing the similar parallelism that exists in types of art of the past. It is true that whole periods—e.g. the Renaissance—may exhibit a preference for one type of art: but if we take the whole history of art into consideration, from prehistoric and primitive art down to the present time, all its diversity can be explained, and to a large degree ordered, by reference to corresponding psychological types.[37]

[35] Cf. *Les Arts*, by Pierre du Colombier and Roland Manuel (Paris, 1933), pp. 61–85, where the distinction is worked out in historical terms.

[36] *Leonardo da Vinci: a Psycho-Sexual study of an Infantile Reminiscence*, trans. by A. A. Brill, London, 1922.

[37] The predominance of a particular type in some particular period is one of the most interesting problems which the historian of art has to solve; but it is certain that it can be solved by reference to the prevailing social and economic conditions, and more especially to the effective expression of these conditions in

To these period classifications—these historical styles, as we call them—which in themselves may be predominantly of one or other psychological type, there will always exist individual exceptions. Artists who are decisively orientated towards one of the function-types will express this function in spite of the prevailing style, and these artists, by their very peculiarity or isolation, perhaps best illustrate our thesis. The extraverted thinking type, expressing himself in a naturalistic style, is found in most ages, though whole phases of art, such as Arabic art, exist in which the type has been entirely suppressed. The same is true of the introverted thinking type, whose counterpart in modern art we found in the impressionist school.[38] Impressionism is a widely distributed phenomenon in the history of art, and beyond the French impressionists there are Delacroix and Constable, Caravaggio and Tiepolo, a whole tradition in Chinese painting, and even the cave paintings of prehistoric times.

The extraverted feeling type is naturally found among the art of primitive peoples, for their '*participation mystique*', which is normally a projection of feeling into an object (to such a degree, Lévy-Bruhl claims, that the subject is no longer able to differentiate his own personality clearly from that of the object), becomes objectified feeling itself when the object is an artefact, made by the subject. But art corresponding to this type is much rarer in civilized epochs, and it is perhaps significant that, according to Jung, examples of the extraverted feeling-type are almost without exception women.[39] The relative prevalence of this type among women would thus account for the relative scarcity of plastic artists among them.

From the introverted feeling-type, on the other hand, has proceeded some of the greatest art known to the world. For this is the type which gives feeling-values to transcendental ideals, such as

strictly enforced ideological categories. It is only in a free democratic society, such as has existed (if only approximately) in Western Europe and the United States of America for the past hundred years, that we find the gradual emergence of types of art directly corresponding to types of men. Otherwise what happens is that the élite in whose hands the power of the state is concentrated demand a type of art (e.g. the naturalistic) which is in accordance with their political ideology. The process has been seen in operation very clearly in Russia and Germany during recent years. For a demonstration of the interaction of social forces and the art of a particular epoch, see Frederick Antal, *Florentine Painting and its Social Background* (London, 1947) and, in the general history of art, Arnold Hauser, *The Social History of Art* (London, 1951).

[38] Cf. also p. 141.

[39] *Op. cit.*, p. 448.

God, freedom and immortality, and thereby becomes capable of expressing these ideals, not in logical concepts, but in plastic images. Not only the great mystics, but the great builders of the gothic cathedrals, represent this type. William Blake and Odilon Redon are individual artists of the same type.

The sensation types are perhaps not so easily differentiated as to their general attitude, though as a function-type they are very easily identified. The expressionism which has been so characteristic of modern German art was also equally characteristic of medieval German art, and reaches its extremity in Grünewald. He, definitely, belongs to the introverted type; of the great Isenheim altarpiece, for example, it might well be said, in the words used by Jung to describe the psychological type, that an image is conveyed whose effect is 'not so much to reproduce the object as to throw over it a wrapping whose lustre is derived from age-old subjective experience and the still unborn future event'.[40] It is perhaps also worth observing that Grünewald betrays a preference for tetanoid-features (cf. the drawings of heads in the Kupferstich-Kabinett in Berlin). There would seem to be no difficulty in relating the physiological features of the disintegrated T-type, as described by Jaensch (cf. pages 80–1), with the psychological characteristics of Jung's introverted sensation-type.

El Greco is another artist who clearly belongs to the introverted sensation-type, though there is a strong admixture of introverted feeling in his make-up. Rembrandt is still more difficult to characterize clearly, though sensation certainly plays the chief rôle in his orientation to life, and I think we may say that his general attitude is extroverted (there are biographical details, such as his passion for collecting *objets d'art*, which point in the same direction). But a better representative of the extraverted sensation-type is Rubens, in

---

[40] The capacity of this type of art for spiritual transcendence is well illustrated by the following observation of Grünewald's *Crucified Christ*: 'Why is the aspect of this bearable? Why does it not release a torrent of horror, which sweeps away all pleasurable contemplation? Because, in spite of the utmost closeness to nature, not the tortured body but the picture of it rises before us; because the master communicates to us his vision and, thereby, his religious fervour in such purity and so decisively, that our imagination, removed far away from disturbing, unrelenting actuality, experiences the distant, sublime myth; and the fearsomeness becomes deeply affecting drama. In the picture Christ dies not once, not here: on the contrary, everywhere and always; hence never and nowhere.' Max J. Friedländer, *On Art and Connoisseurship.* Trans. by Tancred Borenius (London, 1942), pp. 25–6.

whom the sensuous enjoyment of the object, as an external reality, reaches its highest plastic expression.

If Rubens, with his appreciation of objective sensuous values, is the best representative of the extraverted sensation-type, then as representative of the extraverted intuitive type we may take an artist like Piero della Francesca. He, too, was orientated by the external object, but his relationship was not one of 'sensuous hold', but rather one of intuitive apprehension; he was more concerned with its concreteness, its formal qualities, with the abstract proportions of the object and the relationship which existed between one object and another, or that might be made to exist by his plastic experiments. But this extraverted intuitive type of plastic activity is more usually expressed in architecture and except in so far as they are governed by purely functional (i.e. thinking) considerations, most architects of the classical tradition belong to this type.

The introverted intuitive type is identified by Jung with the 'fantastical' artist. 'Intensification of intuition naturally often results in an extraordinary aloofness of the individual from tangible reality; he may even become a complete enigma to his own immediate circle. If an artist, he reveals extraordinary, remote things in his art, which in iridescent profusion embrace both the significant and the banal, the lovely and the grotesque, the whimsical and the sublime.'[41] This does not seem to be a very precise differentiation, and one cannot help feeling that if Dr Jung had been familiar with modern types of abstract art he would have been able to give illustrations of a more definite nature. For actually we are concerned here with what Plato defined as the highest and most absolute form of aesthetic perception,[42] a neglected aspect of his theory of art which I have commented on elsewhere,[43] and which has been reaffirmed in our own time by aestheticians like Croce and Bullough. The fact that such art has rarely been recognized as a distinct form of plastic expression (in architecture, painting and sculpture) is perhaps accounted for by the fact that in music it is the *normal* mode of expression. Music can, of course, express the other function-types, but it finds its normal and its most profound development in the expression of the introverted intuitive mode of consciousness. It may be observed

[41] *Op. cit.*, pp. 508–9.

[42] *Philebus*, 51 B.

[43] *Art Now* (1948), pp. 91–3. Cf. also page 64 above.

that Jung generally seems indifferent to the evidence provided by the art of music.

11. CONCLUSION

These parallelisms between types of ancient and modern art on the one hand, and types of temperament or personality on the other hand, may not be exact, and in any case we cannot too often repeat that *in their purity* all such types are hypothetical. But enough evidence has been brought forward to show that several distinctive types, both of art and of personality, do exist and are interdependent, and this is a factor of supreme importance in any consideration of the educational aspects of art. Art, we may say, has almost universally been taught according to one standard—the standard of the extraverted thinking type. In more progressive schools the standard of the introverted thinking type has been implicitly recognized. In a few others a complete freedom of expression has been allowed, though without any attempt at classification or integration. But obviously the teacher should be in a position to recognize the type-attitudes in all their variety, and to encourage and guide the child according to its inherited disposition. Education, at this stage, should imply the widest principle of tolerance. To what extent art should be used as a key to pathological conditions will be considered in another chapter, but this would obviously be a task beyond the range of the normal teacher. The first aim of the art teacher should be to bring about the highest degree of correlation between the child's temperament and its modes of expression.

This is not to exclude the question of values, or of the necessary judgment which follows from the comparison of values. Aesthetic values do undoubtedly exist, distinct from hedonistic values: the beautiful is not the same as the agreeable. Beauty can, indeed, be the cause of pain, as in tragic art generally, and as in expressionist art. Bullough has shown conclusively that the perceptive attitude which he associates with the 'character' type is the aesthetic attitude *par excellence*, for of all the four attitudes distinguished by him, this alone is free from purely personal factors, 'from accidental memories and irrational associations'; and these facts, together with its essentially emotional tone, 'invest this type with a kind of objective reality which is generally characteristic of aesthetic experiences'. 'The very fact that the temperament or character, as the interpretation of originally purely subjective affections, is exteriorized and objectivated in the colour, and is thus, together with all its original emotional efficiency, severed from its connection with the individual, represents the case of the most complete fusion of character and colour, together with the maximum of emotional potency.'[44] This description of the character-type corresponds most closely with the extraverted intuitive-type, and it is with the intuitive type in general that we would suggest identifying the highest aesthetic values—an hypothesis which is confirmed, not only by the kind of psychological analysis conducted by Bullough, but by the superior status among the arts traditionally given to architecture. It is important to emphasize that there is nothing 'intellectual' in this attitude, but that on the contrary, it implies the fullest degree of empathetic projection, and the complete integration of percept and image.

But any process of judgment whose purpose is to determine aesthetic values is external to the purely autistic process of expression, and is certainly beyond the mental range of the pre-adolescent child. The purpose of the aesthetic education of children can, therefore, never be the production of a type of art conforming to a canonical or 'superior' aesthetic standard, even though the existence of such a standard be admitted. Such an aim would be merely to force an intellectual development within the very subject destined to correct intellectual bias. What our investigations into the type problem have shown is that the purpose of art in education, which should be identical with the purpose of education itself, is to develop in the child an integrated mode of experience, with its corresponding 'syntonic' physical disposition, in which 'thought' always has its correlate in concrete visualization—in which perception and feeling move in organic rhythm, systole and diastole, towards an ever fuller and freer apprehension of reality. Whether such integration depends, as Jaensch claims, on the retention of an innate eidetic disposition, from which an harmonious relationship of percepts and images can be developed out of their original unity, may be left for further experimental confirmation; what is certain, without the support of such a theory, is that the aesthetic mode of experience is always opposed to the intellectual mode of experience, and that the harmonious or natural man, no less than the harmonious or natural society, can only be built upon the integration of these two modes of experience. And it should be obvious that by integration we do not

[44] *Loc. cit.* (see p. 91 above), p. 462.

mean the intellectualization of art any more than a universal aestheticism: integration implies organic interdependence. To adopt a striking image which Croce uses of poetry and history[45] (which are but further aspects of our two modes of experience), art and intellect are the two wings of the same breathing creature, and together they ensure the progress of the human spirit towards the highest range of consciousness.

APPENDIX B

MENTAL FACULTIES

PARALLEL to those physical classifications of the temperaments of men based on physique are certain classifications based entirely on mental processes, for each type of man can be further distinguished according as his mental activity is practical or moral, intellectual or emotional. Plato divided the soul in this way, and Aristotle, though he insisted on the ultimate unity of all mental processes, believed that the soul had various 'faculties'—the nutritive, the desiring, the perceptive, the locomotive and the thinking—and that the peculiarity of any individual was due to a particular combination of these faculties, and to the relative predominance of one or more of them.[1] Aristotle's classification was elaborated by the philosophers of the Middle Ages, particularly by St. Thomas Aquinas, and it became the basis of what is known as 'faculty psychology'.[2]

[45] *History as the Story of Liberty* (London, 1941), p. 313.

[1] *De Anima*, 412a 3–415a 13.

[2] For a brilliant summary of the development of this aspect of psychology, see Sir Cyril Burt's 'Historical Note' printed as Appendix IV to the Board of Education's *Report of the Consultative Committee on Secondary Education* (The Spens Report), pp. 429–38. Sir Cyril's conclusion is relevant to the whole of our present discussion:
'Even in the broader implications there is now a disposition to feel that the reaction against faculty psychology may have gone a little too far. Granting that the mind is a unity, and not an aggregate of mental powers, it is not a homogeneous unity, but an organization. Valuable distinctions, noted and perhaps over-emphasized by the earlier classifications, are now in some danger of being lost; and the later notion of the mind as a simple mechanism for linking up elements by association, much as subscribers are linked up by the switch-board at a central telephone exchange, is not only a gross over-simplification of the facts, but fails to explain the peculiar individual differences observable between individual pupils. It is found that certain children may be peculiarly deficient, not in all-round intelligence, but in some special group of cognitive operations—e.g. in visualization, in mechanical memorization, in verbal manipulation, in arithmetical computation, and the like. These peculiarities, which have been studied statistically, have given rise to the description of specific mental "factors", operating over and

TEMPERAMENT AND EXPRESSION

A few years ago Professor Spearman drew up a list of the 'faculties' then in use in current literature;[3] under somewhat different names it included all the faculties of Aristotle, but several new ones had crept in. Apart from sensory perception, intellect, memory, imagination and movement, we find language, attention, censorship, foresight, and others. Spearman subjects the whole doctrine of faculties, and of the types of mentality based on the individual's possession of one or more of these faculties, to a drastic criticism. He points out how impossible it is to isolate any particular faculty in an individual, and hence the impossibility of assessing the inter-dependence of any of the faculties. Without correlation there can be no measurement, and without measurement no science.

Spearman's difficulty seems to be logical, and his criticism would be valid only if our object were the same as his—namely, the correlation of mental processes and the measurement of intelligence. But our object is the legitimate one of classification, and if we can determine distinct psychological species within the genus homo, it does not invalidate our classification if these species contain hybrids and sports. My purpose has, therefore, been to review this psychological classification and to show its relation to the mental 'factors' involved in aesthetic modes of feeling and expression without implying thereby that all types of mentality and all kinds of art fit neatly into the scheme. There are intermediate types and composite types, and our analysis is merely the crystallization or formalization of a biological series, of a vital process which is actually continuous and integral.

above "general intelligence". At first sight these new "factors" are not unlike the old "faculties". The chief differences are that the factors are statistical abstracts, not casual entities or anatomical organs in the brain, that the lines of distinction are relative rather than absolute, and that the evidence for them rests on an empirical analysis of data collected by means of experimental tests, not upon mere armchair speculation.' All these questions are dealt with much more fully in Sir Cyril Burt's recent and exhaustive treatment of the subject: *The Factors of the Mind* (London, 1940).

[3] *The Abilities of Man*, pp. 32–4.

Chapter Five

THE ART OF CHILDREN

The art itself is nature.—Froebel

1. FREE EXPRESSION

The child begins to *express* itself from birth. It begins with certain instinctive desires which it must make known to the external world, a world which is at first represented almost exclusively by the mother. Its first cries and gestures are, therefore, a primitive language by means of which the child tries to communicate with others.

But already in the first few weeks of its life we can distinguish between expression which is directed to a specific end—namely, securing the satisfaction of some appetite, such as hunger; and expression which is undirected and has no other object but to exteriorize a more generalized feeling, such as pleasure, anxiety or anger. It is true that these two modes of expression are related: the satisfaction of hunger, for example, induces a state of pleasure which is then expressed in a smile; or the prolongation of hunger induces a state of displeasure or pain which is then expressed in angry cries. But as often as not the states of pleasure and displeasure are not immediately or directly connected or associated with instinctive needs, and the expression is *apparently* disinterested.

We may say, therefore, that the state of feeling which is expressed varies in definiteness, even in an infant. In popular language we already distinguish between a *feeling* and a *mood*. The one is concentrated, the other diffuse. But what is diffuse is not necessarily less urgent; indeed, the very diffuseness of a mood may give rise to a very positive need of expression, for we feel the need to define what is indefinite. For example, the existence in us of 'a vague feeling of anxiety', which is a mood in our sense of the word, will inspire activities of quite a general, and apparently unrelated nature. The child, no less than the adult, has such moods, and desires to express them. Such expression is, of course, ultimately controlled by the somatic (particularly the glandular) and psychological disposition of the child, but because it is relatively indirect and apparently not designed to secure the satisfaction of an immediate need, we call it *'free expression'*. We may perhaps anticipate a later discussion by remarking here that it is not implied that 'free' expression is necessarily 'artistic' expression.[1]

2. PLAY OR ART?

Free expression covers a wide range of bodily activities and mental processes. Play is the most obvious form of free expression in children and there has been a persistent attempt on the part of anthropologists and psychologists to identify all forms of free expression with play. The play theory has, indeed, a very respectable ancestry, going back to Kant and Schiller on the philosophical side, and to Froebel and Spencer on the psychological side. Froebel went so far as to claim that 'play is the highest expression of human development in the child, for it alone is the free expression of what is in the child's soul. It is the purest and most spiritual product of the child, and at the same time it is a type and copy of human life at all stages and in all relations'.[2] In this wide sense we should have no difficulty in describing as a form of play those plastic modes of expression with which we are now concerned; but the tendency since Froebel's time has been to give a much narrower interpretation to play activity. Spencer, for example, regarded children's play as the discharge of surplus energy, a biological theory which was further developed by Karl Groos and Stanley Hall. It is not part of my present purpose to give a critical account of the play theory—this, indeed, has been done fairly recently and very adequately by Dr Margaret Lowenfeld[3] —but it must be stated quite generally that the biological or genetic point of view fails to make the distinction, which from our point of view is essential, between free and functional modes of expression. Dr Lowenfeld provides a very necessary corrective to this functional bias. For example, she criticizes Groos for failing 'to distinguish between movements made by the child in the effort to gain

[1] Cf. pages 206–9.

[2] *Chief Writings on Education*, trans. by S. S. F. Fletcher and J. Welton (London, 1908), p. 50. For a more general survey of the play-element in culture, see J. Huizinga, *Homo Ludens* (London, 1949).

[3] *Play in Childhood* (London, 1935).

control over his body, which are to the child purely functional in purpose, and movements and activities made by the child for the sake only of the pleasure they bring'.[4] In her own view 'play in children is the expression of the child's relation to the whole of life, and no theory of play is possible which is not also a theory which will cover the whole of a child's relation to life. Play . . . is taken as applying to all activities in children that are spontaneous and self-generated; that are ends in themselves; and that are unrelated to "lessons" or to the normal physiological needs of a child's own day.' This is a point of view almost identical with the one to be put forward here: the only difference being that while Dr Lowenfeld regards art as a form of play, we regard play as a form of art. This is not a merely verbal distinction, because our order of words does in effect restore a teleological element which Dr Lowenfeld has altogether rejected. Art we have already defined as mankind's effort to achieve integration with the basic forms of the physical universe and the organic rhythms of life. All forms of play (bodily activity, repetition of experience, phantasy, realization of environment, preparation for life, group games—these are Dr Lowenfeld's categories) are so many kinaesthetic attempts at integration, and from this point of view are akin to the ritual dances of primitive races and like them are to be regarded as rudimentary forms of poetry and drama, with which are naturally associated rudimentary forms of the visual and plastic arts.[5]

3. SPONTANEITY AND INSPIRATION

Perhaps what we need, as a first step in this discussion, is a definition of *spontaneity*, especially in relation to such terms as *inspiration*, *creation* and *invention*. The opposite term to spontaneity is *constraint*, and negatively spontaneity may be defined as doing something or expressing oneself without constraint. The notion is always of an inner activity or volition, and of the absence of obstacles to this inner activity in the external world.[6]

[4] *Op. cit.*, p. 34.

[5] Hartlaub (*Der Genius im Kinde* (Breslau, 1922). p. 23) suggests that play becomes art the moment it is directed to an audience or spectator. Cf. Sully, quotation given on pages 116–7.

[6] The problem of spontaneity in relation to the sider problems of social and political freedom is discussed by Erich Fromm: *The Fear of Freedom*, pp. 258–64.

Obviously inner activity may be of different kinds of degrees. It may be what Spencer and Groos describe as an accumulation of 'energy', the release of this pressure taking the form of bodily activity. The mechanism of this process is presumably sensation, but the energy may equally well be emotional, or rational, or intuitional —that is to say, it may be an activity of any one of the four mental functions, and ideally it would be desirable to have a separate term for the spontaneous or unconstrained expression of each of these forms of mental activity.

In the natural course of growth these mental activities are expressed without constraint, or with only so much constraint as is implied in the act of communication. In that sense the whole of our lives, if they are happy, are spontaneous. But what is implied in the Spencer-Groos theory of play, and in various theories of inspiration and 'free' expression, is that such day-to-day natural expression of mental activity does not take place—that there is in effect a constraint on such activity, a damming of physical or psychical energy, and that a sudden release of the condition of tension becomes necessary. Spontaneity seems to be too wide a term for such a limited and occasional event. Indeed, if we do not live spontaneously, that is to say, freely exteriorizing our mental activities, then something much worse than a state of mental tension or accumulation arises, namely, a neurosis.

The word 'inspiration' might be reserved for the occasional release of mental tension, especially if we do not insist too much on the etymological meaning of the word 'inspiration', and if by 'mental tension' we imply something far more superficial than the state of unconscious repression. At the conclusion of her book on the subject which we have already referred to, Dr. Harding defines inspiration as: 'the result of some unknown factor accidentally met with operating on the mind of the man of science or artist at that particular moment when it is pent up to a certain tension either by accumulation of "visions, colours, forms", or by facts and pondering over them in the unsuccessful attempt to solve a problem. Although inspiration can occur to anyone it will only be manifested in its highest degree in those persons who are capable of this emotional tension.'

This definition we may accept as accurate as far as it goes, but though it does implicitly distinguish between the thinking activity (pondering over an accumulation of facts in the unsuccessful attempt to solve a problem) and the feeling activity (the emotional tension produced by an accumulaton of visions, colours, forms, etc.[7]), it should for the sake of completeness have covered the accumulation of energy (the sensational aspect) and the much more difficult problem of intuition. But extended in this sense, the definition would serve to distinguish clearly between spontaneity and inspiration. Free or spontaneous expression is the unconstrained exteriorization of the mental activities of thinking, feeling, sensation and intuition. Where, however, for some reason these mental activities cannot achieve immediate expression, and a state of tension is produced, the tension may be suddenly and perhaps accidentally released, and then the expression takes on an inspirational character. The supposition is that unconscious processes of organization are possible, and that the tension induced in the higher nervous centres of the brain by the given elements of a problem may of itself 'inspire' a solution, which solution emerges into consciousness the moment the relevant aesthetic organization is achieved. We shall offer direct evidence of such unconscious processes in a later chapter.

It follows that inspiration should have a fourfold character, and indeed there is no difficulty in distinguishing these modes. The sudden solution of the intellectual problem, the 'automatic' or lyrical expression of feeling in poetry, the improvised dance or play activity as a release of suppressed energy, the intuitional apprehension of new relations of form in mathematics, music and architecture—these are the inspired moments upon which human progress in the arts and sciences ultimately depends.

The terms 'invention' and 'creation' may perhaps be incorporated in this definition. The Oxford English Dictionary should be consulted for the various meanings which have at various times been given to the word invention: they range from 'to come upon, or find' —the meaning embodied in the name of the church festival known as the Invention of the Cross—to the current sense of devising or originating a new method or instrument. But all the meanings imply

[7] Dr. Harding's definition owes some of its terminology to a striking description of Alphonse Daudet's views, which she quotes from Léon Daudet's book on his father (*Alphonse Daudet*, trans. by C. de Kay, London, 1898). The following passage from the book (pp. 156–7) is the most significant: his father, Léon says, believed 'that in the case of all creators there are accumulations of sentient force made without their knowledge. Their nerves, in a state of high excitation, register visions, colours, forms, and odours in those half-realized reservoirs which are the treasuries of poets. All of a sudden, through some influence or emotion, through some accident or thought, these impressions meet each other with the suddenness of a chemical combination'.

previously existing objects or facts, with the mind as merely an agent that arranges or combines them in a new order. Here is no question of accumulation or tension: only the spontaneous exercise of normal mental processes is involved, and their expression in constructive activity.

'Creation', on the other hand, should imply the calling into existence of what previously had no form or feature. It is an anomalous word, for strictly speaking there can only be creation out of nothing, as in the myth of the Creation. Otherwise, creation always involves the use and adaptation of existing materials, and therefore the difference between invention and creation can only be one of degree. It would seem best, therefore, to avoid the words create, creative and creation unless the context makes it clear that we are not using them in a literal sense.

4. MONTESSORI ON SPONTANEOUS EXPRESSION

These considerations are not without relevance to our immediate subject, the nature of the activity carried on by children when they get hold of a pencil or a brush and proceed to draw or paint. Obviously, in so far as such children act of their own free will, their activity is spontaneous. But is the product of their activity in any sense inspired—can it in any sense of the word be described as artistic? Or is it, as Dr. Lowenfeld suggests, merely one form of play?

We may best approach this question, which has many implications, by quoting a passage from one of Dr. Montessori's books:

'There can be no "graduated exercises in drawing", leading up to an artistic creation. That goal can be attained only through the development of mechanical technique and through freedom of the spirit. That is our reason for not teaching drawing directly to the child. We prepare him indirectly, leaving him free to the mysterious and divine labour of producing things according to his own feelings. Thus drawing comes to satisfy a need for expression, as does language; and almost every idea may seek expression in drawing. The effort to perfect such expression is very similar to that which the child makes when he is spurred on to perfect his language in order to see his thoughts translated into reality. This effort is spontaneous; and the real drawing teacher is the inner life, which of itself develops, attains refinement, and seeks irresistibly to be born into external existence in some empirical form. Even the smallest children try spontaneously to draw outlines of the objects which they see; but the hideous drawings which are exhibited in the common schools, as "free drawings", "characteristic" of childhood, are not found among our children. These horrible daubs so carefully collected, observed and catalogued by modern psychologists as "documents of the infant mind" are nothing but monstrous expressions of intellectual lawlessness; they show only that the eye of their child is uneducated, the hand inert, the mind insensible alike to the beautiful and the ugly, blind to the true as well as to the false. Like most documents collected by psychologists who study the children of our schools, they reveal not the soul but the errors of the soul; and these drawings, with their monstrous deformities, show simply what the uneducated human being is like. Such things are not "free drawings" by children. *Free drawings* are possible only when we have a *free child* who has been allowed to grow and perfect himself in the assimilation of his surroundings and in mechanical reproduction; and who, when left free to create and express himself, actually does create and express himself.

'The sensory and manual preparation for drawing is nothing more than an alphabet; but without it the child is an illiterate and cannot express himself. And just as it is impossible to study the writing of people who cannot write, so there can be no psychological study of the drawings of children who have been abandoned to spiritual and muscular chaos. All psychic expressions acquire value when the inner personality has acquired value by the development of its formative processes. Until this fundamental principle has become an absolute acquisition we can have no idea of the psychology of a child as regards his creative powers.

'Thus, unless we know how a child should develop in order to unfold his natural energies, we shall not know how drawing as a natural expression is developed. The universal development of the wondrous language of the hand will come not from a "school of design", but from a "school of the new man" which will cause this language to spring forth spontaneously like water from an inexhaustible spring. To confer the gift of drawing we must create an eye that sees, a hand that obeys, a soul that feels; and in this task the whole life must co-operate. In this sense life itself is the only preparation for drawing. Once we have lived, the inner spark of vision does the rest.'[8]

[8] *The advanced Montessori Method* (London, 1918), Vol. II, pp. 304–6.

This passage is evidently written with an unusual degree of feeling, which may account for what appear to be certain confusions of thought. Drawing cannot, or should not, be taught, says Dr. Montessori. It should be a spontaneous activity, a free expression of the child's own self, own thoughts. Thus far Dr. Montessori is obviously conforming to the definition of spontaneity we have just given. But then she goes on to condemn, in violent language, children's drawings which are certainly the product of a spontaneous activity. She applies to these drawings a certain aesthetic standard—condemns them because they are monstrous, ugly, deformed, etc. That is to say, she judges them by some standard of 'beauty' which is assumed rather than stated, but which we may in our turn assume to be the standard of a classical idealism, or perhaps of a naïve naturalism.

To ensure that the child should produce drawings which conform to this standard, we gather that its 'inner life' must first be developed, refined, inspired with some vision of 'eternal existence'; and that at the same time the hand of the child should be trained in muscular ability, so that it can reproduce its spiritualized feelings. There are three preliminary conditions which must be satisfied before the child is allowed to express itself by plastic means—'an eye that sees, a hand that obeys, and a soul that feels'.

I have no wish to question the idealism which inspires the whole of Dr. Montessori's teachings: it has been one of the most significant and valuable contributions to modern education theory and practice. But to reject all 'graduated exercises in drawing' and 'schools of design' with a view to liberating the child's powers of expression and then to substitute 'the development of mechanical technique' and 'the development of the formative processes of the inner personality' is merely to substitute one form of discipline for another, without making clear in what the superiority of the new system consists. That is to say, it is by no means clear why a mechanical technique should not be developed by graduated exercises in drawing; and the development of the inner personality of the child is certainly not restricted by the production of drawings which, though natural and spontaneous, fail to satisfy the canons of 'beauty'. It is perhaps only a question of priority, but before we can proceed with this discussion it is obvious that we must have some clear conception of what actually happens when a child begins to draw spontaneously. It is a question to which psychologists and educationalists have given much attention, but without, in my opinion, coming to any very satisfactory conclusion.

5. WHAT HAPPENS WHEN THE CHILD BEGINS TO DRAW?

Let us first glance at the history of this problem. It begins with Ruskin. In 1857 *The Elements of Drawing* was published, and in this and subsequent works (e.g., *The Laws of Fésole*, 1877–9) Ruskin first drew attention to what might be called the educational possibilities of drawing. It would be fair to say that Ruskin's ultimate object was the production of artists; even when he was teaching at the Working Men's College, he was sustained by the hope that he might discover a Giotto among his pupils. But some remarks of his in the *Elements of Drawing*[9] inspired an English teacher, Ebenezer Cooke, to reconsider the principles of art-teaching in the schools, and two articles which Cooke contributed to the *Journal of Education* at the end of 1885 and beginning of 1886 are the first documents in a long and increasingly complicated process of research. These articles, which precede all other scientific writings on children's art, are so remarkable as an anticipation of subsequent theories, that I have thought it worth while to reproduce some extracts from them in an Appendix (see p. 169).

Even before this time, Cooke had established relations with the leading English psychologist of the period—James Sully, and together they discussed the significance of children's drawings. The subject was beginning to awaken interest in other countries. In 1887 Corrado Ricci published *L'arte dei bambini* at Bologna, and the following year *L'art et la poésie chez l'enfant* by Bernard Perez appeared in Paris.

[9] Ruskin: *Elements of Drawing*, 1857. Preface, § 11: 'I do not think it advisable to engage a child (under the age of twelve or fourteen) in any but the most voluntary practice of art. If it has talent for drawing, it will be continually scrawling on what paper it can get; and should be allowed to scrawl at its own free will, due praise being given for every appearance of care, of truth, in its efforts. It should be allowed to amuse itself with cheap colours almost as soon as it has sense enough to wish for them. If it merely daubs the paper with senseless stains, the colour may be taken away till it knows better; but as soon as it begins painting red coats on soldiers, striped flags to ships, etc., it should have colours at command and, without restraining its choice of subject in that imaginative and historical art, of a military tendency, which children delight in (generally quite as valuable, by the way, as any historical art delighted in by their elders), it should be gently led by the parents to draw, in such childish fashion as may be, the things it can see and likes—birds or butterflies, or flowers or fruit.'

These works already approached the subject from the point of view of child-psychology, but it was Sully's *Studies in Childhood* (1895) which first attempted to give a coherent theoretical explanation to the gathering volume of evidence. As was perhaps inevitable at that time, the theory was evolutionary. Sully deals with several aspects of the child's mind, and when he comes to deal with the child as artist, he traces a typical line of development from selected drawings and makes a first attempt to relate this development to the 'phenomena of primitive race-culture'. Art-activity he regards as continuous but not identical with play-activity. 'The play impulse becomes the art-impulse (supposing it is strong enough to survive the play-years) when it is illumined by a growing participation in the social consciousness, and a sense of the common worth of things, when, in other words, it becomes conscious of itself as a power of shaping semblances which shall have value for other eyes or ears, and shall bring recognition and renown.'[10]

In tracing the evolution of children's drawings, Sully confined himself to delineations of the human figure and of animals, especially the horse, and with a few exceptions he did not go outside the age-range from two or three to about six. He wisely gave preference to drawings made by children in elementary schools, 'as these appear to illustrate the childish manner with less of parental interference than is wont to be present in a cultured home.'

Sully then distinguishes the various stages of development, beginning with aimless scribbling, passing through primitive design 'typified by what I have called the lunar scheme of the human face', and reaching at about the age of six a more sophisticated treatment of the human figure. We shall not review Sully's classification in detail, because it was made the basis of all subsequent classifications and it is better to give a more complete elaboration. But this process of elaboration can be traced stage by stage through Levinstein (1905), Kerschensteiner (1905), Stern (1910), Rouma (1913), Luquet (1913), Krötzsch (1917), Burt (1922), Luquet (1927), Wulff (1927), and Eng (1931). This does not altogether exhaust the list, but it

[10] *Studies of Childhood*, p. 327. Cf. the following definition of play by a modern psychologist: 'Play is a necessity, not merely to develop the bodily and mental faculties, but to give to the individual that reassuring contact with his fellows which he has lost when the mother's nurtural services are no longer required or offered. . . . Cultural interests do ultimately form a powerful antidote to loneliness even where there is no participator present in person; that is to say, cultural pursuits have a social value even where "the other person" is imagined or left unspecified.' Ian D. Suttie, *The Origins of Love and Hate* (1935), p. 18.

represents a structure built up on the foundations laid by Cooke and Sully.

6. THE STAGES OF DEVELOPMENT IN CHILDREN'S DRAWING

We may take, as the most schematic summary of this genetic theory of the evolution of children's drawings, the stages distinguished by Sir Cyril Burt in his *Mental and Scholastic Tests* (pp. 319–22). They are as follows:

(i) *Scribble*—age 2–5 with peak at 3. Subdivided into:

> (*a*) purposeless pencillings—purely muscular movements from the shoulder, usually from right to left.
>
> (*b*) purposive pencillings—the scribble is a centre of attention and may be given a name.
>
> (*c*) imitative pencillings—the overmastering interest is still muscular, but wrist movements have replaced arm movements, and finger movements tend to replace wrist movements, usually in an effort to mimic the movements of an adult draughtsman.
>
> (*d*) localized scribbling—the child seeks to reproduce specific parts of an object—a stage transitional to:

(ii) *Line—age* 4.

> Visual control is now progressive. The human figure becomes the favourite subject, with circle for head, dots for eyes, and a pair of single lines for legs. More rarely a second circle may be added for body, and more rarely still, a pair of lines for the arms. It is usual for feet to be represented earlier than arms or body. A complete synthesis of parts is unobtainable and often unattempted.

(iii) *Descriptive Symbolism*—age 5–6.

> Human figure now reproduced with tolerable accuracy, but as a crude symbolic schema. The features are localized in the roughest way and each is a conventional form. The general 'schema' assumes a somewhat different type with different children, but the same child clings pretty closely, for most purposes and for long periods, to the same favourite pattern.

(iv) *Descriptive Realism*—age 7–8.

> The drawings are still logical rather than visual. The child 'sets down what he knows, not what he sees; and is still think-

ing, not of the present individual, but rather of the generic type'. He is trying to communicate, express, or catalogue all that he remembers, or all that interests him, in a subject. The 'schema' becomes more true to detail; items, however, are suggested more by the association of ideas than by the analysis of percepts. Profile views of the face are attempted, but perspective, opacity, foreshortening, and all the consequences of singleness of viewpoint are still disregarded. There is a gathering interest in decorative details.

(v) *Visual Realism*—age 9–10.
The child passes from the stage of drawing from memory and imagination to the stage of drawing from nature. There are two phases:
   (*a*) two dimensional phase—outline only is used.
   (*b*) three-dimensional phase—solidity is attempted. Attention is given to overlapping and perspective. A little shading and occasional foreshortening may be attempted. Landscapes are attempted.

(vi) *Repression*—age 11–14.
This stage sets in most commonly about the age of 13. Burt (and his view was representative at the time he wrote) regards this stage as part of the child's natural development. Progress in the attempt to reproduce objects is now at best laborious and slow, and the child becomes disillusioned and discouraged. Interest is transferred to expression through the medium of language, and if drawing continues the preference is for conventional designs, and the human figure becomes rare.

(vii) *Artistic Revival*—early adolescence.
'From about the age of 15, drawing for the first time blossoms into a genuine artistic activity.' Drawings now tell a story. A clear distinction between the sexes is now evident. Girls show a love of richness in colour, of grace in form, of beauty in line; youths tend to use drawing more as a technical and mechanical outlet.
But by many, perhaps by most, this final stage is never reached. The repression at the previous stage has been too complete.

Such is the generally accepted account of the development of children's drawings.[11] It has been criticized in some of its aspects,

[11] From a more formal point of view *eleven* stages of development have been

119

particularly by Wulff. Our own criticism will be directed to three fundamental points:

A   The concept of the 'schema'.

B   The genetic theory in general—the neglected correlation of expression and temperament.

C   The supposed inevitability of a stage of 'repression'.

distinguished by Dr. Ruth Griffiths (*Imagination in Early Childhood*, London, 1935, pp. 190–209). She summarizes these stages as follows:

(i) *Undifferentiated scribble.*

(ii) *Rough geometrical shapes appear,* usually circles and squares.

(iii) The making of further objects by the *combination of lines and squares,* and separately of circles. The circles and squares are not yet combined together.

(iv) *Combination of circles and lines* to make many other objects, of which one of outstanding interest is the human figure.

(v) *Juxtaposition of many objects* rapidly drawn and named, but often unrecognizable.

(vi) *Tendency to concentrate on one object at a time,* bolder work, care taken, a degree of detail present.

(vii) *Further juxtaposition,* but clear subjective association usually present, work recognizable.

(viii) *Partial synthesis.* Some items are shown in definite relation to each other.

(ix) *The pure picture.* A tendency also to draw one picture only.

(x) *Multiplication of pictures.* Pure joy of representation.

(xi) *Development of a theme* by means of a series of pictures.

In an accompanying table (p. 211) Dr. Griffiths shows a definite correlation between these stages of development and the mental ages of fifty children. (Binet-Simon scale, Stanford Revision.) We shall discuss the significance of art in relation to intelligence tests later. (See page 253.)

More recently Mrs. Rhoda Kellogg has made a study of more than 100,000 drawings and paintings by children of two, three and four years of age in the Golden Gate Nursery Schools in San Francisco (*What Children Scribble and Why*, 1955). She found that 'beginning with the first stroke of the pencil and continuing to the time when the child can make the finished drawing in which there is a pictorial likeness to the objects drawn, there is evidence of sequential unfolding of drawing ability'. She discovered that the scribbles could be classified into twenty basic types (dot, vertical line, horizontal line, diagonal line, curved line, zigzag line, loop line, spiral line, etc.). Out of various combinations of these basic scribbles emerge six basic designs (Greek cross, square, circle, triangle, odd shaped areas and diagonal cross). These are then combined or aggregated, and representation features are gradually attached to, or associated with, these combines and aggregates. One of these basic designs seems to predominate—the circle combined with the cross, which is the magic circle or 'mandala', 'the dominant religious image of the whole Oriental world'. Mrs. Kellogg shows, in an ingenious chart, how a variety of pictorial representations can be gradually evolved from this single basic design.

These researches would seem to prove that the schema is not arbitrary in its origin: there is in the child's scribbling activity an inherent tendency to form, and even to a specific form that has primordial significance for the unconscious.

7. THE 'SCHEMA'

So far as I can discover, the word schema was first used casually, and without particular significance, by Sully in the following context (*Op. cit.*, pp. 352–3). He has been describing the earliest attempts of children to represent hands and fingers, and after discussing various radial arrangements, he remarks that an important advance on these crude devices is seen where an attempt is made to indicate the hand and the relation of the fingers to the hand. 'One of the earliest of these attempts takes the form of the well-known toasting-fork or rake hand. Here a line at right angles to that of the arm symbolically represents the hand, and the fingers are set forth by the prongs or teeth. . . . Number is here as little attended to as in the radial arrangements. It is worth noting that this *schema* seems to be widely diffused among children of different nationalities, and occurs in the drawings of untaught adults.'

The word thus innocently used on this occasion by Sully was taken up by Kerschensteiner and given portentous significance by him and by subsequent German psychologists.[12] The general meaning of the word, however, is clear enough. Apart from certain rare exceptions, when children first begin to draw intentionally, they apparently make no attempt to translate their visual images into plastic equivalents (imitative or naturalistic representations), but are fully satisfied with certain graphic signs which they identify with their images. These graphic signs may vary from a mark or scribble which has no recognizable relation to the object associated with it, to a linear outline in which all the main features of the object are economically indicated. With their passion for a unitary genetic pattern, all previous writers on the subject have attempted to trace the evolution of the schema, from the first chance recognition of a resemblance in the child's purposeless scribblings, to the first attempt to give such arbitrary discoveries some coherence (Schema der lokalen Anord-

---

[12] It is amusing to observe that thirty-six years later, the translator of Helga Eng's *Psychology of Children's Drawings* (London, 1931, p. 109*n*) deliberates on how this German word *Schema* should be translated into English, and decides on 'formula' as an English equivalent. 'Dr. Eng pointed out that, although "schema", "schematized", etc., are very rarely used in English, some English psychologists have adopted them (!) . . . In spite of this, it was decided to use "formula", etc., as these terms are already in common use in the same sense in connection with drawing and painting generally. It seems unnecessary to introduce a new term, which has the grave disadvantage of being closely similar to a common word, "scheme", having an allied meaning.'

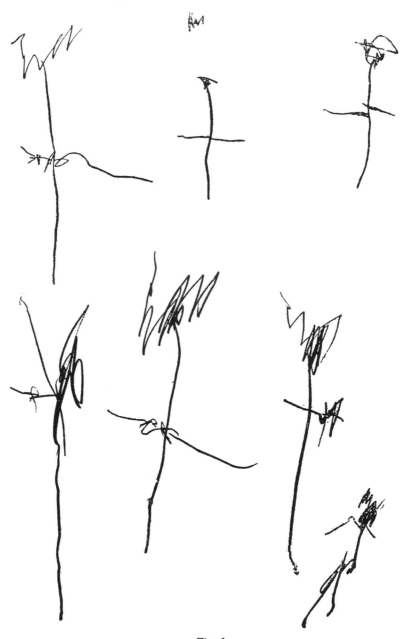

Fig. 1
B, 3, I. First drawings of the human figure

nung), and soon to a deliberate *linear* or one-dimensional schema, and then to an *outline* or two-dimensional schema. Variations in the rate at which different children develop along these lines is accounted for by supposing that some children are more 'visually gifted' than others.

My own observations do not altogether support such a neat evolutionary theory. In the first place, I have not found that the first recognizable representational drawings necessarily emerge by chance from the scribble stage. The drawings by a boy of three years one month illustrated in Fig. 1 were contemporary with the child's first scribbling, but were a separate activity, and clearly indicated a separate intention. They were drawn with great deliberation, and care was taken to connect the limbs to the body 'securely'. But the same child would give a name to a completely non-representational scribble. From the beginning the child finds it possible to invest both an abstract symbol (any mark or object whatsoever) and a summary 'schema' with all the vitality or reality of an image, and in this, of course, he conforms to the animism of primitive man. Under the influence of this environment (the 'naturalistic' taste of his parents and teachers) the modern child sooner or later discards the abstract symbol, but I find that some children persist with it, not only longer than others, but in conjunction with their more representational schemas. What Luquet, for a later stage of development calls a 'duplicité de types', is, in my view, present from the beginning, and this fact has a fundamental bearing on any psychological analysis of the child's activity.

Luquet[13] is discussing the drawings of children of about eight years old when he arrives at what he describes as 'an almost incredible fact, liable to disturb all preconceived ideas based on a too simple conception of the child's mind, but the truth of which cannot be denied. Not only does the child recognize that other people draw in a style different from his; not only does he expect such people to observe the same fidelity to their style as he does to his; but further, when he draws for another person, he adopts for that occasion the style of that person instead of his own. . . . The universality of this curious fact, which one might call "duplicity of styles", is put beyond doubt by looking at the drawings which we find on walls and pavements. These "graffiti" emanate from children of all ages; sometimes even from adolescents and adults; most of the artists have had school-

[13] *Le Dessin enfantin* (Paris, 1927), pp. 65–6.

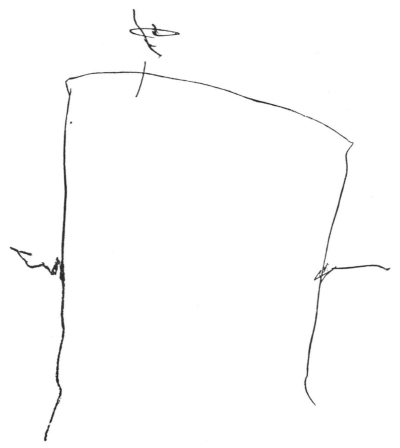

Fig. 2
Second stage in drawing human figure, by the same boy as Fig. 1,
one month later

ing, and many of the drawings are done in the interval between two lessons. Now, among them we find a considerable number of those figures without a body, none of which would be acceptable to a teacher. It is necessary then to admit that the child artist uses simultaneously for the same subject two different styles of representation: one for his own personal satisfaction, the other for the satisfaction of other people.'

This duplicity, which may be observed from the very beginning of the child's graphic or plastic activity, may be explained as a distinction between (a) what the child does for the satisfaction of his own inner needs, and (b) what he does as a social gesture, as a sign of sympathy with or emulation of, an external person or persons.

The second activity is *imitative*, and all authorities are agreed that from the first scribble onwards, a large element of imitation of the adult enters into the child's drawing. He imitates, not only what the adult draws, but the muscular actions of the adult's hand and fingers. There can be no doubt that this imitative instinct plays a large part in the development of a child's drawing in the direction of realism. There is evidence to show that if a child is accustomed to abstract patterns or paintings, or if the parents are themselves abstract painters, the child will develop an abstract style: it has not been proved that the normal child has an irresistible desire to make naturalistic representations of objects. There are historical periods during which a non-figurative art prevailed (the Neolithic age, the Celtic and Arabic civilizations), and such periods prove that a non-representational tradition can be 'natural' or 'normal' at all stages of individual development. There is no reason to suppose that an infant of the New Stone Age drew humpty-dumpties, and the little Moslem child would presumably not be allowed to indulge in any such naturalistic 'schemas'.

So far as I am aware, no one has ever made the experiment of bringing up a child in complete immunity from all types of representational art other than its own, and from all adult examples of graphic activity. Such an experiment, if it were possible, would provide valuable evidence. The nearest approach to such evidence is that provided by Münz and Loewenfeld in their observations of the art of weak-sighted and blind children.[14] Unfortunately the evidence for the totally blind relates to subjects already fairly advanced in age, whose haptic experience is already sufficiently coherent for naturalistic representation, and who, moreover, have been subjected to a training with a strong representational bias. I see no reason to suppose that such subjects, if urged to express themselves in abstract symbols, would not have developed a plastic language of a non-representational type.

We may certainly conclude that the graphic activity in the child may be devoid, not merely of any representational intention, but

[14] V. Loewenfeld: *The Nature of Creative Activity*, and L. Münz and V. Loewenfeld: *Die plastische Arbeiten Blinder* (Brunn, 1934).

equally of any imitative instinct. Whatever the child may draw under influence or instruction, he does also draw for his own obscure purposes, and it is the nature of this independent activity which must first be established.

8. KINAESTHETIC IMAGINATION

But before we proceed to our analysis, let us distinguish a separate activity which might be confused with this graphic activity. We have already seen that Burt describes a stage (i) (*b*) of 'purposive pencilling'. It arises from the pleasure the child takes in its arm movements, and in the visible trace of the movements left on the paper. Krötzsch[15] has given a careful analysis of the development of this purely kinaesthetic activity which he regards as mainly a spontaneous one of the muscles, the expression of an innate bodily rhythm, but for our present purpose we need only note the fact that it does gradually become controlled, repetitious and consciously rhythmical. The line becomes the zig-zag, the zig-zag a wavy line, the wavy line returns on itself and becomes a loop, and from the loop develops the spiral and the circle. At this point the rhythmical activity is interrupted, for the child, so it is assumed, suddenly recognizes in the circle the outline of an object—the human face. The kinaesthetic activity is supposed to end and the representational activity to begin.

We have already criticized this evolutionary theory, but it may be further objected, that the kinaesthetic activity does not actually end. A closer observation of the child shows that it continues as an independent activity. In one case which I observed (a boy of 3), I noticed that when 'cars' were drawn at his request, he would sometimes take the pencil and scribble thickly and fastly over the wheels. When he drew his own first cars, he would repeat this performance. What he was doing was to associate the kinaesthetic activity of scribbling with his motor image of the revolving wheels. The same child would

---

[15] *Rhythmus und Form in der freien Kinderzeichnung* (Leipzig, 1917). I have been unable to consult this work, but it is summarized by Wulff, Stern and other writers on the subject. For a more recent and extreme theory of the motor origin of children's drawing see R. Arnheim, *Art and Visual Perception* (London and Berkeley, California, 1956). Cf. p. 135, 'Drawing, painting, and modelling are a part of human motor behaviour, and they may be assumed to have developed from two older and more general kinds of such behaviour—physiognomic and descriptive movement.'

draw long lines and describe them as 'cars going along the road'.[16]

Another objection to this theory of 'sudden recognition' is that long before the child evolves the schema, he will give a name to his scribble. Krötzsch assumes that this is due to adult influence, a view adopted by Wulff.[17] But like Loewenfeld[18] I have frequently observed that children quite spontaneously give names to their scribbles; I do not, however, find that they always subsequently discover some similarities in the scribble to justify the name. There seems to be general agreement that at first naming takes place *after* the scribble has been completed, and that only at a later age does the child announce what his scribble is going to represent. The age at which naming just begins seems to vary widely: Margaret, the child observed in such detail by Dr. Eng, began at the age of 1, ix, 10 (1 year, nine months, ten days). There does not seem to have been the slightest adult suggestion in this case. She began to name her scribbles *before* making them only a few days after first naming the scribbles *after* making them.[19]

9. THE IMAGE AND THE SIGN

We shall never be able to determine exactly what does happen at this stage of the child's development, but the hypothesis I wish to put forward can be supported by certain analogies from the history of art. I think it might be also supported by considerations drawn from the origin of writing, but I would rather ignore this evidence, which would, even if I were competent to present it, be highly speculative.

I suggest that we have three terms at our disposal: the image, the sign or symbol, and the representation.

We have already considered the nature of the image, and its func-

---

[16] This observation was anticipated by Froebel—cf. *The Education of Man* p. 36: 'The ball that is rolling or has been rolled, the stone that has been thrown and falls, the water that was dammed and conducted into many branching ditches—all these have taught the child that the effect of a force, in its individual manifestations, is always in the direction of a line.

'Thus the representation of objects by lines soon leads the child to the perception and representation of the direction in which a force acts. "Here flows a brook," and saying this, the child makes a mark indicating the course of a brook. . . . Very significantly the child says, "Here comes a bird flying," and draws in the direction of the supposed flight a winding line.' Cf. also Arnheim, *op. cit.*, p. 138.

[17] *Die Kunst des Kindes*, p. 2.

[18] *Op. cit.*, p. 19.

[19] *Psychology of Children's Drawings*, pp. 5–8.

tion in the process of thinking. We found reason to believe that in young children the image is of unusual vividness, and may in a large number of cases be eidetic. But during the course of the child's maturation, the image gradually loses its intensity and individuation, and is replaced by concepts, whose function it is to facilitate the process of thought and reasoning. But we found that in the higher processes of reasoning, where intuition and the perception of pattern or wholeness of relationships is called for, the image still plays an important part.

If we desire to represent an image, so that the image in our mind can be seen and appreciated by other people, we must translate it into a medium of communication. Such media are either aural, visual or kinetic. The principal aural medium is speech, which has evolved from representational or imitative sounds, but in addition to this purely functional medium man has elaborated the arts of song and music, which we may regard as a more subtle kind of language. Kinetic communication is made through the medium of gesture, elaborated into the arts of ritual and dance. Visual communication, with which we are more particularly concerned, aims at a representation of the formal features of the image—its outline, mass and colour —in a plastic material like paint or clay, or a glyptic material like stone. The success of this method of communication is usually judged by the *verisimilitude* of the representation, though various stylistic mannerisms are permitted.

But in addition to these forms of communication, mankind has elaborated various *signs* or *symbols*, which may be aural or kinetic, but are more usually graphic or plastic. These signs or symbols are not imitative, avoid verisimilitude, and only become media of communication by agreement between two or more persons. The word 'tree' is a sign. It is a sound, or some marks made on paper with ink to represent this sound, which by common agreement and tradition, have come to mean, among the limited number of people who understand the English language, 'a perennial plant with single woody self-supporting stem or trunk usually unbranched for some distance above ground'. When I speak or write the word 'tree' I may or may not bring to mind a memory-image of a particular or a generic tree—that is a psychological problem which does not concern us now. The point is that I can, if required, communicate an image of a tree by the use of a purely abstract sign, the word 'tree'.

Signs or symbols can be still more arbitrary (for words have an evolutionary history, and are only rarely invented *ad hoc*). If I make the mark * (an asterisk) in the course of writing this page, the reader knows, by previous agreement, that I intend to draw his attention to something outside the normal course of the text—to a footnote, for example. The symbol then stands for a verbal statement or command such as 'Look down at the bottom of the page'. If I see a cross on a building, I know at once that the building is, or has been, associated with the Christian religion, a vast complex of emotions, images and ideas all reduced to this convenient and economical sign. The field of art is strewn with such symbols, some of them representing images or concepts which we can no longer identify, or can only identify by acquiring special knowledge. If, for example, a peasant were to dig up a gem of the third century A.D. engraved with a fish, he would see a fish and nothing more. But a scholar would be able to tell him that the fish was one of the earliest symbols for the person of Jesus Christ, and that it was based on the fact that the letters of the Greek word for fish make an acrostic for the five Greek words meaning 'Jesus Christ, Son of God, Saviour'; and the psychologist and ethnologist could further inform him that long before the time of Christ the fish was used as a sexual or fertility symbol in various parts of the world.

Signs or symbols, therefore, vary in their degree of esotericism or obscurity, and the more primitive or repressed the tribe or religion may be, the more esoteric its symbols tend to be, *even to the point of being entirely non-representational or abstract*. From a general aesthetic standpoint I have dealt with such symbols in another book,[20] but I must refer to them again, for their significance is of fundamental importance for an understanding of children's drawings. One of the best examples of this abstract symbolism comes from the native tribes of Central Australia, and since I wrote *Art and Society*, additional material of great value has been collected by Mr. C. P. Mountford, of the South Australian Museum.[21] In Mr. Mountford's words: 'The drawings of the Central Australian aborigines are peculiar in that, instead of depicting the particular animal, human being or object in a naturalistic manner, a conventional symbol is used. For example, the U within U design is often used to indicate a human or semi-human

[20] *Art and Society* (London, 2nd edn., 1945), pp. 30 *ff*., and Plates 16 and 17.

[21] See *Transactions of the Royal Society of South Australia*, Vol. LXI (1937), pp. 30–40, 84–95, 226–40; LXII (1938), pp. 241–54. *Records of the South Australian Museum*, Vol. VI (1937–8), pp. 1–28, 111–4.

ancestor; the circle or spiral, a waterhole, hill or totemic place; the tracks of certain creatures, the animal itself.'[22] Mr. Mountford then warns the reader against 'attempting to interpret aboriginal rock paintings or carvings without the help of the artist who produced them, or alternatively, an aboriginal who knows their meanings intimately. Symbols, which in one drawing represent a waterhole, will in another illustrate a hill or a camp. It is obvious that the exact meaning cannot be even guessed at, although, in general, certain symbols are used extensively to illustrate the same or similar objects.' This agrees with the earlier observations of Spencer and Gillen, quoted in *Art and Society* (pp. 34–5).

What is more significant for our present purpose is that this description of the savage's artistic activities agrees with our observations of the child's earliest artistic activities. He, too, draws lines and spirals and other geometrical marks and gives them a name; and he too will at different times attribute different meanings to the same scribble. It may, of course, be argued that the savage's drawings express a religious symbolism, if only of a primitive magical order, and their abstraction is determined by their magical purpose; and Mountford, indeed, quotes a case of an aboriginal whose drawings, formerly of a conventional 'primary' school type and, as a result of his contact with civilized people and schools, quite undistinctive, became abstract and symbolic after he had returned to his tribe and undergone an initiation ceremony.[23] What happened here, in effect, was that the aboriginal exchanged the graphic language of one society for the graphic language of another, the difference being that the first language was diffused and naturalistic, the second arcane and abstract. Both had for him a comparable significance in relation to the societies of which they were characteristic.

I am not suggesting that the young child creates a systematic symbolism: his symbols may be arbitrary and disconnected, but nevertheless, they are a social language of a rudimentary kind, and for adults it is a language which must be interpreted. Incidentally, in reply to a query I addressed to him, Mr. Mountford tells me that the children of the Australian aborigines also draw from an early age, and that their drawings, in general, resemble those of the adults.

[22] Cf. the case, quoted on p.126, of the boy of three who represented cars by lines, i.e. by their tracks. Fig. 3a (p.154) shows the use of the U design by an English child.

[23] *Records of the S.A. Museum*, VI (1938), pp. 111–4.

The point I wish to make by this comparison is that a child's first drawings, which may at first be quite abstract or non-figurative, and which then become recognizable symbols or 'schemas', have no basis in immediate *visual* experience.[24] They are not an attempt to translate an image into graphic or plastic form: they are objects with imaginary associations. They are only representational in the sense that a geometrical sign may stand for a visual image or for some other mental element—just as, in the case of the aboriginal, a spiral may stand for a waterhole (or equally for a gum-tree) or parallel lines for a range of hills (or equally for the track of an animal).

10. THREE HYPOTHESES

The exact relation of the schema to the image in the child's mind is admittedly difficult to determine. We have a choice of three hypotheses:

(i) The generally accepted theory that the child's drawings, from the first stroke to the final stage of visual realism, represent progressive efforts to achieve the accurate imitation of memory images or percepts. This theory we have already found to be inconsistent with the observed facts.

(ii) The child, unable to translate his images into adequate graphic or plastic representations, is satisfied with a merely associative relationship between a mark he makes (sign or symbol) and an image. This would account for the variability of the images associated with one particular symbol, but it does not explain the child's progressive attempts to elaborate his symbols, nor the persistence of the schema long after an ability to imitate the object in a naturalistic manner has been acquired.

(iii) The child is seeking to escape from the vividness of his eidetic

[24] Further evidence of this fact is provided by the Rorschach 'ink-blot reactions', a stimulus to fantasy formation which has been used by several investigators in attempts to measure temperament and personality. Cf. H. Rorschach: *Psychodiagnostik: Methodik und Ergebnisse eines wahrnehmungsdiagnostischen Experiments* (2nd ed., Berne, 1932). Dr. Griffiths, in her experiments with this test, found that the analogy which the child finds almost immediately 'is so strong upon him in some cases, that it becomes almost of the nature of identity. Thus the blot does not merely resemble a horse, or a rat, or an aeroplane, it *is* such. . . . So much is this so, that many children having given the blot a name, and imbued it with all the characteristics of the fancied object, are unable to break free from this idea to find a second association. . . . There are degrees in the strength and force of this identity as observed in different subjects, and in the same subject on different occasions'. *Imagination in Early Childhood*, p. 237.

images, from an omnipresent realism. He wants to create something relatively fixed and personal, an escape from reality, something which is 'his own', and not an uncalled image. He has a feeling or 'affect' which is independent of his conceptual thought (in so far as this has been developed) and of his perceptual images. It is no doubt a residue of his perceptual and other bodily (proprioceptive) experiences, but it is not yet communicable. He is 'charged' with this feeling or affect, for which images are inadequate, or perhaps too adequate, and for which he has not yet evolved the sophisticated machinery of conceptual thought. He therefore creates—and it is here if anywhere that the use of this word is justified—a visual symbol, a cipher in this language of line, which will express his feelings, communicate its quality to others, fix it in the shifting world of appearances.

Normally, as the child acquires the machinery of conceptual thought, the vividness of his images declines: concurrently, the realism of his drawings increases. There would seem to be something in the nature of a law of compensation, vividness of expression becoming more and more necessary or tolerable as abstractness of thought increases, abstractness of expression becoming less and less necessary as a foil to the vividness of the spontaneous images which until then have crowded the mind.[25] From this point of view we may agree with Hartlaub[26] that the schema or symbol is a natural product ('Naturprodukt') of the child's mind rather than a special faculty of abstraction called into being by special circumstances (such as those described by Worringer, page 87) above.

It is this third hypothesis which I propose to adopt, and for which I shall seek further support. But the revolutionary significance of such a theory should be realized. Writing in the light of the first and still too 'logical' interpretation of these facts ('the child draws what he means, thinks, knows—not what he sees'), and before their exact nature had been analysed, William Stern observed that they threw 'a dazzling searchlight on the insufficiency of older theories concerning the beginnings of human apprehension and experience. The belief that contemplation, pure and simple, forms the beginnings of all apprehension, and that, from it, abstract knowledge and judgment slowly develop, can no longer be maintained. . . . It is found that, to begin with, the pictorial representation is only looked upon as the

---

[25] For the distinction between voluntary and spontaneous imagery, see G. H. Betts, *Distribution and Functions of Mental Imagery*, p. 5.

[26] *Op. cit.*, p. 81.

symbol of something meant, something thought of, and that it is only after much effort that the power develops of keeping the pictorial representation of things as they appear to the senses free from all "intentional" features, i.e. those that correspond to the drawer's knowledge and ideas.'[27] We may add that this power develops *pari passu* with the control of the mental process of imagining; when the mind can call up images at will (and suppress them at will) then it can bear to represent things 'as they appear to the senses'. Meanwhile, up to the age of adolescence, nothing could be more unnatural than a naturalistic mode of expression.

11. THE EVIDENCE OF WEAK-SIGHTED AND BLIND CHILDREN

The important investigations of Münz and Loewenfeld, to which reference has already been made, have a decisive bearing on our problem. Their observations clearly demonstrate that in the drawings of children, we are concerned with two distinct types, due to distinct intentions on the part of the child. Though the discovery was made by the observation of weak-sighted and blind children, it is important to remember that Loewenfeld proves that *the distinction is of universal validity*, and can be applied, not merely to the drawings of normal children, but to the historical phenomena of art generally.

The two types are called *visual* and *haptic*. The visual type 'starts from his environment', and his concepts are developed into a perceptual whole 'through the fusion of partial visual experiences'. This latter clause means that a visual representation is not necessarily an instantaneous, impressionistic apprehension of form from one fixed point of view: it may be the translation into concrete plastic form of a visual concept—the synthesis of many points of view.

The *haptic* type, on the other hand, 'is primarily concerned with his own body sensations and with the actual space round him'. The haptic artist is primarily concerned, not with an object in the outer world, but with his own inner world of sensation and feeling. Such a type is not necessarily blind or weak-sighted: he merely does not *use his eyes*. 'The farther optical experience recedes into the background

---

[27] *Psychology of Early Childhood*, pp. 352–3. It is odd that such a careful psychologist as Stern should have been so ready to ascribe 'knowledge and ideas' to the child of three or four years.

the less important does the eye become as the intermediary of the concept. To the same extent the importance of the environment diminishes and experience is more and more confined to the processes that go on in the body as a whole, bodily sensations, muscular inner-vations, deep sensibilities, and their various emotional effects. As the importance of the sense of sight diminishes, so that of the sense of touch as the intermediary between sensations and the concept in-creases'. 'Haptic perception' therefore implies a 'synthesis between tactile perceptions of external reality and those subjective experiences that seem to be so closely bound up with the experience of self'.[28]

Loewenfeld provides a wealth of material to illustrate this distinc-tion: among our own illustrations haptic sensibility is most clearly revealed in Plates 9*b*, 26, 27*a*, 28*a*, 28*b*, 38, 49 and 51*b*.

Loewenfeld's investigations throw much incidental light on the general development of artistic activity in children. We will only mention the following as more immediately concerning us:

(i) In the early years (phase of the schema) visual impressions play almost no part in the drawing, whilst bodily experiences, on the other hand, strongly influence the various forms of expression.

(ii) This bodily experience is the integrating factor in the majority of children, and when, in the ninth and tenth years, the child gains increasing conceptual knowledge of the external world and its significance, his capacity for co-ordinating visual and other impressions in his drawing decreases. 'This period . . . represents the time at which the confidence of the child in its own creative power is for the first time shaken by the fact that it is becoming conscious of the significance of its environment.' (p. 74.)

(iii) Since up to the age of nine, 'proportions, and in many cases also changes in representative symbols, are to the widest pos-sible degree dependent on the subjective attitudes called on by an experience', it follows that 'naturalistic tendencies and conceptions . . . are totally unsuitable means for the under-standing of children's drawings'. (p. 38.) This fact, to a large extent, invalidates the treatment of the subject by previous investigators. Even when apparently most 'objective' and 'scientific', fully recognizing the 'schematic' character of child-

[28] *The Nature of Creative Activity*, p. 82.

ren's drawings, these writers, from Levinstein and Kerschensteiner[29] to Wulff, use in their classifications and criticism a naturalistic criterion which is altogether foreign to the intention of the child. The child has his own 'order of values', an order which is abstract or symbolic, and integrated by the intensity of his experience, and not in the least degree controlled by external 'facts'. This is shown, not only in the general character of children's drawings, but also by deviations in the linear arrangement of the schema itself, and by what Loewenfeld calls 'the over-emphasis of meaningful parts', and even in the way objects are grouped in 'space'. Space itself, as Loewenfeld shows in a series of brilliant analyses of specific children's drawings, may be *affective*.

What, therefore, we must realize is that the child's graphic activity is a specialized medium of communication with its own characteristics and laws. It is not determined by canons of objective visual realism, but by the pressure of inner subjective feeling or sensation. From the very beginning the drawings of children are wholly and spontaneously of this kind. They only change because a naturalistic attitude is gradually imposed on children, first by the necessity of coping with an external world—by the need they experience of objectifying their perceptual world so that they can measure it, assess it, deal with it, *subdue* it; and secondly, by the impulse to imitate the naturalistic modes of representation which they see practised by theii parents and teachers. In so far as the former need is met by conceptual modes of thought, the image merely disappears, or is devitalized, and no need for representing it graphically or plastically is experienced; and in actual fact only a few children, belonging to a specific psychological type, acquire any considerable skill in naturalistic representation.

As for the rest, they may be painfully taught to make a naturalistic representation of objects, but they have no *spontaneous* impulse to do so, and if they indulge in any graphic activity of a spontaneous origin, it is always 'schematic' in character. This 'duplicity', which is so clear in children, continues to exist in a surprising number of adults. Such people will protest that they 'cannot draw', but if compelled to do so then produce drawings of an infantile schematic character. Feeble-

---

[29] Kerschensteiner places as a frontispiece to his book Dürer's precocious self-portrait drawn at the age of thirteen, and his whole outlook seems to be coloured by this preliminary ideal.

minded people, and normal people in their 'absent' or 'doodling' moments, draw quite spontaneously in this regressive manner.[30]

12. THE CONCEPTUAL FALLACY

We have, in the preceding pages, followed the usual practice of discussing 'the child', as though there existed a universal norm. It is true that we have been compelled, again and again, as in the last paragraph, to admit exceptions. But we are now in a position to abandon this unscientific attitude, and try to bring the hypothetical norm and the specific variations within the framework of type psychology, as outlined in the last chapter.

Previous attempts at classification have not gone beyond what is fundamentally the antithesis of percept and concept. Impaled on this elementary dilemma, writers have hitherto been compelled to see in the 'schema' the child's first attempt to represent a concept— ('First I think, and then I draw my think' was the anecdotic justification for such a theory, though it has never been stated at what age this mythical statement was made). The fallacy goes as far back as Sully, who writes for example:

'All this shows that the child's eye at a surprisingly early period loses its primal "innocence", grows "sophisticated" in the sense that instead of seeing what is really presented it sees, or pretends to see, what knowledge and logic tell it is there. In other words his sense-perceptions have for artistic purposes become corrupted by a too large admixture of intelligence.'[31]

Similarly, Luquet describes the third phase of drawing as 'réalisme intellectuel' (the first is 'le réalisme', the second 'le réalisme manqué'). We cannot stop to criticize the use of the word 'réalisme' (it is used in a metaphysical rather than an aesthetic sense), but the word 'intellectuel' is used in the same sense as Sully uses it, that is to say, to denote 'abstract elements which only have existence in the mind (l'esprit) of the artist'.[32] If a child, to take an example which Luquet regards as conclusive, when asked to draw a field of potatoes draws a rectangle filled with small circles, it does not imply, as Luquet supposes, that the child ignores the evidence of its senses, the green plants above the ground, in favour of an intellectual conception of

[30] Cf. H. Prinzhorn, *Bildnerei der Geisteskranken* (Berlin, 1922).

[31] *Studies of Childhood*, p. 396.

[32] *Le Dessin enfantin*, p. 166.

the invisible tubers in the ground: it means rather that for the child the primary association of the potato is the tactual one, or merely the usual visual one—the potato in the kitchen, not the potato growing as a plant in the ground. He therefore draws, not what he thinks, nor what he is supposed actually to see, but the sign or symbol which has been gradually precipitated in his mind as the residue of his total sensational responses to the potato as an object. What he draws, therefore, is a sign that conveys the affective counterpart which he individually associates with the potato.

This is perhaps to question the rational basis of perception. Piaget, for example, in a discussion of Luquet's phrase[33] affirms that 'to perceive is to construct intellectually, and if the child draws things as he conceives them, it is certainly because he cannot perceive them without conceiving them'. It may be that Luquet and Piaget, who both write in French, use *intellect* in a wider sense than the ordinary implications of the word in English, for I do not see how we can apply the word to a process which is in effect the spontaneous association of a symbol with an experience. Intellection only follows with the criticism and comparison of such symbols. The symbol itself may be quite arbitrary and have no objective validity so long as it adequately represents the 'affective component'[34] which is the fundamental residue of our experiences in the subconscious. Arnheim distinguishes between 'perceptual concepts' and 'representational con-

---

[33] *Moral Judgment of the Child*, p. 185.

[34] I owe this phrase, 'affective component', to Dr. Samuel Lowy, whose *Foundations of Dream-Interpretation* (London, 1942) seems to me to throw considerable, if indirect, light on the psychology of children's drawings. The following passage, for example, lends support to the theory of the schema advanced here:

'Our ideas are not only thought, but also felt, experienced. This affective component is the contribution of the "living ego" to the photographic image of the external impression, and constitutes in general a constant counterpart of the "lifeless" concept. Every event, every experience, every representation of an external object and person, exerts a formative influence on the individual psychic life *only* in so far as it occasions in us "affects" of various qualities and quantities. Not the concepts and not the impressions of the external world in their objectivity, but the affective values, associated with and released by them become functioning factors of our psyche. These affective counterparts of our concepts—the result of the complex ego-attitude to the external world and to all perceptions in general—make these external impressions properly *our very own*; they determine the exact disposition of concepts, images and ideas in us; these effective counterparts constitute the cement which binds the association links together; they are responsible for both the quality and the intensity of the influence, exerted by individual psychic elements on the totality of our thinking and acting.' (*Op. cit.*, pp. 8–9.)

cepts'—'that is, the conception of the form by which the perceived structure of the object can be represented with the properties of a given medium. . . . The formation of adequate representational concepts makes the artist'. In defence of his use of the word 'concept' in this connection, he adds: 'I am not subscribing to the intellectualistic theory of the artistic process. Neither perception nor representation in a given medium is based on intellectual abstraction. Nothing but our particular one-sided tradition suggests that concepts are formed only by the intellect. All the cognitive instruments of the mind operate by grasping overall features of a phenomenon or a group of phenomena through form patterns of a medium. The medium may consist of the stock of "perceptual categories" or the shape patterns of a means of representation or the abstractions of the intellect. The word "concept" refers to an operation performed by all kinds of cognition rather than serving to reduce them all to intellectual processes.'[35]

Later writers, particularly Hartlaub and Bühler, have elaborated the contrast between perceptual and conceptual modes of apprehension by incorporating the eidetic factor, and by supposing that an eidetic disposition accounts for 'artistically gifted' children—that is to say, the rare children who have a precocious ability to make accurate copies of objects—and they relate this two-fold distinction to Verworn's classification of primitive art as physioplastic or ideoplastic. Wulff criticizes this classification on the grounds that, in general, eidetic disposition is incompatible with artistic activity—he assumes, against the evidence we have mentioned in Chapter III, that the eidetic disposition is rarely found among creative artists.[36]

---

[35] *Op. cit.*, pp. 133–4.

[36] Actually what distinguishes the artist with a capacity to reproduce objects in all their naturalism is not a vivid (eidetic) imagination, but a capacity to translate such images into a particular medium—what have been called 'images de traduction'. This rare faculty is not a function of memory or eidetic images, but the power to see equivalent images in a material like paint or stone. I prefer a phrase like 'interpretative images' to Arnheim's 'representational concepts'. Cf. L. Arréat, *Mémoire et Imagination* (Paris, 1904), pp. 28–9, quoted by E. Bullough, 'Mind and Medium in Art', *Brit. J. Psych.*, XI (1920–1), pp. 26–46:

'Un peintre figuriste, qui ne *sait* pas l'animal, a des chevaux à placer dans une composition. Il s'applique alors à l'étude du cheval: il prend des croquis, et se met dans la tête des "images". Un cavalier expert pourra ensuite critiquer son tableau en connaisseur. Il garde donc en mémoire, lui aussi, des images précises, auxquelles il a comparé celles du peintre. Il ne serait pas capable cependant de dessiner un cheval ni de le peindre. A quoi tient précisément cette différence? Il ne suffit pas de dire que c'est fa··· d'exercice, car la faculté même d'apprendre marque un

It is true, as we have already found, that eidetic imagery does not inspire the impulse to originate—rather the reverse. But we must distinguish the impulse to originate from the impulse to imitate, which, apart from a rhythmical instinct, is the only basis for artistic activity admitted by Wulff. The reality seems to be what Martin Buber has called 'der Urhebertrieb'—the impulse to originate,[37] which is a quite distinct and independent impulse, not to be confused with or explained by the psycho-analytical concepts of 'libido' or 'will to power'. His failure to distinguish between these two impulses vitiates the whole of Wulff's elaborate analysis of the art of children, leading by but one more route to the same intellectualist conception of education against which this book is a protest. In the course of his long thesis, Professor Wulff makes many very acute psychological observations, but in the end the only purpose he can give to art education is that it should teach the average child to represent the reality of his immediate perception, as he sees it and not as he imagines it. Art must conform to this imitative function, and it only earns its extra-scientific (or extra-photographic) value from the ability which the artist acquires to convey the highest possible degree of conceptual knowledge in immediately apprehended visual form.

Such a conception of art education is dictated by *a priori* and intellectualistic schematism, and is imposed on the facts. It is nearly always a schematism that is only conceivable in terms of this singularly limited conception of art, and of an altogether unscientific conception of 'man'. Among all the investigators of our subject it is only Loewenfeld who perceives that there is a direct and valid relationship between modes of expression and the affective components of each individual child's temperament and disposition.[38]

véritable privilège. C'est d'abord faute *d'images d'interprétation* ou *de traduction*: j'entends par là des schemas visuo-moteurs laissés par l'étude dans le cerveau du peintre, et grace auxquels sa représentation mentale peut prendre figure aussitôt sur le papier ou la toile—des symboles actifs, en quelque sorte, qui sont comme les idées générales "pittoresques".'

[37] *Rede ueber das Erzieherische* (Berlin, 1926), pp. 8–15. Buber himself does not seek any materialistic explanation of the origin of this impulse, but it may perhaps be suggested that it is some kind of compensation for the reproductive instinct. This would agree with the fact that the impulse is generally speaking confined to pre-adolescent children, to childless women, and to men. It is not artistic sensibility that is lacking in most women—in this respect they are probably more and not less receptive than men; what they lack, in general, is this impulse to make things for the mere love of making.

[38] Cf. *The Nature of Creative Activity*, p. 22 and *Creative and Mental Growth*, pp. 142–51. According to Stern (*Psychology of Early Childhood*, p. 351) Krötzsch

13. AN EMPIRICAL CLASSIFICATION OF CHILDREN'S DRAWINGS

In attempting a classification of children's drawings, I decided not to begin with a series of pigeon-holes marked 'psychological types', placing the drawings into them as seemed most appropriate, but rather to adopt a purely stylistic classification of the drawings themselves, and to see then whether this classification corresponded to any of the existing classifications of psychological types. I examined several thousands of drawings, from all types of schools, and as I proceeded, I gave a descriptive label to what, in each case, seemed on purely stylistic grounds to constitute a separate category. I eventually found myself with twelve categories, and as I proceeded I did not find it necessary to extend the series, though naturally it was often doubtful into which of two categories a particular drawing should be placed. This first classification was as follows:

    (i) Organic
    (ii) Lyrical
    (iii) Impressionist
    (iv) Rhythmical pattern
    (v) Structural form
    (vi) Schematic
    (vii) Haptic
    (viii) Expressionist
    (ix) Enumerative
    (x) Decorative
    (xi) Romantic
    (xii) Literary

The superficial qualities on which I based my categories were these:

(i) *Organic.* Direct visual and sympathetic relationship with external objects; preference for groups rather than isolated objects; perception of natural proportions and organic relations (trees seem to *rise* from the ground; human figures are in action and their action is complementary to that of other figures; a flower will droop on its stem rather than stand up stiffly, etc.).

also, in his *Rhythmus und Form in der freien Kinderzeichnung*, 'considers children's spontaneous drawings . . . as affording evidences of character; the child has his drawing "hand-writing" long before his real handwriting has become sufficiently formed to have any graphical significance'.

Examples: Plates 18*a*, 37*a*, 35, 44.

(ii) *Lyrical*. Embodies most of the qualities of (i), but seems to prefer static subjects (still-lifes) and treats these delicately; colours low in tone. More characteristic of girls' drawings than of boys'.
Examples: Plates 34, 48.

(iii) *Impressionist*. I used this term in the general sense in which it is applied to the Impressionist school of painting. Preference for the observed characteristic detail rather than the conceptual whole. Can be lyrical, but not usually very markedly rhythmical. Conveys 'atmosphere'.
Examples: Plates 17*a*, 39, 56*a*.

(iv) *Rhythmical pattern*. The drawing imposes a pattern on the observed facts. The artist takes a motif (e.g. boy snowballing) and repeats the motif, reversed and otherwise varied, until the picture-space is filled. The motif may be based on observation, and be in itself of an organic or lyrical nature: but it is made subordinate to a general pattern.
Examples: Plates 40, 42, 52.

(v) *Structural form*. A comparatively rare type, in which the object is reduced to a geometric formula—but a formula which nevertheless takes its origin in observation. It is the 'stylization' of a theme, a perception of pattern *in* the natural object, rather than the use of the natural object to make a pattern.
Examples: Plates 8*b*, 43*a*.

(vi) *Schematic*. The geometric formula, with no obvious relation to the organic structure. The 'schema' of the early phase which has become fixed—elaborated, perhaps, as a design, but not related to the object in any but a symbolic way.
Examples: Plates 1*b*, 18*b*, 56*b*.

(vii) *Haptic*. As defined by Loewenfeld (cf. quotation on p. 90). The drawing is not based on any visual perception of the object, but is nevertheless not merely schematic. It is the representation of tactual and other non-visual images derived from internal physical sensation.
Examples: Plates 9*b*, 26, 27*a*.

(viii) *Expressionist*. When an attempt is made, not merely to express egocentric sensation (cf. subjects like 'Listening', 'Being Throttled', etc., illustrated by Loewenfeld, *Nature of Creative Activity*, Pls. 8, 29, etc.), but also to represent an external object as it presents itself to the sensations of the artist (e.g. a forest, a street scene, a crowd), then some control is exercised by other than tactual and somatic sensations. The visual perception, though distorted and caricatured, is nevertheless the point of departure.

Examples: Plates 28*a*, 29*a*, 36, 38, 43*b*.

(ix) *Enumerative*. The artist is wholly controlled by the object, and is unable to relate it to any sensation of 'wholeness' or 'atmosphere'. He therefore painstakingly records each separate detail, and as many details as he can see or remember, and distributes them evenly and without any particular emphasis over the available space. The effect may be superficially realistic, but it is the realism of the architect's drawing rather than of the artist's perception.

Examples: Plates 16*b*, 21*b*.

(x) *Decorative*. The artist is primarily concerned with colour and two-dimensional form, and exploits these to produce a gay pattern.

Examples: Plates 21*a*, 47, 55.

(xi) *Romantic*. The artist takes a theme from life, but heightens it with fantasy. Involves inventive reconstruction and recombination of memory and/or eidetic images.

Examples: Plates 33, 53, 54.

(xii) *Literary*. The artist takes a purely fanciful theme, either actually from a literary source, or one suggested by the teacher, or one invented by himself, and uses his imagination (his capacity for evoking and combining eidetic or memory-images) to represent this theme and communicate it to others.

Examples: Plates 31, 32.

14. REDUCTION OF THE CATEGORIES

These categories were never intended to be exclusive, and the brief descriptions I have given of them are not intended as precise definitions. I found that, without any undue allowance, all the drawings I examined fitted into one or other of the twelve categories, but there were many occasions when it was difficult to decide between, say, the romantic and the literary, or the lyrical and the impressionist. My feeling was, however, that the hesitation arose from the lack of a clear division between the categories rather than from any vagueness in the character of the drawings themselves. My next step, therefore, was to see whether, from a logical, rather than an empiric point of view, I could reduce the number of categories.

The first three categories have in common a naturalistic basis:

they all imply a respect for the concrete qualities of the external object as apprehended by the sensuous perceptions of the artist; but one, the organic category, enters into the vital substance and mode of being of the object, and tries to represent this by reproducing the dynamic structure of the object. This is a well-defined group, though not typical of many children under the age of nine.

In considering the impressionist group, we once more encounter the historical ambiguity of the term. If it means a fidelity to immediate perception, it cannot in the present context be separated from the organic category. But as often as not it implies a communication of sensations we feel as belonging to the external object and in that sense is identical with an expressionism conditioned by the object. We can include the first aspect of impressionism within the organic; the second is the objective or extravert counterpart of the haptic or expressionist category, and corresponds closely to the definition of 'empathy' given by Spranger (cf. Note, pp. 24–5).

But what of the *lyrical* category? The more I examined it the more difficult it became to justify its separate existence. In so far as lyricism implies measure, as in a song, it comes within the rhythmic category to be discussed below; and in so far as it implies sensuous ecstasy or enjoyment, it can be identified with either the impressionist or the organic category. I therefore decided I could eliminate a separate lyrical category.

The next three categories all bear a verbal resemblance to one another, and a logical analysis will show that they can all be included within an antithesis which opposes a rhythmical (temporal) to a formal (spatial) structure. The difference again relates to the direction of the artist's activity. If he begins with an external object (e.g. a boy snowballing) and then uses this organic motif to construct rhythmical forms, he produces one kind of picture; but if he begins with a formal motif (e.g. a circle or a triangle) and adapts his subject to this form, he produces another kind of picture. I decided that 'schematic' was the unnecessary word, particularly because it had other uses in our discussion, and that the remaining categories were adequately described as *rhythmical pattern* and *structural form* ('rhythmic' always implying the *repetition* of quantities or measures in a 'temporal' sequence: 'structural' an absolute relationship of individually distinct forms).

'Haptic' and 'expressionist' obviously demanded logical scrutiny. I decided that the distinction I had made between a sensation pro-

143

ceeding from an object situated outside the artist and a sensation proceeding from within the artist's own physical constitution has no logical validity, and, in the case of the child, no actual existence.[39] It was not even a difference of direction, of extraversion and introversion, for even a somatic sensation, arising within the body, is an external phenomenon vis-à-vis the receptive area of the cortex: the sensation produced by the touch of a stone is not different in kind, when it comes to expressing the sensation, from the sensation of a constricted throat. We may perhaps best describe it as a distinction between the expression of tactual sensations and of visual perceptions, and 'haptic' and 'impressionist' are the best terms for such an antithesis.

The 'enumerative' category could not be reduced in any way. I passed on to a consideration of the last three categories, and here there was no difficulty in combining the romantic and the literary: it was a distinction of subject-matter rather than of treatment. The theme might be taken from life or from literature, but in both cases, it was treated subjectively. Because of its historical associations, I abandoned the word 'romantic'.

'Literary', which remained, was not an entirely satisfactory term, for it is used to include themes which have their origin in direct observation; and therefore, in spite of all its dangers, I decided to use the term 'imaginative'.

I was now left with the following eight categories:

> (i) Organic
> (ii) Empathetic
> (iii) Rhythmical Pattern
> (iv) Structural Form
> (v) Enumerative
> (vi) Haptic
> (vii) Decorative
> (viii) Imaginative

In thus reducing the categories, I must confess that I had in my mind the possibility of finding a correspondence between my cate-

---

[39] Cf. Piaget in *A Handbook of Child Psychology* (ed. Murchison), p. 534: 'Child *realism*, in fact all realism, may be defined as a sort of confusion between the inner and the outer, or the tendency to fix in objects something which is the result of the activity of the thinking subject. We know how slow to develop is the consciousness of self in a small child. Everything he feels, knows, and sees seems to him common to the whole world and part of external reality. For him nothing is inner and subjective.'

gories of children's drawings and the psychological types discussed in the last chapter, and that I needed for this purpose to reduce my categories to eight. Having succeeded in doing this, I next proceeded to test the categories against the types.

The requirements were (1) that they should correspond to the four types of aesthetic appreciation as defined by Bullough; (2) that further they should express the four types of mental function distinguished by Jung; and (3) that they should express the extravert and introvert directions of these mental functions.

The purely dynamic aspect of the categories was soon discovered. 'Haptic' and 'imaginative' were almost by definition subjective attitudes, and the 'decorative' and 'enumerative' categories were obviously determined by objective considerations. 'Impressionist' could not be anything else but a subjective attitude, and 'organic', though it involved the element of feeling, projected this feeling into the determinate external form. The dynamic difference between 'rhythmical pattern' and 'structural form' was obviously a difference between an active and a passive attitude, but I could not be sure of the correspondence with extravert and introvert attitudes until I had determined the relevant mental function.

15. RELATION OF THE CATEGORIES TO FUNCTION TYPES

Beginning, then, with the function-types, in their extraverted and introverted aspects, I sought first for the extraverted thinking type, and found it in my *enumerative* category. This category corresponds closely to Binet's *type descripteur* ('content with a pure and bald description of the details of the object, without even seeking to grasp their significance, much less their relation or the meaning of their collocation'). This seems to me to be a thinking or intellectual activity divorced from any feeling for relationships or wholeness, and therefore from any introspective reaction. The drawing is wholly determined by the external object, and the object does not even possess organic relationship with other objects.

If the thinking, however, takes account not only of the object, but of its organic relationships; if the mind, that is to say, penetrates into the form and function of the object, then the result is a drawing which is still objective and naturalistic, but vital and organic: the individual, as Bullough says of his character type, to which this organic category partly corresponds, 'projects himself into the object and rediscovers himself in it'. In the enumerative type there is no such projection, no element of self: only the eye acting like a recording instrument. In the organic style the eye is rather a channel of communication between the psyche of the individual and the object observed.

Feeling, if extraverted, inheres in the medium itself: it exploits colour and expressive form—i.e. form which is an expression of energy rather than of intuitions or ideas. Art which is an expression of extraverted feeling is primarily decorative. Natural forms are used only in so far as they express feelings of joy, melancholy, etc.; and generally in the form of motives which symbolize these feelings (bright flowers to express gaiety, etc.).

Feeling, however, can be expressed more subjectively, that is to say, not in media which are taken directly from the 'fixities and definities' of the objective world, but in modes originating within the artist's mind. Both in poetry and painting, the characteristic element of this mode of expression is the spontaneous image, which gives the name 'imaginative' to the whole category.

It is identical with Coleridge's 'secondary imagination' ('it dissolves, diffuses, dissipates, in order to recreate; or where this process is rendered impossible, yet still at all events it struggles to idealize and to unify. It is essentially *vital*, even as all objects (*as* objects) are essentially fixed and dead'); and distinct as such from the primary imagination (' the living power and prime agent of all human perception') and from fancy (' a mode of memory emancipated from the order of time and space').[40]

From our previous discussion of the subject (see pp. 8, 90) it will be obvious that the haptic type of expression is the introvert aspect of the function of sensation; and empathy (in the sense defined by Spranger—cf. Note, pp. 24–5) is the extravert aspect of the same mental function.

Intuition is perhaps not a highly developed function of the child's mind, but it undoubtedly exists in certain types.[41] It is present in a high degree in such exceptional types as the musical prodigy, and perhaps in all children who show an aptitude for musical expression.

[40] *Biographia Literaria*, Chap. xiii.

[41] 'The eduction of relations manifests itself in some of the earliest perceptions of childhood': W. Line, *The Growth of Visual Perception in Children. Brit. J. Psych.*, Monograph Suppt. XV, Cambridge, 1931.

It is no less certainly present in those children, by no means rare, who develop a spontaneous rhythm in their drawings (see, e.g. Plates 31 and 41). In such cases the motif has been derived from the world of external reality, and the building up of a rhythmical pattern is then an extravert activity (the technique of 'writing patterns' evolved by Marion Richardson provides the best example of such activity in children). But the expression of intuitive 'states of mind' is also found in other types of children's drawings, though it needs a trained eye to see it. The balance of forms in Plate 42, the placing of the masses in relation to the space in Plate 44, the control of perspective in Plate 20a (by a child of six!), the creation of a spatial continuum by purely linear composition in Plate 20b (a rare case), all point to the possession by the child of an inner sense of abstract relationships.

We thus complete the correspondence between our categories and the Jungian psychological types. It may be expressed diagrammatically as follows:

THINKING	extravert	= enumerative
	introvert	= organic
FEELING	extravert	= decorative
	introvert	= imaginative
SENSATION	extravert	= empathetic
	introvert	= expressionist (haptic)
INTUITION	extravert	= rhythmical pattern
	introvert	= structural form

16. RELATION TO PERCEPTIVE TYPES

It remains to test our categories against the four types of perception distinguished by Bullough. We have already established a correlation between Bullough's types and Jung's, so a further comparison with our type of drawing is merely an extension of our analysis.

It will be recalled that the most constant tendency in Bullough's *objective* type was towards a purely intellectual appreciation of colour. Mixed colours, for example, are analysed by this type into their components. The type has no definite preferences—he is prepared to like any colour; and is generally unable to place himself in any close, inward, or personally interested relation to the object. Allowing for the mixed character of the material to be apprehended (as against the simple character of single colours) this type corresponds to our *enumerative* category.

The characteristic of Bullough's *physiological* or intra-subjective type was a direct personal reaction to the organic effects of colour. The criteria were the stimulation and temperature aspects of colour, and very frequently its brightness, and preferences were in the last resort decided by the general constitution of the individual, accordingly as he like being stimulated, or soothed, or preferred warmth or coolness.

This type corresponds closely to our empathetic category, and would include the colour reactions which are associated with the impressionist school of painting (fidelity to the 'vivacity' radiated by the object).

In Bullough's *associative* type, the mental suggestions aroused by the colour tended to be so potent that the colour itself was in danger of being forgotten, of becoming 'a merely inducing factor to the subject's representation'. The colour, we might say, sets in train an imaginative activity, and it becomes difficult not only to keep the originating factor in mind, but even to avoid losing all trace of it ('it dissolves, diffuses, dissipates, in order to recreate'). The important factor is not the thing-in-itself, the object, but the purely subjective feelings associated with the object. Any expression of this reaction becomes, therefore, an expression of associated feelings, and is an imaginative activity, certainly corresponding to our imaginative category.

The correlation with the *character* type presents more difficulty. Bullough himself found it hard to distinguish this type from the objective type—both show an absence of abstract preferences for any particular colour. The difference lay in the quality of the appreciation which 'shows the strange combination of *personal* elements . . . with *impersonal objective* elements . . . the fact that—so to speak— the individual projects himself into the object and rediscovers himself in it . . . appreciations of this type are distinguished at the same time by a maximum of emphasis and by a minimum of *personal* feeling. It is the same paradox which Kant expressed by his famous "disinterested pleasure", a contradiction in terms, which yet is after all, one of the best short descriptive formulas of the curious mixture of impersonal objectivity and intense personal participation, characteristic of the aesthetic attitude in general.'[42]

---

[42] *Brit. J. Psych.*, II, pp. 457–8. Cf. pp. 93–4.

The general nature of this activity is obviously intuitive, and in some sense a combination of both the introverted and extraverted attitudes. But from the point of view of the material actually surveyed, it would also apply to the introverted thinking type, which corresponds to our 'organic' category. The difficulty arises from the fact that Bullough was only considering types of apperception or apprehension, whereas we are also looking at the same material under the aspect of expression. Both points of view are legitimate: indeed, they are but the extravert and introvert aspects of the same process. But in drawing any comparison between our eight categories and Bullough's four types, we must be prepared, not only for a surplus of categories, but for a lack of precise correspondence, for Bullough does sometimes tend to include both subjective and objective aspects within his classification, and in his last 'character' type seeks what is in effect an integration of these two aspects.

With these provisos in mind, we may draw up the following table of correspondence:

BULLOUGH	CHILD EXPRESSION
Objective	= Enumerative
Physiological (intra-subjective)	= Empathetic and decorative
Associative	= Imaginative
Character	= Organic + rhythmical pattern + structural form

This leaves two of our categories unaccounted for, the expressionist and the decorative, but a little consideration will show that one of these is *a priori* excluded from Bullough's apperceptive types, because it is essentially un-visual. The expressionist type is haptic, as Loewenfeld has shown (*op. cit.*, pp. 32–6), and Bullough's experiments were based entirely on the visual perception of colours. As for the decorative category, it does not make a convincing appearance in any logical scheme. Decoration, except in so far as it involves an abstract relationship of form and colour, which would bring it within the structural category, implies a certain compromise between means and end, the 'feelingful' adaptation of colour and design to a given form or space, and is therefore not a 'disinterested' aesthetic category in Bullough's sense. (The word 'decorative', one should remember, is even sometimes used as a term of contempt in modern art criticism.) But in our scheme 'decorative' is used to describe certain arrangements of form and colour which are an extravert expression of feeling, and which belong therefore to the stimulation and temperature aspects of colour appreciated by Bullough's physiological or intra-subjective type.

It must be emphasized once more that none of these types or categories is found in a pure state: at best they indicate a *predominant* attitude or tendency in the individual, and there may be considerable overlapping, both in apprehension and in expression. But that the types do exist in children, and can be identified by their modes of expression, cannot be doubted, and the fact is of enormous potential value for the theory and practice of education.

17. THE AGE FACTOR

Before passing to a general consideration of the pedagogical significance of these facts, we must consider whether the types are already apparent in very young children, and if so, at what age they are identifiable. That a child is born with a *potentiality* for type-differentiation in a particular direction seems to be the assumption of most psychologists: they differ only in the degree of importance they assign to the possibilities of variation from the original disposition (*Urbild*). Kretschmer, for example, states that 'from earliest childhood' there is a recognizable schizoid personality (and therefore presumably also a recognizable cycloid personality) and that at puberty a characteristic psychosis develops out of it.[43] Jaensch considers that 'many individuals—the "disintegrate" of our typology—receive the structure of their perceptual world as a completed heritage. Those with more plastic, impressionable natures, only develop it during their life. . . . In these individuals, functions that later are separate still interpenetrate one another to a high degree and influence each other. That is why we call them "integrate". The integrate type is an earlier one from the evolutionary point of view. The younger children are, the more fully do they show this characteristic integration. Integration also dominates the behaviour of primitive peoples.'[44]

[43] *Physique and Character*, p. 153.

[44] *Eidetic Imagery*, pp. 92-3. Jaensch, that is to say, maintains that the relation of the very young child to the external world is always 'coherent' and that the gradual disintegration of this coherence accounts for 'abnormal' (that is to say, pronounced B and T types). But it would not be fair to assume that Jaensch would not allow for variants within the normal type (though his psychology and pedagogy are under suspicion of being directed to the production of a uniform racial type) and the inference is that these variants are related to the innate

The general truth of the matter has been well expressed by another German psychologist, R. Gaupp: 'Whoever has had a good deal of experience with human beings and possesses psychological insight, can often recognize quite early in childhood the psychic characteristics or temperament of an individual, though a peculiar disposition may first be clearly revealed at puberty. Among those who were my friends and acquaintances in youth I am not able to name one whose disposition has since changed essentially.'[45]

Karl Dambach, who conducted numerous experiments to determine types in children, found that it was possible to differentiate clearly between cyclothymes and schizothymes at the age of ten. He gives the following activities as characteristic of the two categories:[46]

Cyclothymic children prefer to play with other children rather than read books;

prefer group games—do not like to be left alone;

most of them like to change their games frequently;

they are not so sensitive, or so affected by sad stories;

mix well, do not brood, open-hearted, general favourites;

easily moved to anger, but not to passion;

dream about their games and comrades;

prefer practical activities like housework, drawing, etc.;

like to work in the garden or kitchen;

soon forget their troubles and make up their quarrels.

Schizothymic children prefer to play alone, or with one good friend;

prefer building games, trains, ships and animals;

can keep at the game for a long time;

avoid places where there are a lot of people, are shy;

like sad stories, fear death, and if not too stupid, think about God, etc.;

some of them quarrel a lot and weep when things are taken from them, but there is another type which is good-natured and never gets excited;

not forthcoming, more particular in their friendships;

their dreams are fantastic and often express wish-fulfilments;

physical constitution of the individual rather than to the gradual differentiation of a psychological disposition.

[45] *Psychologie des Kindes*, 5th ed. (Leipzig, 1925), p. 63.

[46] 'Die Mehrfacharbeit u. ihre typologische Bedeutung.' 1 Abt. *Zeitschr. f. Psychologie*. Ergaenzungsband 14 (Leipzig, 1929).

prefer counting, copybook writing, religious services and singing
to drawing or housework;
help their mothers in the kitchen, etc.;
afflicted with night anxiety.

Dambach further observes that no child with poor capacity for
attention was cyclothymic, and none with strong capacity for attention was schizothymic. He comes to the conclusion that on the one
hand we have that strong ability to direct attention, inclination to
concentrate on form to the neglect of colour, associative talent—all
symptoms of the basedowoid types (among eidetics), of pyknic
physique and cyclothyme temperament—whilst on the other hand
we have slight ability to direct attention, inclination to concentrate
on colour to the neglect of form, perseverative talent—all symptoms
of the tetanoid type (among eidetics), of non-pyknic physique and
schizothyme temperament—and that these two sets of characteristics indicate two types of constitution *which can already be recognized in childhood.*[47]

Another psychologist of the same school, Gerhard Pfahler, also
claims that a differentiation of schizothyme and cyclothyme types
has been established with unmistakable clarity among school-
children of 10–11 years.[48] The extreme position is represented by
Sheldon: 'It is our impression that the level of the somatype is below
that at which environmental influences operate after birth, and that
the question of changing the somatype is comparable (although not
equivalent) to that of changing the race of an individual. We believe
that the somatype designation offers a basic and reasonably stable
taxonomy of individuals.'[49]

The question we must now ask is whether these types, which can be
established by question and answer methods, involving self-analysis
on the part of the children at the age of ten or eleven, can be deter-

[47] *Op. cit.*, p. 236.

[48] 'System der Typenlehre: Grundlegung einer paedagogischen Typenlehre.
Abt. *Zeitschr. f. Psychologie* Ergaenzungsband 15, p. 311.

[49] *Varieties of Temperament*, pp. 433–4. Sheldon's support might be claimed for
my general point of view. Cf. *Varieties of Human Physique*, pp. 259–61. 'Children
of different constitutional components probably need different educational influences, just as trees which lean in different directions need to be supported from
different angles . . . it might still be claimed that we do not know how to treat
children. Perhaps we shall never know how to treat them until we learn to tell
them apart.'

mined at a much earlier age by means of the free expression revealed in drawings. It is my belief that they can.

18. THE USE OF EARLY DRAWINGS FOR TYPE DIFFERENTIATION

Most of the early observers of children's drawings noticed exceptions of various kinds to the usual types. Sully, for example, after stating that a child's first attempt to draw a man usually takes a circular or ovoid form, then observes that very occasionally children draw a square head.[50] He suggests that this is due to the training received by the child at school in drawing horizontal and vertical lines; the example he illustrates is the work of a Jamaica girl of five. He also illustrates as an exception a drawing by an adult negro which omits the contour of the head altogether, the features being merely indicated by circles and patches which represent eyes, cheeks, ears, etc., but this is a type which can also be found among children's drawings (see Plate 4*b* and compare Loewenfeld, *Nature of Creative Activity*, Fig. 3).

In fact, even the most superficial observation of a sufficiently large number of drawings by children aged three and upwards indicates that though certain types predominate, there is a wide variation of modes of expression, and that far from there being a typical 'schema' for the young child, it would be more exact to say that every child has its own schema. This fact has already been noted by Lowenfeld, who writes:

'But the individuality of the schema has its roots, not only in the body, in autoplastic experience. In many cases it expresses the psychological constitution of the child. In the schema of an anxious child of delicate sensibilities I could trace this anxiety in the round, un-closed, uncertain lines just as much as I could find the characteristic resoluteness of another child in its rectangular representation of the body. Both schemas seem to me characteristic of the child's total personality structure. These facts show clearly that *even the earliest schematic representations are closely bound up with the individual self.* They are not arbitrary signs but are intimately related to both the bodily and the mental constitution.'[51]

---

[50] *Studies of Childhood*, pp. 335-6.
[51] *Op. cit.*, p. 22.

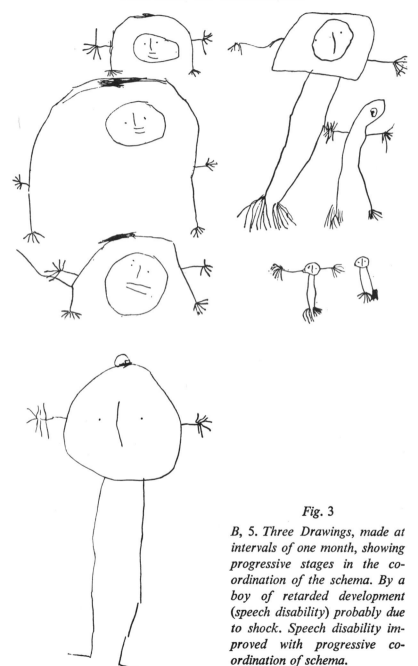

Fig. 3

B, 5. Three Drawings, made at intervals of one month, showing progressive stages in the co-ordination of the schema. By a boy of retarded development (speech disability) probably due to shock. Speech disability improved with progressive co-ordination of schema.

Figures 1 to 4 and Plates 1 to 8*a* illustrate variations in the schema of children between the ages of 3 and 5. Notes on the temperaments of the children, as observed by the teachers, show that in each case there is a correspondence between the drawings and the psychological constitution of the child. But this can best be illustrated by getting a

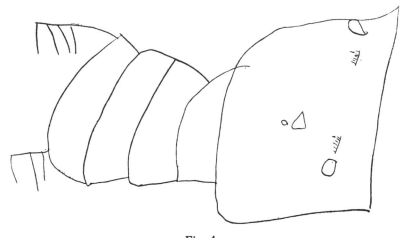

Fig. 4
B, 5, III. Figure drawing by an epileptic boy

group of children of approximately the same age, under identical conditions of environment and materials, to draw the same subject. The subject may be one associated with the children's daily experiences (such as 'My House') or one which involves more imaginative effort (such as 'The trees stood stately and tall', or 'A garden full of flowers'). The results of two experiments of this kind are illustrated in Figures 5 and 6 and Plates 11 to 15. Plates 16*a* and 16*b* are extreme contrasts from another such series: the enumerative unco-ordinated drawing typical of the extravert thinking type (the boy, according to the teacher, 'tends to be extravert, very self-confident') and the balanced structural form typical of the introverted intuitive type (a girl described by the teacher as 'overburdened with responsibility'); compare also the stories invented by these same two children given on page 163. The four houses illustrated in Figures 5 to 6 very clearly express the relative types. (*a*) is a sociable and well-balanced girl; for her houses are not isolated, but symmetrically grouped; a path leads to the door and there are flowers in the garden and birds and clouds (both 'stylized') in the sky—from which we might deduce: extraverted feeling type with decorative mode of expression. (*b*) is a steady un-imaginative boy, and his house is solid, well articulated and schem-

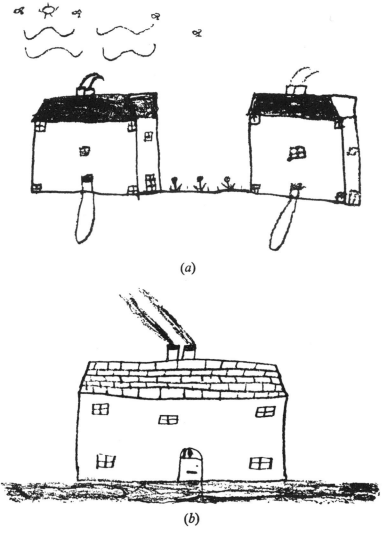

(*a*)

(*b*)

Fig. 5
'*My House*' (*a*) G, 6; (*b*) B, 7

(c)   (d)

Fig. 6
'*My House*' (c) G, 6; (d) B, 6

atic; windows well distributed, tile divisions on the roof accurately
alternated: extraverted thinking type with enumerative mode of
expression. (c) is another sociable girl, but excitable and active, and
her house is accordingly very much 'busier', with gay flowered curtains in the windows and lots of people on the balcony: extraverted
sensation type with impressionist mode of expression. (d) is an
hysterical boy with a stammer; his house is unbalanced, with a
chaotic confusion of windows and smoke which zig-zags into
infinity: introverted sensation type with disintegrated haptic mode of
expression.

A more complete series is illustrated in Plates 11 to 15. The notes
accompanying these plates record the disposition of each child as re-
ported by the teacher, and at the end of each note I have suggested
the corresponding category of the drawing. These categories are only

determined on a general balance of characteristics, and some of the drawings exhibit subsidiary features which suggest intermediate types. For example, Pl. 13*d*, which I have called expressionistic (introverted sensation type), has impressionistic qualities which are of a more extravert tendency, and this tendency is also revealed in the teacher's characterization of the girl, for though she has the same general disposition as her twin sister (Pl. 13*c*), she is less timid and shows a *tendency* to lead, though no real initiative.

This particular correlation of temperamental disposition with graphic modes of expression is based on a single drawing for each child, but obviously for a more accurate analysis it would be necessary to examine many drawings spread over a specific diagnostic period. From many such investigations, carried out by competent observers, it might be possible to construct a graphic key to temperament, so that the individual psychological constitution could be identified with reasonable accuracy by the teacher (somewhat on the lines of a scientific graphology such as becomes possible in later life). But this is not our purpose. Apart from the fact that the use of such a key would demand a high degree of discrimination (for as we have repeatedly emphasized, there are no clear-cut types, but only individuals who, in certain phases of their development, more or less conform to our theoretical types) such schematic methods of identification are no substitute for that total observation of the psychology of the individual which demands, not the use of a key or even of textbooks, but qualities of insight or intuition which are personal to the teacher or the parent. The various modes of expression provide material for assessing those factors which together constitute, even in the early years of life, the temperament and personality of an individual. That the values indicated by such an assessment have no necessary correspondence to the values indicated by ordinary school tests of intelligence must be obvious, and this fact has, indeed, long been recognized.[52] A rearrangement of the drawings illustrated in Plates 11 to 16 according to aesthetic merit would have little relation to the order in which they are reproduced, which is the order of attainment in ordinary class tests. We must postpone until the next chapter, any discussion of this conflict of values as it is perpetuated in the existing educational system, merely noting for the moment that those values which we have shown to be the most reliable and the most direct and

[52] It was demonstrated by F. C. Ayer in *The Psychology of Drawing*, Baltimore, 1916.

convenient clues to personality and temperament are altogether excluded from the examinations that determine which children shall proceed from the primary to the secondary stage of education. They are not used even in the determination of humanistic or technological aptitudes.

19. NON-VISUAL MODES OF EXPRESSION: (I) PLAY ACTIVITY

Though in this study I have been concerned mainly with the visual and plastic arts (drawing, painting and modelling), it is, of course, essential to take into account other forms of aesthetic expression which might reinforce the evidence provided by drawings, etc. These are mainly of three kinds: (1) play activity, (2) verbal inventions, and (3) music.

Since Froebel first pointed out the fundamental importance of play activity in the development of the child, this aspect of the child's life has been observed in considerable detail. It is sufficient to refer to the work of Karl Groos, Piaget, Karl and Charlotte Bühler, Melanie Klein, Susan Isaacs, Margaret Lowenfeld, Margret van Wylick, and Ruth Hartley. Under the influence of psychoanalysis educationalists have been compelled to give a far wider scope to the function of play in the growth of the child. 'Play is not only the means by which the child comes to discover the world; it is supremely the activity which brings him psychic equilibrium in the early years. In his play activities, the child externalizes and works out to some measure of harmony all the different trends of his internal psychic life. . . . Educators have long appreciated the vast significance of play, and many different aspects of its value have been brought out by different thinkers. It has remained for psychoanalysts, and in particular those working with young children, to show in the greatest detail how play is indeed the breath of life to the child, since it is through play activities that he finds mental ease, and can work upon his wishes, fears and phantasies, so as to integrate them into a living personality.' This quotation from Dr. Isaacs[53] shows that the value of play as an index to individuality has now been fully recognized, but it is, of course, no part of the reductive technique of psychoanalysis to formulate typological categories—a fact which distinguishes the therapeutic technique from its doctrinaire superstructures. It is understandable,

[53] *Social Development in Young Children* (London, 1933), p. 425.

therefore, that the study of play activity should from this point of view have been almost entirely occupied with the construction of a developmental theory. That is to say, all the characteristics of play are classified either from a merely descriptive point of view (e.g., functional, fictional and representational) or as characteristic of a particular age group. It is only exceptionally that play is related to temperamental variations. Margaret Lowenfeld, towards the end of her book, devotes a chapter to 'Children Who Cannot Play', and makes some general observations on the relationship between the child himself and the form his play takes. From this point of view she divides children into three groups, namely:

(i) Children whose play is entirely isolated and personal, and which needs for its performance only the most shapeless of materials.

(ii) Children whose play is still individual, but which creates out of the material it uses a definite objective world with which it associates itself.

(iii) Children who play out with fellow-players themes mutually agreed upon.[54]

But the point of view is still that of genetic psychology. That is to say, Dr. Lowenfeld regards these types of children as characteristic of different stages in the process of social adaptation, the natural and fully integrated child at one extreme, the 'unnatural' neurotic child at the other extreme. She agrees that play has an outer and an inner aspect—'an outer aspect, which is the form which appears to the playfellow or adult observer, and an inner or psychological aspect, which is the meaning that type of play has for the child'. She claims that her classification is a combination of both points of view, with an emphasis upon the psychological. She gives as a summary of her classification: 'play that expresses the bodily impulses of the child; that apperceives his environment; that prepares the child for life; that enables him to mix harmoniously with his fellows.' She admits interrelation between these groups, but neither in the classification itself, nor in the book as a whole, is there any consistent attempt to relate types of play to types of children. Play is regarded as a function of childhood rather than of the child. It is true that Dr. Lowenfeld

[54] *Play in Childhood* (London, 1935), p. 281. Cf. Stern, *Psychology of Early Childhood*, pp. 309–23, for a similar classification. *Understanding Children's Play* (New York and London, 1952), by Ruth E. Hartley, Lawrence K. Frank, and Robert M. Goldenson, pays considerable attention to individual variations, but is mainly therapeutic in intention.

recognizes the child's play as 'the externalized expression of his emotional life', and as such she even suggests that play 'serves for the child the function taken by art in adult life'. But play *as expression* remains unanalysed, and unrelated to basic psychological types.

The very detailed and interesting analysis of methods of playing made by Dr. van Wylick[55] has a similar genetic bias. The main attention is directed to differences between ages, and not between types. It is only incidentally that the existence of type distinctions is mentioned. For example, in analysing the quantitative differences in the kinds of play-material used by children of age groups from 4 to 8, Dr. van Wylick found that while the relative use of animals, houses, trees and fences had a developmental significance, the use of human beings could not be related to the progressive age-groups. She suggests[56] that possibly human beings have an important 'characterological' significance, but she does not develop this suggestion.[57]

[55] *Die Welt des Kindes in seiner Darstellung* (Vienna, 1936).

[56] Pp. 36–7.

[57] In his interesting analysis of the subject-matter of children's drawings, Dr. Ballard found that the interest in human beings was at its lowest about the age of nine, and greater before that age than after; after the age of twelve there is a further falling-off. He does not suggest any characterological variations other than those based on sex. Girls draw human beings more frequently than boys before the age of nine, less frequently after that age.

From an examination of 20,000 drawings Dr. Ballard found that the order of preference in subjects was as follows:

Boys: Ships, miscellaneous objects, plant life, houses, human beings, vehicles, animals, weapons, landscapes.

Girls: Plant life, houses, miscellaneous objects, human beings, animals, ships, vehicles, weapons, landscapes.

It would be interesting, after the passage of more than thirty years, to test these results against an investigation on a similar scale. The differences would be some indication of the effect of social environment on the child's mind. My own impression is that vehicles have advanced considerably up the list of boys' preferences, for all ages, and that ships no longer occupy anywhere near the first place.

Dr. Ballard does not compare the stylistic differences that can be observed between the drawings by girls and boys of the same subject. In spite of the characterological variations which will tend to result in the drawing of an extravert girl being more 'masculine' and the drawing of an introvert boy being more 'feminine', a rough generalization is possible (just as it is possible for male and female characteristics in adult life, or male and female characteristics in art and literature). In children's drawings of the same subject we must look for the sex differentiation in such features as the relative emphasis of particular details, the character of the 'line', and the choice of colours. In the drawings of a house, for example, it will generally be found that boys emphasize the functional aspects (doors, windows, chimney) and the dynamic aspects (smoke from the chimney), use a thick forceful line and strong colours; whereas girls emphasize details

20. NON-VISUAL MODES OF EXPRESSION: (II) VERBAL INVENTIONS

This aspect of free expression, to which early writers like Perez, Preyer, and Sully gave a good deal of attention, has been studied more recently by F. Giese,[58] Ruth Griffiths[59] and Marjorie Hourd[60] and by various American writers (Hartman and Shumaker,[61] Hughes Mearns,[62] Harold Rugg[63] and Madeleine Dixon[64]) but never from a typological standpoint. The subject is outside the scope of our present studies, but obviously it has a considerable bearing on the general pedagogical significance of type psychology.

The material is either spoken or written, and in either case essentially the reproduction of an 'interior monologue'. As material, it suffers from certain disadvantages. If spoken, it involves, for its recording, the presence of an adult whose activities (taking down notes) may distract the child or even lead to a deliberate 'playing up to' the adult (comparable to sophistication in drawing). If the verbal fictions are written by the child—and this rarely becomes possible before the age of six—then the fantasy may be inhibited by the difficulty of this technique of expression (letter formation, spelling, etc.) and by the fact that the symbols are strictly limited in number. A child's vocabulary may consist of only two or three hundred words: its visual images are comparatively unlimited, though the invention of 'images de traduction' to represent them may present the same kind of difficulty as the learning of names—it is doubtful if a child ever attempts to draw an object *before* he can name it. It is much more difficult for a child to make a representational picture of an

(curtains), environment (garden, trees), use a thinner line and more delicate colours. These are rather obvious expressions of sexual characteristics and are only significant for the determination of hetero-sexual tendencies. ('What London Children Like to Draw,' *J. Exper. Pedagogy*, I (1911–12), pp. 185–97; 'What Children Like to Draw,' *ibid.*, II (1913–14), pp. 127–9).

[58] *Das freie literarische Schaffen bei Kindern und Jugendlichen*, 2nd ed., 1928.

[59] *Imagination in Early Childhood* (London, 1935).

[60] *The Education of the Poetic Spirit* (London, 1949).

[61] *Creative Expression: The Development of Children in Art, Music, Literature and Drama* (New York, 1932).

[62] *Creative Youth* (New York, 1925).

[63] *The Child-Centred School*, by Harold Rugg and Ann Shumaker (London and New York, 1928). *Culture and Education in America*, by Harold Rugg (New York, 1931).

[64] *High, Wide and Deep: Discovering the Pre-School Child* (London, 1939).

object than to associate with that object, or even than to invent for that object, a symbol, whether aural (word) or graphic (schema). What **is** certainly important in this connection is to record any verbal fantasies which the child spontaneously associates with his drawings: as already indicated, there may be no representational connection between the drawing and the fantasies associated with it, but the fantasy plus the drawing is obviously a unity from the point of view of typological interpretation, and it should be possible to establish a correlation between the classification of the drawings according to the categories indicated in this chapter and a classification of the accompanying verbal fantasies according to Binet's types of apprehension, as expanded by Müller (cf. p. 93). That is to say, an enumerative drawing would be accompanied by a descriptive story, an impressionist drawing by an emotionally-descriptive story, and so on.

For example, the following stories[65] were invented by the two children whose drawings are illustrated on Plates 16a, b about the same time as the drawings were made:

G 7 I   (i) Mummy and Stella and Sally and Daddy are in the house. Sally has a skipping rope and Stella has a doll.

        (ii) Mummy and Stella and Sally and Daddy are in the house. They are playing cards.

        (Note: Stella is called by her pet name 'Sally' at home, and she therefore personifies herself under both names at the same time.)

B 7 VIII   (i) Once upon a time an elephant's mother said he could go into the woods for a walk. He thought he would go to the river. He met a crocodile. They decided to have a boxing match but the elephant knocked the crocodile on the nose and sent him home crying.

        (ii) The enemy aircraft factory is attacked by the fleet air arm. The Nazi air force tried to shoot us down but they went down in flames before they could.

These stories complete and confirm the diagnosis of types given in connection with the drawings. The girl's stories are wholly occupied with herself and her parents, the self is even duplicated, and the action is intimate, 'in the house'. The boy's stories are objective, about things and animals external to the boy himself, 'open air', crude and dramatic.

<hr>

[65] I am indebted to Miss Beatrice Culham for these very apt illustrations.

163

21. NON-VISUAL MODES OF EXPRESSION (III) MUSIC

This aspect of free expression has been studied from our point of view by Heinz Werner,[66] P. Lamparter[67] and H. Jacoby[68]. It may be said that the importance of music as a medium of expression has been generally recognized, and we need only refer once more to Dalcroze's work to indicate the extent to which the subject has been made the basis of educational methods. But so far as I have been able to discover, it is only Lamparter who has investigated the use of expression in music as an index to the psychology of the child.

In general we may say that with the exception of the work of the Marburg school of psychologists, all investigations into the significance of the modes and material of free expression in children have been conceived from a uni-serial, genetic or developmental point of view. It is far from my intention to question the utility of this point of view in general, but nevertheless an exclusive adherence to it has been responsible for some of the worst faults of our educational system. 'The' child as such does not exist, and any system of uniform education based on such a mythical figure is merely a rack on which the all too plastic mind of the individual is distorted.

It may be objected that our 'types' are equally mythical, and we have admitted that however much they may be subdivided (and Jung, for example, is finally not satisfied with less than sixteen types) they remain theoretical categories for which no corresponding individual can be found. It is not a question of correspondence, but of convenience. What we have, as fundamental realities, are two factors determining growth. One is the vital force itself, to which corresponds a process of maturation in body and mind with quite general laws; the other factor is the unique make of the individual, which compels this force to make certain deviations from the general law of development. That 'unique make' is the subject investigated by somatology and individual psychology, and we believe that by scientific classification we can reduce the chaos of individualities to some semblance of order. It is true that we can never classify all the minute

---

[66] *Die melodische Erfindung im fruehen Kindesalter.*

[67] 'Die Musikalitaet in ihren Beziehungen zur Grundstruktur der Persoenlichkeit.' Exp. Beitraege zur Typenkunde. Bd. III, *Zeitschr. f. Psychologie*, Ergaenzungsband 22 (1932).

[68] 'Die Befreiung der schoepferischen Kraefte dargestellt am Beispiel der Musik.' *Das werdende Zeitalter*, Vol. IV (Gotha, 1925).

variations due to the peculiar combination of chromosomes in the cell from which the individual develops; but even these have *average* characteristics. No less multiform are the deviations due to environment and upbringing, and especially to the process of social adaptation which each individual has to make between birth and maturity. But all these deviations follow courses that slowly are being traced by psychoanalysis, and it is possible to determine certain prevalent directions which they take. Individual psychology does no more than attempt to trace lines of greatest frequency. But it does claim that these lines are significant, and that we must be aware of them before we can begin to modify the general line of human development. Social psychology, that is to say, must always be corrected and amplified by the more particular science of individual psychology. It follows, therefore, that any general system of education must be flexible enough to provide for the special needs of the various types of children. It is my contention in this study that those types can be determined by the observations of the child's modes of free expression. It is only when the child's psychic individuality has been so determined that the further step can be taken of educating that child along the lines of its inherent potentialities. It is not sufficient to say, with Edmond Holmes, that the function of education is to foster growth: we must first determine what form of growth is appropriate to the particular organism in our care. To the specific number of actual types correspond a specific number of vocational functions, and the purpose of education, from this point of view, is to lead from the actual type to the corresponding function.

22. THE PURPOSE OF EXPRESSION

In this chapter we have been analysing the child's modes of expression, considered as a dynamic mental *process*; we have not considered the *purpose* of that expression—the impulse or drive behind the process.

It is not sufficient to say that the child desires to represent something—an object he sees or a feeling he experiences. The question is: why should he desire to externalize his perception or feeling? Why is he not satisfied with a merely inward or imaginative representation of the object or feeling?

We have mentioned certain factors which make the activity of expression technically possible—the expenditure of muscular energy and the imitations of the graphic or plastic activities of grown-up people. But these factors do not explain why the child should desire, not merely to make a muscular movement with a pencil in hand, and to give this movement intentional direction, but further to give an individual and personal meaning to the sign he makes.

In short, we have to recognize that expression is also *communication*, or at least an attempt to communicate, and the question we are asking, therefore, is why does the child desire to communicate?

Communication implies the intention to affect other people, and it is therefore a social activity. Any adequate explanation of it must therefore rest on a psychology that considers, not only the individual, but the individual's relation to the group.[69] Actually, the tendency of modern psychology is towards an integration of individual and social psychology.[70] The most fundamental discovery of modern psychology is the fact that the individual can only be explained in terms of his social adaptation—a process which begins with his suckling and weaning, and is not completed until he is an integrated member of a social unit, or series of social units (family, trade union, church, parish, nation). To Dr. Susan Isaacs in particular we owe a careful study of this process of adaptation in young children.

From this new point of view communication becomes an easily explicable phenomenon. Dr. Suttie gives a simple and, for the present writer, a very convincing formula, though Freud, Ferenczi, Jung, Groddeck, Burrow, Susan Isaacs and Edward Glover all have similar or alternative explanations. According to Dr. Suttie, the directing motive in individual development is the attempt to overcome the separation anxiety which begins with the process of weaning, and in all his social activities—art, science and religion included—the individual is seeking a restoration of, or substitute for, that *love of mother* which was lost in infancy.[71]

Included in this hypothesis is an explanation of the conative aspects of expression: expression is not an outpouring for its own sake,

---

[69] Earlier educationalists assumed an automatic interplay of perception and expression—the more that is taken in, the more that must be poured out. Holmes, for example (*What is and What Might be*, p. 184) writes: 'Perception and expression are not two faculties, but one. Each is the very counterpart or correlate, each is the very life and soul, of the other'.

[70] Cf., e.g. Trigant Burrow: *The Social Basis of Consciousness* (London, 1927).

[71] *Origins of Love and Hate* (London, 1935), p. 71 and *passim*.

or the necessary correlate of perception: it is essentially '*an overture demanding response from others*'.[72]

We shall have occasion to discuss this theory in more detail in a later chapter, but for the present it gives us a convincing formula for the motive behind a child's free expressional activities. All types of children, even prodigies of skill in naturalistic representation, use their drawings, not as the expression of their perceptual images, nor of their pent-up feelings, but rather as a 'feeler', a spontaneous reaching-out to the external world, at first tentative, but capable of becoming the main factor in the adjustment of the individual to society. In the narrower sense, the sense elucidated by Jaensch, it is a process of replacing the 'primary eidetic unity' by a balanced world of sensation and ideas; but the primary eidetic unity is merely the cognitive aspect of the primary physical unity of mother and child, and the replacing of the primary or physical unity by a secondary and social unity—the establishment, that is to say, of a harmony between society and the individuals composing it—is the fundamental task of education. The process of adjustment is always one of 'Einbildungs-kraft', of creative imagination, and it is for this very practical reason that we maintain that art is the basis of any efficient technique of education. In this chapter I have been concerned more particularly to emphasize the typological nature of the problem, and to show that art is the best guide for a system of education which has some regard for the natural varieties of temperament and personality. In the captions that accompany the Plates an attempt is made to show the practicability of this technique, but admittedly this is only an indication of a method which should be pursued on a far wider scale and over a considerable period of time. In particular, the progressive development of modes of expression parallel to types of disposition should be correlated in a number of individual cases over the whole developmental period—say from the age of 3 to 18. Such an investigation is only within the capacity of either a research institute or the Ministry of Education itself, and here I can only express a personal conviction, which I hope has been supported by the evidence I have been able to present, that such an investigation would result in discoveries of great pedagogical significance.

---

[72] Suttie, *op. cit.*, p. 35. It will be seen that from this point of view the term 'self-expression' is misleading. In the normal child, self-expression is always social expression, and one of the principal aims of education is to prevent such social expression degenerating into ego-centricity.

One question in particular must await an investigation of such an organized kind: the modification in aesthetic modes of expression which are likely to occur during the phase of adolescence. As we have seen, it is usually assumed that a profound change occurs in the average child at about the age of 11, which change involves the desuetude of aesthetic modes of expression. Admittedly a profound change of a psychological nature does take place at this age. From our point of view it may perhaps best be described as the discovery of logical thought—the mental revolution so vividly described by Bergson, Claparède and Piaget. The child acquires the power of breaking up, or dissociating, his first unitary perceptions, and logical thought begins with this capacity to isolate and compare component details. From this comparative or correlating activity (Spearman's 'education of relations') proceeds the abstract thought or concept, and it must undoubtedly be true that the change thus introduced into the mental processes of the child has a profound effect on his modes of expression. But to assume that visual or plastic (imagist) modes of expression are thereby eliminated is to beg the question. They *may* show a tendency to disappear; but it is perhaps this very tendency that our educational methods should oppose, preserving not only the function of imagination, but even more necessarily the essential unity of perception: not only the continuously vitalizing interchange of mind and the concrete events of the natural world, but also the continuous nourishment of the individual psyche from the deeper levels of the mind.

If we have no *a priori* notions of what art should be—if we realize that art is as various as human nature—then it is certain that a mode of aesthetic expression can be retained by every individual beyond the age of 11 and throughout and beyond the adolescent period in general —*if* we are prepared to sacrifice to some extent that exclusive devotion to the learning of logical modes of thought which characterizes our present system of education. The art of the child declines after the age of 11 because it is attacked from every direction—not merely squeezed out of the curriculum, but squeezed out of the mind by the logical activities which we call arithmetic and geometry, physics and chemistry, history and geography, and even literature as it is taught. The price we pay for this distortion of the adolescent mind is mounting up: a civilization of hideous objects and misshapen human beings, of sick minds and unhappy households, of divided societies armed with weapons of mass destruction. We feed these processes of dissolution with our knowledge and science, with our inventions and discoveries, and our education system tries to keep pace with the holocaust; but the creative activities which could heal the mind and make beautiful our environment, unite man with nature and nation with nation—these we dismiss as idle, irrelevant and inane.

APPENDIX C

EBENEZER COOKE ON 'ART TEACHING AND CHILD NATURE'

Extracts from a review of the discussion—Art Section, International Conference, Health Exhibition, 1884. Journal of Education, Dec. 1, 1885 (pp. 462–5) and Jan. 1, 1886 (pp. 12–15).
'Go to nature,' the artist's cry of reform, means usually to nature objective only. It should include the nature that goes also.

The teacher's knowledge of the pupil's nature is not less important than the system on which he teaches.

So deeply is the child interested in colour, no teaching of drawing adapted to child nature can exclude it. Is it fair to say colour cannot be taught, while the powers needed for its acquisition are unused, undeveloped? All intellectual growth results from exercise of faculty or function.

It is life or death, education or instruction, as it is treated. It is possible to use the apparatus and neglect the spirit. It is more difficult to evolve expression, to exercise imagination, to stimulate voluntary mental activity, than to teach mechanically. Drawing can easily be used for the lower purpose. The teacher who is literal, or slave to a system, may regard it as a series of copies of lines, with little aim beyond exactness, cramming order in, not evoking it, attempting no exercise of imagination, but suppressing it by neglect. Imagination some teachers consider their enemy. Accuracy is ever opposed to it.

Design precedes drawing. Before the child can make a line, he can use one ready made, as a stick or ring. By handling as well as seeing the concrete examples, he gains clear ideas of elements and notions of arrangement. With the power of representation comes ability to make numbers, varied lengths and directions. With simple elements, yet of the nature of generalizations, and widely applicable, the child constructs designs, and enjoys. To arouse consciousness of this innate power of discovery, to fix surely the lesson that it can teach itself, or receive instruction from nature, as it accepts the conditions, is to give the child a strong power for life in dealing with things, and a stimulant to self-activity.

THE ART OF CHILDREN

Mr. Ablett, in Board Schools, takes the elements of script letters, and with these draws, designs, and writes at once.

No line can be drawn without imagination. Every fact passes through it, between the seeing eye and doing hand. Both are alike injurious if the teacher is merely the instrument of a system, not a living teacher knowing the child.

To draw from imagination, we were told, is useless (a usual and approved canon). One girl objected to the exercise; her mother supported. The offensive word was changed to 'memory'; the objection ceased, though the exercise required was the same. For memory has not such a bad character. It is supposed to represent images of things exactly as they were seen. It is an insult to suggest that the things are not seen accurately and fully. Yet, sight is, perhaps, more faulty than imagination, which depends on it. We see only that which we bring power to see; and we must see rightly to acquire the power.

Imagination, even in design, is not unrestrained; observed fact controls it. The highest imaginative art does not transcend general truth. Science and imagination are not opposite, but complementary to each other.

Nature is one. Organic and inorganic agree in plan. Froebel studies crystals, and embodies their forms and construction in his inventional drawing. All his designs result from a repeated and varied unit. He reconstructs on the method of nature, with elements or units, not with fragments.

The choice is between accuracy and interest, technical skill and child-nature. Agreed that truth must be had, but relative. The moral of the whole thing is rather—how to get it. . . . The child's attention is aroused and sustained by interest. It is a power not to be neglected. The teacher who includes child-nature in his subject—its progressive capacity, its extending interests, as they develop—will try and get this and all natural forces on his side. Steam and electricity are our servants, because we learned from them their nature—entered into it, and worked in sympathy with it—did not oppose it. The nature of the child can no more be altered by us. We must study, sympathize and conquer by obeying it.

170

Chapter Six

UNCONSCIOUS MODES OF INTEGRATION

Human consciousness is in perpetual pursuit of a language and a style. To assume consciousness is at once to assume form. Even at levels far below the zone of definition and clarity, forms, measures and relationships exist. The chief characteristic of the mind is to be constantly describing itself.—Henri Focillon.

In our discussion of psychological types, we promised to consider the pedagogical significance of certain factors of an unconscious nature of whose presence we become aware in any diagnosis of type. To discuss these phenomena thoroughly would lead us too far from our immediate subject, and it is a problem which must in any case be left to the professional analyst. But in the course of this investigation certain evidence has come to light which must be recorded and correlated as far as possible with our general conclusions. The hypothesis to be presented is very speculative, and though in my own opinion it provides the final link in my chain of evidence, it is not essential to the general argument, and this chapter may therefore be omitted by the cautious reader. To give this evidence its proper setting, and for the benefit of those among my readers who are not familiar with the literature of the subject, I must begin with a very brief summary, which I shall at the same time attempt to make synthetic, of the modern theories of the unconscious.

1. THE GENERAL THEORY OF THE UNCONSCIOUS

The possibility that our mental life is not a simple unity must have occurred to man at an early stage in his development—from the very moment he began to consider the significance of his dreams. That possibility is evident to the members of those primitive communities which still survive in the world, and is an integral part of their ani-

171

mism or magical religion. Those records of people 'possessed of an evil spirit' which we find so often in the Bible; the *daimon* recognized by Plato and other Greek philosophers—these are but the first attempts to describe mental processes which are not part of what we regard as our normal state of consciousness.

A review of what might be called the pre-Freudian theories of the unconscious was made by F. von Hartmann,[1] but since von Hartmann's time (his book was first published in 1868), the hypothesis of the unconscious has been explored in great detail by the method of psychoanalysis, and most people are prepared to admit that it has been given a firm scientific foundation. Even the extreme physiological school, as represented by Pavlov, has to admit the presence of mental activities beyond the reach of its investigations.[2] Comprehensive and convincing as is the success of the theory of conditioned reflexes as an explanation of mental phenomena, the problems raised by dreams, and by the constructive activity of the imagination, remain outside its scope. It is for precisely these problems that the hypothesis of a mental activity submerged below the level of consciousness offers the only solution.

For the standard psychological theory of the unconscious we must turn to Freud, but before we describe the Freudian conception of the mind in any detail, let us consider for a moment the obvious facts. What, in the first place, do we normally mean by consciousness? A state of awareness. But a state of awareness implies a subject (or self), an object, and an instrument to connect the two. The subject is the physical totality of a perceptive human being; the object is anything external to its system of perception (including not only something separate from the human being's body, but also a separate part or function within his organism); and finally the various organs of sensation which enable a relationship to be established between the subject and the object.

The normal assumption is that sensation, by itself and passively, gives the subject an awareness of the object; but a little reflection will show that this is by no means always the case. We are continually seeing and hearing, smelling and touching, objects of which we remain

[1] *The Philosophy of the Unconscious* (new edition, London, 1931).

[2] 'In recent years, when the right of the physiologist to a comprehensive study of human higher nervous activity has been universally admitted, Pavlov ceased to demand that a fine should be levied for the use of the word "consciousness". He habitually employed this word himself in relation to man.' Frolov: *Pavlov and his School*, pp. 189–90.

unconscious. We do not become conscious of the contents of our sensations without an effort of some kind—a certain attentive concentration. Without such an effort, sensation remains more or less non-conscious.[3]

This is best shown by a consideration of the early development of the child's consciousness. It is doubtful, indeed, whether one can speak in any real sense of a child's consciousness. Certainly, the child is not unconscious: but it is not yet conscious of its own self. It cannot even spontaneously localize its own organic sensations. 'A pain in the foot does not immediately draw its attention to the foot, etc. It is rather a wandering pain which is not localized and which everyone is thought to share. Even when localized the infant no doubt for a long time still regards it as common to all; it cannot spontaneously realize that it alone is able to feel the pain.'[4] Thus Piaget, whose careful analysis of the child's early 'solipsism' has been referred to more than once. Piaget shows conclusively that *the child is unconscious of its self*, of its separate entity, and that it only builds up a consciousness of its self by a process of dissociation, that is, by means of a mental or intellectual construction. The child, that is to say, begins by confusing its self with the world and only gradually comes to distinguish the two terms from each other.

This conception of the origin of the consciousness of self is not essentially different from the psychoanalytical theory of mental structure. Freud's ego, for example, is always conceived as a secondary differentiation of the id, or unconscious, formed under the influence of what he calls the principle of reality. Incidentally, I know of no better description of this process of differentiation than that given by Piaget, in the context already quoted:

[3] Cf. Sir Charles Sherrington, *Man on his Nature* (Cambridge, 1940), pp. 308–9. 'The proprioceptive percept . . . seems a mental product derived from elements which are not experienced and yet are mental in the sense that the mind uses them in producing the percept.'

[4] *The Child's Conception of the World*, p. 126. Piaget distinguishes four stages in the continuous process of this evolution:

(1) A phase of *absolute realism*, during which no attempt is made to distinguish the instruments of thought and where objects alone appear to exist.

(2) A phase of *immediate realism*, during which the instruments of thought are distinguished from the things but are situated in the things.

(3) A phase of *mediate realism*, during which the instruments of thought are still regarded as a kind of things and are situated both in the body and in the surrounding air; and finally:

(4) A phase of *subjectivism* or *relativism*, during which the instruments of thought are situated within ourselves.

'There is . . . in the beginning neither self nor external world, but a *continuum*. The social factors also tend to the same result; from its earliest activities the baby is brought up in a social atmosphere, in the sense that its parents, especially the mother, intervene in all its actions (feeding, suckling, gripping objects, language) and in all its affections. Thus according to this point of view every action is part of a context, so that the consciousness of self does not accompany the child's early movements in any innate manner, but is only gradually revealed as a function of the contacts experienced with the behaviour or others.'[5]

This *relational* conception of consciousness and unconsciousness seems to me to receive nothing but firm confirmation from the investigations of Pavlov into the physiological structure of the brain. Pavlov distinguishes three centres of systems which have arisen in the central nervous system during the process of evolution. The first of these is the system of subcortical centres of ganglia 'most closely adjacent to the cortex'. 'This is the region of complex unconditioned reflexes or instincts, in psychological terminology the region of emotions or wishes, which is closely connected, as is recognized by endoctrinologists, with the chemistry of the organism and its changes during the various cycles of life. It is these centres that give the organism a sufficiently firmly based orientation in relation to the environment and ensure equilibrium, but this orientation is strictly limited to a small number of situations (hunger, self-defence, sexual excitation) and is far from adequate for establishing higher degrees of adaptation.

'Above the first system, and on the basis of it, is a second cerebral system, that of the centres of conditioned or temporary reflexes . . . this system, represented by the general mass of the grey matter in the cerebral hemispheres, has the advantage of ensuring a considerably wider orientation of the organism and of connecting it through the activity of its sense organs or receptors with all the phenomena of the external world. . . . In the vast majority of animals, however, this essentially represents the climax of higher nervous activity.

'In animals, this higher region of the cortex represents an *immediate* projection of the external world; it is an assembly of *analysers*. In the case of the human brain, however, during the process of its development, during the process of verbal human intercourse and the conquest of labour by means of tools, yet another physiological

[5] *Op. cit.*, pp. 235–6.

174

super-structure makes its appearance, viz. an organ which is formed on the basis of the above-mentioned second system, an organ which synthesizes, and generalizes, the activity of the immediate projections, and serves as the material substrate of a new capacity of much later origin, the capacity of abstraction.'[6]

This analysis of the structure of the brain suggests the possibility of a physical location for the three levels into which Freud has divided the mental personality—the id, the ego, and the super-ego. Phylogenetically and ontogenetically, it accounts for the gradual emergence of consciousness, which Pavlov defines as 'a nervous activity of a certain part of the cerebral hemispheres, possessing at the given moment under the present conditions a certain optimal (probably moderate) excitability. At the same time all the remaining parts of the hemispheres are in a state of more or less diminished excitability. In the region of the brain where there is optimal excitability, new conditioned reflexes are easily formed, and differentiation is successfully developed.'[7] The latest researches of psychology and physiology thus converge to support the hypothesis that consciousness is a mental super-structure or differentiated area, something which has evolved out of the relation of man to his physical and social environment, as a refinement of a pre-existing basic mental structure.

It is a tremendous discovery, whose significance for education and the wider problems of sociology has not yet been adequately realized. If consciousness is relative, the product of social experience and individual education, then it becomes evident that the degree and quality of that consciousness is modified, or can be modified, by any fundamental changes in environment or training. The most fundamental change of this kind was marked by the invention or evolution of *speech*, and it is interesting to learn that Pavlov, towards the end of his life, accorded speech a definite place in the chain of evolutionary factors, and was on the point of making a special analysis of this function when death interrupted his plans. From our special point of

[6] Frolov, *op. cit.*, pp. 78–80. Cf. also Pavlov, *Lectures on Conditioned Reflexes*, Vol. II, pp. 44–59; 'A Brief Outline of the Higher Nervous Activity'.

[7] *Lectures on Conditioned Reflexes*, Vol. I, p. 221. Continuing, Pavlov uses a metaphor which John Dos Passos has described as 'one of the most stimulating and mind-clearing paragraphs I have ever run across'. It reads: 'If we could look through the skull into the brain of a consciously thinking person, and if the place of optimal excitability were luminous, then we should see playing over the cerebral surface a bright spot with fantastic waving borders, constantly fluctuating in size and form, surrounded by a darkness more or less deep, covering the rest of the hemisphere.'

view, it would be essential to determine the function of the various types of language (e.g. concrete and abstract) in relation to the evolution of culture. On one occasion, as related by Frolov, Pavlov defined his attitude to this important question in the following way: 'Human thought appears before us draped as it were in three coverings. The first is the most modest, but at the same time the nearest to truth—this covering is movement. The second or middle covering is more ornate—this consists of written signs and graphic signs and graphic symbols. Finally, the third is the most luxuriant, *but also the most superficial*—this is the covering of verbal signals, the symbolism of speech, which is removed from the immediate expression of thought by both the preceding.'[8] From the phrase I have italicized, it is evident that Pavlov would have had something extremely significant to contribute to our subject. It would seem not only that speech was given to man to hide his thoughts, but that thought itself is a disguise for feeling.[9]

2. THE DYNAMISM OF THE UNCONSCIOUS

The theory of the unconscious would not carry us far in the understanding of the human personality if it posited merely a number of static layers of the mind. But actually this is far from the case. We should realize that the simple and almost traditional conception of a bi-partite division of the mind into conscious and unconscious levels has been superseded by a tri-partite division, for which the Freudians use the terms 'ego', 'super-ego', and 'id'; but further, these different levels no longer build up into a neat stratification, like the stories of a house, but rather are fluid levels of different density which shift and interpenetrate in the most intricate manner. For a more or less *static* conception of the mental personality, modern psychologists have substituted a conception which is thoroughly *dynamic*; and in this respect too, the psychologists are fully supported by the physiologists. What we are now given, as a picture of the mind, is a veritable battlefield of contending forces, forces which are, so to speak, paraded

[8] *Op. cit.*, p. 9.

[9] Which is the sense of Goethe's famous saying: 'Gefuehl ist alles, Name ist Schall und Rauch.' (Feeling is all, name is but sound and smoke.) But Kierkegaard is even subtler, 'I do not believe that either Young, or Talleyrand, or a more recent writer [himself], are right in saying of language that its purpose is to conceal thought, for I believe that its purpose is to assist and confirm people in refraining from action.' *Stages on Life's Way* (trans. W. Lowrie, Oxford, 1941), p. 312.

in these formations which we call conscious, unconscious, etc., but which at any given moment are engaged in violent activities, for which only terms like inhibition, repression, resistance, excitation, irradiation, induction, concentration, etc., are adequate. Not all these processes are of immediate interest for us, but in order to make use of the relevant terminology we must glance a little closer at the structure of the mind as analysed by modern psychologists and physiologists.

I think the quickest way to summarize the Freudian theory of the structure of the mental personality is to make a plan of it. I know that some people dislike plans and diagrams—but I think this one will save a lot of verbal description. It differs from the diagram usually given in psycho-analytical text books, but I hope in the direction of simplicity and clarity.

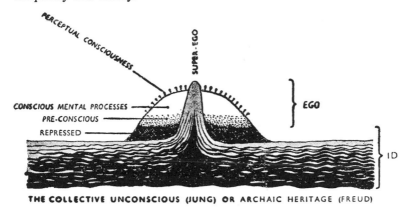

Fig. 7.—Diagram illustrating the supposed levels of the mental personality

We must imagine the lower darker levels as a continuous stream, and the projection above this level as a bubble floating on and with the stream. The stream is the common psychic life of the human race, and the bubble is the mental personality of a single unit or individual within the race. What I have represented as clearly divided geological strata should rather be imagined as fluid levels merging gradually into one another.

On the surface of this bubble, represented by antennae-like projections, is the perceptual consciousness or awareness as given by the various senses and registered in the cerebral cortex. Below this comes the level of conscious mental processes, due to our ability to analyse and correlate our sensations. But the products of these conscious mental processes do not remain continuously conscious: they sink, as we say, into the memory, and are more or less deeply buried in a state, or at a level, from which they can be recovered, especially by the method of analysis. This reservoir of memory-images or sense-impressions, plus the conscious mental processes, together make up the *ego*, the personality of the individual. But below the *pre-conscious* level, as Freud calls the submerged but accessible part of the ego, is a deeper layer of *repressed* instincts or passions normally inaccessible, and which are revealed fragmentarily in dreams and neurotic symptoms. This is the *id*, and it merges into a still lower level where, according to Freud, vestiges of the existences of countless former personalities may be found. That is to say, the id is, to a considerable extent, a generic psychic endowment, a mental component of phylogenetic origin, distinct from the specific psychological disposition of the individual. Freud has described it as the 'archaic heritage' of each individual (see quotation on page 181).

It will be noticed in the diagram, that a spearhead projects from this lower level, passes through the pre-conscious and conscious levels of the ego, and emerges above everything as the ego-ideal or super-ego. Freud suggests that some of the repressed forces in the id, which, as a whole, he characterizes as 'a chaos, a cauldron of seething excitement', are allowed, in a transformed state, to escape through the ego. It is the process known as *sublimation*, and the source, according to Freud, of all our moral, religious and aesthetic ideals. Sublimation is the transformation of selfish, instinctive drives, wishes and desires into socially useful or socially approved thoughts, ideals and activities. It is the force which unites the bubble to the stream, which keeps the individual in the swim.

Such a diagram may satisfy us as a cross-section of the mental personality, but what it cannot do is to represent the continuous state of change within the actual organism: nor can it give us the least inkling of the forces which set everything in motion—which make the stream flow in a certain direction, which produce the bubble on the surface of the stream, and the reflections on the surface of the bubble, and all the swirling elements inside the bubble. There one must simply rely on one's imagination. But certain facts are clear. It is clear, for example, that the bubble does not control the force or direction of the stream—that the ego, that is to say, is not capable of controlling the id. At the same time we must assume that the ego may state its problems, set up its opposition, and thus create a condition of tension between bubble and stream which demands a release, a solution. The conscious process of intellection may, that is to say, present the total mental make-up with an unresolved conflict. The conflict is then resolved by unseen forces—the unconscious then works unconsciously. Freud definitely recognizes this possibility. 'We have evidence that even subtle and intricate intellectual operations which ordinarily require strenuous concentration, can equally be carried out pre-consciously and without coming into consciousness. . . . There is another phenomenon, however, which is far stronger. In our analysis we discover that there are people in whom the faculties of self-criticism and conscience—mental activities, that is, that rank as exceptionally high ones—are unconscious, and unconsciously produce effects of the greatest importance . . . not only what is lowest, but also what is highest in the ego can be unconscious.' (*The Ego and the Id*, pp. 32–3.)

3. THE SUPER-EGO

Sublimation is thus the transformation of instinctive egoistic drives, wishes and desires into socially useful or socially approved thoughts, ideals and activities. In different individuals the degree of unconsciousness in the process may differ, but certainly the process is, to a large extent, always unconscious, and would lose its force, or what we call its sincerity, if it became deliberate and cultivated. Freud finds the need or origin of this process in the Oedipus complex: at least he finds it advisable in general to assume the existence of the complete Oedipus complex, especially where neurotics are concerned. As this complex, formed in infancy, is repressed or disappears, it is replaced by certain tendencies which can be identified with the rôle of the father or the mother: they represent the authority formerly exercised by the parents, and it is this aspect of the ego which becomes the ideal or super-ego. The process is compulsive: it must take place if the individual is to live at peace with his parents and with society; and it is precisely the social factors, which we call discipline, religious teaching, education generally, which aid or effect the process of transformation.

Psychoanalysts sometimes forget or ignore the general (as opposed to the individual and sexual) factors involved in the process, but Freud himself is quite clear on this point: 'If we consider once more the origin of the super-ego as we have described it, we shall perceive it to be the outcome of two highly important factors, one of them biological and the other historical: namely, the lengthy duration in man of the helplessness and dependence belonging to childhood, and the fact of his Oedipus complex, the repression of which we have shown to be connected with the interruption of libidinal development by the latency period and so with the twofold onset of activity characteristic of man's sexual life. . . . We see, then, that the differentiation of the super-ego from the ego is no matter of chance; it stands as the representative of the most important events in the development both of the individual and of the race; indeed, by giving permanent expression to the influence of the parents it perpetuates the existence of the factors to which it owes its origin'.[10]

The important point to note in this theory of Freud's is that the super-ego is not an intellectual construction based on our conscious experience of the external world: *that* is the ego itself. It is tempting to think of id, ego and super-ego as so many degrees in self-awareness, but this is not Freud's theory. His super-ego bypasses the ego. Consciousness is evolved by the direct inter-action of the cerebral hemispheres and the intake of percepts: the super-ego is an internal solution of internal conflicts, though some of the conflicting elements may be inherited, originating from the unconscious experiences of former generations. The super-ego is the direct representative of the unconscious, of the id, and hence the possibility, indeed, the inevitability, of a conflict with the ego, a conflict between what is perceptual and real and what is imaginative and ideal. We thus come back, from a new direction, to our conception of education as a process of integration. Obviously the individual must resolve his conflict, must achieve what we call 'peace of mind', an equilibrium be-

---

[10] *The Ego and the Id* (London, 1927), pp. 45–6. It is at this point that Freud makes his famous protest against those who identify psychoanalysis and materialism. 'Psychoanalysis has been reproached time after time with ignoring the higher moral, spiritual side of human nature. The reproach is doubly unjust, both historically and methodologically. For, in the first place, we have from the very beginning attributed the function of instigating repression to the moral and aesthetic tendencies in the ego, and secondly, there has been a general refusal to recognize that psychoanalytical research could not produce a complete and finished body of doctrine, like a philosophical system, ready made, but had to find its way step by step along the path towards understanding the intricacies of the mind by making an analytic dissection of both normal and abnormal phenomena.'

tween the external and the internal world. As we shall see in the next chapter, Freud may be accused of a certain helplessness, a certain timidity, in approaching this problem. He despairs of humanity because he takes humanity as he finds it, already deformed, already socially disintegrated. He does not seem to realize that the *natural method of integration is education*: psychoanalysis is the therapeutic method to which we must resort when education has failed.[11]

There is one aspect of the id, and thereby by implication of the super-ego, which is of great importance for our present discussion. I give it in Freud's words. 'Owing to the way in which it is formed, the ego-ideal has a great many points of contact with the phylogenetic endowment of each individual—his archaic heritage. And thus it is that what belongs to the lowest depths in the minds of each one of us is changed, through this formation of the ideal, into what we value as the highest in the human soul. . . . Thus in the id *which is capable of being inherited*, are stored up vestiges of the existence led by countless former egos and, when the ego forms its super-ego out of the id, it may perhaps only be reviving images of egos that have passed away and be securing them a resurrection.'[12]

We thus reach the notion of a *collective unconscious* which Jung has developed to an extent which most Freudians deplore. I was sceptical of this extreme theory myself until I discovered, in the course of examining children's drawings in connection with this present work, a mass of evidence which undoubtedly supports Jung's theory, and even carries it a step forward.

4. PERSONAL AND COLLECTIVE UNCONSCIOUS

I am going to leave on one side the whole problem of sublimation. I am not concerned in this chapter with the higher levels of transformation, which are a result of that psychic conflict to which Freud

[11] The general relations between education and psychoanalysis are discussed by Dr. Susan Isaacs, *Social Development in Young Children*, pp. 403–56. Cf. also: M. N. Searl, 'Some Contrasted Aspects of Psychoanalysis and Education', *Brit. J. Educ. Psychology*, Vol. II (1932). After drawing her distinctions between the work of the educator and the analyst, Dr. Isaacs observes (p. 412): 'it should be clear that no one person can combine the two functions to the same child, and that, moreover, it will be an unwise thing for a teacher or a mother or a person in a real relationship of authority to a child to attempt to undertake the work of an analyst, even by ever so little. An admixture of education and analysis tends to ruin both, and can do little for the child but confuse and bewilder him, and increase his conflicts.'

[12] *Op. cit.*, 48, 52.

has given the name *Oedipus complex*. In the course of individual development, the direction of the erotic impulse becomes fixed on the self (narcissistic), or on the father, or on the mother (involving rivalry towards the father); these 'identifications' are repressed, and the libidinal energy is diverted into various forms of social adaptation. That is to say, according to Freud it is the Oedipus situation which gives rise to those idealistic tendencies in humanity which we know as religion, morality, custom, etc. The theory of sublimation is, of course, of enormous importance to all educators, but the process I want to isolate now is still more basic, more elementary and perhaps even more important. Just as sublimation is the process which secures an equilibrium between the individual and his social environment, so, I suspect, the process I am going to describe secures an equilibrium between the individual and his physiological constitution—the essential equilibrium, that is to say, between mind and matter.

There is still another unconscious activity which we are not concerned with at the moment, and which I must therefore eliminate— I mean the process of symbolization and dramatization which goes on in our dreams, and even in our day-dreams. Relatively, this activity represents a later stage of development in the unconscious. The activity now to be described is a primary, or rudimentary, form of unconscious mental activity, not hitherto posited in psychology. I am going to suggest that there is an elementary stage during the course of which there occurs in the unconscious a formation or crystallization of plastic images out of the basic material provided by the internal or proprioceptive sensations of the higher nervous system. The concrete visual symbols, associated with our conscious experience of the external world, which form the ordinary material dealt with in psychoanalysis, belong, according to this hypothesis, to a later stage in the development of unconscious modes of mental activity.

I must first ask the reader to consider a little more closely the significance of the phylogenetic element in the psychic constitution of each individual—the significance of the fact that as individuals we are not altogether unique, but possess mental elements in common. This fact, though, as we have seen, fully admitted by Freud, has been explored more thoroughly by Jung. Jung divides the unconscious into a more or less superficial layer which he calls the *personal* unconscious, and a deeper layer, which does not derive from personal experience and achievement, but is inborn, which is the *collective* unconscious. 'I have chosen the term "collective" because this part of the unconscious is not individual, but universal; in contrast to the personal psyche, it has contents and modes of behaviour that are more or less the same everywhere and in all individuals. The collective unconscious, so far as we know, is self-identical in all Western men and thus constitutes a psychic foundation, super-personal in its nature, that is present in every one of us.'[13]

These two layers of the unconscious are distinguished by their contents. The contents of the *personal* unconscious are the so-called *feeling-toned* complexes, caused by the impact of the personal disposition of the individual on his environment, and are by no means limited, in Jung's view, to sexual conflicts. We might say, in the terms of our diagram, that they are due to the friction between the bubble and the stream. In Jung's words: 'they are "vulnerable points" which we do not like to remember, and still less to be reminded of by others, but which frequently come back to mind unbidden and in the most unwelcome fashion. They always contain memories, wishes, fears, duties, needs, or views, with which we have never really come to terms, and for this reason they constantly interfere with our conscious life in a disturbing and usually harmful way.' But complexes do not necessarily or always imply inferiority—they may act as an incitement to new effort. In this sense they are 'focal or nodal points of psychic life which we would not wish to do without. Indeed, they must not be lacking, for otherwise psychic activity would come to a fatal standstill'.[14]

The contents of the *collective* unconscious are quite different. They consist of images impressed on the mind from earliest times, 'vestiges of the existence led by countless former egos' (to repeat Freud's phrase), and when transformed into *conscious* formulas, they take the form of tribal lore, myth, fable or fairy tale. To the psychic reality underlying these universal manifestations Jung gives the name archetype. Archetypes do not consist of inherited ideas or images, but of inherited predispositions to reaction. They are centres of influence, or fields of force within the unconscious, and any elements sinking into the unconscious, 'are subjected to a new, *imperceptible order*, inaccessible to conscious cognition'. Jung identified this inner order with the reality underlying Yoga exercises and other Eastern modes of

[13] *The Integration of the Personality*, pp. 52–3. The evidence which I shall give presently suggests that there is no need for the word 'Western' in the last sentence.

[14] *Modern Man in Search of a Soul*, p. 91.

concentration and meditation: and he suggests that 'it is this absolute inner order of the unconscious that forms our refuge and help in the accidents and commotions of life, if we only understand how to "get in touch" with it'.[15] In an illuminating analogy, Jung compares these archetypes to 'the axial system of a crystal, which predetermines as it were the crystalline formation in the saturated solution, without itself possessing a material existence. This existence first manifests itself in the way the ions and then the molecules arrange themselves. . . . The axial system determines, accordingly, merely the stereometric structure, not, however, the concrete form of the individual crystal . . . and just so the archetype possesses . . . an invariable core of meaning that determines its manner of appearing always in principle, never concretely.'[16]

The idea that there should exist in the individual mind psychic tendencies which are *a priori*, as it were, and independent of the particular existence of the individual, must at first seem very far fetched, and the hypothesis of a collective unconscious has, in fact, proved extremely repugnant to the scientific mind. Many of Freud's followers are not willing to follow him into what they regard as a metaphysical diversion, and for Jung's more developed hypothesis they have nothing but scorn. The basis of their objection, in so far as it is not unscientific prejudice, is anthropological. These critics admit that unconscious images or dream-symbols are of two types, one type peculiar to specific individuals, or specific cultures, the other type universal, and found so widely distributed in place and time that there can be no question of diffusion. But, they say, such universal symbols and complex archetypal images (to use Jung's term) are expressions of the total Oedipus situation, and their universality is explained by the universality of the family as an institution. For wherever the family exists, or has existed, there you will find the Oedipus complex. But, it would seem that these 'scientific' psychologists, in insisting on the universality of the Oedipus complex, are venturing on a hypothesis fully as metaphysical as the theory of the collective unconscious; and indeed, are they not merely giving

[15] Jacobi, *The Psychology of C. G. Jung*, pp. 41–2.

[16] *Eranos Year Book*, 1938, p. 410 (quoted by Jacobi, *op. cit.*, pp. 43–4). In what follows I may seem to imply that the primordial images or archetypal patterns are necessarily *plastic*. They are, of course, found in any mode of imaginative expression, above all in poetry. I should have felt it necessary to refer more often and more specifically to the poetic evidence had it not been very adequately presented by Miss Maud Bodkin in her *Archetypal Patterns in Poetry* (London, 1934).

another name to the same phenomena? If a certain tension between the individual and his environment has been constant during all the millennia through which mankind has evolved, and if this tension has given rise to the same process of unconscious symbolization during all these millennia, then it is surely a mere quibble to argue that these phenomena do not constitute a collective psyche, but only a collection of similar psyches. One might as well argue that such a thing as a forest does not exist as a unit because it can be proved to be made up of a definite number of individual trees; or that a nation does not exist and cannot act as an entity because it consists of a determinate number of individuals with separate existences, separate feelings and separate wills. From all of which we may conclude, I think, that if the hypothesis of the collective unconscious is to be attacked, it must be on the basis of a logical analysis of the actual concept of collectivity. If we accept the term, then I cannot conceive of a more justifiable use than in relation to mental phenomena that are at once unconscious and universal.

In any case, any scepticism which I personally entertained about the hypothesis of a collective psyche has been removed by the evidence which I am now going to present for the reader's consideration.

5. PRIMORDIAL IMAGES IN THE CHILD'S MIND

The number of collective images or archetypes is relatively limited, but among those most frequently revealed by analysis is the mandala theme. 'Mandala' is a Sanskrit word, meaning a circle or magic ring, and its symbolism embraces all concentrically arranged figures, all circular or square circumferences having a centre, and all radial or spherical arrangements. It often takes the form of a flower, a cross, or a wheel, with a distinct tendency to assume a four-fold structure. As a symbol, the mandala occurs not only throughout the East, but also in Europe during the Middle Ages.

A traditional Chinese example takes the form of the Golden Flower, 'the most splendid of all flowers', and is like a complicated version of the heraldic rose of the Tudors. The specifically Christian ones show Christ in the centre of a circular design, with the four evangelists or their symbols at the cardinal points. The mandala arrangement is, in fact, extremely frequent in all early Christian art— in Byzantine art, Celtic art, the Gothic art of Northern Europe generally. Of course, it might be argued that the very fact that Christian iconography includes *four* evangelists, and that the Cross as a symbol divides any design of which it is an essential part into four compartments, *imposes* a mandala-like treatment on the artist. That is obvious; but we must go a little deeper than this, and ask *why* four evangelists, *why* a four-limbed cross (and not, for example, a T-shaped cross). Once we begin to ask such questions, it begins to look as though, before Christian iconography imposed a four-fold treatment of his design on the artist, some anterior force had imposed a four-fold tendency on the evolution of Christian iconography.

Jung gives other instances of the occurrence of the mandala—among the ancient Egyptians, in Jacob Boehme's book on the soul, in the sand drawings used in the ceremonies of the Pueblo Indians, in a paleolithic 'sunwheel' recently discovered in Rhodesia—but the most beautiful mandalas are those of the East, especially those belonging to Tibetan Buddhism. 'I have also,' he writes, 'found mandala drawings among the mentally diseased, and they were patients who certainly did not have the least idea of any of the connections we have discussed.'[17]

I was one day looking at the drawings of the children (girls) in a secondary school when the teacher asked me if I would like to see some of their 'mind-pictures'. She produced a large number of watercolour drawings all measuring approximately 6½ inches square, and among these I was at once struck by the presence of a number of perfect mandalas. But on being questioned the teacher disclaimed all knowledge of mandalas, or indeed of Jung's psychology, and stated that she 'used these mental pictures simply as a means of teaching self-expression, creation and technique'. The procedure, as described by the teacher, was as follows:

'When I take a class in "Mind Pictures" I tell them to close their eyes and relax and try to feel at peace, not thinking of anything—to try to get away from physical things as one does just before going off to sleep. Some girls get a mind picture quite soon, in a few minutes (sometimes instantly), others take ten minutes or even longer, and some do not see them at all. I try to make them understand that if they do not see one they must be quite honest and say so, and that they are not in any way "odd" if they do not see them.' In answer to a

[17] *The Secret of the Golden Flower* (London, 1938), p. 97. This book, one of the shortest but most significant of Jung's works, is a commentary on a Chinese text translated and explained by Richard Wilhelm. The text promises to 'reveal the secret of the Golden Flower of the Great *One*', and is essentially a book of mystical instructions.

question as to the possible eidetic nature of these images, the teacher added: 'I think it is impossible to say which are imagined. I *see* colours and shapes in my own mind quite often, and I should think that children probably see them more readily than an adult.'

The ages of the girls in question varied from 10 to 16, but the majority of the drawings were done between the ages of 12 and 14, the average age being 13.1. It is not a question of one group of girls: these mind pictures have been made by different classes over a period of nearly twenty years, and present a phenomenon of uniformity and normality. It is true that a very small number of children do not seem to be able to achieve the necessary degree of concentration, and produce sophisticated designs of no significance—they are the children who are by disposition 'fidgety' or 'scatter-brained'. But the great majority of the children produce the drawings readily, without suggestion and without any kind of conscious imitation or copying.

An examination of some hundreds of these drawings shows that they possess general characteristics, and can be divided into four groups. These groups overlap, and indeed, it is possible to arrange the drawings into a progressive series, without any sharp or definite transition between the groups.

    (i) The first group shows cellular forms, amoeba-like in shape, often with concentric rings of different colours, and with a nucleus; there are patches of small and closely associated cells, like frog-spawn; net-work; loose trailing tendrils; shapes like star-fish, with prehensile groping extensions; some more definite enclosed womb-like forms.[18]

    (ii) In the second group the forms are more dynamic; the cells whirl round like catherine-wheels; lines of force, like flowing water or escaping flames, burst through the containing forms, or they are penetrated by sharp daggers and cones; tendrils coil round these pointed shafts.

    (iii) In the third group a certain degree of organization is perceptible: instead of irregular cells, perfect circles and spheres; the spheres seem to float in space.

    (iv) Finally the circle or sphere is isolated, becoming the main object of the picture. It is split up into regular geometric com-

[18] Compare the following descriptions by Jung: 'I know a series of European mandala drawings in which something like a plant seed surrounded with membranes is shown floating in water, and, from the depths below, fire penetrating the seed, makes it grow, and causes the formation of a large golden flower from within the germinal vesicle.' *Op. cit.*, p. 99.

partments, usually on a basis of four, and finally becomes a definite and sometimes elaborate mandala.

Typical drawings from all these groups are illustrated in Plates 22 to 25.

Among the general characteristics may be mentioned the persistent appearance in all the groups of the cross or four-fold division; the rarity of natural or representational forms; an astonishing complexity of composition; a general brightness of colour, to which, however, there are some striking exceptions. The colours, incidentally, are obviously symbolic: that is to say, they are not usually very subtle or harmonious, and in this respect are quite distinct from the normal paintings of the same children. But they show a consistency in the case of each individual child.

6. UNCONSCIOUS PROCESSES OF INTEGRATION

Obviously these drawings supply much evidence which is only of interest in the analysis of the individual child—an aspect of the matter which I cannot go into now. I have attempted, with the aid of the teacher concerned, to make a correlation between the different groups and the general psychological disposition of the children who drew the mind-pictures. It is a hazardous proceeding, but I think it can be stated quite definitely that there is no significant degree of correlation between the degree of organization shown in the drawings and Spearman's 'g' factor, or any ordinary intelligence test. But the evidence tends to show that the more organized images are only achieved by children of a balanced, equable nature. The more elaborate and coherent mandalas are the work of children whom the teacher describes as 'quiet', 'reliable', 'unobtrusive', and 'artistic'. Some of the more disruptive and scattered designs can be assigned to anti-social, non-co-operative and even delinquent types. But the evidence is not invariable. Plate 22*b*, for example, illustrates a mind-picture by the girl who drew the perfect mandala shown in Plate 25*d*. The first drawing was done in the same form and under the same conditions as the second drawing, but I should not hesitate to place it in the first group of formless, unorganized mind-pictures. Incidentally, the colour-schemes of the two disparate drawings are very close, and colour, in my opinion, so long as it is projected from the unconscious, is probably the most reliable index of psychological disposition. It is possible that the same *colour-tones* penetrate all levels of the psyche; whilst the *form* into which colour itself is organized may differ according to depth. That is to say, the unorganized picture might come from a relatively superficial or preconscious level, whereas the mandala is only accessible when the child falls into a more deeply penetrating trance; or vice versa. I am not suggesting that any child's unconscious can be permanently tidy. We must suppose a permanent tendency for undifferentiated energies in the nervous system to seek order or repose. What we are concerned with is not a state of mind, but a power or ability to organize or stabilize nervous energy *when necessary*. The mind of man, one cannot too often emphasize, is a system of compensations and balances. It is the freedom of the scales that matters, so that depression on one side can always be redressed by a counterweight on the other side—so that the chaos produced by a mental shock can be controlled by an automatic reaction towards order.

These mind-pictures no doubt have a wider psychological significance which cannot be explained here. The mere fact that primordial images which we generally associate with Eastern or Medieval mysticism appear spontaneously in the minds of English children, is an awkward discovery to be assimilated into our present educational philosophy.[19] But for us the real significance of these mind-pictures is their revelation of processes of integration within the mind of the child and below the level of consciousness. The unconscious is seen seeking an archetypal order, an order which is not individual, but a correlate of the physical structure of the sensory apparatus itself. This order is intrinsic. It is not dependent on external perceptions, nor on images derived from external perception, though these may intrude. Basically it is a crystallization of abstract forms and symbolic

[19] It might be suggested that I am relying too much on the technique of one teacher, or on one type of child. The drawing illustrated in Plate 1*b* from an entirely different source, is perhaps a sufficient refutation of such a charge. The spontaneous product of a girl of five, of working-class origin, it was described by her as 'a snake going round the world and a boat'. I myself have seen this girl, and though perhaps a little above the normal in intelligence, a more innocent and unsophisticated child would be difficult to find. The drawing is not only a mandala: it is a symbol for which the unconscious mind of the child had already found a verbal equivalent, for the snake surrounding the world is one of the most ancient of primordial images (the Uroboros). See Erich Neumann, *The Origins and History of Consciousness* (London and New York, 1954) for a discussion of the significance of this symbol. A very similar drawing was made by one of Jung's patients and is illustrated in *The Integration of the Personality* (London, 1940) Plate V.

colours, an order introduced into the plastic chaos which, in the child's unconscious, corresponds to the 'big buzzing confusion' which was all William James could imagine to exist in the conscious mind of an infant.

How does the basic plastic imagery arise? The cell-like and tissue-like form of many of the mind-pictures suggests that it may originate in proprioceptive sensations which are registered unconsciously in the psyche (similar to the images of fiery rings, etc., produced by pressure on the eyeball), and some of them—relatively very few—do suggest an optical origin. In some cases such an origin may be freely admitted. But a cause so occasional and incidental cannot account for the complexity and symbolic content of the majority of these mind-pictures. Obviously the 'pictures' do not come from without; they are internal phenomena of some kind and must have a basis in the physiology of consciousness. But they are then organized: they crystallize into a formal pattern, discover an appropriate configuration or 'Gestalt' and we must seek some explanation of their form and structural organization.[20]

Jung, as we have already seen, does not exclude a psycho-physical isomorphism as a basis for the formation of primordial images or archetypes, and he deliberately resorts to physical terminology to describe the process. The archetype is compared to the axial system of a crystal which determines the stereometric structure, though not the concrete form, of the individual crystal. Jung assumes that the physical structure of the brain-cell does in actual fact provide the normal system in accordance with which the mental elements of the brain take on a concrete shape—become steady and steadying symbols amidst the fragmentary traces of recorded experiences. What determines the survival value of these traces, apart from the dissolving influence of metabolism, is precisely the problem which psychoanalysis attempts to solve.

That the pattern into which the traces are integrated should tend towards fourfoldness or quaternity need not cause us any more surprise than such 'neat' facts as the periodicity of the elements or the mathematical regularity of crystals and of organic forms such as the cell of a bee's honeycomb. The original property in matter and energy which organizes the universe in space and time, and which even a purely mechanistic science must posit,[21] extends to those forms of

[20] See Appendix D (pages 202 to 206).

[21] Cf. Lawrence J. Henderson, *op. cit.*, p. 308. The concluding paragraph of this

energy which we call psychic. Not only are the cosmic and biological processes continuous and co-extensive; the mental processes in man are also part of the same dynamic unity. What I am seriously suggesting, therefore, is that *there exists within the mind of the child, no less than of the adult, a psychic process or activity, taking place below the level of consciousness, which tends to organize the irregular or rudimentary images present in the organism into a harmonious pattern. Further, I suggest that the form assumed by this pattern is determined by the chemical structure of the molecules which are the material basis of the brain and by their reactions to the electromotive forces which accompany neuro-visual activity.*

The corollary to this proposition, making it relevant to our educational interests, is that *psychic equilibrium, which is the basis of all equableness and intellectual integration, is only possible when this integration of formal elements below the level of consciousness is allowed or encouraged to take place, which it notably does in all forms of imaginative activity—day-dreaming, spontaneous elaboration of fantasy, creative expression in colour, line, sounds and words.*[22]

scientific classic may be quoted in general support of the present argument. 'There is . . . one scientific conclusion which I wish to put forward as a positive and, I trust, fruitful outcome of the present investigation. The properties of matter and the course of cosmic evolution are now seen to be intimately related to the structure of the living being and to its activities; they become, therefore, far more important in biology than has been previously suspected. For the whole evolutionary process, both cosmic and organic, is one, and the biologist may now rightly regard the universe in its very essence as biocentric.' For a more recent statement of similar views by a scientist, see F. Wood Jones, *Design and Purpose* (London, 1942).

[22] A professional psychoanalyst to whom I submitted this chapter comments: 'The patterns are probably "symbolic expression" of physical structures and processes, and, in addition, of the intrinsic mental content. They are expressions of the united psycho-physical molecular events—or, as one might say, *of the animated physical events* and structures. The supposed subconscious harmonizing process is, therefore, essentially identical with *the continuous intrapsychic process.* The conscious "awareness" of these deep events constitutes the higher intellectual content of the mind—the intellectual, personal manifestation, as it were, of the subconscious creatively-harmonizing processes. In consequence, the encouragement of such day-dreaming, of such relaxing art, might certainly, to some extent, further and aid the development of the mental-spiritual personality. 'If it is true, that the patterns produced by the children are reflexions of *elementary structures* and of elementary physico-chemical processes, then it implies the following: If the child, in state of relaxation, produces figures and paintings, the central feature of which is such an elementary pattern, then this elementary figure represents in brief the total psycho-emotional state of the whole personality, obtaining at that given moment. We know that free drawings, following only a momentary inspiration, express as do dreams a cross-section of

Generally speaking, integration should be 'allowed' to take place. We must learn the secret of action in non-action, which plays such an important part in Eastern philosophy and religious instruction. 'The key is this,' says Jung: 'we must be able to let things happen in the psyche. For us, this becomes a real art of which few people know anything. Consciousness is for ever interfering, helping, correcting, and negating, and never leaving the simple growth of the psychic processes in peace. It would be a simple enough thing to do, if only simplicity were not the most difficult of all things. *It consists solely in watching objectively the development of any fragment of fantasy.*'[23]

The connection with all that has gone before in this treatise will now be seen: this last sentence which I have italicized is a perfect description of the method of education which I have been advocating, and which I shall describe in more detail in the next chapter. In so far as this method depends on a certain attitude of the teacher and a certain technique of teaching, it will be described in Chapter IX. But the psychological mechanism was implicit in Jaensch's conclusion that 'productive thinking must have a close relation to artistic-production' (see p. 58). It is also implicit in the Gestalt psychologist's theory of 'differential sensitivity', which recognizes an aesthetic factor in perception, by means of which experience is organized into appropriate and persisting patterns—patterns which have the same characteristics of symmetry and balance, of proportion and rhythm as these mental pictures, and which are the secret of that 'fortunate variation' in behaviour which is the basis of any progressively successful adaptation to environment, the basis, that is to say, of all forms of skill and grace.

Very disparate systems of psychology not only support but are to an enlightening degree synthesized by the discovery of unconscious processes of integration within the dynamic structure of the mind. The presence and function of these processes seems to me to have been clearly demonstrated. I have suggested that their primary causation is to be sought in the interaction of electro-physical motive

the totality of a present condition. So, in the process of self-perception, the reflex of the molecular element represents the complicated total psycho-physical organization. Consequently, the cultivation of "artistic relaxation" in the above-described fashion, in stressing the significance of the molecular element, in bringing to awareness the processes within the molecular element, might in fact contribute to the development of the "whole" of the personality: at least, of a definite layer of the whole personality.'

[23] *Secret of the Golden Flower*, p. 90.

forces and the constitution of the mind-matter. What still remains to be demonstrated is the relation of these processes to the total psychic development of the individual.

This is obviously beyond the scope of the present work: it would, in effect, be a complete analysis of the human psyche. All that I can presume to attempt here is to show the relevance of our particular researches to such a wider study. I do not need a new hypothesis: my general contention, now enormously strengthened by this particular evidence, is that the progressive apprehension of, and comprehension of, our environment, is only possible by means of aesthetic patterns. Experience only falls into shape and becomes memorable and utilizable in the degree that it falls into *artistic* shape. Consciousness is only socially integrated in the degree that it is an aesthetic apprehension of reality. From a chaos of unco-ordinated sensations we plot this centre which is the self or ego; and from the deeper chaos which is unconscious, instinctive, and to some extent collective, we find emerging the symbols and abstractions which eventually constitute the super-ego. Ego and super-ego have efficiency and biological validity only in the degree that they achieve the harmony and stability of aesthetic patterns, and the most fundamental patterns prove to be those which we share with other people, as part of our common or collective being. Below the level of consciousness, and extending to a level of experience which is more than individual, a wider and deeper chaos seeks the harmony and stability of the aesthetic pattern. We rise to comprehension, to understanding and wisdom, only by virtue of our capacity for the differential and qualitative apprehension of formal values; equally, on the most primitive level of our unconscious being, we seek conformity with the organic laws of nature and the cosmic laws of matter. We only achieve mutual relatedness and collective unity in so far as the contents of the individual unconscious are allowed to arrange themselves according to the pattern of the universal archetypes, the primordial images which are also aesthetic in form or quality. Such is the element of *value* we find implicit in the world of facts and it is possibly the only value *that cannot be excluded* from a progressive evolution of life.

7. THE SOCIAL RELEVANCE OF THESE PROCESSES

To see the full relevance of the unconscious processes of integration, we must consider in more detail the fact that they are not individual or personal, but isomorphic and collective, a function of normal psycho-physical processes of adjustment. Jung is perhaps to be criticized for adopting the words 'archetypal' and 'primordial' to describe the images which emerge from the unconscious, for such terms suggest a reversion to something primitive. What is original and basic is primary but not primitive. What is common to the psychic structure of mankind is the only secure foundation for a community of behaviour and aspiration. It is the neglect of this fact which explains the weakness and unreality of all idealistic philosophies and political theories. The rational systems of state socialism will always remain unreal and unsuccessful precisely because they are logical and not artistic constructions—because they are theoretical and not organic patterns. The superior cohesion of primitive communities (and even of animal communities) is due to the fact that they evolve their patterns from their collective unconscious.

That the ego, the 'I' of consciousness, does not represent the human organism as a whole is the inescapable conclusion to be drawn from modern psychology, but the significance of this fact for our educational practice has not even begun to penetrate our schools. Once we have realized, in Trigant Burrow's words, that 'what man now takes to be the physiology of his feeling is only the vocabulary of this feeling',[24] we shall cease to rely on grammar and logic, or at east, we shall seek to balance intellect and feeling in some more inclusive method of education. It is mere illusion to suppose that in some way, as a result of the evolutionary process, the feelings have been superseded, or sublimated, and that our only concern is the idealistic or humanistic super-structure. It is not merely that we have disguised our feelings as symbols—this may be a desirable convenience, 'a highly salutary trick', and would be harmless if it were a continually renewed activity. But what in effect we have done is to accept a limited number of symbols as an adequate account of the total reality, and what escapes our consciousness is what ultimately destroys us, individually in the form of insanity, socially in the form of war.[25]

[24] *The Structure of Insanity* (London, 1932), p. 31.

[25] 'We are faced with an emergent process in the affairs of men, and the efforts of the economists and statesmen to adjust social inequalities of opportunity and of resources are but visionary and impractical schemes in the absence of a medical and biological reckoning with the subjective dissociations of feeling and of interest that are the basis of these social inequalities.' Trigant Burrow, *op. cit.*, p. 73 (1932).

'Before the introduction or invention of language, of socially agreed signs and symbols, or before the adoption by man of the projective, intellectual mechanism of attention as we now know it, the organism's adjustment to its surroundings was effected, as we know, by means of certain general tensional alternations. These reactions constituted an integral, a systematic or an organic mode of adaptation or attention. Through this process of attention the organism as a whole encountered its environment as a whole. That is, the total object of the environment engaged the total interest or feeling of the organism. In response to this integral species of attention the organism performed its various "instinctive" functions—the function of locomotion, of rest, the function of nutrition, of elimination, of herd or family interplay, of sex activity as of the corresponding interludes of sex quiescence. By virtue of these functions, alternately cumulative and dissipatory, the animal procured its food, gathered for the winter, sought shelter, found repose, grew tense or relaxed, slept or awakened. There was thus maintained that physiological balance of tensions and releases, through which the total organism secured its "internal adjustment to external conditions".

'This organic reciprocity, this synergy between organism and environment is, of course, no less the biological basis of the organism's total function today. This organic rapport between internal tension and external stimulus tends equally today to maintain in man, as in lower animals, an equal balance of adjustment between inner and outer processes. Of special interest to the present theme, however, is the fact that, in their racial homogeneity, these internal tensions constituted for man, as for the lower orders of animals, a medium of inter-individual communication as comprehensive and as efficient for the purpose of the organism as a whole as the sophisticated symbols of interchange that have come to serve the purpose of man in his social inter-communication today. Whatever "mental" agreements have come to be interpolated socially in the course of man's functional evolution, this organic mode of attention that mediated the adjustment of the organism as a whole still maintains unabated its physiological primacy.'[26]

This seems to me to be a very clear description of the functioning of man's organism in relation to his environment, a natural process which has become quite distorted by the sophistications of modern civilization, and particularly by the formulism of modern education.

[26] *Ibid.*, pp. 22–4.

If individual and social harmony is to be restored, and cultural growth continued, then we must strive to recover on a physiological and psychological basis what Burrow calls 'the total organism's internal feeling-behaviour'. How that can and must be done has been shown by this psychologist in his very significant but little appreciated work, *The Social Basis of Consciousness*.

I have read this difficult book three times since its appearance in 1927, baffled and discouraged by its crabbed style, but always with a deepening sense of its truth and importance. I have also read all the criticisms that were written of it, mainly about the time of its appearance, and, in so far as they were antagonistic, mainly by Freudians. I have the greatest respect, as must be already evident, for the genius of Freud, but I have found that he fails to provide us with an adequate solution for the problem just stated—the cure of our modern mass-neurosis; and at the point where Freud fails us, there I think Dr. Burrow, who is himself a pupil of Freud's, comes to our rescue, and provides us with a solution which is, as D. H. Lawrence wrote, 'surely much deeper and more vital, and also much less spectacular than Freud's.'[27]

Burrow's central idea is that the cultivation of consciousness has involved the development of 'separateness'—the individual has cut himself off from the collective unconscious. He has set up an image of 'self' as distinct from other selves—consciousness is *self*-consciousness and means a splitting off from the *group*-consciousness of which the individual was an unconscious part—or rather, with which he was unconsciously possessed. He has only been able to achieve this separateness by repressing his instinctive life, and this repression is responsible for his mental disease—his psychoses and neuroses. According to the prevailing doctrine of psychoanalysis, the remedy for such disease 'lies in the successful adaptation of the personal satisfaction of sexuality expressed both in direct physiological release and in the equivalents of sublimation'. In Burrow's opinion, this therapy leaves out of account the disorders of instinct due to 'the obstruction of man's tribal or congeneric life and to the consequent interruption

---

[27] *Phoenix* (London, 1936), p. 38. Lawrence was much influenced by Trigant Burrow, and in this way some of Dr. Burrow's ideas have been diffused among people who have never heard his name. The sociological emphasis thus introduced into modern psychology has been reinforced more recently by writers such as Karen Horney (*The Neurotic Personality of Our Time* and *New Ways in Psychoanalysis*) and Erich Fromm (*The Fear of Freedom*). See also Ira Progoff—*Jung's Psychology and its Social Meaning* (London and New York, 1953).

of the creative expression of his personality as a societal unit'. The remedy lies in getting rid of the unconscious sense of separateness, in restoring the sense of social unity or togetherness. Therefore, for the Freudian method of individual analysis, Dr. Burrow substitutes a method of group analysis, by which he does not mean an analysis of the group, but 'a phyletic principle of observation', that is to say, group activities which involve the group's analysis of any one of its component individuals. He means, in other words, the provision of natural outlets for those forms of expression which are instinctively social in man through common avenues of concerted work and play, through the creative interests of his common societal activities. He means, in short, precisely those methods of education which are advocated in this book. 'What must be broken is the egocentric absolute of the individual' (D. H. Lawrence).

Burrow does not deal at great length with the prevention as distinct from the cure of this 'separateness' which is at the root of our social disunity: as a doctor he is more concerned with analysis or therapy than with education. But he fully recognizes that the preventive method of a right system of education (involving, of course, a right organization of society) is the only adequate reform. His book is, by implication, and sometimes directly, a tremendous indictment of the whole of the existing methods of education, not only as they exist in the schools, but in the family and in society generally. He traces 'the deeply entrenched root of our human pathology' to the mental conflict suggestively induced in the child at an early age by requiring its conformity, on pain of retribution, to a system of 'right and wrong', 'good and bad', which has no basis in its organic group consciousness. The child is 'tricked into complicity' with the prevalent code of behaviour around him, a code wholly to the advantage of parents and society, whose self-interest is disguised as morality. Out of this situation is born a 'factor of pretence' which is the ultimate element in the dissociation of consciousness.

'One would think, as we look about us today at the utterly destructive processes, social and political, that have been incited throughout entire nations of individuals, "brought up" in this vicarious fashion, that the spectacle would give us pause. But we have had a too-thorough bringing-up ourselves. Our own bringing-up has seen to it that we shall look about us and learn what *is*, but that we shall only respond to the suggestion about us and acquiesce in what *seems*. If we should really look about us and see unflinchingly into the meaning of things, our children would do so too, but that would be subversive of their proper up-bringing. This is the self-contradictory element in the adult's "education" of the child. In truth it is not possible to "bring up" a child at all. One may let a child grow up, naturally, as a plant, tending only the soil about its roots, or one may hinder its growth. But to bring a child up by moulding its personality to one's own is organically contradictory. A child comes up, if at all, only of himself or in accordance with the law of his own growth.'[28]

It is not possible to follow Trigant Burrow into his subtle analysis of all the consequences of this falsely evolved 'separateness', but let us note that the chief consequence, as described by him, is a bidimensional or theoretical representation of the world, an artificial illusion which we substitute for the organic reality. This analysis is completely in agreement with the conclusions arrived at by a very different method of analysis by Jaensch and his school and however much these conclusions differ from the metapsychological doctrines of Freud, they are based on an acceptance of what is scientifically established by the Freudian method of analysis. They are also wholly consonant with Jung's theory of the collective unconscious, for Burrow himself insists that the collective unconscious is the anterior factor to which the individual factor involving neurosis is but the reflex response—'as the central issue upon which my entire position must stand or fall is the conviction that the *responsibility for the neurosis rests upon the societal consciousness in its ontogenetic phase within each of us*'.[29] Finally, Burrow's analysis is at no point inconsistent with the physiological facts as represented by an empiricist like Pavlov—the bidimensional or theoretical illusion which we normally substitute for the organic wholeness of our common life being but an elaborate structure of conditioned reflexes. We can then see that the analysis of the process of education made by Burrow, which I am now going to quote, has the support of the entire body of psychological facts that I have attempted to synthesize.[30] This is the crucial passage from Burrow's work:

'Extending into every phase of our social life, it is this bilateral

[28] *Social Basis of Consciousness*, p. 56.

[29] *Op. cit.*, p. 245. Author's own italics.

[30] That it also has the support of the *sociological* facts is very evident from the outstanding work of Karl Mannheim. See his *Man and Society* (London, 1940), *passim*, and especially his *Diagnosis of our Time* (London, 1943), Chapters IV and V.

motive that is likewise the failure of the schools. With credit, praise or privilege and their opposites (depending upon whether the child "succeeds" or "fails" as judged by the bidimensional standard of good and bad, of praise or blame constituting the arbitrary *picture* of his personal conduct), it happens that, through an unconscious substitution of the image of the child's person for the function of the child's personality, the entire incentive of the schools becomes ulterior and artificial. The so-called liberal schools of today are in no better case. Despite their much ado about advanced methods that will give greater freedom to the child they afford mere imitations of freedom. But this is freedom in aspect, not in function. It is merely the ideal of freedom contemplating its own image. Thus it is futile to attempt to alter our situation through recourse to mere progressive methods of education. The elimination of formal standards of efficiency is likewise unavailing. For the ulterior is present still. We find it present in the bidimensional attitude that actuates the entire pedagogic system with its underlying idea of *preparation*. Apparently it is not realized that this element of the preparatory or ulterior is the criterion also of the teachers, being likewise the basis of their own promotion as it is the standard of promotion in the world at large. But whatever is preparatory is based upon the illusion of the personal image. It is commentative, premeditated, moralistic, and substitutes a mental impression of life in place of life itself. When we offer an image of life for which we seek to "prepare" the child, the very basis of our educational programme becomes pictorial and untrue. Life knows naught of images in the personal sense. Life is the functioning of interests in constructive activities. The rewards of such activities flow naturally out of them and consist in a common earning for daily needs in common daily pursuits. The child, if given the opportunity, will learn to construct useful and beautiful things and his only reward will be the natural reward accruing from the intrinsic value, social and aesthetic, of the work produced. When schools will have become the productive plants of natural childish industry, there will not any longer be the absurd invention by the schools of ulterior rewards such as now supply the artificial stimulus necessary to lend vitality to their essential dullness. It will not be necessary for teachers to stimulate the industry of their pupils through resort to extraneous "merits" in palliation for their own lack of joy in the natural creativeness of spontaneous childhood.'[31]

[31] *Op. cit.*, pp. 92–3.

We shall deal briefly with the rôle of the teacher in Chapter IX, but from the point of view of the child everything that Dr. Burrow says in this paragraph lends support to the philosophy of education outlined in this book. We have conceived education as precisely that functioning of interests in constructive activities which he sees as the essential basis of a healthy organic society—and we have shown that the value of such activities is not merely reciprocal in the social organism, the natural agreement of component parts with each other and with the whole, but that it is intrinsic in a biocentric universe, a property of mind and matter when they react upon each other to organize a relevant structure. We are down to the fundamental formulas of life, in the individual and in society, and there we find our aesthetic principle presiding. There is no escape from it. It is the principle of whatever design and purpose our wisdom can discern in the universe, and to ignore it, or deny it, is to plunge mankind into the chaos and ineptitude so often realized in its discordant history. In such a descent there is a limit to the possibilities of survival. In this sense our great psychologists have been gloomy and impressive prophets. 'The gigantic catastrophes that threaten *us* are not elemental happenings of a physical or biological kind, but are psychic events. We are threatened in a fearful way by wars and revolutions that are nothing else than psychic epidemics. At any moment a few million people may be seized by a madness, and then we have another world war or a devastating revolution. Instead of being exposed to wild beasts, tumbling rocks, and inundating waters, man is exposed today to the elemental forces of his own psyche. Psychic life is a world-power that exceeds by many times all the powers of the earth. The enlightenment, which stripped nature and human institutions of gods, overlooked the one god of fear who dwells in the psyche.'[32] So Dr. Jung wrote in 1932. Still more presciently, in 1923 Dr. Burrow wrote: 'In what has just been experienced sociologically, as the World War, man is afforded an organic warning of the impending disintegration which lurks unseen beneath the surface crust of immediate and temporary social adaptations within the depths of his unconscious. In that far-sweeping manifestation there are felt the first rumblings of a sociological disturbance that bodes the utter destruction of our old order of habituations, and in that desperate expression of man's social unconscious there is evident the need in which he stands of an earnest and far-searching self-analysis. For as

[32] *The Integration of the Personality*, pp. 293–4.

overwhelming as is the catastrophe of the present war—and present it is—this catastrophe is but the detonator preceding the crash that is to come—a crash that has been gathering momentum within the unconscious of the race through centuries past and that will descend upon the world with inevitable fury in the absence of a more societal and inclusive reckoning among us.'[33]

From the education of children to the catastrophe of the world war and the more enduring catastrophe of the world revolution—it may seem that we have strained the connecting links and that the whole structure of this thesis is illusory. But no: the secret of our collective ills is to be traced to the suppression of spontaneous creative ability in the individual. The lack of spontaneity, in education and in social organization, is due to that disintegration of the personality which has been the fatal result of economic, industrial, and cultural developments since the Renaissance. The personality has become disintegrated because the growth natural to it has been thwarted —thwarted by coercive discipline and authoritarian morality, by social convention and mechanical toil—until instead of the wholeness of the expansive tree we have only the twisted and stunted bush. But man is more complex than a tree, and the effects of repression are far more disastrous. Man not only turns against himself, but against his fellows. The forces of his destructiveness are social as well as individual: when the individual is not bent on destroying himself, he attempts to destroy the weight of oppression, which he will identify with some specific group or nation. 'It would seem,' writes another psychologist, 'that the amount of destructiveness to be found in individuals is proportionate to the amount to which expansiveness of life is curtailed. By this we do not refer to individual frustrations of this or that instinctive desire, but to the thwarting of the whole of life, the blockage of spontaneity of the growth and expression of man's sensuous, emotional, and intellectual capacities. Life has an inner dynamism of its own; it tends to grow, to be expressed, to be lived. It seems that if this tendency is thwarted the energy directed toward life undergoes a process of decomposition and changes into energies directed towards destruction. In other words: the drive for life and the drive for destruction are not mutually independent factors but are in a reversed interdependence. The more the drive toward life is thwarted, the stronger is the drive toward destruction; the more life is realized, the less is the strength of destructiveness. *Destructiveness is*

[33] *Op. cit.*, p. 132.

201

the outcome of unlived life.'[34] Support for my thesis could not be more apposite, more forceful. It is only education in its widest sense, as guided growth, encouraged expansion, tender upbringing, that can secure that life is lived in all its natural creative spontaneity, in all its sensuous, emotional and intellectual fullness.

APPENDIX D

A NOTE ON PSYCHO-PHYSICAL ISOMORPHISM

THE Gestalt school of psychology has explored the possibility that a parallelism (or 'isomorphism') exists between individual human experiences and the physical structure of the cortex. That perception, sensation and all neural experiences induce corresponding activity in the brain cells is, of course, an elementary fact about which there is no dispute, and the phenomenon of memory shows that these experiences leave a more or less permanent trace in the brain cells. What the Gestalt psychologists are concerned to establish, on the basis of recent investigations into the modes of action of the nervous system, is that the relation between phenomenal experience and cortical events is not an insulated stimulation of individual cells: it is a structural event within the cortical continuum. Chemical reactions in the cortical 'field' are caused by electric stimulus in a particular part of that field, and the physical pattern that results is 'macroscopic', affecting the field as a whole. The patterns thus induced are strictly comparable to the patterns which can be observed in electrolysis. 'Considered as a conducting medium nervous tissue is an electrolyte, which means that any current which passes through the tissue involves the displacement of ions. It is a peculiarity of electrolytical conduction that surfaces within the medium through which ions cannot freely pass are, as a rule, at once polarized: Ions are, in minute layers, accumulated and absorbed on such interfaces; in consequence of it new forces arise which counteract those of the current; and owing to the change in ionic concentration chemical reactions may occur at those boundaries. The accumulation of ions at each point of a surface is proportional to the density of current at this point. Thus the current deposits on interfaces in its path an adequate picture of the pattern or distribution with which it passes through these surfaces. As time goes on this curious process of self-registration is continued. If the current remains unaltered, the *same* picture is deposited continually; as soon as the current changes its pattern a correspondingly *new* design develops on the surfaces. Thus the current writes its own history. Many years ago, when interest in macroscopic physics was more vivid and electrolytical conduction still a comparatively new subject, physicists would find great pleasure in studying the often beautiful records which currents sometimes leave where they pass from an electrolyte into an electrode.

[34] Erich Fromm: *The Fear of Freedom*, p. 158.

UNCONSCIOUS MODES OF INTEGRATION

'Physiological observations show that living tissue is strongly polarized by electric currents. Nothing else can be expected in a medium in which homogeniety is an exception and interruption by interfaces the rule. We know, however, that in the nervous system physiological function itself is for the most part associated with currents. Since these do not differ from ordinary physical currents, they have necessarily the same effects. It follows that a current which develops in the nervous system polarizes the interfaces through which it passes, and that the pattern of such polarization is the pattern of the current itself as it passes through the region in question. To the extent in which such self-registration is not deleted by subsequent events, cortical currents will therefore leave their diary spread all over the interfaces of the tissue.'[1]

Professor Koehler goes on to deduce some very significant psychological consequences from these facts, but we must ignore these in favour of the light which these same facts throw on our more limited problem. For such physical 'records of function' would serve to explain why the mind of the child, in a state of 'blankness'—that is to say, a state of non-perception—can discover and reproduce concrete patterns within his consciousness. The patterns subsist in the cortical continuum, residues and combinations of the millions of patterns which have been recorded there in the past (individual or collective). But as Koehler points out, there is no reason to suppose that the patterns traced in the cortex of experience are inert objects. 'Pervaded by forces, and possibly sometimes by currents, the record will tend to revise its own text spontaneously. If we consider that it is also under the permanent dissolving influence of metabolism, we can only expect the final edition to be a sketchy abstract of a distorted story.'[2]

Here, then, we have a feasible explanation of the mind-pictures which does not depart from scientific probability. They are the revised texts, the final editions, of the electrostatic patterns produced in the cortex by normal phenomenal experience. They can be recovered and reproduced by a technique of inwardly directed awareness or concentration which is easily taught to the child.[3]

[1] W. Koehler: *The Place of Value in a World of Facts*, pp. 239–41.

[2] *Ibid*, p. 244.

[3] It does not seem that the 'mind pictures' discussed here have any relation to the stroboscopic patterns recently investigated by W. Grey Walter (see *Perspectives in Neuropsychiatry*, ed. D. Richter, London, 1950). According to J. R. Smythies (*Analysis of Perception*, London, 1956, p. 69) 'these are usually composed of a large number of zig-zag dark or coloured lines vibrating with incessant movement upon a light ground. These lines may form a design like the spokes of a wheel or whirlpool, or catherine wheel effects may be observed. The zig-zag lines may sweep from one side of the visual field to the other. Another dominant form of the patterns is a complex mosaic of most intricate structure. Interspersed amongst these line patterns arrangements of coloured dots may be observed. At some frequencies great sheets of brilliant colours may appear and spread over the field.'

Such patterns are induced by a flash of light of extremely short duration. When the light is flashed at between 6–30 flashes per second, the whole visual field

Assuming that this is a valid explanation of why a pattern is discoverable in the mind, there is the further and more difficult question why such patterns should in different individuals, exhibit a certain uniformity. These mind-pictures produced by separate children over a number of years can be classified into definite categories, and these categories can be arranged in a series beginning with designs which might well be called 'sketchy abstracts' or 'distorted stories', but which ends with designs which show a precise geometrical organization.

To explain this phenomenon I can only offer a choice of hypotheses. The first is based on a certain 'law of composition' which seems to be inherent in human perception. Edward Barnhart has shown in an experiment[4] that if a number of people are asked to place a single simple figure on a two-dimensional field (the experimenter used a small black dot on a white rectangle), then the aggregate of such placements invariably takes the form of a simple symmetrical structure whose main density is about the horizontal, vertical and diagonal zones—in general effect, a design rather like the Union Jack. In a circular field the same experiment would presumably give a design still nearer to the mandala. As an explanation of his law of composition, Mr. Barnhart can only suggest 'innate psychological factors governing the perception of relationships and patterns', and refer us to those perception experiments, especially those conducted by Gestalt psychologists, which 'have given evidence of the importance of "organization" in perception and the tendency toward the organization of perceived material into configuration'. Another factor suggested is a demand for generalized types of relationships (such as balance) due to the experience of the subject with design (the subjects, in the experiment, were members of a class in aesthetics).

Another hypothesis, which I advance with the utmost diffidence, is suggested by the fact that the chief chemical component of the brain is carbon, and the formula for a molecule of carbon has a quaternary structure. Jung has noted the 'curious *lusus naturae* that the chief chemical component of the bodily organism is carbon, characterized by four valences'.[5] That this fact is not without significance is recognized by the famous physiologist, Lawrence Henderson, who observes that 'the great diversity of organic substances depends in the first nstance upon the quadrivalence of carbon, which makes of the carbon atom in the organic

becomes filled with these complex patterns. Smythies suggests that these stroboscopic patterns may originate in the complex mechanism of the retina, or alternatively from the 'scanning mechanism' which mediates perception in the cerebral cortex or in the processes connecting the cortex to the visual field. I have not seen experiments with a stroboscope, but no such instrument is needed to induce 'mind pictures' in children, and though there may be some connection with the same neurophysiological processes, the 'mind pictures' represent a different problem of origination and significance.

[4] 'The Structure of Simple Compositions: the Relation of Single Elements' by Edward N. Barnhart. *J. Exp. Psych.*, Vol. 23, No. 2 (1938), pp. 199–213. I am indebted to Dr. Eysenck for this reference.

[5] *The Integration of the Personality*, p. 198.

molecule a focus, from which chains of atoms may extend in four different directions'.[6]

What the relations are between the chemical constitution of carbon and the polarization induced in this same substance by the currents which accompany neural activity is more than our present knowledge of the mental processes can determine. But one might hazard the guess that the primary chemical activity in the cortex has some determining influence on

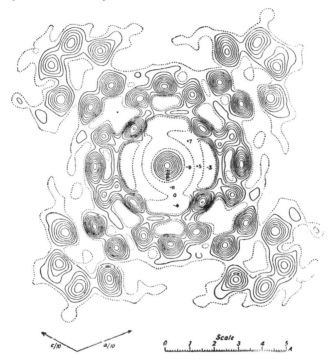

Fig. 8.—Map of a molecule of Platinum Phthalocyanine drawn in the form of a contour map showing the distribution of electron density, or scattering matter, in the molecule

[6] *The Fitness of the Environment* (New York, 1913), p. 209. Cf. also pp. 196–202 where the constitutional formulas given for various compounds of carbon and, hydrogen are comparable in quaternity, regularity and complexity to the Golden Flower and other mandalas. The accompanying illustration (Fig. 8), reproduced by courtesy of Prof. J. M. Robertson and the Chemical Society, is a 'contour map' showing the distribution of electron density in a molecule of platinum phthalocyanine. The more pronounced peaks represent individual atoms, and the hexagonal groups of six at each corner are benzene rings. These are attached to a rather more closely-knit inner system of carbon and nitrogen atoms, while right in the centre there resides a single atom of platinum. The general appearance of the

205

the nature of the pattern deposited on the interfaces by the polarizing current. But all such speculations, though they may explain the formal tendencies of unconscious mental activity, do not, and cannot, account for the further elaboration of these cortical configurations into significant images, or symbols. For an hypothesis adequate to explain this development we must for the present rely on the dynamic psychology of Jung.

map' is exactly that of the mandala illustrated by Jung in Plate 6 of *The Secret of the Golden Flower*.

In the much more general or 'macroscopic' view of our whole material, we have seen how inescapable is the division of mental function into four kinds (thinking, feeling, sensation, and intuition); and we have found even a fanatical mechanist like Pavlov resorting to a four-fold classification of types of disposition. At times one is tempted to exclaim with Sir Toby Belch: 'Does not our life consist of the four elements?' (*Twelfth Night*, II, 3).

Chapter Seven

THE NATURAL FORM
OF EDUCATION

*You must train your children to their studies in a playful manner and
without any air of constraint with the further object of discerning
more readily the natural bent of their respective characters.—Plato*

*Free labour or art is simply nature unravelling its potentialities, both
in the world and in the mind, and unravelling them together, in so far
as they are harmonious in the two spheres. Such labour is therefore a
great corrective to distraction, since it concentrates attention on the
possible, and trains the Will to discriminate and organize its true
intentions.—George Santayana*

Remember that childhood is the sleep of reason.—Rousseau

1. THREE ASPECTS OF ART TEACHING

Some of the matters discussed in previous chapters may seem to
have carried us rather far from our particular subject—the place
of art in education. But the prejudices which surround the subject
are so deep-seated, and so fortified by official regulations and traditional methods of teaching, that any attempt to justify a practical
reorganization of this aspect of education must necessarily be basic,
both in a psychological and a philosophical sense. It is now more than
sixty years since Ebenezer Cooke set out to reform the teaching of art
in England; it is over fifty years since Franz Cizek opened his
Juvenile Art Class in Vienna. About the same time a similar movement sprang up in America, where the pioneer was Arthur Wesley
Dow, whose book *Composition*, first published in 1899, led to a new
conception of art teaching in that country. The movement spread to
other countries in Europe and America, but though it has continuously gained ground, it has not been free from opposition, even on the

207

part of enlightened educationalists. The official attitude, especially in Great Britain, might be described as a rearguard action. Much ground has been yielded, but unwillingly, and it is still mainly in junior schools under a few Authorities and in various types of private school that the new methods of art teaching have been whole-heartedly adopted.

The conflicting points of view spring from a confusion which belongs to the world of art rather than to the world of education, and which has found expression in the warring schools of academicism, naturalism, impressionism and expressionism. As we have seen, what were regarded as mutually exclusive views of art can now be reconciled as the natural differences of the basic psychological types. These differences and their modes of expression have been described. But even when the validity of these types and of their distinctive modes of expression has been admitted, certain general pedagogical problems remain. It may be granted that art teaching should provide for what is called self-expression, but should it stop there? For there are several other possibilities. There is the possibility that what arises as a spontaneous activity may become, under guidance, a specialized ability or technical skill. There is the possibility that this activity or ability may be *applied* to particular material: it will not spontaneously take the form of carving stone or forging metal—it must be directed into these special channels. Nor will this spontaneous activity necessarily conform to other social activities: it must find its level in the general activity of living. It must, above all, find correspondences in the modes of expression of other individuals, and thus be developed into what we call aesthetic appreciation.

It will be seen that there are in effect three distinct activities which are often confused:

A. The activity of *self-expression*—the individual's innate need to communicate his thoughts, feelings and emotions to other people.

B. The activity of *observation*—the individual's desire to record his sense impressions, to clarify his conceptual knowledge, to build up his memory, to construct things which aid his practical activities.

C. The activity of *appreciation*—the response of the individual to the modes of expression which other people address or have addressed to him, and generally the individual's response to *values* in the world of facts—the qualitative reaction to the quantitative results of activities A and B.

These three activities, which are all included in the pedagogical category of 'art teaching', are really three distinct subjects, demanding separate and even unrelated methods of approach.

Generally speaking, the activity of self-expression cannot be taught. Any application of an external standard, whether of technique or form, immediately induces inhibitions, and frustrates the whole aim. The rôle of the teacher is that of attendant, guide, inspirer, psychic midwife.

Observation is almost entirely an acquired skill. It is true that certain individuals[1] are born with an aptitude for concentrated attention, and for the eye-and-hand co-ordination involved in the act of recording what is observed. But in most cases the eye (and the other organs of sensation) have to be trained, both in observation (directed perception) and in notation. It is the usefulness of such acquired skill as an ancillary to the normal logical and scientific curriculum of the school which has led to the fanatical defence of naturalistic modes in art teaching, and to a preference for 'craft' as opposed to 'art'.

As for appreciation, this can undoubtedly be developed by teaching, but as we have seen, appreciation is just as relative to psychological types as is expression, but in so far as by appreciation we mean a response to other people's modes of expression, then the faculty is likely to develop only as one aspect of social adaptation, and cannot be expected to show itself much before the age of adolescence. Until then the real problem is to preserve the original intensity of the child's reactions to the sensuous qualities of experience—to colours, surfaces, shapes and rhythms. These are apt to be so infallibly 'right' that the the teacher can only stand over them in a kind of protective awe.

2. THE AESTHETIC CRITERION

Before we consider the methods of education which would conform to the facts so far presented in this book, there is a preliminary question of values which must be briefly discussed. We have already seen that certain 'free drawings' by children have been characterized as 'hideous', 'horrible', 'monstrous' and 'lawless' by no less an authority than Dr. Montessori. Such drawings 'show only that the eye of

[1] Our 'enumerative' type.

the child is uneducated, the hand inert, the mind insensible alike to the beautiful and the ugly, blind to the true as well as the false' (see quotation on pages 113–4). Dr. Montessori does not illustrate such drawings, but we may assume that she refers in general to the material which we should put in category A as products of the activity of self-expression. At the same time, it is obvious that Dr. Montessori does not necessarily regard our category B as the only alternative to the lawless activity of self-expression: she rather suggests the necessity of a prior training and ethical perfection of the self that is to be expressed. The ethical, she says in effect, must precede the aesthetic, and *then* the child may safely be left to express itself freely in drawings, etc.

This is not, of course, quite the same point of view as that of the traditional 'drawing-master', which is the point of view still enforced in many schools. It may come to very much the same thing in the end, but the traditional or academic attitude is based on aesthetic rather then ethical values. A drawing is either 'good' or 'bad', 'neat' or 'careless', 'accurate' or 'out-of-drawing', according to a standard which, on closer scrutiny, proves to be the unconsciously held standard of naturalism, with perhaps a slight tendency to the classical idealization of the human form.

It would be irrelevant here to discuss the relative value of various aesthetic standards. All that is necessary for our present purpose is to point out that different and irreconcilable standards do exist. We have already suggested that basically these aesthetic standards are the expression of differences in temperamental disposition. But whatever their explanation, the divergent modes of expression indicated by such terms as 'naturalism', 'realism', 'idealism', 'impressionism', 'expressionism' and 'superrealism' have been historically and theoretically justified. Their relative evaluation by some absolute standard may still be in question, but no responsible critic would now deny *some* aesthetic justification to a negro mask as well as to a Roman portrait-bust, to a Byzantine mosaic as well as to an altar-piece by Van-Eyck, to Picasso as well as to Piero della Francesca. The question to determine, therefore, is not whether the drawings of children conform to some absolute aesthetic standard, but whether they can be related to one of several types of aesthetic expression, or even constitute an aesthetic category *sui generis*.

But we have already found that children's drawings do not all conform to one type: that there are at least eight types, and that these types correspond to the psychological dispositions of individual children. That types of art in general have a similar psychological basis is also true, but sociological and ideological factors, which may not be altogether absent in children's art, in adult art modify the direct expression of psychological disposition and enormously complicate the analysis. The universal *similarity* of children's art, type for type, is to be explained by the relative avoidance of these complicating factors by the pre-adolescent mind.

What in effect is necessary, in determining the aesthetic value of children's drawings, is the same objective approach that the student of art gives to all historical manifestations of the creative impulse. Some children's drawings will conform to the standards of impressionist painting, others to the standards of expressionist painting, others to those of naturalistic painting, and so on. Approached in this way, very few children's drawings will be found lacking in, at any rate, an element of aesthetic interest. But there does, of course, remain a difference between the childish and the adult modes of expression within identical categories. Is this a difference in aesthetic value?

Essentially, it is a difference in maturation. That the adult may impart more knowledge and experience in his painting goes without saying; but this is not an aesthetic difference. What does exist besides is a difference which is simply a difference of muscular energy and co-ordination, and which is summed up in the phrase 'technical skill'. In so far as technical skill is the ability adequately to express a mental perception, or a feeling, it will contribute to the aesthetic value of the act of expression. It is for this reason that the acquisition of skill, by methods which we shall presently discuss, is to be encouraged. At the same time it must be admitted that the very process of maturation seems to adjust skill to the requirements of the child at any particular stage of development. The skill is developed by the drawing, not the drawing by the skill.[2] The skill which is adequate for a representational drawing at the age of fifteen would be more than adequate for a 'schema' at the age of five.

[2] Cf. Aristotle, *Nicomachean Ethics*, 1103a: 'Neither by nature, nor contrary to nature do the virtues arise in us; rather we are adapted by nature to receive them, and are made perfect by habit. Again, of all the things that come to us by nature we first acquire the potentiality and later exhibit the activity . . . ; but the virtues we get by first exercising them, as also happens in the case of the arts as well. For the things we have to learn before we can do them, we learn by doing them: e.g. men become builders by building and lyre-players by playing the lyre; so too we become just by doing just acts, temperate by doing temperate acts, brave by doing brave acts.' (Oxford translation.)

There still remains the possibility of a specific aesthetic quality in children's art—a quality which might be generally indicated by the word 'naïvety'. Not all children's drawings are 'naïve'—a considerable number of them are 'clever' or 'sophisticated'. But when we recognize a quality in a child's drawing which we describe as 'naïve', we are indicating a certain 'vision' of things which is peculiar to children, and perhaps to certain rare adults who retain this childlike faculty. I have described it elsewhere as 'the innocent eye', by which I mean an eye uninfluenced by rational or deductive thought, an eye that accepts the correlation of incompatibles, the self-sufficiency of the images which come into the mind uncalled and unchecked by observation. What the child writes, or draws, might best be described as an act of poetic intuition, and it is a mystery beyond our logical analysis. When a child writes: 'The whole face of God is laburnum,' I know that a poetic truth has been expressed, and expressed in a way only available to a child. Similarly, before hundreds of children's drawings, before most of the drawings I have illustrated in this book, I know that I am in the presence of a poetic truth, a truth which only a child could have expressed. And before such drawings I can only say with Frank Cizek: 'The teacher must be the most modest and humble of persons who sees in a child a miracle of God and not pupil-material.'

This does not mean that the teacher must simply stand aside. That might be desirable in a Peter Pan world where children never grow up. But the child is in a constant state of transformation. Its body and brain mature; it adjusts itself inevitably if unconsciously to its social environment. The duty of the teacher is to watch over this organic process—to see that its tempo is not forced, its tender shoots distorted. It follows, therefore, that values must change with the years of growth. What is valuable in and for the child of five will not necessarily be valuable for the child of ten or fifteen. Among other things, the teacher must be prepared to say a reluctant farewell to the charms of naïvety. The problem is to preserve an organic continuity, so that the poetic vision of one age fades insensibly into the poetic vision of the next age: that the sense of value never loses its instinctive basis, to become an ethical code or an aesthetic canon, an artificial appendage to an otherwise purely appetitive existence.

3. THE OFFICIAL ATTITUDE

Considerations of this kind are not absent from the official attitude to the arts in education. In Great Britain, at any rate, successive reports of the Ministry of Education's Consultative Committee have emphasized the desirability of extending and improving the teaching of art and craft in the primary and secondary schools, if only as a corrective to the doubtful effects of an exclusively logical or grammatical training. It is interesting to note that in the thirteen years which separate the Hadow Report on *The Education of the Adolescent* (1926) and the Spens Report on *Secondary Education* (1939) a decisive difference in the treatment of this subject has come about. In the first report 'drawing and painting' are commended as 'affording the pupil a mode of self-expression and a means of interpreting his appreciation of what he sees in the world around him', but they are immediately dismissed in the plea that 'the lines along which this development should take place are well established, and we think well understood, and a detailed consideration of them is hardly necessary'. The Report then goes on to consider in some detail 'the application of drawing to those branches of the work of a Modern School which in our view should be characteristic of such a school. From this point of view, some practical skill in drawing forms a valuable and indeed, an indispensable adjunct to the study of various branches of the curriculum, such as woodwork and metalwork, elementary geometry, elementary science, particularly nature study, biology and mechanics, geography and history. In such subjects, drawing is of value, not only as a means of recording what is seen, and in so doing strengthening the pupil's powers of accurate observation of detail, but also as a means of training the pupil to appreciate the significance of diagrams, maps and plans in the text-book and works of reference which he uses for the various branches of the curriculum' (p. 227). The Report then goes on to distinguish the four main divisions into which the teaching of drawing should fall—viz. object drawing, memory drawing, geometrical and mechanical drawing, design.

This conception of *art as an adjunct* is, of course, so indigenous that it is no surprise to find it embodied in an official document of the year 1926. Nor is it any wonder that this same conception of art should still dominate a large proportion of our schools. What is more surprising, and insufficiently realized, is that the Ministry of Education itself has now abandoned this attitude. Apart from the recommendations of the Reports on Primary (1939) and Secondary Education (1939) which are, after all, merely the recommendations of an external committee, we find in the *Handbook of*

Suggestions for the Consideration of Teachers from the edition of 1938 onwards, a complete understanding and recommendation of what we might still call 'the new point of view'. The emphasis of the 1926 Report is now completely reversed. Section 6 of Chapter VII states:

'It is clear that training in draughtsmanship, although it may still be of value as a means to an end, is not a sufficient end in itself. The love of drawing, painting, and making things seems to be instinctive in every normal child. By such means he expresses ideas about the things which surround him, long before he can use the written word, and this outlet for his lively imagination must be fostered and developed to the full. The spontaneity, the freshness and vigour which are characteristic of the free expression of young children's drawings and painting should be recognized as of greater importance than an imitative accuracy, but it should equally be recognized that for the normal child it is as natural to make progress towards adult standards in the language of drawing as in the written word'. Even when dealing with the Senior School Stage, the *Handbook* suggests that 'there is no justification for the abandonment of expressive or imaginative drawing and painting.

'No teacher would think of equipping children with the vocabulary of a language, a knowledge of its grammar, and the ability to make the symbols used in writing it, and then withhold all opportunity for the expression of ideas by the use of it. Yet it is still possible to find schools where the whole time given by the older children to drawing is spent in acquiring knowledge of the appearance of things and the technique of draughtsmanship, without making any use of this knowledge to express ideas.'

In accordance with these general remarks, the Ministry of Education recommends their teachers to secure 'a reasonable balance between the acquisition of knowledge and skill and their use in the expression of ideas'.

This open recognition of the new attitude towards the methods of teaching art is accompanied by an admission that 'art' should be interpreted in a wide sense, and that there should be no artificial separation between 'art' and 'handicraft', 'which should properly be regarded as part and parcel of one important branch of teaching'. Interpreted in this wide sense, art becomes a subject of greatest significance; indeed, 'nothing in the school curriculum has a closer contact with life. While few people are called upon to use draughtsmanship to any extent, all are called upon to exercise choice between what is good and what is less good in matters of shape and colour and craftsmanship, and to take action, either as individuals or as members of the community, which will affect their environment'.

When so much has been conceded, it might seem ungracious to complain that it is not enough. But it is likely that the separate chapters of the *Handbook* were written by separate authorities, and whilst so much is claimed for art in the chapter devoted to the subject, separate and equal claims are made in the chapters devoted to English Language and Literature, Geography, Nature Study, Science and Mathematics. It should further be noted that the *Handbook* is intended only for teachers in Public Elementary Schools, and no comparable suggestions have been made for Secondary Schools—though the Spens Report expressed the view that a training in the aesthetic subjects was 'as important as the training of the intellect through Languages, Science and Mathematics' (p. 171). What the *Handbook* and the Reports avoid is any adequate correlation of the various subjects included in the curriculum. And by correlation we do not mean merely a proportionate allotment of teaching hours. This purely quantitative aspect has been dealt with in some detail, and the Spens Report, for example, in its experimental time table, allots as much time to aesthetic subjects as it does to mathematics plus science, and more than to languages. But by correlation is meant something more fundamental—nothing less than the introduction of the aesthetic criterion into every aspect of school life. It should be evident from the considerations brought forward in the earlier chapters of this book, that the aesthetic activity as such is the organic process of physical and mental integration: the introduction of value into a world of facts. From this point of view the aesthetic principle enters into mathematics and history, into science itself; and above all it enters into all the social and practical aspects of school life.[3] From the very beginning the aesthetic principle must be applied to the building of the school and its decoration, to every item of its furniture and utensils, to all the organized aspects of work and play. Speech and gesture, action or movement, every mode of behaviour and ex-

[3] It is pleasant to record that since these words were written an experiment which applied the aesthetic principle in this complete sense and with complete success was conducted in a Junior School in Birmingham. The experiment is described in an illustrated pamphlet written by the headmaster of the school, Mr. A. L. Stone, and published by the Ministry of Education (*Story of a School*, H.M. Stationery Office, London, 1949).

pression, has its configuration; and the pattern of this configuration has effect and efficiency in the degree that it has aesthetic value.

4. CREATION AND CONSTRUCTION

It is from this point of view that we must criticize a certain tendency which exists in some schools, and even among certain educationalists, to confuse the values of art and of mechanical construction. The *Handbook* is happily free from this tendency: it deprecates any attempt to treat 'art' and 'handicrafts' as separate sections of the curriculum. They should both be treated as merely different media for the expression of the same aesthetic activity. But in many schools, especially public schools for boys, the studio and the workshop are offered as alternatives, and there is a bias, all the stronger for not being openly expressed, in favour of the workshop—it is considered more 'manly' and as having a more direct vocational value. The distinction merely reflects the 'split' nature of our civilization, a civilization which can complacently tolerate that divorce between form and function, work and leisure, art and industry, which is basically the divorce between mind and matter, between the individual and the collective aspects of consciousness. But without entering into these wider speculations, it should be evident to any observer that the child who is drawing or painting a free representation of its feelings or ideas is engaged in one form of mental activity, and that a child engaged in measuring and cutting lengths of wood or pieces of cloth and joining them together *may* be engaged in a totally different mental activity. The two activities can only be related to each other in the sphere of formal values, in that region of pure aesthetic values in which all forms of expression are reconciled or for ever rejected. The boy who is making a book-case or a tray, or the girl who is making a dress, will only reach that region if what they make by measurement is *in the process of making* determined by a sense of design. That children possess such a sense will not be denied by anyone who has seen their first efforts in construction; but nothing will inhibit that instinctive sense so quickly as the premature use of implements of precision. The senses must first be educated to appreciate the quality in material, the visual proportions in measurements, the tactile relationship of areas and masses. The desire to make beautiful things must be stronger than the desire to make useful things; or rather, there must be an instinctive realization of the fact that beauty and utility, each in its highest degree, cannot be conceived separately. But it is easier to recognize this truth in all its abstractness than to apply it to the practical organization of the school workshop or the school curriculum. As we shall see presently, that unity can in the end only be secured by the right kind of teacher.

5. PRESENT PROVISION FOR ART TEACHING IN SCHOOLS

The present educational system allows for a wide latitude in the teaching of art and craft at various stages, but generally speaking it may be said to allow a bare minimum in the lower stages, and to decrease this minimum progressively as the child advances, except in so far as the child is diverted into the courses of vocational training provided by the Junior Classes in Art Schools, where, of course art or craft has a direct vocational justification. Apart from their vocational aspects, all forms of aesthetic education are progressively eliminated as education merges into an active preparation for life. Art, in the higher branches of our system, is not considered as a necessary part of a liberal education.

Beginning from the bottom, we find that art activities, because they can be so easily assimilated to play activities, occupy a large place in the Infant Schools. A good deal depends on the interest which the individual teachers take in the subject, and on their general ability as teachers; but it would be fair to say that in the degree of their efficiency the Infant Schools make some form of aesthetic activity a major part of their daily programme. Any reforms that are desirable at this stage relate to methods of teaching and not to the content of the curriculum itself.

The formalization of our subject begins in the Elementary Schools. At this stage the Juniors are given *at least* a double period of 45 minutes weekly, and the Seniors *generally* a double period for drawing and modelling, and in addition one or more periods for craft (woodwork and metalwork for boys, needlework for girls).

The double period continues in the Secondary Schools (and generally speaking in those anomalous institutions, the Comprehensive Schools) up to the age of 15. From 11 to 13 the pupils in such schools may be given an additional double period for craft.

From the age of 15 onwards the place of art in the curriculum is determined absolutely by the examination system. From 15 to 17, little or no time is given to the subject unless it is to be taken in the General Certificate examination, when a double period or even more may be allotted to it. Similarly, a double period or more may be given to those pupils in the Sixth Form who are taking art in the 'advanced' level of the Certificate examination. For the rest of the Sixth Form, an entirely arbitrary system prevails: but in most schools a certain amount of time at this stage is devoted to art (even to art history and 'appreciation') and to craft.

We need not pursue the subject any further, because it is nowhere recognized in Great Britain as an essential part of university education. In response to certain vocational needs (museums, art trade, etc.) institutions for the study of what might be described as the science of art have been established at London and Birmingham, and courses of an optional nature exist at Oxford, Cambridge, Edinburgh and Reading.[4] A more general survey of art teaching in our universities is given in Appendix E, but for our present purposes it is sufficient to note that in no sense can it anywhere be described as an integral part of the higher forms of education.

Such is the place of art, in a purely quantitative sense, in the present educational system of Great Britain. Various recommendations for improvement have been made by the Consultative Committee of the Ministry of Education. The Hadow Report on the Primary School suggests (pp. 97–8) that 'handwork and drawings are . . . useful as ancillary means of learning about other things, but they should also hold an important place in their own right. . . . The creative powers, of which even the ordinary child has his share, give his teachers the opportunity of fostering very desirable tastes, desirable not only because they will improve the quality of his adult leisure, but also because they must in the long run tend to keep up the national level in craftsmanship and incidentally assist in the improvement of many products of industry; and this we take to be a consideration of great weight'. And for reasons of such weight the Committee come to the conclusion 'that while drawing has a barely adequate place in the present curriculum for children, that assigned to handwork of all kinds, and especially craftwork, is definitely insufficient, particularly in the case of boys'.

The Spens Report on Secondary Education shows a more imaginative grasp of the problem. Generally it recognizes that in the

[4] Since 1943 art departments have been established at the Universities of Manchester, Leeds and Nottingham.

present curriculum 'didacticism is still overweighted in comparison with originating activity' and that 'the activities which are the richest in the creative element have the strongest claim for a place in the curriculum'. They feel that it is necessary to reaffirm the recommendation they made in their report on *Differentiation of Curricula between the Sexes in Secondary Schools* (1923, p. 138) *'That a more prominent and established place in the ordinary curricula of schools both for boys and girls should be assigned to aesthetic subjects, including Music, Art and other forms of aesthetic training, and that special attention should be paid to developing the capacity for artistic appreciation as distinct from executive skill'*. 'We feel this training to be as important as the training of the intellect through Languages, Science and Mathematics, and should like to see a larger proportion of the school hours available to subjects of this nature.' (p. 171.)

In an official Circular (No. 1294) issued by the Board of Education in 1922 the minimum time suggested as necessary for aesthetic subjects was *five* periods a week, two for drawing, two for manual work and one for music. In the Spens Report this period is increased to *seven* periods a week for a normal course, and decreased to four periods for pupils taking a second or third foreign language from the second year onwards, and for pupils specializing in Science or Mathematics from their fourth year onwards. It may be increased to eight periods for pupils learning a second language who desire to give increased attention to artistic subjects in their fourth and fifth years. These, of course, are merely recommendations which have never been put into effect.

6. THE INTEGRAL METHOD

Such in brief is the actual position of art teaching in the Primary and Secondary Schools of Great Britain,[5] and such is the extent of

[5] The position in Scotland is slightly different, but not to the advantage of art teaching. Cf. 'Art Education in Scotland', by J. G. Corbett McVean (*Athene*, Vol. 1, No. 1, 1939). The position in Wales is dealt with in a report of the Central Advisory Council for Education (Wales) on *Arts and Crafts in the School of Wales* (London, H.M.S.O., 1956). The position in our universities, dealt with in Appendix D, does not differ in any way from the position in the German universities in 1872, as described by Nietzsche (*On the Future of Our Educational Institutions*, Fifth Lecture. Trans. J. M. Kennedy, Edinburgh, 1909). 'In what relationship these universities stand to *art* cannot be acknowledged without shame: in none at all. Of artistic thinking, learning, striving, and comparison, we do not find in them a single trace; and no one would seriously think that the voice of the universities would ever be raised to help the advancement of the higher national

any reforms that are even remotely in prospect. It is evident that the distinction between 'didacticism' and 'originating activity' has become clear to the distinguished educationalists who were members of the Ministry's Consultative Committee, and who may be taken as representative of an even wider and equally authoritative body of pedagogic opinion. This distinction is none other than that which we established on psychological grounds in an earlier chapter. Our conclusions then led us to suppose that those activities which we denote by such words as 'imaginative', 'creative', 'originating', 'aesthetic', do not represent a subject with definite limits which can be treated like any other subject and allotted its two or five or seven periods in a competitive time-table, but are rather an aspect of mental development which is all-embracing—which is, indeed, no aspect but a *mode* of mental development. The imaginative does not stand over against the logical, the originating against the didactic, the artistic against the utilitarian, as a claimant to which a concession must be more or less unwillingly made; the two processes are in absolute opposition, and though the end we desire may be called a synthesis, our contention is that the basis of all intellectual and moral strength lies in the adequate integration of the perceptive senses and the external world, of the personal and the organic, an integration which is only to be achieved by methods of education. In other words the structure of reason, in so far as reason has the biological value which, as we shall see, is better represented by the word *wisdom*, rests upon organic patterns of behaviour, upon 'a way of life' in harmony with 'the law of nature'; and what we call a pattern or a law is evident only to aesthetic judgment—is a 'fittingness' or value evident only to the percipient or apprehending aspects of wisdom which we call *sensibility* and *insight*.

It follows that from our point of view the wrangle over the time-table is as unnecessary as it is unseemly. Our aim is not two or more extra periods. We demand nothing less than the whole 35 into which the child's week is now arbitrarily divided. We demand, that is to say, a method of education that is formally and fundamentally

schemes of art. Whether an individual teacher feels himself to be personally qualified for art, or whether a professorial chair has been established for the training of aestheticizing literary historians, does not enter into the question at all: the fact remains that the university is not in a position to control the young academician by severe artistic discipline, and that it must let happen what happens, willy-nilly—and this is the cutting answer to the immodest pretensions of the universities to represent themselves as the highest educational institutions.'

aesthetic, and in which knowledge and manual ability, discipline and reverence, are but so many easy and inevitable by-products of a natural childish industry.

Obviously such requirements involve a reform of the educational system which is too revolutionary to be substantiated by the observations of one individual, and it is obviously not within my competence to say how such reforms would affect, say, the teaching of individual subjects like mathematics and geography. The integral education which I conceive is relatively indifferent to the fate of individual subjects, since its underlying assumption is that the purpose of education is to develop generic qualities of insight and sensibility, which qualities are fundamental even in mathematics or geography.[6]

The formulation of the aesthetic basis of education in such general terms will inevitably clash with any similar formulation of a moral or religious nature. This question will be dealt with in the next chapter, but here, by way of an interim answer, my point of view may be briefly indicated. In so far as morality or ethics can be separated from religion, they are only susceptible of being taught at the pre-adolescent stage by two methods: (a) as a conceptual system of maxims or dogmas, such as the Ten Commandments or the Church Catechism; or (b) in the form of parables. The first method, for reasons already given in this book, is psychologically misconceived, and can only be made effective by sanctions of fear or reward which undermine the moral basis which they are designed to establish. The good life must be freely chosen if it is to be rightly enjoyed. The second method of inculcating morality involves the aesthetic method: it consists, that is to say, in the translation of conceptual generalizations into the concrete images of a dramatic pattern, and is effective in the degree that it has aesthetic value. The parables of Christ, of Lao-Tzü, of Tolstoy, or of any great moral teacher, are works of art, and are intended to operate (and this is the important point) on the perceptual and non-ratiocinative level of mental consciousness.[7]

[6] That an aesthetic education does develop these generic qualities was clearly demonstrated in the experiment referred to in Note 3, p. 215 above.

[7] Cf. Gustave Thibon: ' . . . there is no worse social misdeed than forcing the masses to holiness. Placed as we are at the very core of a failure of moral habit such as has never before been known in history, it behoves the thinker to beware more than ever of ideal constructions and universal systems and the intoxication of words and 'pipe-dreams'. Moral erethism has been cultivated quite long enough: what we need above all now is a propelling, a *motive* morality. After our too numerous, too protracted and sterile intellectual and affective debauches, it is time to teach people to put the ideal they bear in their spirit, and the feeling they

The relation of our pattern of education to religious education (in so far as that form of education can be divorced from moral education) is again a relation of identity. It is not likely (for reasons that we need not go into now) that the express tenets and ritual practices of a particular denomination will ever be re-introduced into a national system of education. The most that can be attempted, or desired, is the inculcation of a religious spirit or attitude in the child, a characteristic which was expressed above by the word 'reverence'. This was always inculcated into primitive people by music and dance, and other forms of artistic discipline; and can anyone seriously contend that the pre-adolescent child is likely to be so effectively *moved* and *moulded* by any alternative method? It may be my private philosophy that religion implies above all a life in conformity with nature; but philosophers far more ostensibly religious have held the same view, and have thereby committed themselves to some system of education which can also claim to be in conformity with nature, that is to say, based on a direct perception of natural laws, on the *experience* of these laws in activities which originate in the child and acquire significance for the child in the degree that they assume a form or pattern of aesthetic rightness. It is the perception of rightness, and not the knowledge of it, which is possible to, and characteristic of, childhood.[8]

Knowledge, in the sense of logically arranged and memorized information, is necessary to the business of bread-winning. But it is one of the main contentions of this book that such knowledge can be rapidly and efficiently acquired in the adolescent phase of mental development, if the foundations of a natural wisdom have been laid in the pre-adolescent phase.

In practical effect this means that the whole of the primary phase of education should be reorganized on an integral plan in which individual subjects lose their present definite and artificial outlines, to merge in a total constructive or originating activity, in this sense continuing the teaching methods of the Infant and Nursery Schools. The development of the child should be conceived as the progressive

bear in their heart, into their hands and fingers. It is a matter of *incarnating* the human truth humbly and patiently; giving the human truth a body and reality in the life of each and all. The noblest of ideals attains to meaning only in proportion as it gives birth to this simple, lowly, flesh-and-blood effort.' (*What Ails Mankind?* Trans. Willard Hill. New York, 1947, pp. 134–5.)

[8] The social aspects of this question are dealt with in the concluding chapter (see pages 302–8).

enlargement of its social group, first the family, then the kinder-garten, then the successive classes of the primary school. At every stage the group should be intact and organic, carrying on all its activities as a unit.

From an active point of view the progression may be regarded as beginning with *play*, and as being, throughout the whole of the primary stage, nothing but a development of play. There is, of course, nothing very original in such a suggestion, and 'the play way' is a recognized method of education, especially in infant schools. But as I have already indicated, the conception of play on which these dis-cussions and experiments are based is inadequate and sometimes superficial. At the lowest it becomes a pretence of 'not taking things seriously', and every subject is debased to an hilarious game in which the teacher becomes an histrionic buffoon. At its best the method tends to develop a form of sophistication which is only too evident to the child. The play method, if properly pursued, should not imply merely a lack of coherence and direction in teaching—that is playing at teaching, not teaching by play—*but to give coherence and direction to play is to convert it into art*, and it was for this reason that an objection was raised in the last chapter to the theoretical treatment of art as a form of play. Play is rather an informal activity capable of becoming an artistic activity, and of thus acquiring significance for the organic development of the child.

7. FROM PLAY TO ART

It will be found that the varieties of children's play are capable of being co-ordinated and developed in four directions, corresponding to the four basic mental functions, and that when so developed, the play activity naturally incorporates all the subjects appropriate to the primary phase of education.

From the aspect of *feeling* play may be developed by personifica-tion and objectivation towards DRAMA.

From the aspect of *sensation* play may be developed by modes of self-expression towards visual or plastic DESIGN.

From the aspect of *intuition* play may be developed by rhythmic exercises towards DANCE and MUSIC.

From the aspect of *thought* play may be developed by constructive activities towards CRAFT.

These four aspects of development, DRAMA, DESIGN, DANCE (including MUSIC) and CRAFT, are the four divisions into which a primary system of education naturally falls, but together they form a unity which is the unity of the harmoniously developing personality.[9]

Actually they include all the subjects normally taught in elementary schools in separate and unrelated classes. Drama includes the various modes of communication, such as elocution, reading and English. Dance incorporates music and physical training. Design includes painting, drawing and modelling. Craft includes measurement (elementary arithmetic and geometry), gardening, biology, farming, needlework, and some elementary physics and chemistry, structure of materials, composition of foodstuffs, fertilizers, etc.

These aspects of education are aspects of one process, and cannot be departmentalized without harm to one another. The fundamental play is a drama, the unfolding drama of creation and discovery, a drama called GROWTH, and it involves craft, design and dance as necessary co-operative activities.

As a child grows, he will develop a bias, according to his temperamental disposition, along one of the four directions of originating activity. The ideal is, of course, the harmonious development of all the mental functions, but there is not one ideal of human personality, nor even four, but four main groups with different combinations of the three subordinate functions under the dominant trait. But it is not until adolescence that the combination assumes its final pattern, and until that phase of development is reached it is not practicable to partition the educational system according to temperamental disposition—that is to say, to start vocational education. But this does not, of course, exempt a teacher at the primary stage from the necessity of adapting a general system to the requirements of particular types.

Primary education should have as its ideal an individual in whom all the mental functions grow harmoniously together. It is in this sense that we can return with deeper understanding to Edmond Holmes's statement, that the function of education is to foster growth. At the beginning the growth may seem to be uniform, but sooner or later, and at the latest at the stage marked by the end of primary and the beginning of secondary education, branches stem from the trunk, personality is differentiated according to innate disposition, and

[9] Cf. Aristotle. *Politics* (V, iii). 'The customary branches of education are in number four; they are—(1) reading and writing, (2) gymnastic, (3) music, and, although this is not universally admitted, (4) the art of design.'

teaching must follow along the diverse directions in which the human psyche splits and spreads out into the social environment.

8. THE STRUCTURE OF THE EDUCATIONAL SYSTEM*

These general principles, which are based on the detailed psychological evidence offered in the earlier chapters of this work, inevitably involve a practical reorganization of more than the contents and divisions of the curriculum. The whole structure of the educational system is put in question, together with the architectural planning of the school, the methods of teaching and the training of teachers, and the measurement of results. And since we are concerned, not with the production of that artefact, the *scholar*, but with an organic unit of society, the *citizen*, we must plan our educational system against the broad outlines of a social background. Indeed, it is possible that I have from the beginning made certain assumptions which betray a social bias. The difference between the ideal of citizenship in a free democracy and the ideal of service in a totalitarian state is so absolute that from infancy to manhood it implies a complete divergence in educational aims and methods. The world events through which we have lived and are living have had the effect of driving us to define our assumptions about the nature of society and the purpose of government, and though our definitions show far too much confusion of thought, they do agree and gather force on two or three principles. However we may phrase the beliefs, we do agree, on the libertarian side of the world struggle, that society should be ruled by natural law and not by the dogma of a particular race or creed; we do agree that it is possible to organize a society on the basis of voluntary association and mutual aid; and we agree with Aristotle that happiness is the highest of all attainable goods, and the final aim of all our practical activities. These principles, so much a part of our collective ideology, are far from being realized in our political institutions, including our educational system. We oppose the abrogation of these principles with our lives, but we are singularly reluctant to insist on their application. We die for truths we dare not live by.

*The following pages were written before the coming into force of the Education Act, 1944, and the similar Acts for Scotland and Northern Ireland in 1946 and 1947, but this general discussion of principles is not affected by the detailed provisions of these Acts, which are concerned with the reorganization of the system of national education, and not with any fundamental change in its content.

If, therefore, I now proceed to make practical suggestions for the reform of our educational system, they will have no other end than the basic ideals of a libertarian society: the further definition of the organization of that society becoming apparent as we progress from stage to stage; for the final stage of the educational system is not the grammar school or the technical college, or the university, but the society itself.

The first problem to be faced is the practical one of what might be called 'school articulation'. Though rationalized to a considerable extent by the Education Act of 1944, bewildering variety of schools still reflects social prejudices and economic restrictions rather than any natural or reasonable order.

For merely practical or numerical reasons, schools must be divided into separate grades, and the obvious division would be one based on progressive stages in age and maturation. Such a 'natural' division is still recommended by some authorities (e.g. Rudolf Steiner) and it is claimed that the change of the milk teeth at the age of seven, the oncoming of puberty at the age of fourteen, and the cessation of growth at the age of twenty-one, mark the completion of three rhythmical processes of physical development with complementary phases of psychical development. Any divisions in educational methods and organization should take account of these fundamental phases.

The actual growth curve of the child presents a more complicated appearance than this. Fuller details will be found in a Memorandum (Appendix II) which Professor Harris contributed to the Hadow Report on the *Primary School*. The growth curve (for height and weight) shows three 'springing-up' periods followed by three 'filling-out' periods, with divisions at the end of the first, fourth, seventh, tenth, fifteenth and twentieth years.

'Each "springing-up" period has its own peculiar problems, and to a lesser extent each filling-out period has its peculiarities. All these periods are apt to be upset by oscillations of growth, and may be modified by diet, environmental conditions, and disease. The first "springing-up" period presents the dangers of certain nutritional diseases such as rickets, scurvy, infantile diarrhoea and digestive-disturbances. The second "springing-up" period from five to seven years and the first "filling-out" period immediately preceding it are peculiarly associated with the acute infections and fevers of childhood such as whooping-cough, measles, chicken-pox and diphtheria. The second "filling-out" period from seven to eleven or twelve is the period during which the child presents in varying degree the sequelae of these acute infections. The problems presented during this interval concern themselves predominantly with the heritage of the diseases and deficiencies of the preceding years. In particular, dentition, defective vision, enlarged tonsils and adenoids, middle-ear disease, and disease of the lymphatic glands in the chest, neck and abdomen call for urgent attention. This period of consolidation from the age of 7 to that of 11 may be regarded at one and the same time as the opportunity for retrieving past errors of development and for preparing for the heavy demands necessitated by rapid growth during the third "springing-up" period of puberty.

'The type of growth registered by this curve is far from being an adequate representation of the profound changes taking place in any given child, and deals purely with changes in height and weight, Practically every external lineal dimension of the body, with the exception of the head and neck, follows this type of growth. The growth of the skeleton, of the limbs, of the thoracic cage and respiratory organs and of the muscular system as a whole conforms to this *general type of skeletal growth.*

'The growth of the brain, the eyeball and the skull is peculiar. From birth to the age of eighteen months, these organs grow with extreme rapidity; by the age of two years they have reached 60 per cent of their adult size, and by the age of seven almost adult size. This type of growth may be regarded as *neural,* and applies to the brain, spinal cord, eyeball, ear and skull, exclusive of the face.

'The lymphoid tissue of the body, as illustrated by the lymphatic glands, tonsils and thymus, grows rapidly in childhood and continues to grow at a somewhat slower rate until puberty. During adolescence and adult life there is both an absolute and a relative decrease in the amount of lymphoid tissue. In view of the extent to which the lymphatic glands are involved in children at all ages as a result of acute disease and of chronic infections, this third type of lymphoid growth must be of deep significance.

'The fourth type of growth is that presented by the *genital organs.* These organs grow but slowly in infancy, remain almost stationary from two to ten, and grow rapidly in the two years before puberty, during puberty and during adolescence.

'Scammon lays emphasis on the fact that these four types of growth, general or skeletal, nervous, lymphoid and genital are but crude representations of the complexity of the processes involved.

227

'The ductless glands, or glands of the endocrine system, which have provided so many astounding experimental observations and so much feeble theorizing, present a picture which defies analysis. The thyroid gland displays steady growth from birth to maturity, with the tendency to enlargement in relation to puberty and pregnancy as a characteristic. The thymus follows the lymphoid type of growth. The pineal follows the nervous type, and the pituitary follows the thyroid. There is thus no trace of correlation in the growth pattern of the ductless glands.'

I have quoted from this Memorandum at length because it shows how hopeless it would be to base any articulation of the process of education on the physical growth of the child, or any supposedly concomitant psychical development. In the absence of such an organic basis it would seem that we are thrown back on purely arbitrary divisions determined by practical and social considerations, and if, as will presently appear, these divisions correspond to the rhythmical phases of development already mentioned, it is a fortunate coincidence. From an *a priori* point of view there is absolutely no reason why education should be regarded as anything but a unified and continuous process, beginning universally at the age of five or less and not concluding until the child is ready to take its place in the adult society as a productive unit. That is to say, the *terminus* of any child's education would be determined by no other factor save the characteristics of the vocation for which, during the process of education, the child had shown an aptitude or preference.

It might be generally agreed on physical if not on ethical grounds that no vocation whatsoever should be practised by a child under the age of fourteen. This general rule would mark the terminus of primary education.

It might then be generally agreed that certain vocations required an extended education up to the age of 18, gradually becoming more specialized. This rule would mark the terminus of secondary education.

A more restricted number of vocations would require specialized education beyond the age of eighteen, and up to the age of 21 or even 25. This phase would be standardized as tertiary or vocational education (technical colleges and universities).

Such a unified system would still leave for settlement the problems connected with the transition from one stage to another. It seems generally agreed that if a pupil in the primary stage is to pass eventually to the secondary stage, he should be transferred to the secondary school before reaching the normal terminus of the primary stage. Similarly, a pupil in a secondary school who is to proceed to a technical school should begin his technical or professional specialization before reaching the normal terminus of the secondary stage. In other words, the three stages should to some extent overlap. The present system provides for a transfer of the primary pupil at the age of 11+, with a review of those left behind at the age of 13. But as Professor Clarke has pointed out:[10] 'Experience unaffected by "elementary" pre-suppositions and undistorted by special pleading about the "onset" of adolescence would seem to suggest that for the normal child with normal schooling the age of 9 is a more appropriate point for a break than that of 11. By this time he will have gained command of the rudimentary tools of knowledge and his physical system is in a stage of hardening and consolidation which makes him capable of a high degree of sustained energy. Moreover, if the essentials of a worthy common culture, together with at least the beginning of personal and vocational specialization are to be satisfactorily achieved, a six-year period of "senior" schooling is none too long'. Professor Clarke recommends a further break, 'or at least a pause for review', at about the age of 13. 'From 9 to 13 the scheme of studies would have necessarily to remain broadly uniform for all alike, with however increasing watchfulness, taking all the conditions into account, to discover the lines of further education most suitable for each pupil'. At 13 the pupils would be drafted, according to their propensities, to technical or grammar schools.

From the point of view we have reached in this book, we must agree with Professor Clarke that 'the break at 11 + seems to be obviously calculated to make the worst of both worlds, junior and senior'. But from the same point of view we cannot accept the necessity of a break at 9, if that break implies a change in the type of *school*. What seems to be demanded by nature no less than by reason is an undivided primary stage passing insensibly into a secondary stage, at which stage differentiation according to propensity begins to be reflected in school organization. The point at which the stem should begin to divide is the point at which innate dispositions can be clearly defined. This we identify with the onset of puberty, and there, at 13+ or 14, should come 'a pause for review'. The admission, by Professor Clarke and others, of the necessity of 'a pause for review' at this important

[10] *Education and Social Change* (London, 1940, p. 51).

stage of life, seems to mark it as the natural line of division between one phase of education and another. In comparison the stages of 9 or 11+ are purely arbitrary.

In any case, our considerations here must follow such a 'natural' line, and not be diverted by irrelevant questions of an architectural or economic kind. If the primary and secondary schools as they exist do not permit a natural articulation of the educational system, they must be rebuilt.

Similarly, the school leaving age for non-professional and non-technical pupils must not be determined by the economic needs of the family or the productive needs of society, but by the natural laws of physical and mental maturation.

The 'system' of education envisaged in the suggestions of method which follow implies, therefore, four phases of a continuous process:

    I. Infant: up to the age of 7.

    II. Primary: 7–14.

    III. Secondary: 14–18.

    IV. Vocational: 18–21 or more.

The only serious objection that is likely to be raised to this articulation of the organic process of education is that it limits the secondary phase to a short period of four years. But our whole contention will be that the seven years of the primary phase will lay such foundations of sense and sensibility that the existing criteria by which progress in mental development is measured at the secondary stage will no longer be applicable. It will be essentially a phase of differentiation. Some pupils will reach an optimum of differentiation at the age of 15 and be absorbed directly into the productive units of society; others would be further differentiated at the age of 16 and be then absorbed into society; and so on, the final differentiation taking place at the age of 18, when the residue commit themselves to a further phase of vocational education.[11]

9. SUBJECTS AND CLASSES

If the natural facts of the child's growth offer little or no basis for any decisive breaks in the vertical organization of the school system,

[11] The need for a more organic articulation of a system of education is recognized by the appearance, within the present national system, of local deviations known as 'multilateral', 'comprehensive', 'common' and 'bilateral' schools, the purpose of which is to combine under one roof, and under one direction, two or more of the elements (i.e., grammar, technical, and modern) which the Act seeks to separate.

equally there is no justification in nature or reason for any rigid departmentalism in its horizontal organization. That is to say, the accepted convention of education as a collection of competing 'subjects', taught by separate specialists in separate classrooms, is so grotesque that it can represent no principle of organization but merely the chaotic accumulation of an undirected historical process. I am not aware that any attempt is ever made to justify it as a system: it is usually accepted as an inevitable compromise. But actually, as Caldwell Cook once bitterly observed, 'nothing surely could be conceived in educational method so inadequate, so pitiably piecemeal as *the classroom system of teaching subjects.*'

There is, of course, an obvious sense in which one subject merges into another, making any division between them arbitrary. How can history be explained without geography, or geography without political economy, or political economy without natural philosophy, natural philosophy without mathematics and geometry? But this is not quite the basis of our objection to the classroom system. If the purpose of education is to impart information in easily assimilable form, then the classification of this information under separate groups and headings is a reasonable method of procedure. It is a task which must be undertaken if only for the purposes of use and reference. But if, as I have often stressed, the purpose of education is integration—the preparation of the individual child for his place in society not only vocationally but spiritually and mentally, then it is not information he needs so much as wisdom, poise, self-realization, zest—qualities which can only come from a unified training of the senses for the activity of living. In other words, the school must be a microcosm of the world, and schooling an activity which grows insensibly into living. The process is one of *initiation*, and though it may be objected that the word *play* is not a good enough word for such a solemn rite (and therefore we substitute the word *art*) nevertheless Caldwell Cook's description of this method is the best that could be quoted. 'Play, as I mean it,' he says—*art* as I mean it, 'goes far deeper than study; it passes beyond reasoning, and, lighting up the chambers of the imagination, quickens the body of thought, and proves all things in action. The study of books, however thorough, may yet remain but superficial, in the sense that there may be no feeling of reality behind it. "No impression without expression" is a hoary maxim, but even today learning is often *knowing* without much care for *feeling*, and mostly none at all for *doing*. Learning may re-

231

main detached, as a garment, unidentified with self. But by Play (Art) I mean the *doing* anything one *knows* with one's heart in it. The final appreciation in life and in study is to put oneself into the thing studied and to live there *active.*'[12]

Though written a quarter of a century ago, these words still await substantial fulfilment in our educational system, and this book has no other purpose but to repeat, with a new emphasis, the eloquent plea of this pioneer.

Caldwell Cook was a schoolmaster, and his theory arose out of his practice. The present writer has not the same advantage, and in practical methods of teaching he must defer to practitioners like Cook and Dewey, Ferrière and Piaget, Homer Lane and A. S. Neill —defer and refer. Their experiments are full of false starts and temporary failures, but they represent the only road upon which there has been a positive advance in the direction indicated by our more theoretical and *a priori* consideration. It is my belief that their failure to convince the world at large—a world which demands quantitative results, in marks and certificates, rather than a lighting up of the chambers of the imagination, is due to their neglect of *a priori* considerations. These pioneers have proceeded experimentally and intuitively; some of them, Dewey in particular, have erected a pragmatic philosophy on the results of their experience; but they have not sought the basis of a method, as Rousseau did, in the objective facts of human nature. If the art of education is to foster growth, we must first discover the laws of growth; and these are the laws of harmonious progression, of balanced relationships, of achieved pattern.

The indications of method which follows are suggested by these general principles. I believe that many of them have been proved practicable by the pioneers I have mentioned, and are being proved and improved every day by 'progressive' schools in every part of the world. But though presented in a somewhat dogmatic form, I fully recognize that they stand or fall, not by their theoretical coherence, but by the extent to which they succeed in establishing the wholeness and well-being of the community.

10. THE INFANT SCHOOL

The guiding principle of the infant school[13] should be undifferen-

[12] *The Play Way* (London, 1917), pp. 16–17.

[13] The same principle should begin to guide us already in the Nursery School, and generally does in so far as these nursery schools are established on enlightened

tiated play activity. The parent, or the teacher *in loco parentis*, observes the whole activity of the child. There is no division into classes except for convenience of supervision, and no division into subjects, except to provide variety and maintain interest.

At this stage the undifferentiated function of the teacher is already recognized. The official *Handbook*, for example, states bluntly that 'there is no place for the specialist art teacher in the Infant School', and suggests that 'the teacher's part is one of sympathetic encouragement rather than direct teaching'. Indeed, in stating the principles underlying the curriculum, the *Handbook* recommends, in a general way, most of the methods of teaching appropriate to an aesthetic education—for example, 'rhythmical training'. 'Such training commonly takes the form of bodily movement to music, and this is the natural way of introducing it . . . a good preparation for the various forms of dancing . . . through singing or chanting, with or without the accompaniment of music, or playing in percussion bands, the sense of rhythm will be strengthened.' After referring to the the importance of giving the children first-hand experience, and of encouraging them to translate their experience into language, the *Handbook* recommends other forms of expression. 'The children should have full opportunity to express their ideas and experiences through drawing and painting, through handwork, and through miming and other dramatic action. In these ways they can often express themselves more completely and find an outlet for the natural impulse to create something. Through music, dancing, the saying of poetry, or through practising various kinds of decoration and design, they can find vent for feelings of which they are hardly conscious themselves, but which are none the less real.'[14]

In this way the *Handbook* recognizes all the four forms of aesthetic activity of which we suggest that pre-adolescent education should consist. It fails, however, to relate these forms of activity to an integral conception of the functions of the maturing mind, and introduces some undue emphasis on those 'skills' (speaking, reading, writing and numbering) which are purely instrumental, and best acquired incidentally, in the course of originating activities. What the *Handbook* admits in the case of arithmetical calculation, that 'skill of this kind

lines. See Phoebe E. Cusden, *The English Nursery School* (London, 1938), for a detailed account of the enlightened methods now being followed in Great Britain.

[14] 1938 edition, pp. 91–2.

may be cultivated at the expense of the very thing that makes it worth while', is a general principle which holds good for all other forms of skill.

It is not within my competence to speak of actual methods of teaching, but it is obvious to any interested observer that everything, in this system as in others, depends on the nature of the relationship established between teacher and child. A good teacher can do much to redeem a bad system; a good system will be damned by a bad teacher. In this connection I cannot do better than quote the words of Marion Richardson, a great teacher who has made the teaching of art her special sphere:

'The artist discovers in the world around him (that is to say, in his raw material) relationships, order, harmony—just as the musician finds these things in the world of sound. This cannot be done by the conscious, scheming, planning mind. Art is not an effort of will but a gift of grace—to the child at least, the simplest and most natural thing in the world. Whenever people are sincere and free, art can spring up. . . . That is why the child's happiness or otherwise in the presence of the teacher is all important, and why the school of today is, or should be, the perfect setting for children's art. It is not too much to say that unless relationship amounting to love exists between teachers and children, children's art, as it is now understood, is impossible.

'How does this love translate itself into action? For work such as is seen here is not "free expression" as generally understood, which may be merely unconscious imitation, but a disciplined activity in which the teacher's own imaginative gifts play a very important part.

'There is no single answer to this question, the one which everyone asks. Each teacher finds his individual solution to the problem and those who can spare time to visit the schools will be struck by the variety and flexibility of modern methods. One essential is established. The good art teacher will always take his children and their drawings completely seriously. Perhaps this counts for more than anything else and is the means of inducing the children to demand the very best of themselves. They need, especially as they approach self-consciousness, the authority of a grown-up to convince them that their own art is worth while and to warn them against accepting the ready-made and secondhand which surrounds them on every side. This seriousness comes easily to the teacher as he realizes that his work with children may in the end provide for him a key to the understanding of art in its widest sense.'[15]

These words were written with the teaching of drawing and design in mind, but they apply equally well to the other three branches of education—music and dancing, drama and craft. For whatever aspect of education we take, and at whatever stage, the *rapport* established between the teacher and the child is the all-important factor. The growth of confidence, the elimination of fear, the binding force of love and tenderness—these are the elements with which a teacher must work. Not only the assimilation of knowledge, the acceptance of discipline, and the realization of the self depend on the right development of these psychological processes, but what is even more important, the integration of the individual with the group or society to which he belongs. The converging researches of several schools of modern psychology are making this fact clear. As one of the most profound of these psychologists has said, 'the abiding problem and central task of mankind has been maturation and the harmonization of his love-needs with his appetite-needs and the attaining of maximal satisfaction in both. It is a task which must be pursued simultaneously in the developing, adapting *individual*, and in the ever-changing *community*, culture and tradition. Repression can be practised by the individual, and, "in a complementary manner", suppression by the group. This negative solution, however, is impermanent and precarious in both cases, and what is really required is a double process of adjustment, i.e. the individual to society and society to the need of the individual. One might even define the ideal culture and social organization as that which gives the maximum socially permissible freedom of expression and development to human nature (the minimum restriction and coercion) along with the most effective substitution and suppressions *where this is inevitable*.'[16] First the parent,

[15] 'Note' published in connection with an Exhibition of Children's Drawings in the County Hall, London, 12th July, 1938. For further details of the same teacher's methods and ideals, see an article on 'Children's Drawings and Designs' in the *Annual Report* of the London County Council Vol. V (1936), pp. 3–6. Many other articles could be quoted in which teachers give accounts of their methods in teaching art which are of general value. The following have struck me as particularly useful: 'The Creative Mind in Education', by K. Doubleday (*New Era*, Vol. 17, No. 2, February, 1936); 'A Summary of Art Teaching', by E. H. Styhr (*Athene*, Vol. 1, No. 1, 1939); 'The Value of Art teaching in School', by Michael Feild (*Athene*, Vol. 1, No. 5, 1941); 'Art Teaching in Preparatory Schools', by Michael Carr (*ibid.*); and the series of articles on 'Studios at Work' in the same journal.

[16] Ian D. Suttie, *Origins of Love and Hate*, pp. 125–6.

and then the teacher, is the agent of this process of adjustment, and love is the tempering flame. What we teach—if we teach successfully —are but so many substitutes and compensations for the forces which originally fused the child and mother in organic unity. We succeed in so far as we create a wider organic unity whose bonds are no less real and instinctive.

11. THE PRIMARY SCHOOL

These remarks have led us far beyond our immediate subject, which was the principles of teaching in the infant school. But the same principles are valid for the primary school, and indeed for all stages of education (the institution of tutor at Oxford or Cambridge is an admission of the principle that good teaching depends on the establishment of a relationship of mutual confidence between teacher and pupil). And here it must be stated that *a continuity of method* is essential to the system of education I am advocating, and that a continuity of method implies an unbroken hierarchy of teachers. To anyone who approaches the present educational system with an open mind, one of its most striking anomalies is what can only be described as a 'caste' division of the teaching staff. The gulf between the uncertificated and certificated, the elementary and secondary teacher, is deep and unbridgable. And its consequence is a disastrous schism in educational evenness of development if between the primary and secondary stages of education the child passes, not merely from the environment and amenities of one type of building to those of another, but also from teachers with one standard of training to teachers with quite a different standard. The abruptness in the change in the pattern of behaviour, and the difficulty of the required readjustment, must create unnecessary and harmful psychological reactions in the child— reactions which are reflected in invidious social distinctions and divisions. It is probably the child's first introduction to those elements of snobbery and exclusiveness which are to be the basis of his imperfect citizenship.

There are teachers who by disposition and capability are more suited to the teaching of infants, and others who are more suited to the teaching of adolescent youths, and the hierarchy should be differentiated to provide for a variety of vocational aptitudes. But it should be one hierarchy, related to one system of training, and providing within its limits the possibilities of promotion and development which should be characteristic of all democratic institutions. Even from the point of view of the children, it should be possible for a teacher to carry on through the various stages into which the educational system is divided. It is conceivable, that is to say, that the same teacher (of drawing, for example) would move with his or her class through all the stages of primary or secondary education. We want a conception of the teacher as group guardian, rather than as a dispenser of information about a particular subject; and the integrity of the group is probably a far more powerful educational factor than a progressive grading of teachers. This is a subject which must be discussed at greater length on another occasion, the only point which it is necessary to stress now being the continuity of the process of education. We must desist from the common habit of regarding the elementary and the secondary school child as two different animals, for whom different cages and different keepers must be provided. It is the same child, from birth to maturity, and its education should be a single undivided process.

It follows, therefore, that the fourfold method which began in the infant school should continue in the primary school. The child is maturing, absorbing new experiences, new sensations; his eidetic world is beginning to crystallize around concepts, growing in number and utility. His education must keep pace with these organic processes, increasing in range of materials, complexity of movements, scope of discipline. But the moulds do not break: they expand. Drawing, as we have seen, expands and develops naturally; its richness of content compensating for the blankness of conceptual knowledge. Verbal and musical expression increase in the same ratio of complexity, with unity or integration as the continuing aim. But the greatest development will be in dramatic expression and in constructive activities. The 'project', taking in wider and wider aspects of experience and relevant knowledge, will dominate whole weeks and even terms of the school programme.[17] It will begin to embrace history and geography, economics and sociology. It will call upon the constructive abilities of the children, and these in their turn will involve increasingly difficult problems in measurement and calculation,

---

[17] For practical suggestions for this method of teaching, see *Projects for the Junior School*, by R. K. and M. I. R. Polkinghorne and Beatrice Clements (London, 1941). I am aware that serious criticisms have been made of the project method of teaching, but they seem to be based on a formless type of project. As we remarked in discussion the play method, everything will depend on the shape or pattern given to such activities, and on the nature of the interest evoked.

in surveying and building, in physics and chemistry. Incidentally, the school itself, as a theatre, arena or background, becomes an element in education; and its care, its heating and lighting and ventilation, and above all the cultivation of the school garden or farm, provide the opportunity for teaching those elements of science and natural history which are appropriate to the primary stage.

This, it will be said (now as always) is fine in theory, but is it practicable? Its practicability has been proved by many experiments, which only fail to reach the ideal because they are partial, and unco-ordinated by any general theory of human development or social organization. But as evidence of the practicability of this kind of education I would prefer to quote, not any of those experiments in progressive education carried out under artificial conditions of selection and environment (whose value is not questioned), but a description of a one-room school inspected by an American educationalist. It comes from an unpublished study carried out by Florence Tilton under the direction of Dr. Leo Brueckner and Dr. Wesley Peik, of the University of Minnesota:[18]

'I am thinking now of a lovely little white schoolhouse set on a hill surrounded by a wood in Hennepin County, Minnesota. The instant I entered that doorway I knew I had entered a school where art was a part of daily living. The formal set arrangement of desks, so common in one-room schools, was banished. Instead, desks were grouped. All along one wall was a large frieze with figures painted in what was very evidently child work. The colour scheme was restful; the teacher was dressed in good taste; well-arranged books added colour to the room; there was an air of happy comradeship as the children made covers for a history booklet. The teacher began plying me with art questions. She was concerned about how appreciation was to be developed without pictures. She expressed the opinion I had long held that arranging a display of child work was something children should do themselves because they could learn thus how to balance sizes and shapes of paper in a given space. She was aware of the opportunities for teaching colour in their daily life. When questioned about how she organized her work, she said she taught one subject such as lettering to the entire group, but varied the work, giving simple applications to the small children, more difficult ones to the

---

[18] *A Field Study of Art Teaching in One-Room Rural Schools of Hennepin County, Minnesota*, 1936. Quoted in the Fortieth Yearbook of the National Society for the Study of Education (1941), pp. 587–8.

fourth, fifth and sixth grades, and the most difficult applications to the seventh and eighth grade children.

'In this school art is an integral part of living. Children are taught to be conscious of beauty in all things. They endeavour to make their environment beautiful. They accept appraisals of school work for its artistic merit as naturally as they accept appraisals of speech. They believe that all things, to be effective, must be beautiful. They learn how to create beauty through daily choices in dress, the arrangement of their books and playthings. They enjoy colour, simplicity of line, dark and light pattern and forms of many kinds through association with beauty. These they find in nature, in pictures, in sculpture, in architecture, and in manufactured articles. They experiment with modelling in clay, in wood, and in plaster. They weave simple patterns on looms they themselves have made. They express their imaginative ideas both as individuals and as groups. Through working together to accomplish common objectives of beauty for their school, they learn how to subordinate selfish desires to group objectives. They are developing hobbies and interests. When a study is made of a foreign country, they learn what types of costumes are worn, what are the typical colour arrangements, how the forms of artistic expression of a people are influenced by their geographical background, the facts of their history, their emotional characteristics, and their economic status. In all social studies the contributions of art are studied. The teacher thinks of art as one of the areas of learning, developed through four approaches; namely, the appreciative, the creative, the informational, and the technical. There is a well-adjusted balance between work designed to foster self-expression and opportunities to make art choices. All work is child-originated. There is no dictation, no tracing, very little copy-work; but much more imagination, much work for the development of mental images. The power to do things skilfully is kept growing throughout the school period. The children are taught those knowledges and abilities judged by experts to be most socially useful. This teaching is by the rural teacher, not by a special art teacher.'

Such, it seems to me, is the realizable pattern of education, in London or New York as well as in Hennepin County, Minnesota. That single-handed rural teacher, working in a one-room school, is the model for all teachers, elementary or secondary, even university. I will add nothing to the force and Platonic truth of this one example.

THE NATURAL FORM OF EDUCATION
12. THE SECONDARY SCHOOL

The secondary school is but a continuation of the primary school and of its methods of teaching. A wider field is covered, and it is worked with an increasing degree of correlation. But a new factor begins to make itself felt. Society, which has always been the framework within which the pattern of the school is designed, but which has presented itself as a vast human aggregate, now demands a closer attention. It is then seen to be a highly complex organism, consisting of a multitude of interlocked but differentiated cells, each performing a separate if interdependent function. The child is approaching the age at which he must decide into which of these cells he will fit himself when he leaves school. The rest of his education should then prepare him for his place in society, and make his transition from school to society natural and easy.

It may be said in the first place that the majority of these cells will assimilate their human plasm without any special preparation beyond that provided by a general education such as that we have outlined. Education should have given the individual that wisdom which comes from insight and sensibility, and it is the cell itself—that is to say, the activity of craft—which moulds the basic wisdom to its particular needs. Such is the justification of a continuous education, uniform throughout the primary and secondary stages. It endows the child with the *general* capabilities which fit it for society.

But other cells in the social organism have a more specialized function. They need, not merely wisdom, but an acquired *technique*, depending upon intensive learning in a particular subject. That is to say, before the individual can be assimilated to the exceptional cell which he has selected, he must be prepared by a further period of education. The question which educationalists have to determine, for each particular function, is the age at which this special training should begin.

In most cases it should obviously begin before the end of the secondary stage, especially if we extend the secondary stage to the age of 18. A pupil who proposes to pass to a school of medicine at the age of 18 should have specialized in certain branches of science before reaching that age. But rightly conceived, secondary education is not inconsistent with such preliminary specialization. 'Technical instruction must be considered not as the rival of a liberal education but as a specialization of it, which, whether it comes earlier or later in the scholar's life, ought to be, as far as possible, made a means of mental stimulus and cultivation, and will be most successfully used by those whose intellectual capacity has been already disciplined by the best methods of literary or scientific training.' This sentence comes from 1895 *Report of the Royal Commission on Secondary Education* (p. 285), and is quoted with strong approval in the Spens Report (pp. 58–61). A further passage from this early *Report* (pp. 135–6) is even nearer to our own point of view:

'Plato in the *Protagoras* draws a distinction between the man who learns the arts of the grammarian, the musician, or the trainer as a craftsman, for trade, and the man who learns them as a private person or freeman, for education or culture. But even culture is not an end in itself: it makes the private person of more value to society and to the State. All secondary schools, then, in so far as they qualify men for doing something in life, partake more or less in the character of institutes that educate craftsmen. Every profession, even that of winning scholarships, is a craft, and all crafts are arts. But if Secondary Education be so conceived, it is evident that under it technical instruction is comprehended. The two are not indeed identical but they differ as genus and species, or as general term and particular name, not as genus and genus or as opposed terms. No definition of technical instruction is possible that does not bring it under the head of Secondary Education, nor can Secondary Education be so defined as absolutely to exclude from it the idea of technical instruction.'

The problem is therefore one which is covered by the phrase 'flexibility of curriculum'. The course of education, primary and secondary, should provide for the gradual revelation of individual aptitude, and this requires a curriculum flexible enough to meet the emergent needs of each child. At present the curriculum tends to be a more or less rigid frame on which the unformed mind is forcibly stretched: it demands conformity to a single pattern of behaviour, a predetermined standard of 'intelligence'. We should rather look upon the curriculum as a more or less infinite scale of *interests* upon which the individual mind of the growing child can play its melody, according to its impulse to self-expression, self-realization. It is only when that melody can be distinctly heard that we can determine, with any justice, the future of the child and the special training or technical instruction which that future will require.

Incidentally, this metaphor may be continued in illustration of the general philosophy of education expressed in this book. The melody (the inspiration) provides the theme upon which the composer builds up, according to the laws of music, his fugue, sonata, or symphony (the composition). The individual temperament of the child, revealed by its self-expressive activities, is the basis which must be found before the teacher can build up, by his laws of education, a harmonious society of free citizens.

The Spens Report recommended the establishing of a new type of higher school of technical character, wholly distinct from, yet equal in status to, the traditional academic Grammar (Secondary) School. The age of recruitment for these schools should be 11+, and the method of recruitment the same as for the 'Grammar' schools. From 11+ to 13+ the curriculum in these proposed schools should be broadly of the same character as the curriculum in other types of secondary schools. From 13+ and onwards (i.e. to the age of 16+) 'the curriculum should be designed to provide a liberal education with science and its applications as the core and inspiration'.

The Report admits that such a curriculum does not differ greatly, if at all, from that of the science side of the normal Grammar School; the difference would lie in the interpretation to be given to the subjects in a school with a technical emphasis, and would imply 'a first-hand knowledge of the application of science both to the processes of manufacture and to the operation of the devices and plant manufactured'. The Education Act of 1944 recommends the establishment of Technical Secondary Schools with a bias towards the skills required by local or regional industries. Such schools are virtually the same as the Grammar Schools, with a scientific or technological instead of a literary bias.

This tendency to segregate 'grammar' from 'science', academic instruction from technical instruction, conflicts with the general psychological considerations put forward in the earlier part of this book. We discussed in Chapter II the wholly disastrous effects of a logical bias in education—a bias which the segregation of the 'grammar' school (the very name chosen for it is significant) is designed to perpetuate. The Education Act proposes to correct this bias by the creation of an independent system of 'technical' education. The result will be to create one more unbalanced social type, with the new possibility of organized conflict with the grammatical type. For there is no reason to suppose that a technically educated individual will confine his mental processes to questions connected with the engineering and building industries. Indeed, we can already see, especially in America, the emergence of a specifically technical intelligence which claims to think in its own way on all aspects of existence. Essentially materialistic, it extends its almost wholly unconscious philosophy into the spheres of economics and history, and sees no reason why its Weltanschauung should not be made the basis of politics.[19] There are exceptions, but fundamentally the technocrat denies that 'values' (aesthetic, ethical or religious) are a constituent of the objective world. Such people will not admit that these subjective attitudes represent facts of nature which must be included in a strictly scientific system. But science itself must in the end recognize that any division between the facts of mental life and the facts of physics (the assumed basis of the division between grammatical and technical education) is arbitrary. The process no less than the aim of education should be as integral as these natural facts.

It is for this very fundamental reason that any division of secondary education is to be deplored. The true solution is to provide, within an integral scheme of full secondary education, sufficient flexibility in the curriculum so that not only the specific needs of the individual are met, but also the specific needs of society, as represented by the industries prevailing in the region in which a particular school is situated. That is to say, to take extremes, there would not be much point in making provision for a subject like engineering drawing in a secondary school in a rural district; nor for teaching the elements of agriculture in London or New York. The curriculum of the secondary school should always have what might be called regional relevance.

But to return to the main contention of this chapter: the curriculum should not be conceived as a collection of subjects. At the secondary stage as at the primary stage, it should be a field of creative activities, with instruction as incidental or instrumental to the aim of these activities. If at the infant stage these activities may be described as *play* activities, and at the primary stage as *projects*, then, at the secondary stage they merge into constructive *works*.[20]

[19] Their position has been defined by Wolfgang Koehler in *The Place of Value in a World of Facts*.

[20] This suggestion has the very welcome support of Professor J. A. Lauwerys in an article contributed to *The New Era* (Vol. XXII, pp. 200–6, 1941): 'It might be wise to return to the principles of the Fisher Act, the chief objection to which was that it was born before its time. Would it be possible to lead adolescents *gradually* into gainful occupation, e.g., could they do 2 hours remunerative work at 13, 4 hours at 16, 6 hours at 18? The advantages of such a scheme are even more obvious than its difficulties, which are chiefly organizational in kind, and thus fairly easily overcome. Control would remain with the Educational Author-

At the conclusion of their book[21] which reviews some of the earlier experiments with this tendency carried out in America, John and Evelyn Dewey make some general observations which coming from practical educationalists of their reputation, may serve to reinforce the more theoretical considerations put forward here:

'Mere activity, if not directed toward some end, may result in developing muscular strength, but it can have very little effect on the mental development of the pupils. . . . The children must have activities which have some educative content, that is, which reproduce the conditions of real life. This is true whether they are studying about things that happened hundreds of years ago or whether they are doing problems in arithmetic or learning to plane a board. The historical facts which are presented must be true, and whether the pupils are writing a play based on them or are building a viking boat, the details of the work as well as the main idea must conform to the known facts. When a pupil learns by doing he is reliving both mentally and physically some experience which has proved important to the human race; he goes through the same mental processes as those who originally did these things. Because he has done them he knows the value of the result, that is, the fact. A statement, even of facts, does not reveal the value of the fact, or the sense of its truth—of the

ity, not with the employer, and any money earned should be spent for the benefit of the children.' Professor Lauwerys adds a footnote with a surprising but very apposite quotation from Karl Marx (*Capital*, Vol. I, Part 4, Chap. XIII): 'If the element of exploitation could be removed from it, child labour ought to become an essential part of education. "As we can learn in detail from a study of the life work of Robert Owen, the germs of the education of the future are to be found in the factory system. This will be an education which, in the case of every child over a certain age, will combine productive labour with instruction and physical culture, not only as a means for increasing social production, but as the only way of producing fully developed human beings".' It will be remembered that Bernard Shaw came to a similar conclusion in 'Parents and Children' (the Preface to *Misalliance*): 'There is every reason why a child should not be allowed to work for commercial profit or for the support of its parents at the expense of its own future; but there is no reason whatever why a child should not do some work for its own sake and that of the community if it can be shown that both it and the community will be the better for it. Productive work for children has the advantage that its discipline is the discipline of impersonal necessity. The eagerness of children in our industrial districts to escape from school to the factory is not caused by lighter tasks or shorter hours in the factory, nor altogether by the temptation of wages, nor even by the desire for novelty, but by the dignity of adult work, the exchange of the humiliating liability to personal assault from the lawless schoolmaster, from which the grownups are free, for the stern but entirely dignified pressure of necessity to which all flesh is subject.'

[21] *Schools of To-morrow* (1915), chapter XI.

fact that it is a fact. Where children are fed only on book knowledge, one "fact" is as good as another; they have no standards of judgment or belief. . . . Thus we see that it is a mistake to suppose that practical activities have only or even mainly a utilitarian value in the schoolroom. They are necessary if the pupil is to understand the facts which the teacher wishes him to learn; if his knowledge is to be real, not verbal; if his education is to furnish standards of judgment and comparison.'

Here, as elsewhere, Dewey is thinking chiefly of the inculcation of moral values—the moral value, for example, of working for the sake of what is being done rather than for the sake of rewards. Whilst not seeking to deny the moral value of these methods of education, the psychological truth is that their primary value is aesthetic. Knowledge is presented to the child through the senses, in acts, and it is in the degree that these acts acquire a significant pattern that they are memorized and utilized in the biological process of mental growth. The point is that the perceptions involved are the same for beauty and for understanding. We come back to the theory of Professor R. M. Ogden, quoted in an earlier chapter (see page 60). The internal structure of behaviour, in so far as that behaviour is effective, skilful, and therefore retained, is essentially aesthetic. Or, in his words: 'the adequacy of any response in which the dominant feature is not the discernment of an objective but a course of action, is determined by the aesthetic feeling which marks it. Furthermore, this feeling does not attach to any arbitrary action resulting from repetition, but only to such rhythms of response as constitute what we have metaphorically called "a melody".[22] And that is the whole justification of education by means of practical activities—that thereby the responses which are appropriate are *felt* as such, and the essential rhythm of life is unconsciously and inevitably acquired.[23]

In the end, therefore, we are unable to suggest a theoretical justification for any essential difference in the educational methods of primary and secondary schools. There is an increase in scope and complexity, but growth and the assimilation of experience are continuous, and the methods of fostering them do not change. But as the

---

[22] *Psychology and Education*, pp. 144–5.

[23] I regard it as one of the curiosities of philosophy that when John Dewey, late in life, came to the subject of aesthetics (*Art as Experience*, London, 1934), he nowhere, in the course of an imposing treatise, established a connection between aesthetics and education.

transition from school to society occurs—and it may occur at ages ranging from 15 to 25—so the school experience becomes the social experience. There should be no essential break—the process of learning should lead imperceptibly into the process of earning. At one moment the individual is a schoolboy, at another a productive member of the community; but it should not be easy to determine the moment of transformation.

This is not to deny that the stages of the pupil's progress should be marked by some form of test or diagnosis, and to this problem we shall devote a separate section (see pages 249–54). But first we must anticipate the criticism that the integral curriculum, which might be approved for the primary stage of education by a majority of educationalists, cannot be said to make adequate provision for the necessary contents of a secondary curriculum. The plea for specialization or departmentalization at this stage is insistent and almost unanimous.

To this criticism we can reply generally that any system of education which is truly integral is also universal. That is to say, no subject is alien to it, since it takes the whole of knowledge as its proper sphere, and each developing individual absorbs with ease those aspects of knowledge which are most relevant to his mental disposition.

Let us for a moment envisage the ideal organization of a secondary school based on our integral pattern. Under the headmaster there would be four senior masters, or masters of method, in charge of the four main activities—drama, design, music, craft.

Under these four masters of method would be a number of assistant-masters, for whom the old-fashioned name of preceptor might be revived, for their function would be to take their place at the head of a class or group of pupils, and initiate them into particular aspects of the group activities. Under the master of design would come a preceptor in drawing; under the craft master, preceptors in mathematics and science; under the music master, preceptors in eurhythmics and dancing; and under the master of drama, preceptors in history, literature and elocution.

Such an organization of the curriculum provides for all the existing subjects, with the possible exceptions of geography, foreign languages, certain aspects of science, and scripture.

But these gaps are more apparent than real. Geography is certainly best taught by the project method: by the construction of scale models showing typical physical features, by the actual surveying of a tract of country, and in conjunction with historical projects and pageants. It falls naturally into the integral pattern. So do those various aspects of science which might seem to risk being neglected if subordinated to a craft-master. Biological subjects inevitably find a place in the kind of projects we have in mind; for it should be realized that the whole school must itself be conceived as a project—as, indeed, the final integration of all the activities taking place within its confines. And the school, as we shall see later, is to be conceived as an organic community, to every practicable extent self-supporting. The ideal school will have its gardens and its farm, and it is in connection with these productive activities that a large part of natural history will be taught.

Foreign languages are admittedly not an organic function of the school community, except in circumstances which it would be too idealistic to envisage. I refer to the suggestion that, as a practical measure for promoting international understanding, a widely developed scheme of exchange pupils should be instituted between the various countries of Europe. Then the learning of langugages would become a practical necessity for purposes of inter-communication, and the presence in each school of children speaking a foreign but native language would be the most effective way of teaching that language to the other children, always remembering the basic method of group activities to which we are committed. Otherwise languages would play a subordinate part under the master of drama: they would be taught in connection with the dramatic historical projects relating to a particular country.

This admittedly reduces languages, especially dead languages, to a relatively subordinate position in the secondary school curriculum, but in the present writer's view it is difficult to see any justification for the considerable position they now occupy. It is a problem with many aspects, some of them difficult and most of them extremely controversial. Probably the only aspect upon which there would be general agreement is the purely literary one. If our object is to gain an *intimate* knowledge of the aesthetic values of a foreign literature, and perhaps to some extent an equally intimate knowledge of the refinements of thought expressed in that language, then it can only be done by learning the language, and learning it thoroughly. It is also possible that the exact use of one's own language depends to some extent on an adequate knowledge of the roots which that language has in the languages of the past.[24] But in any case, knowledge of that kind cannot be acquired at the secondary stage of education, except by exceptionally gifted individuals: it is, in fact, a subject for specialization, and as such is one of the divagations which may begin at the secondary stage, but which can only be completed at the technical or university stage.

But the teaching of languages, dead or living, is not usually defended on aesthetic grounds. It may be promoted on commercial or utilitarian grounds, in which case it is again a subject for specialization. But more usually it is recommended as a 'formal training' or 'mental discipline'. It is this aspect of the teaching of languages, especially dead ones, which has led to such extensive and often embittered controversy.

Obviously we cannot deal with this problem at any length in the present study. The reader must be referred to the memorandum by Dr. H. Hamley which is given as Appendix V to the Spens Report and to the extensive literature there detailed. But we may take it as established by experimental psychology that there is no evidence at all to show that training in one subject produces a general ability which can then be transferred to, i.e. applied to, a totally different subject. All abilities are individual and specific, conditioned by the data in each particular case. This does not altogether dispose of the value of formal training, as Dr. Hamley makes clear, but it does mean that the claim of any particular subject must be examined on its merits, and in accordance with its verifiable results. The value of a language as a disciplinary or formal training must be compared with the value of logic or mathematics; there is evidence to suggest that the more conscious mental science of logic or mathematics may have a far more direct result than the indirect method of mental training involved in learning Latin or Greek. For our part we would also say that the merits of each subject must be judged in relation to the psychological disposition of the individual pupil. There are certain types which are mentally impervious to languages or mathematics. Further, the subjects must be considered in relation to the age of the pupil: what might have value at the age of fifteen might have disastrous effects at the age of ten. What, in effect, we return to, are the psychological considerations put forward in our third chapter. The

[24] This neglected aspect of the problem was discussed by T. S. Eliot in his Presidential Address to the Classical Association, 1942. (Printed by the Oxford University Press.)

fallacy underlying all the pleas for formal training or mental discipline is merely one more aspect of that pedagogical ideal, which, as Jaensch pointed out, 'rests on the untrue assumption that productive logical thinking proceeds *because* of the laws of logic and also has its psychological basis in them, since it proceeds in *accordance* with them, and its results agree with them'. The truth is that productive logical thinking, *even in the most exact sciences*, 'is far more closely related to the type of mind of the artist and the child than the ideal of the logician would lead us to suppose'. The whole tenor of our researches shows that there is neither creative art nor productive thought without an identity of concept and percept, a *fusion*, as Jaensch calls it, of the person with the object, 'so that every lifeless system of signs ranged in between is felt to be a hindrance'. Jaensch then adds a sentence which clinches the matter for us here: '*The grammatical structures of language are such a system of signs, unless concrete imagination infuses life into them.*' Our contention therefore is, that unless language can be related to the concrete imaginative projects under which we subsume the whole educative process, languages should not play any considerable part in primary education. That they can be related to such projects is our belief, but the relation is then one of concrete poetic values, and never of formal training.

This leaves us with scripture as the only subject in the curriculum not accounted for in our integral pattern. In so far as scripture means religious education, it will be dealt with in the concluding chapter. In our meaning of the word, religion is the final degree of integration, the stage at which the individual consciousness becomes completely integrated with the collective consciousness of the group. But if by scripture is meant the literary and historical contents of the Bible, then it falls naturally into the same pattern as the general categories of literature and history. Its relative position in these categories will be determined by our sense of human values.

13. THE NATURE OF INTELLIGENCE

We come finally to the problems associated with mental and scholastic tests. If the reader has already seized the implications of our general argument, he will now realize that for us these are essentially unnecessary problems. But let us consider them in some detail. There are really three distinct problems.

(*a*) Education is a national investment. It is a trust vested in a department of state, and the state (or more concretely, its citizens) must be satisfied that the system is productive—that it is making better and more useful citizens than ever existed before a system of compulsory education was introduced, or would exist if the system were now abolished. What is required is a general test of social relevance or utility.

(b) Education is a progressive hierarchy. Certain callings need a more prolonged intensive course of education, and therefore tests must be devised to grade pupils so that the best go highest. This is a *vertical* differentiation.

(c) Education is a preparation for life. It must prepare the youth of the nation for a suitable vocation, and therefore tests must be devised which sort the human material into appropriate callings. This might be described as a *horizontal* differentiation.

These three distinct problems are usually confused. They are confused by the scholastic procedure itself, for there are not three types of test, but only one. Whether by examination tests, or by what are sometimes called 'diagnostic periods', the aim of all such procedures is to measure a quantity called 'intelligence'.

In his brilliant analysis of this term, Professor Spearman has shown that in modern usage it simply does not possess any definite meaning at all. Once it was dissociated from the classical concept of intellect, which has been defined as the power to conceive universal ideas, intelligence was abandoned, in Spearman's forceful phrase, to the psychology of the streets. It is not part of our present purpose to discuss how any exact meaning or scientific dignity is to be restored to the concept: it is sufficient to point out that it has no agreed meaning, and that the multitude of tests designed to measure it can therefore present no results of universal validity.

Examinations and tests are defended, however, as a rough and ready measure of 'utilizable skill', and in so far as this is a social and pragmatic aim, it may be accepted as the only practicable method of classifying individual abilities. But the value of the test will be almost in inverse ratio to the presence of anything we could describe as 'intellect'. That is to say, test of the speed and accuracy of a shorthand typist, or the skill of a motor-driver, can be accurate enough for all practical purposes. But once we pass to tests of ability of a more general kind, we must be resigned to the inevitable presence of wide degrees of unreliability and inconsistency. The researches of the International Examinations Inquiry Committee have shown that the greatest difficulty exists in assessing precisely those subjects like the English essay or history in which a high quantity of 'mental energy' is involved; and even 'the general idea that mathematics and science subjects can be marked with greater precision than humanistic subjects is apparently not founded on a sound basis'.[25]

It may be confidently asserted, that so long as our criterion of intelligence remains so vague, no method of testing intelligence, whether by examinations, boards of examiners, individual examiners or psychological tests, can be devised. The conclusion of the Inquiry Committee was that 'it is as impracticable to recommend an *a priori* cure for the defects of the present examination system as it would be to recommend an *a priori* cure for a disease. It is only by careful and systematic experiment that methods of examination can be devised not liable to the distressing uncertainties of the present system'.[26] But experiments, however careful and systematic, will be futile so long as we remain undecided about the ultimate purpose of examinations. As methods or instruments of precision examinations can conceivably be made both consistent and valid; but what is the substance to be measured, and how much of it will qualify for efficiency?

It is significant that the Examinations Inquiry Committee set a high value on the English Essay examination, though the marking of it is proved to be very inconsistent. Their reason for this preference is that they feel that the essay examination covers elements of craftsmanship and quality which are not tested by the examinations in other subjects. The Committee even tried the experiment of having a series of essays marked solely by 'impression', thus admitting the possible validity of a purely subjective criterion. (The results showed that marking by impression tended to be lower than marking by details, and at the same time to involve greater discrepancies, due entirely to the different standards of the various examiners.) What is implied by this admission is, of course, the significance of certain aesthetic elements, and it is a pathetic confession that only in the English essay, and then only by chance, did this element receive any recognition in, for example, the Special Place Examination by means

[25] *The Marks of Examiners* (London, 1936), p. 243. Cf. also the following publications of this Committee: *An Examination of Examinations*, by Sir Philip Hartog and Dr. E. C. Rhodes (1935); *Essays on Examinations*, by Sir Michael Sadler, A. Abbott, P. B. Ballard, Sir Cyril Burt, C. Delisle Burns, Sir Philip Hartog, C. Spearman and S. D. Stirk (1936).

[26] *Op. cit.*, p. xviii.

of which the Local Education Authorities used to determine which pupils from elementary schools were to have the benefit of secondary education.

It will not be found that the aesthetic element, or sensibility in general, plays much part in psychological or pedagogical definitions of intelligence. Rousseau's distinction between the *raison sensitive* and the *raison intellectuelle* has been fogotten, and all theories of intelligence are based on the supposition that reason is always intellectual. The fact that the child is not capable of intellectual reasoning makes no difference to educational theorists, who proceed on the assumption that he must be made capable of it. Even Spearman, who formulates as one of his three principles of cognition, that 'when two or more items (percepts or ideas) are given, a person may perceive them to be *in various ways* related', does not seem to realize that the qualifying phrase which I have italicized admits an entirely new principle. It does not suffice to admit, as he does, that the relations may be arranged either randomly, or systematically. It does not suffice to dignify a systematic arrangement with such names as 'form', 'pattern', 'configuration' and the like. The significant fact to be recognized is that an arrangement is perceived to have a pattern or necessary configuration only by the exercise of that faculty we call sensibility or insight. Nor do we need to rely on the much questioned postulates of 'faculty' or even of 'Gestalt' psychology to justify the reality of this mental process: it is the foundation of all discriminative behaviour, and of all learning.[27]

Now it may be argued that if we test *what has been learned* by the child, we thereby test *the ability to learn* and *the quality of what is learned*, that is to say, *the ability to evaluate what has been learned*. But this is obviously an error. 'What has been learned' is the sum of what has been retained by the memory, and no one has yet ventured, I think, openly to identify intelligence with memory—though

[27] The process has been beautifully defined by R. M. Ogden: 'Beginning with a vague whole, the articulateness of which is somehow felt to be greater than the articulateness of its surroundings, the response of the organism will focus upon any outstanding or prepotent feature of this whole. This outstanding feature, or focus, is an accent of excitement; it may be inherent in the whole, or it may be arbitrarily introduced by external conditions that permit one direction of response and deny all others. In either case, the organism learns to respond to a direction within the apprehended whole. In other words, the organism perceives a gradient in the particularized situation-response. The quality and nature of this gradient, once it is perceived, is transferable, and its prepotent aspect will thereafter dominate any future situation in which this same gradient is given.' *Psychology and Education*, p. 260.

many tests of intelligence seem to be based on such an assumption. (Incidentally, memory itself is not independent of aesthetic factors. I was once present at a demonstration of phenomenal memory, at which the subject showed himself capable of reproducing the recurring decimals of π to any extent; after proceeding for several hundred 'places', he could take up the series at any given point ahead. On being questioned, the subject confessed that he remembered the figures by means of a 'rhythm'. The close relation of musical and mathematical ability is significant from this point of view.)

The quality of what is learned, and the ability to recognize degrees in quality of what is learned, cannot be tested by quantitative means. In recognition of this fact various tests have from time to time been devised for testing aesthetic response, or artistic appreciation, the best-known being the Meyer-Seashore Test. My own experience in using these tests at Edinburgh University was not very encouraging. Whilst in a small number of cases uniformly positive reactions were obtained, the results in the majority of cases were of a baffling inconsistency, and the element of 'chance', due to guessing, was obviously considerable. All such tests depend on the presentation of contrasts: the choice is between a balanced pattern and an unbalanced pattern; between coherent and incoherent designs; between harmonizing and discordant colours; and so on. It is possible to make the distinctions by rational processes of thought, with no subjective feelings involved; moreover, the distinctions have a certain generic character which is soon 'learnt'. This latter objection applies particularly to those tests which assume a conventional standard of good and bad taste. The subject knows, or soon perceives, that 'simplicity', for example, is regarded by the tester as a virtue, and the simpler form (as between two teapots, for example) is chosen on this basis of *a priori* knowledge, and not on the basis of any direct feeling or sensibility.[28]

[28] It is a sufficient commentary on the whole conception of intelligence tests that the Goodenough Test, which uses children's drawings as a basis, and which produces results which can be closely correlated to the standard intelligence tests (Stanford-Binet, Army Alpha, Trabue Completion, etc.) explicitly excludes the aesthetic element. 'Artistic standards have been entirely disregarded', is the emphatic declaration of the deviser of the tests. An intelligent drawing is not necessarily a beautiful drawing; nor a beautiful drawing necessarily intelligent. It is a paradoxical assumption, but it is characteristic of the attitude adopted in all intelligence tests. The paralogism seems to be the following: science can only deal with measurable quantities; science is identical with intelligence; therefore intelligence is limited to measurable quantities.

A general objection to examinations and tests of all kinds is that they require a special localized effort and intensive preparation for this effort which is an uncertain test of general ability. A man who can win the 100 yards sprint cannot necessarily walk twenty miles a day. It is for this reason that various educationalists have proposed a 'diagnostic period', either as a supplement or alternative to the test and examination. Over a certain period the pupil's general activities are observed and unobtrusively assessed. No doubt such a method is subject to the same human fallibility as any form of examination, for it involves an examiner's subjective judgment, but it is certain that the results are more valid. But even this method will be useless unless it takes sensibility no less than intellect into account.

If the diagnostic period is used in conjunction with the methods of teaching advocated in this chapter, it cannot fail to take sensibility into account. There is only one way of judging an individual's part in a group activity, and that is by observing its co-operative integrity. It either fits or does not fit into the pattern. The awkward child, the insensitive child, the undisciplined child—in short, what in the psychology of the streets is called the unintelligent child—will stick out like a broken spoke in a wheel.

We should examine for unfitness, not for fitness; for regrouping, not for promotion. The group activities of the school should be organized to correspond with the multiform activities which make up the variety of our social life. In some 'cell' of this macrocosm the most Ismaelitish, the most delinquent child will find his comrades, and together they will discover their pattern, their *esprit de corps*, and with this discovery, the possibility of growth and achievement.

Returning to the three aspects of the problem which we outlined at the beginning of this section, our general survey should now enable us to see, firstly, that the social value of education cannot be measured by the 'intelligence' of individual units; education is a preparation for communal activities, and the best education, from the point of view of society, is the one which leaves the individual as a freely co-operating unit in a group. If we are to keep the social relevance of education in mind, co-operation, and not competition, must be the guiding principle.

The progressive differentiation of individuals is a natural result of growth or maturation. If it is necessary to separate the sheep from the goats at any stage, then this should be done on a vocational basis.

THE NATURAL FORM OF EDUCATION

As children are gradually absorbed into society, from the age of 15 or 16 onwards, the residue go on to higher stages of education. But children should not be evicted at any stage, on the assumption that their education is completed, and that society must find a place for them, if only in the ranks of the unemployed. The leaving-age must be determined by the chosen vocation, not the vocation by the age. If this principle is accepted, then the distinction between a vertical and a horizontal differentiation of ability is seen to disappear. All differentiation is horizontal, according to diagnosed interest and aptitude: and the vertical is merely the stem which continues to rise after the lateral shoots have branched off.

For the wider concept—which includes sensibility and insight as well as intellect and reasoning, the perception of a pattern in relational cognition, and not merely the awareness of the discrete relations, the *raison sensitive* as well as the *raison intellectuelle*—for this concept we need a better word than 'intelligence'. *Virtue* might do, if, like Aristotle, we were to make a clear distinction between intellectual and moral virtue. But *Wisdom*, which originally implied the knowledge of the way or shape of things, and not so much judgment in matters relating to life and conduct (the original root is still preserved in words like 'likewise', 'otherwise', 'nowise') would seem to be the right word, if we could free it from its association with the Old Men of Gotham and other wiseacres. But nothing is more difficult than the task of renovating a debased word. It is in any case a task that must be left to time; here we can do no more than define the quality. 'Who is as the wise man? and who knoweth the interpretation of a thing? A man's wisdom maketh his face to shine.' The Bible associates wisdom with understanding, with what we call enlightenment, and enlightenment is the true aim of education. Its organic aspect is maturity. 'Ripeness is all'—the attainment of perfect maturation in all mental and physical faculties: such is the final scope of our teaching.

THE NATURAL FORM OF EDUCATION

APPENDIX E

THE PLACE OF ART IN A UNIVERSITY

(From an Inaugural Lecture given by the Author at the University of Edinburgh on 15th October, 1931)

THE place of art in the teaching of our universities has not a very long history. Its beginning may be dated precisely to the foundation of the Slade Professorships at Oxford, Cambridge, and London in 1869. Ruskin was the first Slade Professor at Oxford, and in his inaugural lecture he laid down ideals which, if they had been followed, would have done much to redeem the subject from the neglect it has always suffered in England. The initiative and encouragement given to art studies by the foundation of the Slade professorships has never developed into any considerable school of art scholarship, nor is it easy to trace any cultural influence on the general standard of English education. The Slade professorships have declined rather than increased in influence, and the average graduate of an English university remains abjectly ignorant of one of the primary divisions of human culture. The reason for this stultification of a noble purpose is, I think, obvious: the place of art in a university education will depend on the recognition given to it in the normal curriculum, and unless it is recognized that the history of art is as valid in the completeness of a general culture as the history of literature, or of politics, or of science, it is hopeless to expect the student, besieged on every side by necessary studies, to take up another study, equally complex and time-exacting, in a spirit of love and sacrifice. But now, sixty years after the foundation of the Slade professorships, there is some change of heart. At Oxford a Diploma in the History of Art has recently been instituted, and the Slade professorship has thus been given real sanction, though not a sanction equivalent to an honours school. At Cambridge the subject is being fostered by a very vital school of architecture, and London has taken an even bolder step. Through the generosity of Mr. Courtauld, a separate faculty for the history of art has been founded, with an institute and all the equipment essential for the prosecution of research. This is comparable with the normal equipment of a German or American university, and really marks the beginning of a new era in English art historical studies.

Whether art is a subject which can be properly submitted to such intensive scientific study is often questioned, and before giving you my own opinion, I would like to ask you to glance at the position in Germany, where the study of art in the universities is more highly organized by far than anywhere else. In Germany, with one exception, every university in the country (and there are thirty of them) has a separate faculty for the history of art. The first faculty was founded not long before the Slade professorships, so we might say that whilst the whole of this immense development has been taking place in Germany, England has made no progress at all. At each German university there is an average of about twenty undergraduates studying for a Doctorate in the History of Art, and as many as sixty or seventy taking the subject as a component in an ordinary degree. At large universities like Berlin, Leipzig, and Munich, the staff in the Department of Art alone numbers as many as eight or ten professors and lecturers.

This emphasis on the study of art in German universities may come as a surprise to some of you, but I do not think that we need necessarily regard the development as in every way admirable. There are two aspects of the question. There is the effect which such teaching has on the practical life of the student, and there is the effect which this intensive scholarship has on the proper function of art in education. These are two very different problems, and I will, if you allow me, enlarge on them a little.

The first involves a very general and very acrimonious subject—the extent to which a university education should be directly vocational. In the inaugural lecture I have already mentioned, Ruskin laid it down that 'the object of instruction (at a university) is not primarily attainment, but discipline: and that a youth is sent to our universities not to be apprenticed to a trade, nor even always to be advanced in a profession, but always to be made a gentleman and a scholar'. That seems to us now a very romantic ideal, having very little relevance to the social organization of the modern state. Several years before Ruskin delivered his lecture, no less a person than Cardinal Newman had admitted that the 'gentleman' was an 'antiquated variety of human nature and remnant of feudalism'. And it was Cardinal Newman who, on the same occasion, laid down the true ideal of a university education. 'Our desideratum,' he said, 'is not the manners and habits of gentlemen—these can be and are acquired in various other ways, by good society, by foreign travel, by the innate grace and dignity of the Catholic mind but the force, the steadiness, the comprehensiveness and the versatility of intellect, the command over our own powers, the instinctive just estimate of things as they pass before us, which sometimes indeed is a natural gift, but commonly is not gained without much effort and the exercise of years.'

This then, according to Newman, is the true ideal of a university education—the cultivation of the intellect as such, and its object is nothing more nor less than intellectual excellence. Such excellence, he held, is not only best for the individual himself, but enables him to discharge his duties in society. This great cleric ends by describing the practical aim of a university course as that of training good members of society. 'Its art is the art of social life, and its end is fitness for the world.' When thus expressed, Newman's ideal does not seem to differ much from the romantic ideal of Ruskin. If it is not romantic, it is at least quietist, passive. I do not wish to suggest for a moment that we should abandon the ideal of a liberal education, the ideal of an education that refuses to be servile to a narrow functional conception of life. But we must recognize that the character of life has changed since Newman's time. It has become much more urgent, more practical. Youth to-day is faced, not by the complacent world of Victorian prosperity, but by a world of bankrupt states, a world distraught by political revolutions, by economic uncertainty, by the disappearance of ethical authority. The world still needs its scholars, pursuing learning for its own sake; but how can the world guarantee its scholarship if the very foundations of society are insecure? The university must fit its students for society, says Newman. But what if there is no society for which they can be made fit? We have been forced to the conclusion that what the world needs to-day is not the disinterested scholar so much as the man of action; the mind trained to fulfil a particular function; equipment for a definite vocation.

That has been the inevitable tendency of university education during the last few decades. It is a tendency which has been resisted, and will continue to be resisted, by those who are passionately devoted to the liberal ideal in education. I do not for a moment suggest that such resistance is mistaken, or in vain. I share the same ideal. But I venture to think that our strategy is mistaken. I think we must frankly recognize the priority of vocational training in our universities; but having recognized it, I think we must then do all in our power to counteract its evil influence upon character and disposition.

There is no need for me to emphasize those evil effects. The single-track-mind is one of the most pitiable objects in the modern scene. It is not merely that a limited outlook distorts the general vision, and makes the specialist a blind and ineffective member of society; but the limitation of mental interests embodies its own fate. The mind, maintained within blank walls, turns sour and stale; it ferments in its own unhappiness, turns to self-disgust and insipidity. Deprived so long of sensuous enjoyment, it awakes to find itself no longer capable of new interest and keen appreciations. But for the light thrown through its one narrow porthole, it is a dark insensitive chaos. You will all be familiar with the lament which one of the most famous of the past students of this university, Charles Darwin, made in his Autobiography; it is often referred to, but let me quote to you once more Darwin's own impressive words: 'Up to the age of thirty, or beyond it, poetry of many kinds, such as the works of Milton, Gray, Byron, Wordsworth, Coleridge and Shelley, gave me great pleasure, and even as a schoolboy I took immense delight in Shakespeare, especially in the historical plays. I have also said that formerly pictures gave me considerable, and music very great, delight. But now for many years I cannot endure to read a line of poetry: I have tried lately to read Shakespeare, and found it so intolerably dull that it nauseated me. I have also lost my taste for pictures and music.'

Then in the next paragraph of his Autobiography, he attempts to explain 'his curious and lamentable loss of the higher aesthetic taste':

'My mind seems to have become a kind of machine for grinding general laws out of large collections of facts, but why this should have caused the atrophy of that part of the brain alone, on which the higher states depend, I cannot conceive. A man with a mind more highly organized or better constituted than mine, would not, I suppose, have thus suffered; and if I had to live my life again, I would have made a rule to read some poetry and listen to some music at least once every week; for perhaps the parts of my brain now atrophied would thus have been kept active through use.

The loss of these tastes is a loss of happiness, and may possibly be injurious to the intellect, and more probably to the moral character, by enfeebling the emotional part of our nature.'

The drift of what I am saying will now become evident. It is implicit in this lament of Darwin's. To counteract the evils of vocational training and of intellectual specialization in general, it is necessary to cultivate, not merely the intellect as a disinterested activity, but in a far greater degree the sensibility.

I would be grateful if you would accept, for the present, this distinction between intellect and sensibility. It is, I think, a distinction commonly used. It might be expressed in another way as the distinction between knowledge and taste, but I do not, in either formulation, want to imply a separation of the mind and the senses. A healthy intellect or reason is every bit as dependent on the exercise of the senses as is a healthy taste. I mean rather the distinction, made use of by Professor Whitehead, between intellectual analysis and intuitional apprehension. You may remember that towards the end of *Science and the Modern World* Professor Whitehead considers this very problem of the balance of general and specialist education, and comes to the conclusion, that the make-weight which balances the thoroughness of specialist intellectual training should be of a kind radically different from purely intellectual analytical knowledge. He can see no solution of the problem in a combination of the gross specialized values of the mere practical man, and the thin specialized values of the mere scholar. 'Both types have missed something; and if you add together the two sets of values, you do not obtain the missing elements.' What Professor Whitehead asks for is a faculty for the direct perception of the concrete achievement of a thing in its actuality, and he finds this faculty in aesthetic apprehension; but merely passive apprehension is not enough. We must foster creative initiative. Impulse as well as sensitiveness is essential, for 'sensitiveness without impulse spells decadence, and impulse without sensitiveness spells brutality'. And the *habit* of art he defines as the habit of enjoying vivid values.

There, I think, we have an ideal which we can apply in a university through its Chair of Fine Art, but before I develop this theme, let us return to the German scene again.

The high place which the study of the history and theory of art has taken in the German educational system has led to an intensive organization and definition of the subject. It has led to a division into three well-defined methods of approach, which we might describe as the psycho-philosophical, the morphological, and the historical. The first method makes its approach from the subjective activity involved in the appreciation of art, and is *aesthetics* properly speaking. The second method of approach is purely objective and is concerned with the work of art itself—the problems of technique, the anatomy of form, and so forth. This is the general science of art, and in German has a distinct label—allgemeine Kunstwissenschaft. The third method is the historical method itself.

Aesthetics, although it has a limited experimental field, must to a large extent rely on introspection as a method of study, but it can be further distinguished as either descriptive or formal; that is to say, it attempts either to explain the psychological process of the mental activity involved in art, or to formulate logical definitions and laws of an *a priori* kind. Naturally, in the country of Kant, formal aesthetics does not lack its modern adepts, but the general tendency has been more realistic. The science of art (Kunstwissenshaft) is again divided into the general and the particular —the general science studying the common forms of art irrespective of their material manifestations, the particular science taking one particular art, and analysing it with special reference to its peculiar technical attributes. This more specialized branch of the science of art has been greatly fostered within the last fifty years by the development of institutions like museums and art galleries, all of which have taken on the character of research stations for this progressive science. Then, altogether apart from aesthetics and the science of art, you have the general history of art, which is, of course, studied in great detail, period by period. And there are many periods in the history of art. You will now see how it is possible to employ as many as ten professors and lecturers in the Art Department of a single German university.

No one is more grateful than I am for the mass of erudition and research which has been lavished on this particular subject, the history and theory of art, by German scholars. They are supreme in this field, and all our studies are dependent on their work. As pure scholarship one can have no possible reserves in praising all this activity. A new field of exact scholarship and intellectual analysis has been created, but from the point of view which I am now considering, that is to say, the place of art in a liberal education, it appears that we have merely added another vocational course to the number already competing for the interest of the student. A new professional career has been created—that of the *Kunstforscher*, the art expert and museum curator. It is a profession which must in the nature of things be limited in numbers, and even if we add to it the numerous class of art teachers, we still find the profession utterly unable to absorb the large numbers of students who every year pass out from the German universities with degrees in the history and theory of art. That seems to reduce university education to an absurdity; specialism expanding beyond the real needs of the community, and so passing into the world a graduate who has neither the social adaptability of the graduate with a general education, nor the utility of an economically justified professional scientist.

I do not think there is any prospect of a similar over-production in this kingdom. The new Courtauld Institute in London should suffice to produce year by year as many professional art experts as the country can absorb, and it is to be hoped that eventually some liaison will be created between the Institute and any other universities where a Chair of Fine Art exists, so that any student who wishes to adopt the profession of the art expert may pass on to the Courtauld Institute through a recognized channel. That is to say, the Courtauld Institute should act as a clearing-house for the advanced art scholarship of the whole kingdom.

If that is generally accepted, it leaves our course much clearer. It leaves us free, in fact, to cultivate in this University, and through this Chair of Fine Art, the very element which Professor Whitehead demands as a corrective to the evils of specialized education. Let us return to his words:

'What is wanted is an appreciation of the infinite variety of vivid values achieved by an organism in its proper environment. When you understand all about the sun and all about the atmosphere and all about the rotation of the earth, you may still miss the radiance of the sunset. There is no substitute for the direct perception of the concrete achievement of a thing in its actuality. We want concrete fact, with a high light thrown on what is relevant to its preciousness.

'*What I mean is art* (*and aesthetic education*). It is, however, art in such a general sense of the term that I hardly like to call it by that name. Art is a special example. What we want is to draw out habits of aesthetic apprehension. . . . The habit of art is the habit of enjoying vivid values.'

It might seem that the qualification made in the latter part of this quotation detracts a little from the application I now want to make. Art, says Professor Whitehead, is a special case of what he means. He wishes to encourage a much wider use of the aesthetic faculties: to make the aesthetic apprehension which we exercise normally in the case of a work of art the general habit in our apprehension of reality.

Let us admit that qualification. But how else, I would like to ask, can you develop and train the habits of aesthetic apprehension but by means of the appreciation of poetry, music and the Fine Arts. And the appreciation of the Fine Arts is incomparably the most objective, the most practical and infinitely the most valuable of these methods. This may be shown in two ways: there is first the significance of the Fine Arts in the general culture of a nation; and there is a special quality in the Fine Arts which not only explains this significance, but enables us to apprehend it in a peculiarly direct manner. From the first point of view, we may say that only in the Fine Arts do you get an adequate and definite embodiment of what might be called public virtue. Again let me remind you of Ruskin, whose name I must continue to invoke: 'The art of any country (he said) is the *exponent of its social and political virtues.*' 'With mathematical precision (he said in another lecture), subject to no error or exception, the art of a nation, so far as it exists, is an exponent of its ethical state.' Now, however we define virtue (and it is possible that our conception of it would be very different from Ruskin's). I think this statement of his, which is almost the central dogma of his whole teaching, is true in the precise degree claimed by Ruskin.

There must, of course, be some definite reason for the superiority of the Fine Arts in this respect—for their superiority as an index to culture. I think that reason may be found in the fact that in the Fine Arts you have spiritual sensibility in direct contact with matter. All other arts are expressed immaterially; music and poetry are created within the mind, and though they must be communicated through a medium, that medium is only a bridge of symbols between the mind of the poet and his reader, between the musician and the listener. But in the Fine Arts the concept and the medium are one; there is no symbolic language; you cannot conceive your work of art except in terms of a solid and tangible material. That compels the artist to a definiteness which is not merely a definiteness of meaning, but also of matter. The values are all objective; necessarily so. The work of art is indeed what Professor Whitehead desires: the concrete achievement of a thing in its actuality, with a high light thrown on what is relevant to its preciousness.

The Fine Arts, therefore, represent culture at its most coherent stage; and a work of art embodies the values of that culture with the greatest possible vividness. The enjoyment of art is thus the most valuable way in which we can draw out habits of aesthetic apprehension.

That, it might be said, is all very well as an ideal, but we are practical educationalists. The deed of foundation of the Watson Gordon Chair of Fine Art lays down that 'the Professor occupying the said Chair for the time being shall be bound to give a course of instruction to students by lectures during the University session on the history and theory of the Fine Arts including Painting, Sculpture and Architecture and other branches of Art therewith connected'. He must give such a course of instruction; and at the end of his course he must examine his students to show how they have benefited by his instruction. He must produce what are known as practical results. Can this be done by teaching the enjoyment of art? Enjoyment—is that the object of a university course?

I believe that it is, and I would like to suggest to you briefly a way in which I think a course of instruction in the Fine Arts can give enjoyment and at the same time fulfil the practical requirements of a university curriculum.

The dominant motive of the course is to be the development of sensitiveness in relation to works of art. But a course must have coherence and direction. These could be provided either by a theory of art, or by the history of art. I think it is better to take the history of art as the underlying structure, because any theory of art must be largely personal, and though all teaching is inevitably personal, and indeed *should* be personal if it is to be inspiring, yet in this matter of aesthetic apprehension it is above all necessary to create in the student a form of activity rather than to inspire an attitude. That form of activity is itself very personal, because, as I have already indicated, it is intuitional in nature and not rational or analytical. I believe that the mind, free from all intellectual prejudices, needs no other preparation for the appreciation of art. I would therefore begin a course on the History and Theory of Fine Arts by asking my students to free their minds from every conception they may have formed of the nature of art. I would then, with the help of the wealth of illustration which is now available to a lecturer in the history of art, begin to show them examples of what art has been, beginning at the beginning, with the art of primitive man, and coming down the ages, through Asia, Egypt, Greece, and all the lands of the earth wherever a culture has arisen, until we meet the art of our own time. On the way we should note how the art of each period enlightens the culture of each period; we should note the formation of styles and the cultivation of mannerisms;

we should trace the influences which spread from age to age and from land to land. We should, too, with reference to individual works of art, note how the artist has exploited his material; the beauty of each technique and the function of each work of art in relation to the life of the people, their economy and their religion. All these things we should note in a possessive spirit, because a work of art, like a living organism, cannot live in isolation from its environment, and the works of art which we are to enjoy must all be living works of art. In such an atmosphere, which is not an atmosphere of analysis and research, but, I insist, an atmosphere of creative initiative, the aesthetic sensitiveness is awakened, the habit of enjoyment is formed.

But the process must not end there. Art, just because it demands an intuitional apprehension, cannot be dismissed as history. It is a present activity, and I should regard my duties as but half done if, in teaching the enjoyment of the art of the past, I did not also lead my students to enjoy the art of the present day. Art to-day is a testimony to our culture, a witness to its positive qualities and to its limitations, just as the arts of the past are to the cultures of the past. We cannot fully participate in modern consciousness unless we can learn to appreciate the significant art of our own day. Just because people have not learned in their youth the habit of enjoyment, they tend to approach contemporary art with closed minds. They submit it to intellectual analysis when what it demands is intuitive sympathy. They have no pureness of heart and therefore they cannot share the artist's vision. That is a sad state, and it seems to me that it is one of the primary functions of a university like this, which sends out its thousands of young men and women to be the teachers and preceptors of their fellow-men, to send them out with open eyes and active sensibilities, so that what they see they may enjoy. For what they *seeing* enjoy (*id quod visum placet*), that is art. It is one of the qualities of enjoyment that it is infectious, and everywhere we should try to diffuse an awareness of the vividness of this habit of enjoyment which is art. It will then be possible to lift our heads above the ugliness which, like the rising flood after a storm, has followed in the wake of the Industrial Revolution. These islands were once beautiful, and full of pleasures; the ugliness that then descended on them was a disease of the spirit. It was due, more than to anything else, to the divorce which philosophy and even religion made between spirit and matter. Art, even more than any other faculty, is stultified by such a divorce, for art is literally, as I have already insisted, spirit informing matter. If you no longer believe that spirituality can form an organic unity with matter, then you can no longer believe in art. It is surely a significant fact that the decay of art in Europe has proceeded step by step with the growth of dualistic doctrines in theology, philosophy and science. I am not suggesting that the way to recover our art, to bring beauty back to life, is to readopt a medieval religion, or a pre-Cartesian philosophy, and to ignore the logic of science altogether. All forms of sentimental medievalism are false to the spirit of the age. But if only as a scientist in my subject, I am compelled to observe that in historical times art has been a force in a nation's life precisely when a certain form of religion has been a force; and it does not suffice to say merely *some* form of religion, because many forms of religion are inimical to art. The religion must be one which postulates the organic unity of spirit and matter. Only in such a way can religion inspire that respect for the senses, that cultivation of joy, that communal delight in colour, music and harmonious movement, which is the mark of all great artistic epochs. Hitherto we have been too much accustomed to regard art as dependent on religion, but from the point of view I am expressing, it is possible to regard religion as equally dependent on art, and I am sure that on a broad survey of the history of religion and art, this mutual dependency could be established. In the end, art should so dominate our lives that we might say: there are no longer works of art, but art only. For art is then the way of life.

Chapter Eight

THE AESTHETIC BASIS OF DISCIPLINE AND MORALITY

One of the most important tasks of culture is to submit man to the influence of form, even in his merely physical life: to make this life aesthetic by introducing the rule of beauty wherever possible; because only from the aesthetic, and not from the physical state, can morality develop.—Schiller

1. THE TRADITIONAL CONCEPT: (A) MILITARY

The word 'discipline' had originally the same meaning as education; it was the instruction imparted to his disciples by a master of any subject. When education ceased to be personal and became general or systematic, the subjects taught (literature, rhetoric, arithmetic, geometry, astronomy, music, etc.) were known as the liberal disciples or arts. We have already seen how these disciplines gradually degenerated into artificial studies far removed from the organic realities of human life: and at the same time that education lost its biological function—the inculcation of a natural and harmonic control of body and soul—it assumed, as a compensation for its failure, the right of arbitrary compulsion. Society was no longer, either ideally or practically, based on natural law: its codes, stabilized from habits and conventions, became an end in themselves, and the business of education was to subdue the untamed spirits, the 'unruliness' of young children, and to train them to conformity. Education became, in Tolstoy's deeply perceptive phrase, the 'tendency to a moral despotism raised to a principle', the expression of the 'tendency of one man to make another just like himself'.[1] So far has the concept of discipline degenerated that its present meaning could not be stated more concisely than in the words of the Concise Oxford Dictionary:

[1] *Pedagogical Articles*, p. 110. Quoted by McCallister, *The Growth of Freedom in Education*, p. 5.

265

'order maintained among schoolboys, soldiers, prisoners, etc.' The discipline which was the receptive relationship of pupil to master has become identifiable with the barking of a sergeant-major on the barrack-square.

It may be that in fact the application of a discipline of force is no longer typical of our schools. It is said that the rule of the birch and the rod is over, but if so it is a revolution which has never been ostentatiously celebrated by schoolboys. But even if the cruder conceptions of discipline no longer prevail in civilized communities, there is still considerable confusion between what we might call the educational, the moral and the military implications of the term.

From a military point of view, discipline has been defined as 'enforced obedience to external authority', and is made dependent on a system of punishments and rewards. Discipline 'always involves control exercised from outside', and is for that reason distinct from *morale*. 'Whenever there is discipline, the punishment is inflicted by some authority outside the man or the group that is submitted to discipline. Whenever the authority comes from inside the man himself, we get *morale* rather than discipline, though the distinction is less sharp in fact than it may be made in theory.'[2]

Morale, as defined by the same authority, is 'obedience to authority under external circumstances which impose great strain, the source of authority being within the man, or the group, that is obedient'.[3]

When Professor Bartlett comes to consider the methods by which discipline may be enforced, he distinguishes the direct method (the use of punishment) and the indirect method (the establishment of some form of unquestioned prestige), but expressly excludes the method of education because this leads to morale and not to discipline. Discipline, in the military sense, has become completely dissociated from its original educative sense.

We need not review the various methods of enforcing discipline, but it is possible, on the basis of experience, to question its efficacy. There is no doubt that parades, drill, badges, insignia of rank, uniforms, are all instrumental in forming what we may call a system of conditioned reflexes. Individuals and groups can be trained to respond to such stimuli as constantly and accurately as Pavlov's dogs. But such stimuli are only valid so long as the artificial conditions of environment under which they are normally given persist. Should

[2] F. C. Bartlett: *Psychology and the Soldier* (Cambridge, 1927), pp. 118-9.
[3] *Ibid*, p. 152.

those conditions be suddenly and violently disturbed, the carefully built-up automatic responses will fail.

Military psychologists are aware of the necessity of constantly re-conditioning the nervous mechanism of their human material. Professor Bartlett, for example, says: 'A period of rest, interposed between periods of fighting, is peculiarly demoralizing. Then is the time for rigorous and vigorous parade drill. This is useful, not in order to produce more efficiency in certain muscular exercises, and certainly not because these regular and stereotyped evolutions are directly applicable to the fighting which will follow, but because of its suggestive influence in maintaining an attitude of controlled, alert, trained respect for authority without which no body of men will for long hold together and be an effective unit as a fighting group.'[4]

I believe that this reasoning is decisively contradicted by the experience of modern warfare, and my own observations in the last war led me to be extremely critical of the military theory of discipline.[5] But let us return to Pavlov's dogs for a decisive demonstration of the breakdown of discipline under external circumstances which impose great strain—the breakdown, as Pavlov would say, of the cortical mechanism under the influence of complex external actions.

On September 23, 1924, the city of Leningrad, in which Pavlov's laboratories were situated, was inundated by remarkable floods. 'Water unexpectedly penetrated into the building where the feeding-room of the dogs was situated. The laboratory attendants hastened to the rescue of the animals. Each dog was of account and was highly prized because of the important work in which it has been used for several years.

'The animals were kept in low cells with doors situated close to the floor. When the attendants arrived in the feeding-room, the cells were already at least two-thirds full of water. The water had forced the dogs to the ceiling of the cells; they were floundering about or swimming in the water but there was no way out.

'It was by no means easy to rescue the animals. They stubbornly resisted, and no wonder, for it was necessary first of all to submerge the dog's head under water in order to drag the dog out through the opening at the level of the floor. The majority of the animals had great difficulty in enduring these experiences.

[4] *Psychology and the Soldier*, p. 132.
[5] Cf. *Annals of Innocence and Experience* (London, 1940), Chap. 5.

'All the dogs were saved, but as a result of the flood some quite exceptional consequences were observed in several animals. Pavlov's collaborators, A. Speransky and Rikman, noted that after the flood conditioned reflexes to ordinary stimuli, such as light or sounds, had disappeared. *It was as if they had never been formed.* Only very gradually by means of numerous repetitions was it possible to restore these reflexes.'[6]

In other words, the discipline of the dogs, built up by rigorous and vigorous drill, had completely disintegrated, and in exactly the same way I have seen the discipline of men, built up by vigorous and rigorous parade drill, disintegrate under the strain imposed by a bombardment or a hail of machine-gun bullets. We fell back, in those circumstances, on such *morale* as we had been able to establish in spite of the inhuman conditions imposed by the system of military discipline: we fell back on what Professor Bartlett calls 'persuasive leadership', and which he thinks more appropriate to civil than to military life. Why he should think so is a little difficult to understand, for he admits that '*morale* produces a steadier, more persistent, less fluctuating type of conduct than discipline' and 'may continue when all external sources of command have broken down'.[7] What he does not seem to admit is that the 'obedience to external authority', enforced by leaders who maintain their position by virtue of the established social prestige attaching to their office (the *institutional* type), or by virtue of their personal capacity to impress and dominate their followers (the *dominant* type), is wholly inconsistent, in the same individuals and groups, with the relationship of mutual trust and understanding characteristic of the *morale* established by a leader of the persuasive type.

(B) MORAL

This is not the place to pursue our theme in its military and political implications: we shall find the truth driven home with sufficient force in the moral and pedagogical spheres. The possibility that an identical basis may be found for ethics and aesthetics has been discussed positively by Schiller and negatively by Kierkegaard. I must here merely declare myself on the positive side of the argument, and refer the reader to Schiller's 'Letters on the Aesthetic Education of

[6] Frolov, *Pavlov and his School*, pp. 214–5.

[7] *Op. cit.*, p. 152.

Man'[8] for a philosophical discussion of the evidence.[9] In the present context we must restrict ourselves to a brief examination of the effects of a discipline of constraint on the psychic disposition of the child, and to a comparison of such discipline and its effects with the alternative possibility of a discipline based on aesthetic activity.

Sully warned us long ago that there has been more hasty theorizing about the child's moral characteristics than about any other of its attributes. His own conclusions were tentative and pragmatic. The child, he found, is on its moral side wanting in consistency and unity. 'It is a field of half-formed growths, some of which tend to choke the others. Certain of these are favourable, others unfavourable to morality. It is for education to see to it that these isolated propensities be organized into a system in which those towards the good become supreme and regulative principles.'[10] He realized that the early years are the important ones, and that the task is not one which can be handed over to a paid substitute or an institution, but is intimately bound up with the feelings of tenderness and trust inspired by the child's mother.

The conclusions of psychoanalysis are not radically different, though they have thrown much light on the genesis and evolution of moral sentiments in the child. Whether we accept the extreme Freudian view, according to which all moral restraint is a product of the actual process of mastering the Oedipus complex, or merely accept the simpler and more general view which regards the acquisition of a moral sense as one aspect of the necessary adaptation of the individual to the social group, the process always involves a phase of opposition for the individual. It is a conflict in which one part of his nature is subdued to the requirements of an external code. Whilst not denying the necessity of a moral code, and not at the moment questioning the existing formulations of that code, we must examine the methods by means of which it is instilled into the mind of the child.

The child is amoral: he has instincts which may be good or bad according to our adult code. But he cannot, at the early age he first

[8] 'Ueber die aesthetische Erziehung des Menschen in einer Reihe von Briefen,' *Saemtliche Werke*, ed. Höfer, Munich, 1913, Vol. XI. English translation with introduction by Reginald Snell: *On the Aesthetic Education of Man* (London, 1954).

[9] Cf. Snell, *op. cit.*, p. 12: 'The whole burden of the argument in these letters is, in a single sentence, that Man must pass through the aesthetic condition, from the merely physical, in order to reach the rational or moral'.

[10] *Studies of Childhood*, p. 266.

comes into conflict with it, apprehend our code in any cognitive sense: he can only learn to observe it by experience, which in present practice means the experience of a system of rewards and punishments. He learns to associate certain lines of conduct with reactions of tolerance or encouragement in the adult; other lines of conduct with reactions of displeasure and aggression. He learns that the former acts are 'good', the latter 'bad'. But what psychic deformations are involved in this disciplinary process?

2. THE ORIGINS OF MORAL DISCIPLINE

We like to think, and are encouraged by philosophers and moralists to think, that the distinction between 'good' and 'bad' is based on sound reason as well as common sense. According to Leon Chwistek, this erroneous assumption derives from Socrates. 'In addition to his emphasis upon sound reason, Socrates entertained the conception of the perfect good. This conception is irrational and cannot be reconciled with sound reason. Men recognize almost intuitively the difference between good and bad because they have been taught to make such distinctions since childhood; nevertheless such evaluations are superficial.'[11]

Superficial? This is perhaps not the right word to describe a psychic transformation in the individual that is elaborate in its mechanism, takes place over a number of years, and implants in the mind a phenomenon so deep-seated as the conscience. We must admit that the whole process is irrational, and that the moral systems which are constructed in the process are fantasies that have no necessary basis in observed facts. But the 'teaching' of moral distinctions is not parallel to the teaching of subjects like mathematics or geography, nor is the knowledge acquired as easily demolished by rational criticism as Chwistek assumes.

We shall refer to two theories of the origin of moral behaviour in the child, one based on the empirical observation of children (Piaget) the other on the analysis of the individual (Freud), before coming to

[11] *The Limits of Science* (London, 1948), pp. 26–7. Cf. Trigant Burrow: 'It was the lot of each of us as infants or children to be given an alternative symbol or designation which was to cover all conditions affecting the behaviour of man. This designation or word or idea was called "good" conduct as contrasted with conduct symbolized as "bad" . . . Whatever was connoted by these terms has to be taken wholly on faith. For the alternatives, good and bad conduct, in contrast to the physiological behaviour of the total organism, are utterly lacking in scientific criteria.' *The Structure of Insanity*, pp. 38–9.

the fundamental criticism of Burrow and my own suggestions for an integration of moral and aesthetic discipline.

The psychoanalytical account of the process, once it is expressed in general terms, seems both reasonable and adequate as an explanation of the existing conventions. We are given two fields of force, the individual mind and the world external to this individual mind. A state of mutual tension arises between these two fields of force, and an adjustment becomes necessary. This adjustment is carried out by means of two psychic mechanisms, which have been called *introjection* and *projection*. Introjection is the positive process of building up a moral sense in the individual mind; projection is analogous to to Einfühlung (empathy) in aesthetics, and is the investing of other people with the moral attitudes and feelings which actually operate in ourselves. It is, as Susan Isaacs defines it, 'perceiving that part of oneself which gives rise to internal tension and anxiety, not as in oneself, but as out in the external world'. Psychoanalysts usually restrict the term to the projection of feelings of conflict and antagonism, but the same mechanism surely applies to feelings of sympathy and attraction, and the mechanism then leads to that state of mutual respect from which alone, as we shall see, a stable moral discipline can develop.

The mechanism of introjection begins literally with the taking-in of the parent that is to say, with the taking-in of food from the breast. To quote Dr. Isaacs again: 'In his own phantasy the child does literally take not only the mother's nipple and breast, but the mother herself, and the father, into himself. He loves and dreads them there within him. They are now a part of his own psyche, and yet not himself, not, at any rate, his primitive wish-self. They, or that part of him which is identified with the parents, remain *parents* even though they are within him.'[12] Or as Dr. Isaacs expresses it still more explicitly: 'A part of himself begins to act towards the rest as (he feels) the parents act (or may act) towards his person as a whole. It becomes the *parents-in-him*, and in his phantasies is indeed the parents in him. The feeling of guilt is the dread of this part of oneself that *is* the parents, that (in phantasy) judges and condemns and reproaches and punishes; and in punishment does to oneself all that one wanted to do to others. A great part of the feeling of guilt is thus unconscious, inaccessible to one's ordinary self-awareness.'[13]

[12] *Social Development in Young Children*, p. 304.
[13] *Op. cit.*, p. 270.

The child, according to this reasoning, takes the parents into himself, and transforms them into an inner court of appeal, in order that he may avoid the frustration which will overcome him if he opposes his primitive individualistic instincts to the external world. The conscience is a mediator between the individual and the group. But why then should the individual be afraid of his conscience? Why this universal sense of guilt and shame?

Dr. Isaacs deals with this difficulty in a footnote which deserved more prominence in her book: 'It will be noted that at various points, I speak of the child's *dread of his super-ego*. This may seem strange in view of the fact that the super-ego itself is held to arise from the need to escape the overwhelming pain of frustration. Both are true, however. In the first instance the child becomes a parent to himself in order to control those instincts which, if given their head, expose him to the pain of frustration, that is (to him) to an attack by the cruel, hostile parents in the external world. The function of the internalized parent is to save him from retribution from the external parents. But since the internalized parent, or super-ego, is itself built upon the most primitive aggressive tendencies, it becomes also a source of scarcely less dread and internal danger. The cure is, thus, very little better than the disease.

'The child then seeks to get rid of this internal danger by all the other mechanisms at his resource, and in the first instance, by *projection* of the super-ego itself. In the early phases of development his mind moves constantly back and forth between these two mechanisms of introjection and projection, according to the external situation. Moreover, both processes continue at work throughout the whole of his development. The child gains relief as a result of the projection of his most primitive super-ego on to the *real* parents, since they do not in fact fulfil his most primitive phantasies, and he can re-introject these real people again and again, with an increasing tincture of reality, as his perceptions of them develop and his experience is built up. There are thus many different layers to the super-ego, and it is the most primitive from which the greatest anxieties arise.'[14]

This perhaps carries the discussion into more detail than is justified in the present context. The important point to note about this theory is that it provides an explanation of the origin of the conscience, of the growth in each individual of a sense of 'good' and 'bad', and a

[14] *Op. cit.*, pp. 306-7.

biological justification for the encouragement of the good in preference to the bad. The ideal of goodness may be irrational, but it does enable the individual to adapt himself without frustration to the society into which he is born. It might be defined as socialized love, just as badness is socialized hate; and both are mental expansions of the physical parent-child relationship. But why, except to satisfy a theoretical preference for antitheses, should goodness be balanced by badness, love by hatred?

Dr. Isaacs, it will be seen, suggests that there are instincts within the child which must be controlled, or otherwise they will expose him to 'the pain of frustration . . . to an attack by the cruel, hostile parents in the external world'. This dramatic presentation is justified as a description of what actually takes place. But is it merely naïve to ask why the relationship of love, which is natural to the state of nurture and protection into which the child is born, should ever be transformed into hate? Is the Oedipus complex to be regarded as inevitable, or as merely the product of bad educational methods in the home? There is an alternative view, to which I have already referred—and which I find more consonant with the facts presented in this book. It is the view taken by Jean Piaget, Trigant Burrow, Ian Suttie, and to some extent by Karen Horney and Erich Fromm. It is expressed in these words of Suttie's: 'Both Freud and Adler . . . regard the infant as "bad" by nature and as having to be made "good" by external compulsion, or else allowed outlet for its badness. I consider that the germ of goodness or of love is in the individual (of every species which has evolved a nurtured infancy) from the very beginning, and that our traditional method of upbringing frustrates this spontaneous benevolence and substitutes a "guilt-anxiety" morality for natural goodness. I consider further that the traditional attitude is so deeply ingrained in Freud's and Adler's outlook on life that they cannot admit the existence of love as other than a prudent avoidance of the anger of others'.[15]

If in this passage we substitute 'discipline', for 'traditional method of upbringing', the problem gains in definiteness, for the traditional method is disciplinary—a system of maintaining order among schoolboys, soldiers, prisoners, etc.—and does not allow for the spontaneous emergence of co-operation and self-government within the group. Naturally there is still room within such a system for 'leadership of the persuasive type', and a practical child psychologist like Dr. Isaacs

[15] *Origins of Love and Hate*, p. 52.

sees that this kind of leadership is necessary to attain 'the haven of friendly co-operation'.

'The stern parent who rules only by fear and prohibition, and does not offer the children the positive means of making good, cannot give them this happiness or further their social development, even though she checks their open hostilities. Unless she provides the materials for their making and creating, and encourages active social skill in them, thus showing her faith in their wish to make good, she will not be able to create an expanding social world in and for her children. . . . She is a true educator only when and in so far as she becomes the parent who offers the means and encouragement to make good; that is to say, when her super-ego function works unobtrusively towards active and constructive ends in the group of children.' But everything, as Dr. Isaacs would agree, depends on the actual means employed in this group activity. It depends, I would say, on substituting for the conception of discipline, not only the relationship of mutual love, but also techniques of creative industry.

'It is the ineptitude of virtue,' writes Dr. Burrow, 'that it is but the bi-dimensional reverse of vice.' It does not suffice, that is to say, to implant in the child an ego-ideal based on the image of the parent or adult. This, as Freud himself was compelled to admit, merely leads to conflicts between this ideal and the ego, between what is mental and what is real, between the internal and the external world. Our whole aim should be to avoid this conflict and the neurosis born of it. Our object should be to devise a method of education or upbringing which from the beginning secures the organic confluences of the mind within and the world without. And to do this we must abolish the very concepts of 'good' and 'bad', 'right' and 'wrong', and the whole disciplinary system of praise and blame, reward and punishment. *But that does not imply that we should not put anything else in their place.*

'It is my conviction,' writes Dr. Burrow, 'that the deeply entrenched root of our human pathology is to be traced alone to the conflict incurred through this suggestively induced image of right and wrong, and that it is profitless, therefore, to seek beyond the impasse of this unconscious alternative for the ultimate source of neurotic reactions.'[16] Dr. Burrow seems willing to admit that if this 'induced image of right and wrong' had any absolute validity, there might be a

---

[16] *Social Basis of Consciousness*, p. 53. The same conclusion is reached by a more orthodox Freudian like Professor J. C. Flugel. Cf. his *Psychoanalytic Study of the Family* (London, 1921), *passim.*

case for making our children conform to it. But we know, unconsciously if not consciously, that the image is irrational and cannot be reconciled with any absolute established by reason. The absoluteness of the system is merely a *pretence*, working for our concrete benefit in our immediate social situation. The fact that we may not be aware of the pretence does not act as a limitation on its pernicious effects: unconsciousness is merely in this case a measure of unreality, of artificiality. The more grandiose the formulation of a code of morality and the more collective in its acceptance, the more unconscious its workings become. But its falsity is evident enough in little things, and especially in the daily conflicts of the nursery and school. Dr. Burrow exposes its shams relentlessly:

'What the adult arbiter of the child really has up his sleeve is the child's conformity to *him* and *his* convenience. Accordingly, the parent or guardian lays down the proposition that a good little boy doesn't destroy costly bric-à-brac or that only a bad little girl would play in the mud with her nice clean rompers on. Both these postulates are utterly false as every sponsor of them knows. But that is not the point. The point is that such statements are incomparably adapted to the ends of adult commodity. The truer rendering of the proposition in either instance would be to the effect that the misdemeanour in question would occasion inconvenience or chagrin to the parent. But so sincere a statement on the part of the parent might alienate the child's jealously coveted affection, as we commonly term the infantile dependence we secretly tend to beget. Hence, the real motive of interdiction must be hidden from the child and a comprehensive edict cunningly invoked such as will place an effectual check upon him and yet amply safeguard the parental interest. It is this bogus morality which, by our unconscious social consent, the conscripted phantom called "good and bad" is unanimously commissioned to represent.

'Because of this attitude of pretence in others whereby the child is tricked into complicity with the prevalent code about him, there is begotten this self-same reaction of pretence within him. This illusion that is in the air he learns to assimilate from others through imitative affinity, and from now forward the ruse becomes self-operative. What began as a social coup is continued as an individual policy. The silent intimation of a mysteriously pervasive immanence of "good and bad" having now been engendered, the child henceforth responds automatically, not alone to the signals of make-believe about him, but to the signals of make-believe within him. For in unconsciously succumbing to the contagion of the autocratic system of "right and wrong" about him, this hobgoblin of arbitrary make-believe becomes equally systematized within his own consciousness. Accordingly, the pretence involved in interdictions of conduct (fear-blame reaction) is accompanied by the mental suggestion of "wrong" or "bad", and the pretence underlying the inducements of conduct (hope-praise reaction) is accompanied by the mental suggestion of "right" or "good"—*that is, of good or bad as it reverts upon the individual from the point of view of his personal advantage as reflected in the image of the parent.*'

A proper consideration of this problem would involve a review of the principles of ethics of the most fundamental kind, and is certainly outside the scope of this book. The points I regard as established, not here but in the works referred to in the course of this chapter, are these.

1. The concepts of 'good' and 'bad' are arbitrary, and not established by any process of logical reasoning.

2. The concepts of 'good' and 'bad' ('right' and 'wrong') are induced into the mind of the child during the course of its upbringing, either unconsciously by the process of 'introjection' or consciously by a system of rewards and punishments.

3. The result is a state of psychic ambivalence peculiarly liable to tensions (psychoses) and disruptions (neuroses) in the individual, and a state of unconsciousness in society equally fraught with the possibilities of breakdown (revolts and wars).

3. FROM CONSTRAINT TO CO-OPERATION

The purpose of the rest of this chapter is to suggest, not an alternative system of ethics (for our ethics are aesthetics), nor a method of avoiding the consequences of the established system (psychoanalysis or group-analysis), much less the economic and political correlates of a healthy social mind, but merely some essentials which have been overlooked in the formulation of a practical pedagogy based on reciprocity rather than constraint. But before we define these essentials we must first give some account of Piaget's important investigations.

Piaget proceeds quite independently of psychoanalytical methods, though not in opposition to them. He observes the behaviour of children, patiently and methodically, and makes his deductions from the evidence he thus accumulates. He is not a behaviourist in the narrow sense, for he proceeds to philosophical conclusions; but he is a strict empiricist, and his conclusions deserve the closest attention.

In his inquiry into the origins and development of moral judgment in the child,[17] Piaget begins with watching a game of marbles. He ends with a fundamental criticism of the current theories of Kant, Durkheim, and other moralists, psychologists and sociologists. The general conclusion he reaches may best be given in his own words:

'. . . The morality prescribed for the individual by society is not homogeneous because society is not just one thing. Society is the sum of social relations, and among these relations we can distinguish two extreme types: relations of constraint, whose characteristic is to impose upon the individual from outside a system of rules with obligatory content, and relations of co-operation whose characteristic is to create within people's minds the consciousness of ideal norms at the back of all rules. Arising from the ties of authority and unilateral respect, the relations of constraint therefore characterize most of the features of society as it exists, and particularly the relations of the child to its adult surroundings. Defined by equality and mutual respect, the relations of co-operation, on the contrary, constitute an equilibrial limit rather than a static system. Constraint, the source of duty and heteronomy, cannot, therefore, be reduced to the good and to autonomous rationality, which are the fruits of reciprocity, although the actual evolution of the relations of restraint tends to bring these nearer to co-operation.'[18]

This may seem to reduce to something innocent enough, but in the pedagogical sphere it involves these clear consequences:

1. The social life developed by children among themselves gives rise to a discipline infinitely nearer to that inner accord which is the mark of adult morality than does any *imposed* system of morality. There exists a clear distinction between a morality of obedience and a morality of attachment or reciprocity, and the latter is the morality of harmonious societies.

2. The adult's relation to the child must always be that of a collaborator, never that of a master.

3. Co-operation is essential to intellectual no less than to moral

[17] *The Moral Judgment of the Child*, Trans. by Marjorie Gabain (London, 1932)
[18] *Op. cit.*, p. 402.

277

development. For the laying down of ready-made rules we must substitute the elaboration of rules through experimentation and reflection, carried out in common, and the school thus becomes a place where such co-operative activities are possible. 'Autonomy is a power that can only be conquered from within and that can find scope only inside a scheme of co-operation.'

4. Absolute condemnation of the examination system, 'which helps more than all the family situations put together to reinforce the child's spontaneous egocentrism'.

5. Gradual elimination of every trace of expiation from the idea of punishment, reducing the latter to simple acts of reparation, or simple measures of reciprocity.

6. Reaffirmation of Plato's observation that in the moral as in the intellectual domain we really possess only what we have conquered ourselves.

4. SOCIOLOGICAL IMPLICATIONS OF RECIPROCITY

These are the chief conclusions to be drawn from Piaget's observations of the development of moral consciousness in young children. The wider implications of his discoveries can only be briefly noted. They include a theory of the evolution of the idea of justice in social communities, and the drawing of a parallelism between the most evolved stage of this evolution and the politics of democracy.

The phylogenetic evolution corresponds to the ontogenetic development in children, beginning with a unilateral relationship in which authority is absolute, justice is retributive, and punishment an expiation. During the second stage, a sense of equalitarianism based on mutual respect is developed, justice becomes distributive, and punishment fitted to the crime. Finally, mere equalitarianism makes way for a more subtle conception of justice which we may call 'equity'; it consists in never defining equality without taking account of the way in which each individual is situated (age, previous services rendered, etc.). At this stage 'solidarity between equals appears once more as the source of a whole set of complementary and coherent moral ideas which characterize the rational mentality'.[19]

In other words, responsibility, which in the primitive community

[19] *Op. cit.*, p. 324.

278

is *general*, 'visited upon the children unto the third and fourth generation', or even, as in the doctrine of Original Sin, implicating the whole of the human race, gradually becomes *individualized*. And at the same time the idea of justice, from being absolute and objective —the law of the gods—becomes spiritualized, an affair for the conscience of the individual man. Essentially it is the same process as described by Freudian psychology: the absolute constraint which is due to the introjection of the parental image is transformed into a sense of responsibility to the ego-ideal, and is thus generalized into abstractions which we share with other individuals. 'The great lesson of comparative sociology', deduces Piaget from an examination of sociologists like Durkheim and Fauconnet, 'is that there exist at least two types of responsibility—one objective and communicable—the other subjective and individual, and that social evolution has gradually caused the second to predominate.'

Piaget's criticism of Durkheim is that he makes an unwarranted identification of constraint and co-operation. 'He entirely ignores the existence of spontaneously formed children's societies, and of the facts relating to mutual respect. Consequently, elastic though Durkheim's pedagogy may be in principle, it simply leads, for lack of being sufficiently informed on the subject of child sociology, to a defence of the methods of authority.'[20] It also leads to an authoritarian conception of society incompatible with the principles of democracy—to a conception of society rigidly held together by the bonds of duty rather than to a conception of society based on that sense of justice which arises from mutual respect and co-operation. 'The essence of democracy resides in its attitude towards law as a product of the collective will, and not as something emanating from a transcendent will or from the authority established by divine right. It is therefore the essence of democracy to replace the unilateral respect of authority by the mutual respect of autonomous wills.'[21]

Burrow, in *The Social Basis of Consciousness*, carries this analysis a stage further. He makes what is in effect the same distinction between a morality of constraint and a morality of reciprocity, but he would not be so ready to admit that a morality of reciprocity is possible under existing social conditions. What he sees in modern society is a vast unconscious acceptance of a morality of constraint, only differing from the absolute authoritarianism of primitive societies in

[20] *Ibid.*, pp. 358–9.
[21] *Ibid*, p. 366.

the degree to which it is unrecognized. From his earliest days the child is introduced to an artificial set of rules, of distinctions between good and bad, right and wrong, etc., and is made to realize affectively (he is not yet capable of *rational* realization) that his personal advantage depends on the observance of these rules. Life for the child then becomes, not something lived organically, as animals live their lives, but a flat and two-dimensional scheme, a black-white chessboard across which the child must make certain strict and arbitrarily imposed moves. The child's entire universe of feeling is thus limited to a game in which his personal gain or loss is determined by his ability to obey the rules or pay the forfeit. We thus substitute at the very outset of life 'a primary condition of unreality for the inherent reality of life'.

This contraction of the organic fullness of life to a system of alternative modes of action determined by one's own pleasure and one's own pain is the source of our neurotic ills. For this personal bias, this reduction of life to a self-reflection which is projected into the social environment, entails a division of the personality which is nothing short of a compulsion neurosis, the scope of which involves our entire social consciousness. What is good for me is what is socially approved; what is bad for me is what is socially disapproved. If the social consciousness about me is willing to connive with my individual consciousness and applaud my egoistic self-strivings, then all is well: if not, my state is indeed an unhappy one.

The natural state is an organic social consciousness, in which all sense of mental oppositeness is dispelled. What we have now is self-consciousness, 'the fallacy of a self as over against other selves'. It is this state of split-consciousness which is at the root of all our troubles. 'Suddenly aware of himself, and of other selves over against him, man is a prey to the division inside himself. Helplessly he must strive for more consciousness, which means, also, a more intensified aloneness, or individuality; and at the same time he has a horror of his own aloneness, and a blind, dim yearning for the old togetherness of the far past.'[22]

According to Dr. Burrow, a new sense of social identity, of togetherness, is to be acquired by methods of group analysis. The individual tension cannot be released by individual treatment, because the tension arises within a group and can only be released by a change in group relationships. People must co-operate to rid them-

[22] D. H. Lawrence, *Phoenix*, p. 379.

selves of their mutually created neuroses. To quote Lawrence's clear interpretation of Burrow again: 'The cure would consist in bringing about a state of honesty and a certain trust among a *group* of people, or many people—if possible, all the people in the world.'

But our business as educators is not with the cure but with the prevention of the social neurosis, and prevention consists in not allowing the feelings of separativeness to develop in the individual. This can only be done by making our education from the very beginning group-education, and at this point the analysis and recommendations of Burrow and Piaget come together and reinforce one another. The aim of education is the creation of a sense of mutuality. 'For it is only when we can get a man to fall back into his true relation to other men, and to women, that we can give him an opportunity to be himself. So long as men are inwardly dominated by their own isolation, their own absoluteness, which after all is but a picture or an idea, nothing is possible but insanity more or less pronounced. Men must get back into *touch*. And to do so they must forfeit the vanity and the *noli me tangere* of their own absoluteness: also they must utterly break the present picture of a normal humanity: shatter that mirror in which we all live grimacing: and fall again into true relatedness.'[23]

5. PEDAGOGICAL IMPLICATIONS

The application to pedagogy of the principles thus established becomes obvious. Piaget is wholly in favour of introducing autonomous group methods into schools, and agrees with the great German pedagogue F. W. Foerster, in finding it unbelievable that at a time when democratic ideals are proclaimed in every sphere of life, they should have been so little utilized as instruments of education. He believes that the future of education lies with the Activity School ('that in which the child is not made to work by means of external constraint, but where he works of his own free will'), and recommends his readers to study the methods of Sanderson, Dewey, Cousinet, etc. These methods all depend on group work, but Piaget does not himself define the characteristics of such group work, beyond saying generally that it consists in allowing the children to follow their pursuits in common, either in organized 'teams' or simply according to their spontaneous groupings.

Piaget must be aware that the activity of a group should, if it has

[23] D. H. Lawrence, *op. cit.*, p. 382.

to have any coherence, be guided by a scope or intention, however undefined or 'intuitive' that scope or intention may be. The children he observed playing marbles, for example, did not pursue their game merely to exercise their limbs, or for the kinetic pleasure of placing and displacing a number of balls. There is an early stage, Piaget recognizes, of a purely motor or individual character, 'in which the child handles the marbles at the dictation of his desires and motor habits'. It may be compared to the scribbling stage in drawing. But this purely individual activity leads, as in drawing, to the 'ritualized schema'. Then by stages the player grows out of his egocentricity, observes other players, gradually begins to co-operate with others, and finally in conjunction with a group arrives at a reciprocal agreement embodying definite rules. Piaget proceeds to draw a wealth of psychological conclusions from a close analysis of this evolutionary process, but it does not seem to me that he stops to examine what, from our point of view, is of supreme importance —*the pattern of the game*. For the rules evolved by the group are not arbitrary: they have style, economy, harmony; they all cohere to the one end (e.g. to drive a given number of marbles out of an enclosure). Most of us have forgotten the rules of marbles, but we may consider the quite comparable rules of football and cricket. In each case there is a ritual, the appreciation of which demands, not merely knowledge, but also aesthetic sensibility. The football fan's jargon of 'style' and 'form' is not baseless: it has far more reality than the similar words which cling like dead husks to academic culture.

The rules of the game are merely the definition of a perceived pattern, and the pattern is valid and acceptable to a group because all the members of the group agree that it is agreeable, satisfying, fit to the intention of the game.[24] Now, obviously Piaget should logically

[24] The various rôles within the game allow for the spontaneous assorting of varieties of temperament. The normal conception of discipline makes no provision for such differences. Cf. the following important observation of Sheldon, *The Varieties of Human Physique*, pp. 260–1: 'Watch young children in a nursery school. There are often a few vigorous-bodied somatotonics who take the lead in all enterprises, a few round, healthy-looking viscerotonics who join in with excellent fellowship, and a few little pinch-faced cerebrotonics who constitute a watchful and unsocialized periphery. These little cerebrotonics seem to want to stay on the side lines and watch. Their eyes are sharp as needlepoints and nothing seems to escape their quick attention, but they do not want to be pushed into the swim. They are under stern internal check, and they seem to want to see without being seen. Should these children be sent to nursery schools and forced into the social press with a score of other children? Should they be sent to boys' camps and girls' camps? We do not know about these things. Modern educators

demand that the group activities which he wishes to make the basis of education should satisfy the same conditions. They should have a pattern which inspires the same unity of intention, the same concentration of energy, the same pleasure in the performance. They should involve 'style' and 'form', just as a game of marbles or football does. But Piaget nowhere, that I have discovered, makes this point; nor do the other exponents of the Activity Method. And this, of course, explains, where explanation is necessary, the failure of this method, and the slowness with which as a consequence it has been adopted in the public educational system. *It is only in so far as group activities take on the aesthetic patterns and organic vitality of the groups spontaneously formed by children themselves (and by adults when they are playing like children) that these activities will achieve a moral and intellectual superiority over more authoritarian forms of education.*

6. CONCLUSION

It will be seen, therefore, that from this moral and disciplinary approach we reach the same conclusion as before. True discipline is a spontaneously evolved pattern of behaviour. Any other form of behaviour that goes by this name is merely arbitrary constraint, imposed by fear of punishment, unstable in its equilibrium, and productive of individual and social tensions. The way to rational harmony, to physical poise, to social integration, is the same way—the way of aesthetic education. This was the teaching of Plato—clear and unequivocal in spite of the smoke-screens and sophistries of his latter-day commentators. Plato meant exactly what he said: that an aesthetic education is the only education that brings grace to the body and nobility to the mind, and that we must make art the basis of education because it can operate in childhood, during the sleep of reason; and when reason does come, art will have prepared a path for her, and she will be greeted as a friend whose essential lineaments have for long been familiar.[25] Moreover, Plato did not see or offer any alternative to art as an instrument of early education—it is the only instrument that can penetrate into the recesses of the soul.

might want to ponder this problem. It may be that late-maturing personalities need a high degree of privacy and seclusion and protection during the formative years. It is possible that loneliness is as essential to the full development of a creature "mentally inclined" as sociability is essential to a viscerotonic or aggressive self-expression to a somatotonic youth.'

[25] *Republic*, III, 401. *Laws*, II, 653–6, VII, 797–816. *Protagoras*, 326.

Plato's teaching on this matter was taken up in the modern world by Schiller, and in all his philosophical works, but above all in his *Letters on the Aesthetic Education of Man*, we have again a clear and explicit statement of this doctrine of education: that until man, in his physical and sensuous modes of being, has been accustomed to the laws of beauty, he is not capable of perceiving what is good and true—he is not capable of spiritual liberty. Many other witnesses to this truth might be called[26] but none so unequivocal as these two, whom I value more than any others; and I am very content to rest in their company.

[26] I cannot refrain from enlisting Milton's powerful and perhaps unexpected support. The following aesthetic conception of discipline comes from *Reason of Church Government*, Book I, Chapter 1, Bohn Edition, Vol. II, p. 441: 'Nor is there any sociable perfection in this life, civil or sacred, that can be above discipline; but she is that which with her musical chords preserves and holds all the parts thereof together. Certainly discipline is not only the removal of disorder; but, if any visible shape can be given to divine things, the very visible shape and image of virtue, whereby she is not only seen in the regular gestures and motions of her heavenly paces as she walks, but also makes the harmony of her voice audible to mortal ears. Yea, the angels themselves, in whom no disorder is feared, as the apostle that saw them in his rapture describes, are distinguished and quaternioned into their celestial princedoms and satrapies, according as God himself has writ his imperial decrees through the great provinces of Heaven. The state also of the blessed in paradise, though never so perfect, is not therefore left without discipline, whose golden surveying reed marks out and measures every quarter and circuit of New Jerusalem.' I am well aware that Milton's particular views on education, though assigning a considerable part to 'the solemn and divine harmonies of music', have little in common with the aesthetic education advocated here.

Chapter Nine

THE TEACHER

Not the professor, but the artist is your true schoolmaster.—Caldwell Cook

1. MARTIN BUBER ON THE CONCEPT OF CREATIVITY

On the subject of teaching, the little that I can say is based on external observation and reflection rather than on practical experience. Nor is this little that I have to say in any degree original: it has all been said with subtlety and profundity by a great modern philosopher who, at an international conference held at Heidelberg in the year 1925 to consider 'the unfolding of creative powers in the child', spoke on this very subject.[1] As his lecture seems to be quite unknown to educationalists in this country, I shall give some account of its general argument and then emphasize the particular aspect which I find so relevant to the problem we have been discussing.

Buber begins by examining the concept of 'creativity' on which, as he says, modern educators rely so much. He shows that it was only fairly late in history that this concept, formerly reserved for the divine action of calling the universe into being, was metaphorically transferred to human activities, more especially to works of genius in the sphere of art. It was then recognized that this tendency to create, which reaches its highest manifestation in men of genius, was present, in however slight a degree, in all human beings. There exists in all men a distinct impulse to make things, an instinct which cannot be explained by theories of libido or will to power, but is disinterestedly experimental. Buber gives as an example of the manifestation of this instinct, the manner in which an infant will attempt to utter words, not as given things, which he has to imitate, but as original things to be attempted for the first time—'sound-image after sound-image

---

[1] Martin Buber, *Rede ueber das Erzieherische*, Berlin (Lambert Schneider) 1926. A translation by Ronald Gregor Smith has been published since this chapter was written in a volume entitled *Between Man and Man*, London (Routledge) 1946, pp. 83–103.

breaks forth, emerges from vibrating throat, from trembling lips, into the surrounding air, the whole of the little vital body vibrating and trembling, shaking with a paroxysm of outbreaking selfhood.' Obviously such an instinct to originate must be taken into account in the process of education, but Buber points out that it is not the free exercise of the instinct that matters, but the opposition it encounters. Here Buber gives the reader a foretaste of his characteristic mysticism. If, he says, the originating instinct operated in a passive world, it would create things which would then become merely external, objective. Under such circumstances it is a force which goes out from the centre of the person and into the object made, and there it peters out. But nothing comes in—and hence the ironic myth of Pygmalion. Man as creator is a lonely figure. Even if his creations are appreciated by other men, he remains isolated. 'It is only when someone takes him by the hand, not as a "creator", but as a fellow-creature lost in the world, and greets him not as an artist but as comrade, friend or lover, that he experiences an inner reciprocity. A system of education built up solely on the instinct to originate would bring about a new and the most painful isolation of men.' A child learns much from the making of things which he cannot learn in any other way, but there is something he cannot learn in this way, and it is the essential thing in life. He can gain an objective sense of the world from his own creative activity, but what he cannot acquire in this way is a subjective sense. That can only come from a mutual relationship, established by what Buber calls the instinct for communion (Verbundenheit)—an instinct which again owes nothing to the libido or will to power, which is not a desire to enjoy or dominate another person, but which is at one and the same time a giving and a receiving. 'The child, who, lying with half-closed eyes, waits anxiously for his mother to speak to him—his longing springs from something other than the desire for the enjoyment or domination of a human being, and it is also something other than a desire to do something on his own; in face of the lonely night, which spreads beyond the window and threatens to break in, it is the desire to experience communion.'

2. THE PUMP AND THE FUNNEL

Buber fully admits that the liberation of creative powers in the child is a precondition of education, but distinguishes between a specific impulse to originate and a more general spontaneity. All educators recognize the necessity of not repressing spontaneity, but they leave the child beating his wings in the void. Buber then takes as an example the very subject with which we have been most concerned in this book. In a drawing lesson a teacher using the old method of 'constraint', begins with prescripts and approved models which lay down what is unquestionably beautiful, and all he has to do afterwards is to decide how nearly his pupils have approximated to these standards. But the teacher in a 'free' school places, say, a spray of broom in a jug on the table and lets his pupils copy it; or he might first place it on the table, ask them to look at it, and then take it away and ask them to draw it from memory. In either case, the results for each pupil would be quite different. But now comes the delicate, almost unperceived, but all-important stage: criticism and instruction. The child comes up against a definite, if unacademic, scale of values: against a more particularizing, but still clear-cut, knowledge of good and bad. The more unacademic, the more particularizing, this scale or knowledge may be, the more vivid it appears to the child. In the old days, a declaration of legitimacy found the child either resigned or rebellious; now, however, the child himself has already ventured far with the work before he is enlightened by the teacher. By his own experience plus the enlightenment he subsequently receives, he is truly educated and made reverently aware of the nature of the object.

This almost unobserved encounter, this utmost delicacy of approach—perhaps the raising of a finger, a questioning look—is one half of the educational activity. But these modern theories of education which emphasize freedom do not see the importance of the teacher's function, whilst those which are based on the principle of authority neglect the importance of the other half (the child's experimental activity). The symbol of the funnel has merely been exchanged for that of the pump.

The dispositions which, if it were possible to analyse them, one would find in the soul of a new-born infant, are nothing but aptitudes to receive and conceive the outer world. The world engenders the person in the individual. Thus the world—the whole environment, nature and society—'educates' man: it draws out his powers, allows him to respond to and be convinced by the world. What we call education, conscious and willed, means the *selection of a feasible world* by the individual—means to give the directing force to a selection of the world made under the guidance of the teacher.

THE TEACHER

3. EDUCATION AS SELECTION

There was a time when there was no specific calling of teacher and pupil and none was needed. The master—whether a philosopher or a goldsmith—lived and worked with his apprentices and the apprentices lived with him and they learned, whether they realized it or not, the mystery of the personal life; they experienced a spiritual reality. Apart from a few exceptions, this form of education is irretrievably gone. But nevertheless the 'master' remains the prototype of the teacher. For the teacher, if he is to act consciously, must act 'as if he did it not'. Merely a raised finger, a questioning look, is the limit of his proper activity. Through him the selection of a feasible world reaches the pupil; but the teacher fails to get the right response from the pupil if he forces this selection on him in an attitude of intervention. He must have made his own harvest of experience; and what he gives from his store must have an air of quiescence. Active intervention splits the being in his charge into a listening and a resenting part; but the secret influence of the whole personality has the power of completion, of unification.

The world influences the child as nature and as society. The elements educate him—air, light, the life of plants and animals; and relationships educate him. The true educator comprises both; but he must be to the child as one of the elements.

4. FREEDOM AND UNION

Buber then returns to his first point—that freedom is a condition of education, and not more. Approaching the subject from its negative aspect, he points out that the antithesis of compulsion or constraint is not freedom, but communion or attachment. Freedom is a possibility, a recurring possibility. Coerced by fate, by nature, by man—the opposite to such states is not to be free from fate, nature or men, but to be united with them. In order to be able to do this one must naturally be first free and independent, but independence is a path and not a dwelling place. Freedom is the vibrating needle, the potential zero. Compulsion in education—that implies disunitedness, disunion, humiliation, rebelliousness; but communion in education—that implies just unitedness, that is to say, the capacity to be open and to become enclosed. Freedom in education is nothing else but possessing the ability to become united. It is the run before the leap, the tuning of the violin before it plays. The struggle for freedom, to which men may rightly dedicate their lives, should be regarded as a struggle for the right to experiment: liberty is not an end in itself, not a policy or a programme. To be free of all ties is a misfortune—to be borne as a cross, not as a crown of glory. It means that responsibility, instead of being shared by many generations, must be personal. To live in freedom is a personal responsibility, or it is a mere farce.

5. QUESTIONING AND ANSWERING

This fragile course between birth and death can, however, be run successfully if it takes the form of a dialogue. In living we are questioners; by thinking, speaking, doing, producing, influencing we try to become answerers. For the most part we fail to answer, or only babble incoherently. But when the word comes to us and the answer flashes out, there is then some sign of human life in the world. In so far as we can give the correct answers, we establish a sphere of responsibility. In so far as the relationships we enter into are traditional ties, rules, directions, to that degree our responsibility is shared. But to the degree that we 'become free', to that degree the responsibility is personal and we can expect no support. To the degree that we give answers, we answer *for*: response entails responsibility.

From this standpoint Buber can reach to a much profounder understanding of the rôle of the teacher. He discusses two existing principles of education—and dismisses them both. The first is based on the 'will to power'. The teacher approaches the child as the bearer of fixed values. He represents the established cosmos of history against this element, the pupil, new-born from chaos. This is obviously a relationship which can be easily abused, degenerating into an exploitation of the individual will-to-power, the tyranny of the average teacher. But when this tendency has run its course, that is to say, reached its climax, the relationship may easily be converted into its complete opposite, on which is based the second of the existing principles of education dismissed by Buber. The teacher suddenly faces the pupil as individual to individual, and he is filled with a secret longing to be loved for himself. The attitude of domination is changed for the attitude of enjoyment, but both attitudes are false attitudes for the ideal teacher, whose relationship to his pupil must be absolutely disinterested. Education based on love is education based on choice—the elective affinity of the lover; but the true educator does not choose his pupil—he just lights upon him. When he enters the schoolroom for the first time, he sees before him, bent over their desks, a confused crowd, figures ill-bred or well-proportioned, little animal faces, some mean, some noble—but quite unselected. His glance—the glance of a teacher—embraces everything and absorbs everything. Now, if he is a true teacher, he will not begin to divide and classify according to his inclinations or preferences. He will be guided by his knowledge of values. But even then his choice will be stayed by the specific humility of the teacher, for whom the particular existence of each of his pupils is the decisive factor to which his hierarchy of values is subordinated. For in the very variety and manifoldness of the children he will find evidence of the creative reality.

6. TEACHER AND PUPIL

Teaching demands a high degree of asceticism: joyful responsibility for a life entrusted to us, which we must influence without any suggestion of domination or self-satisfaction. Each intercourse will have its own laws and structure, its own reality, which is not inconsistent with comprehension and permeation. But, like any relationship that expresses the spirit of service to life, this pedagogical intercourse must be kept impersonal. For if the private spheres of either of the partners enter into it, if its structure and its tensions are not carefully preserved, then the way is open to a dilettantism without foundation, and finally to disintegration.

The matter-of-fact ascetic relationship of teacher to pupil must not be taken to exclude all emotive communion. Here Buber introduces another concept, for which he uses the term *envelopment* (Umfassung). This means, between two people, the actual experience of the partner's situation, and particularly of his feelings and his reactions to one's own behaviour. It is distinct from empathy (*Einfuehlung*)[2] because it does not involve a total identification with the other person's feelings or situation. It means experiencing the give and take of a mutual relationship, both from one's own and the other person's end at one and the same time.

Buber distinguishes various kinds of 'envelopment', but in so far as it is an educational relationship it is a relationship of trust—of trust in the world *because this man exists*. And this man must be really there, not a figment of the imagination. He must be present to

[2] See the definition 5 quoted on pp. 24–5.

answer for the world. The act of understanding, which can be a momentary and spontaneous flash in most relationships, must between teacher and pupil be a constant condition of reciprocity. If the teacher fails to establish the constancy of this reciprocity, he will be subject to arbitrariness in the relationship. But—and in this the teacher-pupil relationship differs from other forms of envelopment —however intimate this relationship becomes, it must remain essentially one-sided, for the pupil cannot experience the act of educating from the point of view of the teacher. Since education is a selection of the world through the medium of one person for the purpose of influencing another person, the person *through* whom this happens, far more than the person *to* whom it happens, is involved in a paradox. What would otherwise be an act of grace becomes an act of law. But it is essential not to allow the educative will to degenerate into wilfulness. One can observe, in the accounts of the teaching methods of a great pedagogue like Pestalozzi, how easily the will to educate becomes wilfulness. Wilfulness is due to the temporary suspension or paralysis of that enveloping force which should not merely intervene to regulate, but which should be as it were a constant cover, intrinsic to the relationship. It is not sufficient for the teacher to represent the pupil to himself imaginatively, and thereby experience and appreciate the individuality of his disposition: he must really identify himself with the other personality, and feel and do as he does.

It is because there must always be a unilateral element in this mutual relationship that the 'envelopment' of the pedagogical relationship remains distinct from that which is found in friendship. The teacher sees the situation from both ends, the pupil from one only. The moment the pupil attempts to see things from the point of view of the teacher and to appreciate the bilateral nature of the relationship, then the situation has become one of friendship. This is a later, post-educative stage in personal relationships.

The teacher gradually learns to distinguish and anticipate the real needs of his pupil. And as he gradually becomes aware of what this individual needs and what not, he understands ever more profoundly what the human being needs in order to become human. But the teacher also learns how much of what is wanted he himself is able to give, and how much he cannot give; what he can already give, and what is still too much for him. Thus he learns his responsibility for the particle of life entrusted to his care, and as he learns he educates himself. Self-education, here as always, does not mean that one has solitary dealings with one's self, but that one should consciously occupy oneself with the world around. The forces in the world which the pupil needs for the creation of his personality should be discerned by the educator and educed in himself. The education of a pupil is thus always the self-education of the teacher. Education of men by men implies, Buber repeats, the selection of a feasible world through a personality and for a personality. The educator absorbs the constructive forces of the world. He himself decides, rejects or accepts. These constructive forces are ultimately always the same forces—Buber calls them the forces which derive from the unity of the world with God—and the teacher is the channel through which they are conveyed.

7. APPLICATION TO THE THESIS OF THIS BOOK

I have, in this account of Buber's ideas, necessarily deprived them of much of their subtlety and suggestiveness—if only for the reason that Buber uses the German language in an original manner which does not lend itself easily to translation. But the essential message for us is clear, and when I describe it as essential I mean that the whole structure of education, as envisaged in this book, depends on a similar conception of the teacher. Objections are often made, when these plans for the reform of education are put forward, that the teachers necessary for such a scheme do not exist, and could not be trained within ten years or more. To which the reply is, that the scheme does not need a change of method so much as a change of heart, and that this *could* come overnight to thousands of teachers if only their pride in the present system, or in their present qualifications, were first subdued. Such pride can perhaps only be subdued on a large enough scale by a national catastrophe—not necessarily an irreparable disaster, but a look into the pit of destruction, and a recoil with all the forces of a new constructive vision.

It will perhaps be obvious how well Buber's conception of the teacher's rôle fits in with and completes those psychological analyses of the child's development to which I have repeatedly drawn attention. In particular, we seem nearer to an avoidance of that 'taboo on tenderness' which Suttie found responsible for the jealousies and other conflicts which are now such an inevitable feature of adaptation, hindering individual development and marring social harmony.

292

Suttie's solution was more love, prolonged parental tenderness, indeed, a matriarchal society. He recognized, and this was an aspect of his theory which lent support to the present thesis, that the mother-child bond could be gradually enlarged by play-activities into a group bond, and eventually into a social bond. Piaget has gathered convincing evidence to show that children do evolve their own group patterns spontaneously, but there was nothing to show that the play-group would in its turn spontaneously evolve into a co-operative social unit rather than into an anti-social 'gang'. Suttie did not consider to what extent the parent-rôle could be replaced by the teacher-rôle. Obviously any complete 'transference' of the maternal function to the teacher would be attended by its own emotional stresses and would not be conducive to educational efficiency: it would involve the bilateral 'friendship' reciprocity which Buber distinguished from the unilateral reciprocity of teacher-pupil. But if Buber's conception of the relationship of teacher and pupil is accepted, then obviously it can play a considerable part in the 'psychic weaning' of the child. The all-seeing understanding, the constant anticipation of needs, the selective function of Buber's teacher, give us a new and more constructive conception of tenderness. We escape from the pampered atmosphere of Suttie's psychology into a functional and constructive world; and at the same time we avoid the destructive effects of a crude application of power or authority. Buber's conception of the teacher's guiding and selective function allows us to construe tenderness as an active agency instead of a passive emotional state.

In much the same way Buber's teacher enables us to see how the limited inter-individual system of tensions and communications, which Burrow finds productive at best of an aggregation of individuals, can be replaced by an organic mode of adaptation to the social organism as a whole. The selective 'I' of the individual is replaced by the selective 'Thou' of the teacher. The individual takes in his environment through a selective screen, and the pattern of this screen, determining what comes in and what is excluded, is the social pattern. Burrow insists that it should at the same time be the organic pattern, for a society is a biological organism or it is an arbitrary association of individuals which will disintegrate at the first impact of reality. Both Buber and Burrow agree that it is the dissociation of feeling from purpose and action which is responsible for the paralysis of a society or a civilization. It produces a more or less total condition of individual separateness or isolation which prevents the healthy functioning of those very obscure but very real collective reactions on which the organic vitality of the group depends. It was the 'oppositeness' in the teacher-pupil relationship which Burrow found at once so characteristic of our prevailing pedagogical systems and such a menace to our social unity. 'Consider to what an extent our systems of education are really barriers to education. In the very idea of oppositeness the child is instinctively revolted. His organism shrinks from it as from a blow.' It is this 'oppositeness' which Buber's conception of teaching overcomes; the teacher becomes the uniter, the mediator between the individual and his environment, the midwife through whose agency the individual is reborn into society, guided into its most vital currents. But neither the midwife nor the teacher is the conceiver, the gestator, but accepts an already determined entity; and it is only in the degree that he identifies himself with a given disposition that he can ease the social parturition.

Equally it is only in the degree that the teacher is an adequate representative of his social group that he can guide the pupil to the threshold of manhood and of society. But by this we do not mean that the teacher should necessarily be socially conscious in a merely theoretical sense. Courses in citizenship will not qualify him for his task if he lacks that unconscious social integrity which is his sense of a total organism's feeling-behaviour. Buber would call it his acceptance of the will of God; less mystically, we may call it his perception of a pattern in the multiplicity of phenomena.

8. CONCLUSION

I am not a teacher, and have none of the experience which qualifies a man to be, say, an inspector of education; but in the course of preparing this book I have visited a good number of schools as a disinterested observer, and with the particular object of seeing the art classes at work. I have been enormously impressed by the fact, at first puzzling, that the best results could not be correlated with any system of teaching or any academic qualifications in the teacher. Sometimes the best work comes from schools where an art-master or mistress as such does not exist. It was equally evident that the good results did not come from a particular type of school. A collection of the best work would come in arbitrary proportions from public, elementary, secondary and private schools. My first conclusion was that good results depended on the creation, in the school or class, of a sympathetic atmosphere, and to a certain extent I still think this is true. But if by 'atmosphere' one means the amenities which money can buy, it is not true. The right atmosphere can exist in a village school, or in a dingy barracks in some industrial city. The atmosphere is the creation of the teacher, and to create an atmosphere of spontaneity, of happy childish industry, is the main and perhaps the only secret of successful teaching. To do this the teacher may not need more than a minimum of technical or academic qualifications: but he or she does require the gift of understanding or 'enveloping' the pupil which Buber has defined. Beyond that, the teacher only needs what Buber would call the love of God—for the teacher can only intervene effectively between the pupil and the world if he has a principle of selection. In the end the teacher must ask, what is the objective? A gentleman, a citizen, a Christian? The very fact that we can differentiate our objectives shows that they are good only for a particular time or civilization. When these temporary and partial aims fail us, we can only fall back on what Buber like other mystics calls the imitation of God—imitatio Dei absconditi sed non ignoti—a remote but not an impracticable aim, towards which we can proceed step by step, through the realm of beauty to the realm of truth.

Chapter Ten

ENVIRONMENT

*We must seek out those craftsmen whose instinct guides them to what-
ever is lovely and gracious; so that our young men, dwelling in a whole-
some climate, may drink in good from every quarter, whence, like a
breeze bearing health from happy regions, some influence from noble
works constantly falls upon eye and ear from childhood upward, and
imperceptibly draws them into sympathy and harmony with the beauty
of reason, whose impress they take.—Plato (trans. Cornford)*

1. A FEASIBLE WORLD

Buber, as we have seen, defines education as the selection of a
feasible world (eine Auslese der wirkenden Welt) and he conceives the teacher as essentially a mediator between the child and his
environment. We cannot, in our approach to the problems of education, be satisfied with a passive acceptance of this environment. The
efficiency of our mediation is to some extent dependent on our ability
to modify that environment. Education, in fact, is not separable from
our social policy as a whole.

From this point of view it is not likely that our educational reforms will ever overtake the general line of social and political development. This is not a cause for despair: it is a call to action in that
wider sphere. Unless we are primarily citizens, conscious of the common needs of the community, and of the rights and responsibilities
which belong to us as citizens, we can never be good educators. It is
doubtful whether a worker in any field—be he a poet or a mathematician, a physiologist or a farmer—can work effectively in isolation. He needs the stimulus of association, the sense of community,
to call out his highest potentialities. But this is above all true of the
teacher, for fundamentally education is not directed to the increase
of knowledge in the individual, but to the creation of well-being in
the community. It is only in so far as we raise the general level of

health, happiness, inventiveness and wisdom that we succeed in our discriminating task.

These considerations have never been absent from the preceding pages, but there is a certain limited sense in which environment requires more particular, if brief, treatment. This is the actual physical structure of the school. Rousseau's Emile seems to have been taught in a well-furnished country house, surrounded by a well-cultivated garden with all variety of natural phenomena within easy reach. That may be the ideal environment for the unfolding sensibility of a child —personally I believe that it is. But it is not a possible environment for the vast majority of children in a modern industrialized community. And whilst it is possible for a single child, or even for a small group of children, the necessary aggregation of children into schools catering for several hundreds at a time destroys any notion of intimate communion with nature.

We can propose one or two general laws whose truth is so obvious that they should be readily accepted. First, *the environment provided by the school should not be artificial*. If there is a complete divorce between the school and the home, the result will be tension, discontent, even neurosis in the child. But equally we might say that the environment of the home should not be artificial; and what could be more artificial than the brick boxes opening on to cement pavements which are now the homes of millions of children. If we can create a natural environment in the school, we should do so, and then try to bring the home into harmony with the school.

That the school should satisfy the requirements of scientific sanitation, ventilation and of hygiene generally, hardly needs to be mentioned. But aesthetics is also a science, and it should be no less a matter of course that the school should satisfy the simple laws which govern good proportions and harmonious colours. The school in its structure and appearance should be an agent, however unconscious in its application, of aesthetic education. The architecture of schools is of fundamental importance, but again it is an aspect of the problem which cannot be isolated from the wider developments of the art. It is not conceivable, that is to say, that school architecture will develop independently of the general development of architecture. But here the prototypes have already been realized, and in this country and abroad there are model schools which satisfy, whatever their incidental defects, the aesthetic standards of good architecture.

However good the siting and the building of a school, there remain more intangible elements which together make up the atmosphere of the school. The furniture and fittings of a school should properly be a part of the architect's function, and should not be mass-produced without any consideration for the particular setting in which they are to be placed. Many a good school is spoilt by hideous desks or inappropriate lighting. But many other details contribute to the atmosphere of a school: the use of textile hangings, the exhibition of pictures and sculpture, the dresses of the children and the teachers, the display of flowers, the absence of stridency and undue haste. It is by these means that each school can reveal its individuality, and for that reason the children should always co-operate in the creation of their own environment. The best pictures to decorate a school are the children's own pictures, but only if these pictures are treated with respect, properly mounted and decently framed. Children should, of course, be shown the work of mature artists, both of the past and of the present (and preferably not reproductions), but these again should be treated with respect, and shown in an appropriate setting. But it should always be remembered that the school is a workshop and not a museum, a centre of creative activity and not an academy of learning. Appreciation, as I have previously emphasized, is not acquired by passive contemplation: we only appreciate beauty on the basis of our own creative aspirations, abortive though these be.

Finally, and perhaps most importantly, environment must ensure freedom—freedom in the most obvious sense: freedom of movement, freedom to roam. The senses are only educated by endless action. 'Children,' said Rousseau in one of his most perceptive moments, 'will always do something that keeps them moving freely. There are countless ways of rousing their interest in measuring, perceiving, and estimating distance. There is a very tall cherry tree; how shall we gather the cherries? Will the ladder in the barn be big enough? There is a wide stream; how shall we get to the other side? Would one of the wooden planks in the yard reach from bank to bank? From our windows we want to fish in the moat; how many yards of line are required? I want to make a swing between two trees; will two fathoms of cord be enough?'

There are few modern schools that can provide such idyllic aids to mensuration, but the principle involved is universally valid. The child's senses can only be educated in action, and action requires space—not the restricted space of a room or a gymnasium, but the space of nature.

2. A PRACTICAL DEMONSTRATION

We turn, then, to the practical question: is it possible, not merely to conceive, but to build and introduce into the existing educational system, schools which provide the essentials of an educative environment? The answer is yes: it has been done in at least one instance, and a model perhaps not perfect in every detail, but practical, functional and beautiful, does exist on English soil.

This is the Village College at Impington in Cambridgeshire, conceived in principle by the local Director of Education, Henry Morris, and designed by Walter Gropius, formerly Director of the Bauhaus at Dessau in Germany and now head of the Graduate School of Design, Harvard University, and by Maxwell Fry. There are special features in the actual structure and lay-out of this school which are due to the fact that it is a rural school, combining elementary, central and adult educational purposes. But its main features are the general features which should be embodied in the plan of every school. They might be grouped in the following way:

A. *Promenade*: (16 in the accompanying plan) a large vestibule in which all the personnel of the school—teachers, pupils of all ages and both sexes, can meet and mingle as they come and go, on arrival and before departure, corresponding to the *Peripatos* of Aristotle's Lyceum.

B. *The Theatre*, with stage and full sound projection equipment: with seating capacity for the whole school together with parents and other members of the regional community.

C. *The Withdrawing Room* (17)—a place where the pupil can retire to read or meditate undisturbed.

D. *The various workshops and laboratories* (2, 22, 23).

E. *Work rooms* (form rooms and lecture rooms) (9, 24–8).

F. *Recreation rooms* and *gymnasium* (6–8, 18–20, 30).

G. *Refreshment rooms* (canteen, refectory, etc.) (4, 11).

H. *Library* (12).

I. *Services* (cloakrooms, kitchen, baths, medical) (4, 13, 29).

J. *External amenities* (playgrounds, gardens, playing fields).

K. *External services* and *experiments* (vegetable garden, horticultural and stock breeding stations).

3. A QUESTION OF PRIORITY

These are the minimum requisites, necessary for a natural mode

ENVIRONMENT

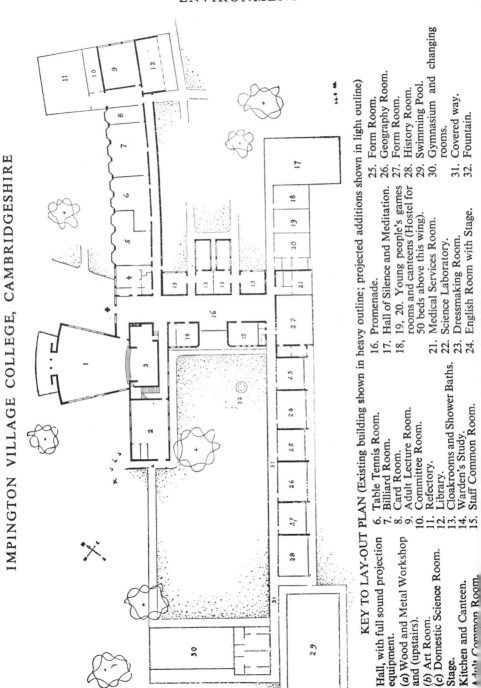

IMPINGTON VILLAGE COLLEGE, CAMBRIDGESHIRE

KEY TO LAY-OUT PLAN (Existing building shown in heavy outline; projected additions shown in light outline)

1. Hall, with full sound projection equipment.
2. (a) Wood and Metal Workshop and (upstairs).
   (b) Art Room.
   (c) Domestic Science Room.
3. Stage.
4. Kitchen and Canteen.
5. Adult Common Room.
6. Table Tennis Room.
7. Billiard Room.
8. Card Room.
9. Adult Lecture Room.
10. Committee Room.
11. Refectory.
12. Library.
13. Cloakrooms and Shower Baths.
14. Warden's Study.
15. Staff Common Room.
16. Promenade.
17. Hall of Silence and Meditation.
18, 19, 20. Young people's games rooms and canteens (Hostel for 50 beds above this wing).
21. Medical Services Room.
22. Science Laboratory.
23. Dressmaking Room.
24. English Room with Stage.
25. Form Room.
26. Geography Room.
27. Form Room.
28. History Room.
29. Swimming Pool.
30. Gymnasium and changing rooms.
31. Covered way.
32. Fountain.

of education. Nothing in this plan is extravagant or luxurious: everything is natural, functional and practical. Although designed for a rural community, the essential features of such a plan hold good for the town school. Here again some groupings of amenities and services may be necessary, so that instead of five or six schools in back streets there will be one large school in its own park. Sufficient space for such parks should be provided as part of any scheme of national planning, and naturally the reorganization of town schools must be part of a general policy of industrial decentralization. New schools will have to be built; our concern as educators is to see that they are practical embodiments of our new ideals. Since from a functional aspect schools are to a large degree identical, the building of new schools can be greatly accelerated by the planning of pre-fabricated units. The question of cost is irrelevant: there is land, there are building materials, there is skill and labour. In a rational society, there is only the question of priority, and no services in such a society, save those nourishing and protecting life itself, should have priority over education.

Great men have emerged from evil environments: perhaps their greatness was in some way an outcome of the struggle of their indomitable spirits with almost insuperable obstacles. But we do not educate to produce a race of supermen, nor can we count on many endowments of indomitable spirit. A democratic educational system is designed for the average, for the multitude of humble spirits, and for such the selection of the right environment, some influence from noble works, is the indispensable preliminary of an education which draws our children 'imperceptibly . . . into sympathy and harmony with the beauty of reason, whose impress they take'.[1]

[1]Anthropology provides some pertinent warnings against the over-valuation of the educational process as such, considered apart from the general cultural environment. Cf., e.g. Margaret Mead, *Growing Up in New Guinea* (Pelican Books, London, 1942, p. 159): 'Not until we realize that a poor culture will never become rich, though it be filtered through the expert methods of unnumbered pedagogues, and that a rich culture with no system of education at all will leave its children better off than a poor culture with the best system in the world, will we begin to solve our educational problems. Once we lose faith in the blanket formula of education, in the magic fashion in which education, using the passive capacities of children, is to create something out of nothing, we can turn our attention to the vital matter of developing individuals, who as adults can gradually mould our oldpatterns into new and richer forms.'

Chapter Eleven

THE NECESSARY REVOLUTION

All the great revolutions in men's lives are made in thought. When a change takes place in man's thought, action follows the direction of thought as a ship follows the direction given by its rudder—Tolstoy (trans. Maude)

It is the first day of June, 1942. The laburnum trees cast their golden rain against a hedge of vivid beech leaves. Everything is fresh and sweet in the cool early sunshine. I have just heard that during the weekend the biggest air-raid in history has taken place.

Over the city of Cologne, where once we left the bones of eleven thousand martyred virgins, our air force on Sunday morning dropped about the same number of bombs. I listen half-consciously to the sounds that reach me here—to the twittering of birds and the voices of children playing in the garden—and try to realize the meaning of these distant events. On the plains of the Ukraine two immense armies have fought to a temporary standstill, and now count their killed and wounded. In Libya hundreds of armoured vehicles, a triumph of human skill, manned by technicians carefully educated for constructive work, churn through the dust and torrid heat in a fury of mutual destruction.

Against such a vacillating background I have written this book, and must now bring it to a close. I have been reminding the reader of 'the importance of sensation in an age which practises brutalities and recommends ideals'[1] and I have built up a theory which attempts to show that if in the upbringing of our children we preserved, by methods which I have indicated, the vividness of their sensations, we might succeed in relating action to feeling, and even reality to our ideals. Idealism would then no longer be an escape from reality: it would be a simple human response to reality.

For an idealist who remains aware of his environment, there are

[1] E. M. Forster on Virginia Woolf (Rede Lecture, Cambridge, 1942).

facts which though less brutal are even more disillusioning. War is not quite always with us, but poverty is, and many desperate evidences of man's injustice and cruelty. Even more difficult to discount is the universal evidence of insensibility. I believe that insensibility is a disease—literally a sclerosis—of endocrine origin; but one has to admit that it is endemic, bred into the physique of millions of our fellows. But its incidence is arbitrary. Insensibility is not a class distinction, much less a national or racial distinction. Insensibility to beauty and truth, to goodness and glory, is found in offices and colleges no less than in slums and railway carriages. Though we must admit the real presence of these diseases of the human spirit, we do not thereby confirm their reality in any absolute sense. For we must assert with Plato that the ideal is the true. The ideal may be manifested only imperfectly and intermittently, but nevertheless the only rational activity in which we can engage, and which can justify our existence, is to strive daily to make the ideal an actuality. Plato thought that in fact it could only be made actual by investing the wisest men with absolute power, and his system of education is in the first place designed to produce such wise men. But once in control, he admitted that his philosophic ruler, in order to put his ideals into practice, would resort to very tyrannical measures, such as banishing to the country all citizens over ten, and making a clean start with the remaining children, 'away from the present habits and manners of their parents'. Measures as drastic as this have been carried out by modern tyrannies (the collectivization of agriculture in Russia, for example) but only under the pressure of inexorable economic forces, and never by democratic consent.

The most a democratic philosopher can hope to do is to inspire a sufficient number of effective fellow-citizens with his idealism—to persuade them of the truth of his ideas. The *effective* among his fellow citizens are those who are organized into corporations or associations for a functional purpose, and in our particular case, this would mean the general body of the teachers and administrators of the educational system. If the *thought* within such a syndicate could change, a change in practice would inevitably follow; and their practice would gradually react upon the whole body of the community. How quick and how effective such a gradual process can be, when it is an educational process, was clearly demonstrated by the authoritarian educational policies established in our time in Russia and Germany. Though a revolution may at first be guaranteed only by force, by means of education it can in ten years be founded on conviction, and in twenty years it will have become an unconscious tradition. It follows that a democratic method of education is the only guarantee of a democratic revolution: indeed, to introduce a democratic method of education is the only necessary revolution.

The difficulty is not to reconcile idealism and reality, theory and practice: the difficulty is to reconcile discipline with freedom, order with democracy. I believe that the only way in which this can be done is the way indicated in this book. Nature does not abhor its own laws: rather, in its laws it exhibits perfect freedom. To conform to such laws should be the aim of any rational society, for human beings are part of nature and they do not resent the laws which nature imposes on them individually—the laws which condemn them to breathe at a certain rate, to eat a definite amount of food in definite chemical proportions, to sleep for a definite period of time. The only problem is to extend these laws to the body-politic, so that it too lives with a natural rhythm and symbiotic balance. I have tried to show in detail how a natural order of education could achieve such individual and social harmony.

There may be critics who will say: 'a natural order is not enough—man must aspire to a transcendental order, otherwise his existence is vain'. I do not think there is anything in this book that would deny such necessity; indeed, everything I have said implies a correspondence of some definite kind between the transcendental and phenomenal realms. Like Professor Koehler's imaginary friend,[2] I cannot regard the human mind as 'a domain of mere indifferent facts'. With him, I believe that 'intrinsic demands, fittingness and its opposite, wrongness, occur among the genuine characteristics of its contents', and that this is true whether we consider the more intellectual or the moral and the aesthetic phases of mental life. 'In all these fields we find the alternative: mere facts or, besides mere facts, right and wrong, in a sense that varies to some extent from one field to the others, but shows everywhere the same fundamental contrast to mere facts. Let us for the moment give the name *value* to this common trait of intrinsic requiredness or wrongness, and let us call *insight* all awareness of such intellectual, moral or aesthetic value. We can then say that value and corresponding insight constitute the very essence of human mental life.'

The kind of education which I have recommended in this book,

[2] *The Place of Value in a World of Facts*, p. 31.

and which I have called 'education through art', has no other object than the cultivation of such awareness of intrinsic value. I cannot believe that any other method so far evoked by educators approaches anywhere near to the adequate training of this faculty. Certainly not those systems of religious instruction which nowadays (understandably in view of our common plight) make such an insistent clamour for re-establishment. My objection to such a form of education is not that it is religious, nor even that it would like to be sectarian, but simply that it is psychologically misconceived and ineffective. That objection should be obvious to anyone who has accepted the analysis of insight which has been given in these pages (and in a sense such an analysis has been our main occupation); but to make my meaning quite clear I would like to quote an extract from a letter which Rabindranath Tagore once wrote to a missionary who was intending to come out to India:

'... I have only one thing to say; it is this: Do not be always trying to preach your doctrine, but give yourself in love. Your Western mind is too much obsessed with the idea of conquest and possession; your inveterate habit of proselytism is another form of it. Christ himself never preached any dogma or doctrine; he preached love of God. The object of a Christian should be to be like Christ—never like a coolie recruiter trying to bring coolies to his master's tea garden. Preaching your doctrine is no sacrifice at all—it is indulging in a luxury far more dangerous than all the luxuries of material living. It breeds an illusion in your mind that you are doing your duty—that you are wiser and better than your fellow-beings. But the real preaching is in being perfect, which is through meekness and love and self-dedication. If you have strong in you your pride of race, pride of sect and pride of personal superiority, then it is no use to do good to others. They will reject your gift, or even if they do accept it they will not be morally benefited by it—instances of which can be seen in India every day. On the spiritual plane you cannot *do* good until you *are* good. You cannot preach the Christianity of the Christian sect until you be like Christ—and then you do not preach Christianity, but love of God, which Christ did.'[3]

What is true of the missionary with designs on the unenlightened 'native' is equally true of the teacher with designs on the innocent

[3] *Mahatma Gandhi's Ideas*, by C. F. Andrews (London, 1929), p. 356. For a similar point of view, but that of a Christian, see Gustave Thibon: *What Ails Mankind?* Trans. Willard Hill (New York, 1947).

child. On the spiritual plane, the teacher cannot teach Christianity, but only be a Christian, and then teach the love of God. He can only do this by virtue of that insight which enables him to distinguish those values—intellectual, moral or aesthetic—which 'transcend' the phenomenal realm. I cannot conceive how the teacher, and in turn the pupil, can acquire such insight except by that process of individual and social integration which has been described here. And the process of integration, as we have seen, consists largely in avoiding those mental attitudes which are implicit in didacticism. The pattern in morality, in art, in society, must be perceived afresh by each nascent sensibility: otherwise the pattern merely kills the life it should contain.

Finally, I must answer the possible complaint that I have done nothing to solve the problem of relativity in human relations. By an insistence on the physical origin of temperamental variations, and by an equal insistence on the validity of the modes of expression peculiar to those temperamental variations, I have introduced a plurality of values into education which will defy codification and standardization. In so doing I have only represented the essential variety of our human nature, and to do more, to insist on a uniform ideal, to which all men should conform, would be to confuse the human with the divine. It is asking men, not to love God, but to be God-like—which is, perhaps, the fallacy typical of modernism in religion. At any rate, it is the error of treating different realms of being as if they were alike, that false humanism from which T. E. Hulme, who was my first preceptor in these matters, saw two sets of errors springing, namely: '(1) The attempt to introduce the *absolute* of mathematical physics into the essentially middle zone of life' which leads to 'the mechanistic view of the world'—a view which includes, I would add, the logical bias in education; and '(2) The attempt to explain the *absolute* of religious and ethical values in terms of the categories appropriate to the essentially relative and non-absolute vital zone', which leads to 'the entire misunderstanding of these values, and to the creation of a series of mixed and bastard phenomena'.[4] Perfection, as Hulme insisted, belongs only to the non-human, and to attempt to achieve it by educational methods is not merely vain, but productive of the utmost mental and social confusion.

From our standpoint in the phenomenal realm in which we live and have our being, we can only *perceive* the values of the trans-

[4] *Speculations* (London, 2nd Ed. 1936), p. 10.

cendental realm; and perception is the essential link between the two realms. We can only become increasingly and ever more accurately aware of these values by training or educating the faculty of perception to the end that it may have the quality of universal insight. That is the end to which all our observations and exhortations have been consistently directed.

In sympathy with the predominant traits of his disposition and temperament, each individual will, as a result of his educated awareness, or insight, find a different pattern in his experience. He will accordingly construct his individual view of the world, the *Weltanschauung* of his type. We can still use the Jungian phraseology to describe such basic attitudes, but we really need a more general terminology for the discussion of the ethical implications of individuality. The series used by Eduard Spranger, for example, is perhaps as convenient as any. Spranger distinguishes six basic types of individuality—the theoretical, economic, aesthetic, social, political and religious.[5] It is far from my intention to go over this ground once again: there is no doubt that Spranger's types can be correlated with Jung's types, and they are equally to be regarded as artificial aids to facilitate discussion rather than as fixed and isolated categories. In particular, they enable us to discuss the relationship of individual to collective morality, and the possibility of a hierarchy of values. Such problems are deliberately excluded from the present book—not because they do not concern us, but because we have limited the purpose of education to the development of the individual's individuality, which development necessarily implies his social integration. But to estimate the relative social value of the theoretical and the social, the economic and the political, the aesthetic and the religious attitudes—that can only be done by the philosopher of history: a De Tocqueville or a Burckhardt, a Spengler or a Croce. I have not disguised the fact that such an estimate of the lessons of history, were I capable of it, would leave me on the side of Jakob Burckhardt, who believed that the only constant factors in history

---

[5] *Types of Men: the Psychology and Ethics of Personality.* Trans, by P. J. W. Pigors (Halle, 1928). Spranger is merely an accessible source for a very general discussion of value in relation to type which has been going on in Germany for some years—viz. in the writings of Dilthey, Jaspers and Scheler. Particularly relevant are the last-named's works on *Der Formalismus in der Ethik und die materiale Wertethik* (Halle, 2nd, Ed., 1921) and *Wesen und Formen der Sympathie* (Bonn, 1926, trans. Peter Heath, *The Nature of Sympathy*, London, 1954).

are the aesthetic factors.[6] States rise, flourish for a while, and fall. Religions, if they do not altogether disappear, are transformed beyond the recognition of their founders and apostles. But art remains—permanent and indestructible, accumulative but ever free—ever, on its immediate fringes, active and expansive. I believe that this spontaneous expression is inherent in life: that collectively, as well as individually, we live out an inherent but evolving pattern—Goethe's 'geprägte Form, die lebend sich entwickelt'.

It follows that if any type should be regarded as the ideal type, it is the artist. But we have seen that there is no such thing as an 'artistic' type: every type has its artistic (i.e. aesthetic) attitude, its moments of spontaneous development, of originating activity. Every man is a special kind of artist, and in his originating activity, his play or work (and in a natural society, we have held, there should be no distinction between the psychology of work and of play), he is doing more than express himself: he is manifesting the form which our common life should take, in its unfolding.

Seer Green, July, 1940–*June,* 1942.
Stonegrave, November–December, 1956.

---

[6] Cf. *Reflections on History* (trans. M. D. Hottinger, London, 1943), p. 58: 'From the world, from time and nature, art and poetry draw images, eternally valid and universally intelligible, the only perdurable thing on earth, a second ideal creation, exempt from the limitations of individual temporality, an earthly immortality, a language for all the nations.'

BIBLIOGRAPHY

This list of references is not an exhaustive bibliography of the subject, but is confined to those works which the author has consulted in the course of writing this book. More complete bibliographies will be found in items 77 and 136. A further list, of books which the author has consulted for the present revised edition, follows at the end of this list.

(1) ALLPORT, G. W. 'Eidetic Imagery.' *Brit. J. Psych.* XV (1924–5), 99–120.

(2) AYER, F. C. *The Psychology of Drawing.* Baltimore, 1916.

(3) BALLARD, P. B. *The Changing School.* London, 1926.

(4) BALLARD, P. B., 'What London Children like to draw.' *Jour. Exp. Pedagogy,* I (1911–2), 185–97, II (1913–4), 127–9.

(5) BARNES FOUNDATION. *Art and Education.* Contributions by John Dewey, Albert C. Barnes, Laurence Buermeyer, Violette de Mazia, Mary Mullen and Thomas Munro. Merion (Pa.), 1929.

(6) BARNHART, E. N. 'The Structure of Simple Compositions: The Relation of Single Element to the Field.' *J. Exp. Psych.* XXIII (1938), 199–213.

(7) BARTLETT, F. C. 'The Function of Images.' *Brit. J. Psych.* XI (1920–1), 320–37.

(8) BARTLETT, F. C. 'Experimental Study of some Problems of Perceiving and Imaging.' *Brit. J. Psych.* VIII (1916), 222–66.

(9) BARTLETT, F. C. 'Feeling, Imaging and Thinking.' *Brit. J. Psych.* XVI (1925–6), 16–28.

(10) BARTLETT, F. C. *Psychology and Primitive Culture.* Cambridge, 1923.

(11) BARTLETT, F. C. *Psychology and the Soldier.* Cambridge, 1927.

(12) BARTLETT, F. C. and others. *The Study of Society: Methods and Problems.* London, 1939.

(13) BAYER, Herbert, and GROPIUS, Walter & Ise. *Bauhaus, 1919-1928.* London, 1939.

(14) BETTS, G. H. *Distribution and Functions of Mental Imagery.* Columbia University, New York, 1909.

(15) BOARD OF EDUCATION. *Handbook of Suggestions for the Consideration of Teachers and Others concerned in the Work of Public Elementary Schools*. London, 1938.

(16) BOARD OF EDUCATION. *Report of the Consultative Committee on Infant and Nursery Schools*. London, 1933.

(17) BOARD OF EDUCATION. *Report of the Consultative Committee on Secondary Education* (Spens Report). London, 1938.

(18) BOARD OF EDUCATION. *Report of the Consultative Committee on the Primary School*. London, 1939.

(19) BOARD OF EDUCATION. *Report of the Consultative Committee on the Education of the Adolescent*. London, 1940.

(20) BODKIN, Maud. *Archetypal Patterns in Poetry: Psychological Studies of Imagination*. London, 1934.

(21) BRIDGES, Katherine M. Banham. *The Social and Emotional Development of the Pre-School Child*. London, 1931.

(22) BUBER, Martin. *Rede ueber das Erzieherische*. Berlin, 1926.

(23) BUEHLER, C. *From Birth to Maturity*. London, 1935.

(24) BUEHLER, Karl. *Die Geistige Entwicklung des Kindes*. 6th edn. Jena, 1930.

(25) BUEHLER, Karl. *The Mental Development of the Child*. London, 1930.

(26) BULLEY, Margaret, H. 'An Enquiry as to Aesthetic Judgments of Children.' *Brit. J. Educ. Psych*. IV (1934), pp. 162–82.

(27) BULLOUGH, Edward. 'The "perceptive problem" in the Aesthetic Appreciation of single Colours.' *Brit. J. Psych*. II, 406 ff.

(28) BULLOUGH, Edward. 'The "perceptive problem" in the Aesthetic Appreciation of simple Colour Combinations.' *Ibid*. III, 406 ff.

(29) BULLOUGH, Edward. 'Psychical Distance as a Factor in Art and as an aesthetic Principle.' *Ibid*. V, 87–118.

(30) BULLOUGH, Edward. 'Recent Work in Experimental Aesthetics.' *Ibid*. XII, 76–99.

(31) BURROW, Trigant. *The Social Basis of Consciousness*. London, 1927.

(32) BURROW, Trigant. *The Structure of Insanity*. London, 1932.

(33) BURT, Cyril. *Mental and Scholastic Tests*. London, 1922, 3rd imp. 1927.

(34) BURT, Cyril. *The Factors of the Mind: an Introduction to Factor-Analysis in Psychology*. London, 1940.

BIBLIOGRAPHY

(35) CAMPAGNAC, E. T. 'Notes on the Significance of Rhythm in Plato's Scheme of Education.' *Jour. Exp. Pedagogy*, II (1913–14), 421–31.

(36) CLARKE, F. *Education and Social Change: an English Interpretation*. London, 1940.

(37) COMMISSION ON SECONDARY SCHOOL CURRICULUM (U.S.A.). *The Visual Arts in General Education. A Report of the Committee on the Function of Art in General Education*. New York and London, 1940.

(38) COOK, H. Caldwell. *The Play Way: An Essay in Educational Method*. London, 1917.

(39) COUNCIL FOR ART AND INDUSTRY *Art and Industry: Report on the Production and Exhibition of Articles of Good Design and Everyday Use*. London, 1932.

(40) COUNCIL FOR ART AND INDUSTRY. *Design and the Designer in Industry*. London, 1937.

(41) CUSDEN, Phoebe, E. *The English Nursery School*. London, 1938.

(42) DALBIEZ, Roland. *La méthode psychanalytique et la doctrine freudienne*. 2 vols. Paris, 1936.

(43) DALCROZE, Emile Jacques. *Rhythm, Music and Education*. Trans. H. F. Rubinstein, London, 1921.

(44) DAMBACH, Karl. 'Die Mehrfacharbeit und ihre typologische Bedeutung.' *Experimentelle Beitraege zur Typenkunde*, Bd. I, ed. by O. Kroh (*Zeitschr. f. Psychologie* (Ergaenzungsband 14), Leipzig, 1929.

(45) DEWAR, H. 'A Comparison of Tests of Artistic Appreciation.' *Brit. J. Educ. Psych.* VIII (1938), 29–40.

(46) DEWEY, J. *School and Society*. Chicago, 1898.

(47) DEWEY, J. *Democracy and Education*. New York, 1916.

(48) DEWEY, J. *Art as Experience*. London, 1934.

(49) DEWEY, J. and Evelyn. *Schools of To-morrow*. London, 1915.

(50) DIXON, C. Madeleine. *High, Wide and Deep: Discovering the Pre-school Child*. London, 1939.

(51) DOWNEY, June E. *Creative Imagination: Studies in the Psychology of Literature*. London, 1929.

(52) DRUMMOND, Margaret. 'The Nature of Images.' *Brit. J. Psych.* XVII (1926–7), 10–19.

(53) DURKHEIM, Emile. *L'Education Morale*. Paris, 1934.

(54) EHRHARDT, Alfred. *Gestaltungslehre: Die Praxis eines Zeitgemaessen Kunst und Werkunterrichts*, Weimar, 1932.

BIBLIOGRAPHY

(55) ELLIS, Willis D. *A Source Book of Gestalt Psychology.* London, 1938.

(56) ENG, Hilda. *The Psychology of Children's Drawings*, Trans. H. Stafford Hatfield, London, 1931.

(57) EVANS, Joan. *Taste and Temperament.* London, 1939.

(58) EYSENCK, H. J. 'The General Factor in Aesthetic Judgments.' *Brit. J. Psych.* XXXI (1940-1), 94-102.

(59) EYSENCK, H. J. 'Type Factors in Aesthetic Judgments.' *Brit. J. Psych.* XXXI (1940-1), 262-70.

(60) FEDERATED COUNCIL ON ART EDUCATION (U.S.A.). *Report of the Committee on Art Instruction in Colleges and Universities,* 1927.

(61) FIELD, Joanna. *An Experiment in Leisure.* London, 1937.

(62) FLUEGEL, J. C. *The Psychoanalytic Study of the Family.* London, 1921.

(63) FOX, Charles. *Educational Psychology: Its Problems and Methods.* London, 1930.

(64) FOX, Charles. 'A Study in Perception.' *Brit. J. Psych.* XV, 1-16 (1924).

(65) FREEMAN, Kenneth. *Schools of Hellas: An Essay on the Practice and Theory of Ancient Greek Education.* London, 1907.

(66) FREUD, Sigmund. *Introductory Lectures on Psychoanalysis.* Trans. Joan Riviere. London, 1922.

(67) FREUD, Sigmund. *New Introductory Lectures on Psychoanalysis.* Trans. W. J. H. Sprott. London, 1933.

(68) FREUD, Sigmund. *The Ego and the Id.* Trans. Joan Rivière. London, 1927.

(69) FREUD, Sigmund. *Group Psychology and the Analysis of the Ego.* Trans. J. Strachey. London, 1932.

(70) FREUD, Sigmund. 'Analysis of a Phobia of a Five-year-old Boy' (1909). *Collected Papers*, Vol. III, London, 1925.

(71) FROEBEL, Friedrich. *The Education of Man.* Trans. W. N. Hailmann. New York, 1895.

(72) FROLOV, Y. P. *Pavlov and his School: The Theory of Conditioned Reflexes.* London, 1937.

(73) FROMM, Erich. *The Fear of Freedom.* London, 1942.

(74) GALTON, Francis. *Inquiries into Human Faculty and its Development.* London, 1883 (Everyman edn. 1907).

(75) GAUPP, R. *Psychologie des Kindes*, Leipzig, 1912, 5th edn. 1925.

BIBLIOGRAPHY

(76) GIBBS, Evelyn. *The Teaching of Art in Schools*. London, 1934.

(77) GOODENOUGH, Florence, L. *Measurement of Intelligence by Drawings*. Yonkers-on-Hudson & Chicago, 1926.

(78) GRIFFITHS, Ruth. *A Study of Imagination in Early Childhood and its Functions in Mental Development*. London, 1935.

(79) HARDING, Rosamond E. M. *An Anatomy of Inspiration*. Cambridge, 1940.

(80) HARGREAVES, H. L. 'The Faculty of Imagination.' *Brit. J. Psych*. Monograph Suppt. X. Cambridge, 1927.

(81) HARTLAUB, G. F. *Der Genius im Kinde*. Breslau, 1922.

(82) HARTMAN, G. & SHUMAKER, A. *Creative Expression: The Development of Children in Art, Music, Literature and Dramatics*. New York, 1932.

(83) HARTOG, Sir Philip & RHODES, E. C. *The Marks of Examiners*, with a memorandum by Cyril Burt. London, 1936.

(84) HARWOOD, A. C. *The Way of a Child*. An Introduction to the Work of Rudolf Steiner for Children. London, 1940.

(85) HENDEL, Charles William, *Jean-Jacques Rousseau Moralist*. 2 vols. Oxford, 1934.

(86) HENDERSON, Lawrence J. *The Fitness of the Environment: an Inquiry into the Biological Significance of the Properties of Matter*. New York, 1913.

(87) HICKS, G. Dawes, 'On the Nature of Images.' *Brit. J. Psych*. XV (1924–5), 121–48.

(88) HOLMES, Edmond. *What is and What Might Be*. London, 1911.

(89) HORNEY, Karen. *The Neurotic Personality of our Time*. London, 1937.

(90) HORNEY, Karen. *New Ways in Psychoanalysis*. London, 1939.

(91) ISAACS, Susan. *Intellectual Growth in Young Children*. London, 1930.

(92) ISAACS, Susan. *Social Development in Young Children*. London, 1933.

(93) JAENSCH, E. R. *Eidetic Imagery and Typological Methods of Investigation*. Trans. Oscar Oeser, London, 1930.

(94) JAENSCH, E. R. *Grundformen menschlichen Seins*. Berlin, 1930.

(95) JAENSCH, E. R. 'Der latente Cartesianusmus der modernen Wissenschaft.' 16. Ergaenzungsband, *Zeitschr. f. Psychologie*, 1930.

(96) JUNG, C. G. *Contributions to Analytical Psychology* (includes four lectures on 'Analytical Psychology and Education'). Trans. H. G. and Cary F. Baynes. London, 1928.

(97) JUNG, C. G. *Modern Man in Search of a Soul*. Trans. W. S. Dell and Cary F. Baynes. London, 1933.

(98) JUNG, C. G. *The Integration of the Personality*. Trans. Stanley M. Dell. London, 1940.

(99) JUNG, C. G. *Psychological Types, or the Psychology of Individuation*. Trans. by H. Godwin Baynes. London, 1938.

(100) JUNG, C. G. and WILHELM, Richard. *The Secret of the Golden Flower: A Chinese Book of Life*. Translated and explained by R. W. with a commentary by C. G. J. London, 1938.

(101) KERSCHENSTEINER, G. *Die Entwicklung der zeichnerischen Begabung*. Munich, 1905.

(102) KIMMINS, Charles William. *Children's Dreams: an Unexplored Land*. London, 1937.

(103) KINTER, M. *The Measurement of Artistic Abilities*. New York, 1933.

(104) KIRKPATRICK, E. A. *Imagination and its Place in Education*. Boston, 1920.

(105) KLEIN, Melanie. *The Psychoanalysis of Children*. Trans. Alix Strachey. 2nd edn. London, 1937.

(106) KLUEVER, H. 'Studies on the Eidetic Type and on Eidetic Imagery.' *Psychological Bulletin*, XXV (1928), 69–104.

(107) KOEHLER, Wolfgang. *Gestalt Psychology*. London, 1930.

(108) KOEHLER, Wolfgang. *The Place of Value in a World of Facts*. London, 1940.

(109) KOFFKA, K. *The Growth of the Mind: an Introduction to Child Psychology*. Trans. Robert Morris Ogden, 2nd edn. London, 1928.

(110) KOFFKA, K. *Principles of Gestalt Psychology*. London, 1935.

(111) KOFFKA. 'Problems in the Psychology of Art.' *Art: a Bryn Mawr Symposium*. Bryn Mawr, 1940.

(112) KRETSCHMER, Ernst. *Physique and Character: an Investigation of the Nature of Constitution and of the Theory of Temperament*. Trans. by W. H. J. Sprott, 2nd edn. revised with an Appendix by E. Miller, M.R.C.S., L.R.C.P., D.P.M. London, 1936.

(113) KROH, O. (ed.). *Experimentelle Beitraege zur Typenkunde*, Leipzig, 1929. Vol. I (1929), includes 'Die Mehrfacharbeit und ihre typologische Bedeutung,' by Karl Dambach, Vol. III (1932), in-

cludes 'Die Musikalitaet in ihren Beziehungen zur Grundstruktur der Persoenlichkeit,' by Paul Lamparter, and 'Typische Formen Bildhafter Gestaltung,' by Hans Lamparter.

(114) LEVINSTEIN, Siegfried. *Kinderzeichnungen bis zum 14. Lebensjahr.* Leipzig, 1905.

(115) LINCOLN, Jackson Steward. *The Dream in Primitive Cultures.* London, 1935.

(116) LINE, W. 'The Growth of Visual Perception in Children.' *Brit. J. Psych.* Monograph Suppt. XV, Cambridge, 1931.

(117) LIVINGSTONE, Sir Richard. *The Future in Education.* Cambridge, 1941.

(118) LOEWE, Adolf. *The Universities in Transformation.* London, 1940.

(119) LOEWENFELD, V. *The Nature of Creative Activity.* Trans. by O. A. Oeser. London, 1939.

(120) LOWENFELD, Margaret. *Play in Childhood.* London, 1935.

(121) LOWY, Samuel. *Biological and Psychological Foundations of Dream Interpretation.* London, 1942.

(122) LUQUET, G. H. *Le Dessin Enfantin.* Paris, 1927.

(123) MCCALLISTER, W. J. *The Growth of Freedom in Education.* London, 1931.

(124) MCMILLAN, Margaret. *Education through the Imagination.* London, 1904.

(125) MANNHEIM, Karl. *Ideology and Utopia: an Introduction to the Sociology of Knowledge.* London, 1936.

(126) MANNHEIM, Karl. *Man and Society in an Age of Reconstruction.* London, 1940.

(127) MANNHEIM, Karl. *A Diagnosis of our Time.* London, 1943.

(128) MEARNS, Hughes. *Creative Youth.* New York, 1925.

(129) MEARNS, Hughes. *Creative Power.* New York. 1929.

(130) MEARNS, Hughes. *The Creative Adult. Self Education in the Art of Living.* New York, 1940.

(131) METZ, P. *Die eidetische Anlage der Jugendlichen in ihrer Beziehung zur kuenstlerischen Gestalthung.* Langensalza, 1929.

(132) MOHOLY-NAGY, L. *The New Vision: Fundamentals of Design —Painting, Sculpture, Architecture.* London, 1939.

(133) MONTESSORI, Maria. *The Advanced Montessori Method.* Vol. I, 'Spontaneous Activity in Education,' trans. by F. Simmonds and L. Hutchinson. Vol. II, 'The Montessori Elementary Material,' trans. by Arthur Livingston, London, 1917 and 1918.

BIBLIOGRAPHY

(134) MUENZ, Ludwig and LOEWENFELD, Viktor. *Plastische Arbeiten Blinder.* Bruenn, 1934.

(135) MURCHISON, C. (ed.). *A Handbook of Child Psychology,* 2nd ed. Worcester (Mass.), 1933.

(136) NATIONAL SOCIETY FOR THE STUDY OF EDUCATION. *Fortieth Year Book: Art in American Life and Education.* Bloomington (Illinois), 1941. Includes 46 chapters divided into the following sections: I—'Art in American Life.' II—The Nature of Art and Related Types of Experience.' III—'Art Education: its Aims, Procedures and Agencies.' IV—'The Preparation of Teachers of Art.'

(137) NATORP, Friedrich. *Grundlagen kuenstlerischer Erziehung.* Augsburg, 1930.

(138) NETTLESHIP, Richard Lewis. *The Theory of Education in Plato's 'Republic'.* Originally contributed to *Hellenica: A Collection of Essays on Greek Poetry, Philosophy, History and Religion,* Ed. by Evelyn Abbott, Oxford and Cambridge, 1880. Separate edition. Oxford, 1935.

(139) NUNN, T. Percy. *Education: its Data and First Principles.* London, 1920.

(140) OAKLEY, C. A. 'The Interpretation of Children's Drawings.' *Brit. J. Psych.* XXI (1930–1), 256–70.

(141) OAKLEY, C. A. 'Drawings of a Man by Adolescents.' *Brit. J. Psych.* XXXI (1940–1), 37–60.

(142) OGDEN, Robert Morris. *Psychology and Education.* New York, 1926.

(143) PAVLOV, Ivan Petrovich. *Lectures on Conditioned Reflexes.* Vol. I: Twenty-five Years of Objective Study of the Higher Nervous Activity (Behaviour) of Animals. London (1928: new edn. 1941). Vol. II: Conditioned Reflexes and Psychiatry. London, 1941.

(144) PEARSON, Ralph, M. *The New Art of Education.* New York, 1941.

(145) PFAHLER, Gerhard. 'System der Typenlehre. Grundlegung einer paedagogischen Typenlehre'. *Zeitschr. f. Psychologie,* Ergaenzungsband 15. Leipzig, 1929.

(146) PIAGET, Jean. *Language and Thought of the Child.* Trans. Marjorie Warden. London, 1926.

(147) PIAGET, Jean. *Judgment and Reasoning in the Child.* Trans. Marjorie Warden. London, 1928.

(148) PIAGET, Jean. *The Child's Conception of the World.* Trans. J. and A. Tomlinson. London, 1929.

(149) PIAGET, Jean. *The Child's Conception of Physical Causality*. Trans. Marjorie Gabain. London, 1930.

(150) PIAGET, Jean. *The Moral Judgment of the Child*. Trans. Marjorie Gabain. London. 1932.

(151) PIAGET, Jean. *La naissance de l'intelligence chez l'enfant. La construction du réel chez l'enfant*. 2 vols., Neuchâtel, 1936–7.

(152) PLATO. *The Republic*. Trans. with introduction by F. M. Cornford. Oxford, 1941.

(153) PLATO. *The Laws*. Trans. with introduction by A. E. Taylor. London, 1934.

(154) PRINZHORN, H. *Bildnerei der Geisteskranken*, 2nd ed. Berlin, 1922.

(155) RASMUSSEN, Vilhelm. *Child Psychology*. Vol. II: 'The Kindergarten Child: Its Conception of Life and its Mental Powers.' London, 1921.

(156) READ, Herbert. *Art and Industry*. London, 1934.

(157) READ, Herbert. *Art and Society*. London, 1937.

(158) RICHARDSON, Marion. *Writing and Writing Patterns*. London, 1935.

(159) ROUMA, Georges. *Le Langage graphique de l'enfant*, 2nd ed. Brussels, 1913.

(160) ROUSSEAU, Jean Jacques. *Emile, or Education*. Trans. Barbara Foxley, London (Everyman edn.), 1911.

(161) RUGG, Harold. *Culture and Education in America*. New York, 1931.

(162) RUGG, Harold. *The Great Technology. Social Chaos and the Public Mind*. New York, 1933.

(163) RUGG, Harold and SHUMAKER, Ann. *The Child-centered School. An appraisal of the New Education*. New York and London, 1928.

(164) RUSSELL, Bertrand. *The Analysis of Mind*. London, 1921.

(165) RUSSELL, Bertrand. *On Education, especially in Early Childhood*. London, 1926.

(166) RUSSELL, R. L. *The Child and his Pencil*. London, 1935.

(167) SCHUHL, Pierre-Maxime. *Platon et l'art de son temps*. Paris, 1933.

(168) SCHELER, Max. *Wesen und Formen der Sympathie*. Bonn, 1926. Trans. Peter Heath. *The Nature of Sympathy*. London, 1954.

(169) SEARL, M. N. 'Some Contrasted Aspects of Psychoanalysis and Education.' *Brit. J. Educ. Psych.* II (1932).

(170) SHAW, Bernard. *Misalliance. With a Treatise on Parents and Children.* London, 1930.

(171) SHERRINGTON, Sir Charles. *Man on his Nature.* Cambridge, 1940.

(172) SPEARMAN, C. *The Nature of 'Intelligence' and the Principles of Cognition.* 2nd edn. London, 1927.

(173) SPEARMAN, C. *The Abilities of Men: their Nature and Measurement.* London, 1927.

(174) SPEARMAN, C. *Creative Mind.* London and Cambridge, 1930.

(175) SPRANGER, Eduard. *Types of Man: The Psychology and Ethics of Personality.* Trans. Paul J. W. Pigors. Halle (Saale),1928.

(176) STEAD, H. G. *The Education of a Community.* London, 1942.

(177) STEINER, Rudolf. *The Essentials of Education.* London, 1926.

(178) STEINER, Rudolf. *The New Art of Education.* London, 1928.

(179) STERN, William. *Psychologie der fruehen Kindheit.* Leipzig, 1914, 1923, 1930.

(180) STERN, William. *Psychology of Early Childhood up to the Sixth Year of Age.* Trans. Anna Barwell. London, 1924.

(181) SULLY, James. *Studies of Childhood.* London, 1896.

(182) SUTTIE, Ian D. *The Origins of Love and Hate.* London, 1935.

(183) TANNAHILL, Sallie B. *Fine Arts for Public School Administrators.* New York, 1932.

(184) TEASDALE, H. 'A Quantitative Study of Eidetic Imagery.' *Brit. J. Educ. Psych.* IV (1934), 65–73.

(185) THOMPSON, D'Arcy Wentworth. *On Growth and Form.* New ed. Cambridge, 1942.

(186) TOMLINSON, R. R. *Picture Making by Children.* London, 1934.

(187) TOMLINSON, R. R. *Crafts for Children.* London, 1935.

(188) TOMLINSON, R. R. *Children as Artists.* London, 1943.

(189) VALENTINE, C. W. 'A Study of the Beginnings and Significance of Play in Infancy.' *Brit. J. Educ. Psych.* VIII (1938), 188–200, 285–305.

(190) VAN WYLICK, Margret. *Die Welt des Kindes in seiner Darstellung.* Vienna, 1936.

(191) VERNON, M. D. 'The Relation of Cognition and Phantasy in Children.' *Brit. J. Psych.* XXX (1939–40), 273–94. XXXI (1940–1), 1–21.

(192) VIOLA, Wilhelm. *Child Art and Franz Cizek.* Foreword by R. R. Tomlinson. Vienna, 1936.

318

BIBLIOGRAPHY

(193) VIOLA, Wilhelm. *Child Art*. London, 1942.

(194) WEBSTER, T. B. L. 'Greek Theories of Art and Literature down to 400 B.C.' *Classical Quarterly*, XXXIII (1939), 166–79.

(195) WHITEHEAD, A. N. *The Rhythm of Education*. London, 1922.

(196) WHITEHEAD, A. N. *The Aims of Education and Other Essays*. London, 1929.

(197) WILHELM, F. *Die Bedeutung der eidetischen Forschung fuer Erziehung und Unterricht*. Leipzig, 1927.

(198) WILLEMSE, W. A. *Constitution-Types in Delinquency*. London, 1932.

(199) WOELFFLIN, Heinrich. *Principles of Art History*. Trans. by M. D. Hottinger. London, 1932.

(200) WOODWARD, William Harrison. *Studies in Education during the Age of the Renaissance, 1400–1600*. Cambridge, 1924.

(201) WRIGHT, Ernest Hunter. *The Meaning of Rousseau*. Oxford, 1929.

(202) WULFF, Oskar. *Die Kunst des Kindes*. Stuttgart, 1927.

ADDENDA TO THE BIBLIOGRAPHY

This list includes titles that have been consulted during the revision of the text for the present (1958) edition, and a number of books which have appeared since the first (1943) edition and which seem to the author to reinforce his argument.

(203) ARNHEIM, Rudolf. *Art and Visual Perception: a psychology of the creative eye*. London, 1956.

(204) BRITSCH, Gustav. *Theorie der bildenden Kunst*. Munich, 1926.

(205) BUBER, Martin. *Between Man and Man*. Trans. Ronald Gregor Smith. London, 1947.

(206) CANE, Florence. *The Artist in Each of Us*. New York, 1951.

(207) DUNNETT, Ruth. *Art and Child Personality*. London, 1948.

(208) FIELD, Joanna. *On Not Being Able to Paint*. London, 1950.

(209) FORDHAM, Michael. *The Life of Childhood. A Contribution to Analytical Psychology*. London, 1944.

(210) GILLIARD, Edmond. *L'Ecole contre la vie*. Lausanne, 1942.

(211) GOODMAN, W. L. *Anton Simeonovitch: Russian Teacher*. London, 1949.

BIBLIOGRAPHY

(212) GRÖZINGER, Wolfgang. *Scribbling, Drawing, Painting: the early forms of the child's pictorial creativeness.* Trans. Ernst Kaiser and Eithne Wilkins. London, 1945.

(213) HARTLEY, Ruth, FRANK, Lawrence, K., and GOLDENSEN, Robert. *Understanding Children's Play.* New York & London, 1952.

(214) HOURD, Marjorie L. *The Education of the Poetic Spirit.* London, 1949.

(215) HUIZINGA, J. *Homo Ludens: A Study of the Play-Element in Culture.* London, 1949.

(216) JAEGER, Werner. *Paideia: The Ideals of Greek Culture.* Trans. Gilbert Highet. 3 vols. Oxford, 1939–45.

(217) KAYSER, Hans. *Akróasis. Die Lehre von der Harmonik der Welt.* Basel, 1946.

(218) KELLOGG, Rhoda. *What Children Scribble and Why.* San Francisco (Golden Gate Nursery Schools), 1955.

(219) KELLOGG, Rhoda. *Finger Painting in the Nursery School.* San Francisco (Golden Gate Nursery Schools), 1955.

(220) LANGER, Susanne K. *Feeling and Form.* New York & London, 1953.

(221) LANGEVIN, Vige et LOMBARD, Jean. *Peintures et dessins collectifs des enfants.* Paris, 1950.

(222) LODGE, Rupert C. *Plato's Theory of Art.* London, 1953.

(223) LOEWENFELD, Viktor. *Creative and Mental Growth. A Textbook on Art Education.* New York, 1947.

(224) MINISTRY OF EDUCATION. *Art Education.* Pamphlet No. 6. London, 1946.

(225) MORRIS, Charles. *Signs, Language and Behaviour.* New York, 1946.

(226) PIAGET, Jean. *Play, Dreams and Imitation in Childhood.* Trans. C. Gattegno and F. M. Hodgson. London, 1951.

(227) PIAGET, Jean. *The Child's Conception of Number.* Trans. C. Gattegno and F. M. Hodgson. London, 1952.

(228) PIAGET, Jean. *The Origin of Intelligence in the Child.* Trans. Margaret Cook. London, 1953.

(229) PIAGET, Jean. *The Child's Construction of Reality.* Trans. Margaret Cook. New York & London, 1955.

(230) PIAGET, Jean, and INHELDER, Bärbel. *The Child's Conception of Space.* Trans. F. J. Langdon and J. L. Lunzer. London, 1956.

(231) PETRIE, Maria. *Art and Regeneration.* London, 1946.

BIBLIOGRAPHY

(232) READ, Herbert. *Education for Peace.* New York and London, 1949.

(233) ROBERTSON, Seonaid M. *Creative Crafts in Education.* London, 1952.

(234) SCHAEFFER-SIMMERN, Henry. *The Unfolding of Artistic Activity: Its Basis, Processes and Implications.* University of California Press, 1950.

(235) SHELDON, W. H. *The Varieties of Human Physique.* New York & London, 1940.

(236) SHELDON, W. H. *The Varieties of Temperament.* New York & London, 1942.

(237) SLADE, Peter. *Child Drama.* London, 1954.

(238) SMYTHIES, J. R. *Analysis of Perception.* London, 1956.

(239) SNELL, Reginald. Introduction to *On the Aesthetic Education of Man,* by Friederich Schiller. London, 1954.

(240) STONE, A. L. *Story of a School.* Ministry of Education Pamphlet No. 14. London, 1949.

(241) THIBON, Gustave. *What Ails Mankind? An Essay on Social Psychology.* New York, 1947.

(242) ZIEGFELD, Edwin (editor). *Education and Art: A Symposium.* Paris (Unesco), 1953.

INDEX

INDEX

INDEX

INDEX

INDEX

326

INDEX

realism, 26, 27, 97–8, 130–1, 136–7, 173n
realism, descriptive, 118
realism, visual, 119
reality, principle, of, 68
reciprocity, 276–82
REDON, O., 102
regional relevance, 243
relativity, human, 306
religious education, 221–2, 305–6
Renaissance, the, 63, 87, 100
repetition, 143
representation, 128
repression, 119
response, 166–7
responsibility, 279
RHODES, E. C., 251n
rhythm, 24, 65–6, 253
rhythmical patterns, 140, 141, 143, 144, 145
RICCI, C., 116
RICHARDSON, Marion, 147, 234–5
RICHMOND, G., 45n
RIEGL, A., 94
ROBERTSON, J. M., 205n
romantic category, 140, 142
romanticism, 27
RORSCHACH, H., 131n
ROUMA, G., 117
ROUSSEAU, 7, 49, 59, 232, 252, 297, 298
RUGG, H., 162
RUSKIN, 116, 257, 261
RUSSELL, Bertrand, 53n

sadism, 6
SADLER, Sir M., 251n
SCHELER, M., 307n
'schema', the, 121–6, 130–4, 208
schematic category, 140, 141, 143, 152–3
Schiller, 1, 85, 109, 268, 284
schizoid temperament, 77–8, 150 3
scholar, the, 225
school, structure of, 197–301
science, 10, 11, 213, 243
science of art, 259–60
Scotland, 219
scribbling, 121; see *Kellogg, R.*
scripture, 249
SEARL, M. N., 181n
secondary education, 225–6, 228, 229, 230, 240–9
selection, 288, 289, 290, 293

self-consciousness, 280
self-education, 292
self-expression, 167n, 208–9
self-government, 266
sensationalism, 49
sensation, 9, 27, 40, 60, 86, 94, 111, 223
sensibility, 220, 221, 245, 252, 255, 259
sensitivity, differential, 192
separateness, 196–8
shape, 16
SHAW, G. B., 244n
SHELDON, W. H., 26n, 75–81, 95, 282n; groups of traits listed by 79–80; on level of soma-type, 152n
SHELLEY, 42, 43
SHERRINGTON, Sir Charles, 173n
SHIRER, W. L., 262
SHUMAKER, A., 162
SIEBOLD, Erika von, 83n
signs, 127–30
SIMSON, O. von, 22n
skill, 60–1, 211, 214
Slade professorships, 256
SMYTHIES, J R., 203n
SNELL, R., 269n
society, 235
social consciousness, 277–81
space, 23
SPEARMAN, C., 45, 71, 107, 168, 188, 250–2
specialization, 240, 246
speech, 175
SPENCER, H., 109, 111
SPENGLER, O., 307
Spens Report, 213, 215, 218, 241, 242, 248
spontaneity, 110–15, 208, 286 7, 295
SPRANGER, E., 24, 26, 307
STEINER, R., 226
STERN, W., 117, 132, 133n, 139n, 160n
STYHR, E., 235n
STIRK, S. D., 251n
structural form, 140, 141, 143, 144, 145
STRZYGOWSKI, J., 87
styles of art, 26, 27
S-type (synaesthetic), 82, 83n
subconscious, 8
subject-matter of drawings, 161n
subjects, 230–2
sublimation, 178–9
SULLY, James, 116–17, 121, 136, 153, 162, 269, 270

INDEX

sun adaptation, 83n
super-ego, the, 179–85, 193
superrealism, 26, 27, 33, 97–8
SUTTIE, I. D., 117*n*, 166. 167*n*, 235*n*, 273, 292, 293
symbolism and symbols, 118, 123, 127–36. 140*n*, 185, 188
symmetry, 24, 61
synergy, 195

TAGORE, Rabindranath, 305
teacher, the, 12–13, 200, 207 *seqq.*, 236, 285–95
technical intelligence, 242–3; technical secondary schools, 242
temperament, 26, 76, 157–9
T-type, 81, 102, 150n, 152
test, Goodenough, 253*n*
tests, intelligence, 250, 251, 252–3
test, Meyer-Seashore, 253
test, Rorschach, 131
tetanoid condition, 80
THACKERAY, 42
theatre, school, 299–300
THIBON, G., 221*n*
thinking (thought), 9, 49–53, 52*n*, 59, 68, 69, 70, 86, 95, 112, 223
THOMPSON, Sir D'Arcy Wentworth, 18, 20
thought (see *thinking*)
TILTON, Florence, 238
time-table (see *curriculum*)
TOCQUEVILLE, A. de, 307
TOLSTOY, 265
totalitarianism, 4
type, associative, 91–4, 148
type, character, 91–4, 104, 147–9
type differentiation, 153–9
type, extraverted feeling, 101, 145, 146, 156
type, extraverted intuition, 99, 103, 147
type, extraverted sensation, 99, 102, 145, 157. 158
type, extraverted thinking, 101, 147, 157
type, introverted feeling, 101, 146, 147
type, introverted intuition, 99, 103, 147, 155
type, introverted sensation, 102, 146, 147, 158
type, introverted thinking, 101, 145, 147

type, intra-subjective (physiological), 91–4, 147–9
type, objective, 91–4
types, aesthetic, 96–104
types, disintegrate, 82–4, 101–3
types, eidetic, 80–4
types, haptic, 89–90, 143, 144, 145, 147
types, function, 145–7
types, individual, 307
types, integrate, 81–2, 84, 89
types, perceptive, 25, 90–5, 147–50
types, psychological, 26, 27, 73–4, 84–6, 147
types, visual, 89–90, 131, 133–5

unconscious, the, 32, 171–206; collective, 177, 181–5
union, unitedness, 280–4
university education, 218, 256–64

VALENTINE, C. W., 91*n*
values, 28, 31–4, 104, 105, 198, 199, 208, 239, 284
VARLEY, 43–4
verbal education, 9
verbal inventions, 162–4
verisimilitude, 128
VERWORN, M., 94–5, 138
VINCI, L. da, 100
viscerotonia (group of traits), 79
visual education, 9; images, 30; realism, 119; visualization powers, 44, 45, 47, 67
vocational training, 218, 228, 230, 255

WALTER, W. Grey, 203n
weak-sighted children, 125–6, 133–4
WERNER, H., 164
WHITEHEAD, A. N., 59, 66, 259, 261
wholeness, organic, 5, 69
WILHELM, R., 186*n*
WILLEMSE, W. A., 26, 74*n*, 79*n*
wisdom, 220. 225
WOELFFLIN, H., 94, 100
WOHLGEMUTH, 46
WOODWARD, W. H., 63*n*
WORDSWORTH, W., 29
workshops, 216–17
WORRINGER, W., 83*n*, 86–9, 132
WRIGHT, T., 44*n*
WULFF, O., 117, 127, 135, 138–9
WYLICK, Margret van, 159–61

328

ABOUT THE AUTHOR

Herbert Read was one of the world's most famous art historians and literary critics. In addition to *Education Through Art,* his most famous work, he has written over twenty books, among them *The Art of Sculpture, Art and Alienation, Anarchy and Order,* and *This Way, Delight,* a children's book.

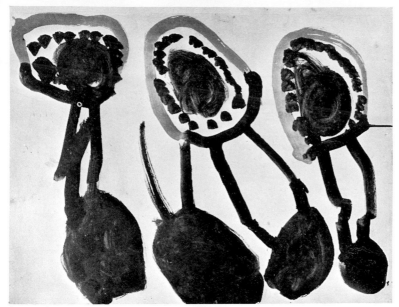

1a   B 3   *'Dollies'*   HOME

Abstract 'schema'. Direct representation of purely affective or 'haptic'
realization of the object. See pp. 90, 133–5

1b   G 5   *'Snake round the World and a Boat'*   HOME

Abstract symbolic drawing, entirely spontaneous in origin. See p. 189

'Father Feeding the Birds'

The 'schema' becomes more realistic, but is still an expression of the sensational affe
The birds are represented by an abstract symbol (wavy line)

B 4   *Portrait*   DUNHURST (P)

arly evidence of intelligent observation
and organic feeling (there is some attempt
to unite the figure with its environment).
The child is described as 'remarkably
observant and intelligent, but most uncommunicative'. Probably introvert thinking type

3b   **G 4**   *'With Love from Esther'*
DUNHURST (P)

By contrast with (*a*), a haptic, sensational
drawing. Note: nose between the eyes,
where it 'feels' to be, and cheeks realized
as separate entities (round outlined blobs
of red), white teeth, no torso. Title given
by the child indicates desire to communicate. Described as 'very imaginative,
sweet-tempered, with a definite will of
her own'. Probably extravert feeling type

4a   G 5 VI   *Figure*   ISLEWORTH (E)

Retention of affect-schema by child of backward intellectual development. Compare Plate 9a

4b   B 5   *Figure*   ISLEWORTH (E)

Disintegrate schema of a child of poor physique with marked want of co-ordination in speech, deportment and general behaviour. Compare next illustration

'*Teacher*'   ISLEWORTH (E)

A drawing by the same child as Plate 4*b* after eighteen months' progress. Lack of co-ordination still shown in patched colouring of dress (red and green)

5*b*G 5

A first figure drawing

DUNHURST (P)

Another drawing showing lack of co-ordination (e.g., disjointed arms). This child often dissociates colour from object in separate patches. Described as 'precocious, quick-witted, and full of "pretty" mannerisms'. Probably extravert thinking type

6   G 5   *'Kitty in the Sun'*   L.C.C. (E)

Evidence of early imaginative activity. Kitty has a clearly articulated body, but the sun has limbs only, radiating from a face. Probably introvert feeling type

7a G 5   *'Mother, Rain and a Flag'*   ISLEWORTH (E)

Another example of the retention of the schema in a child of retarded intellectual development (compare Plate 4*b*), but in this case there is more evidence of rhythmical pattern and of extraverted sensation (the mother is actually very stout; note also the ground line, which is not characteristic of the strict schema)

7b G 5 VI   *'The Family'*   THE MARLBOROUGH SCHOOL (E)

Typical drawing of a robust child of normal intelligence, for comparison with Plates 4*a*, 5*b* and 7*a*. Individual characteristics (e.g. hair) are now differentiated; head and body are distinct entities, but the greater sensational value of the head is indicated by its relatively greater size; note also that the cheeks are still a distinct feature

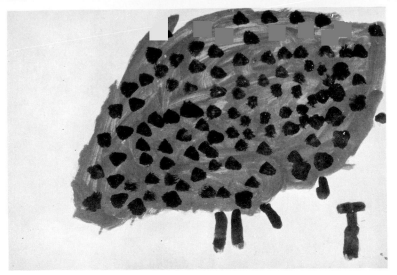

8*a*   B 5   '*Ladybird*'   HOME

The child has projected himself into the object, and is giving intuitive expression to its form and volume. It is the mode of apprehension and representation which in an older child is illustrated below

8*b*   G 15   '*The Cat*'   HIGHBURY HILL HIGH SCHOOL (S)

The volume and structural form of the animal are intuitively apprehended, and thrown out against the formal pattern of the carpet

9a G 5 VI

Figure   ISLEWORTH (E)

Drawing by a girl of exceptionally high standard of intelligence. Expressive profile view of face; accurate observation of limbs, foreshortening of forearm holding basket; swing of the necklace and compensatory fling of skirt; contrasted tonal value of black hair and green dress (pale yellow hat, knickers, gloves and stockings and very pale pink flesh not visible in this reproduction). Probably introvert thinking type likely to develop an organic style of expression. Compare Plates 5b and 7b

9b G 5
'Stirring the Christmas Pudding'
DUNHURST (P)

The ground-level, the level of the table on which the bowl stands, are fixities to which the body of the child must be accommodated. The sensational organ most immediately involved, the neck which conveys the pudding from the bowl to the stomach, is therefore elongated. An example of haptic over-emphasis. See p 135

10*a* G 6
A first figure drawing
DUNHURST (P)

Compare Plate 5*b*. Comparatively a backward child, but one of 'normal, equable temperament', expressed directly in the free rhythmic lines of the drawing. Over-emphasis of buttons, hands and fingers. Probably introvert sensation type

10*b* G 6
A first painting by the same child

A series devoted to the same subject drawn by sixteen different children at the same time and under the same conditions. They are given in the class order, i.e. the order of tested school intelligence. The brief characterization of temperament is given in the words of the teacher. I have added a tentative diagnosis of psychological type and mode of plastic expression. All sixteen drawings are executed in coloured crayons as indicated in brackets. (br = brown, g = green, r = red, bl = blue, y = yellow, p = purple, bk = black.)

11*a*　G 7　Brilliant; attainment age well over 7. French mother. Extraverted intuitive = rhythmical pattern (br, g, r, bl)

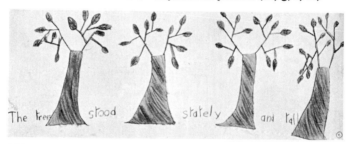

11*b*　B 7　Studious, attentive to detail; reserved, cautious but friendly. Extraverted intuitive = rhythmical pattern (br, **g, r**)

11*c*　G 7　Sociable, confident, reliable; a good leader. Extraverted feeling + sensation = decorative + emphatic (br, **g, r**)

12*a* B 7 Bold, imaginative, excitable, often sensational. Extraverted sensation=empathetic (br, g)

12*b* G 7 Sociable, rather superficial, conversational, great love of colour and dancing. Extraverted thinking=enumerative (br, g, r, y)

12*c* G 7 Solemn, intelligent, but very reserved. Introverted sensation=expressionist (br, g)

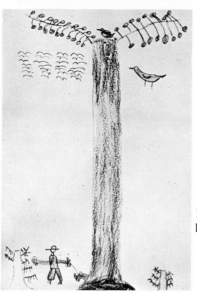

13b   B 7   Boisterous, sociable, generous, a natural leader, but impulsive. Extraverted feeling = decorative (br, g, r, bl)

13a   B 7   Backward through much absence, poor physique, quiet but friendly and co-operative, reliable. Extraverted thinking = enumerative. (br, g, r, y, bl)

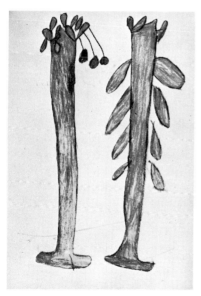

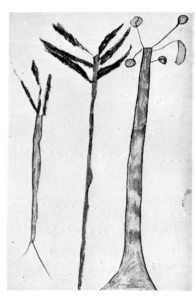

13c   G 7   Self-conscious, timid. Introverted sensation = expressionist (br, r, g, bl, y)

13d   G 7   Twin sister to c, same disposition but less advanced, careful and polite, tends to lead but no real initiative. Introverted sensation = expressionist (br, r, g, y)

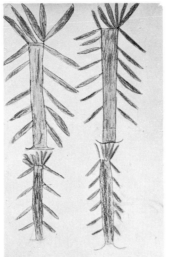

14*a*   (br, p, y, r, g)

G 7 Very poor physique; introvert. Introverted intuitive=structural form

14*b*   (r, g, y)

B 7   Normal,   uninteresting.? Introverted intuitive=structural form

14*c*   (y, bk, g,
                                                         bl, br)

B 7   Affectionate, unsteady, sensitive. Introverted feeling=imaginative

15a G 7 Very poor physique, quiet, happy but not sociable. Introverted sensation = expressionist (y, br, p, g)

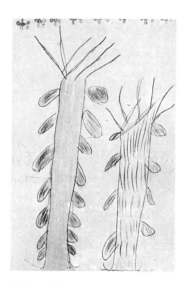

15b G 7 All round poor development, no initiative, over-careful mother. ? Introverted sensation = expressionist form (y, p, g, r)

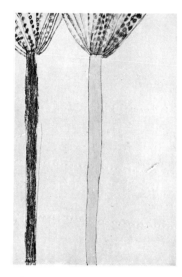

15c G 7 Very poor nutrition, shy, sensitive. Introverted intuitive = structural form (r, y, bk, bl, g, p)

16a   G 7   *'A Garden Full of Flowers'*   ISLEWORTH (E)

16b   B 7 VIII   *The same subject*   ISLEWORTH (E)

An extreme contrast in modes of plastic expression. The girl (I.Q.101) produces a structural form of extreme rigidity, every detail balanced about the radial axes. The boy (I.Q.112) produces a completely unbalanced distribution of details (our enumerative type). See p. 163 for a comparison of stories invented by the same children about the same time as these drawings were made. From this evidence it may be deduced that the girl is of the introverted intuitive type, the boy of the extraverted thinking type—a deduction confirmed by the teacher

17a B 13+
'The Cattle Show'
MILL HILL (S)

Extraverted attitude. The child is trying to record what his eye actually saw. He uses the 'imbricated' method of indicating perspective (building his objects up one behind the other) and thus achieves a certain sense of rhythmical pattern. Probably extravert sensation type (impressionist) with secondary intuitive tendency (rhythmical pattern)

17b B 13+   'Cattle'   MILL HILL (S)

Introverted attitude. The child is trying to realize the contour and mass of each animal as a unique structure, a vital form. Comparable with bushman and neolithic art (cf. Hugo Obermaier and Herbert Kuhn, *Bushman Art* (Oxford, 1930), pls. 10–15). Probably introvert sensation type (expressionist) with secondary intuitive tendency (structural form)

18*a*   B 13+   *'The Cattle Show'*   MILL HILL (S)

Introverted attitude. The child tries to realize the animal as a moving object within an environment, thus showing an organic feeling for wholeness. Probably introverted feeling type (imaginative) with secondary thinking tendency (organic)

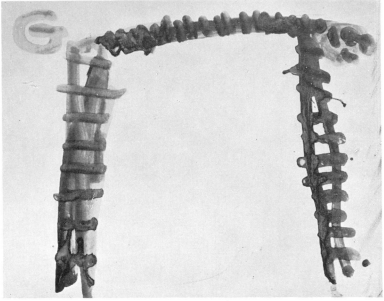

18*b*   G 4 XI   *'Tiger'*   HOME

This drawing, by a much younger child, illustrates the wholly introvert, inorganic basis of the schema. Whatever image of a tiger the child may have, she pays no regard to it, but draws merely the tiger's stripes (blue on red) and thus creates an expressive symbol which corresponds not to her perceptual awareness or conceptual knowledge of the tiger, but to her feeling for the tiger's dominant features, its 'fearful symmetry'

19*a* G 7   *'Daddy'*   ISLEWORTH (E)

19*b* B 14   *'War Wedding'*   LEICESTER (E)

These two drawings illustrate, at infant and adolescent stages, a type of unreflective and naïve expression which is characteristic of many children, and which persists into adult life. It is essentially the mode of expression of the extraverted feeling type, a superficial decorative style, which can develop into a talent for pretty embroidery, etc., but is not capable of the qualities necessary for art of any deeper significance

20a B 6 III

'*New York*' (crayon) HOME

An unusually early example of feeling for spatial depth and vertical 'perspective'. The child had been brought up in the country near London, and had never seen New York. It is an imaginative construction, and the child's work in general was of the introverted feeling type

20b G 16

'*Home from the Sea*' (pen)
LANGFORD GROVE (S)

The same mode of expression at a more advanced stage

21a   G 16+   *'Guernsey Harbour'*   QUEEN'S COLLEGE, HARLEY STREET, LONDON (S)

A more sophisticated and decorative treatment of an architectural subject (done after the teacher's verbal description). Very bright colours

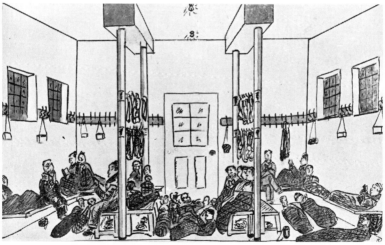

21b   B 16   *'Air Raid Shelter'*   CRANBROOK (S)

The balanced symmetrical form probably imposed by the subject. Essentially an enumerative type of drawing based on an extraverted thinking attitude

22a G 12   22b G 12

'*Mind-pictures*' MILHAM FORD, OXFORD (S)

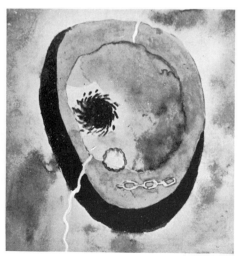
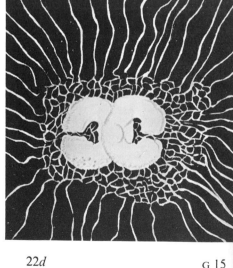

22c G 13   22d G 15

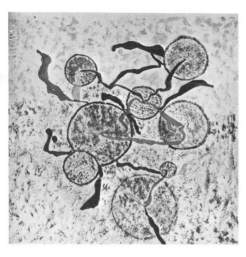

23a   G 11

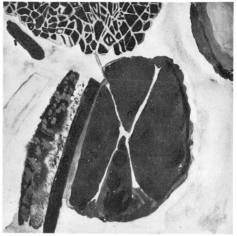

23b   G 12

'Mind-pictures'   MILHAM FORD, OXFORD (S)

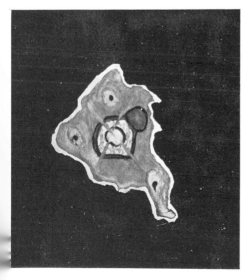

23c   G 11

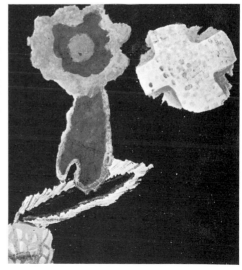

23d   G 14

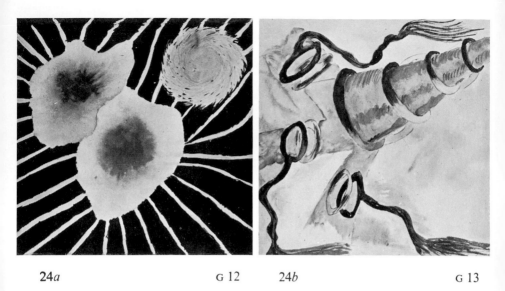

24*a*   G 12   24*b*   G 13

'*Mind-pictures*' MILHAM FORD, OXFORD (S)

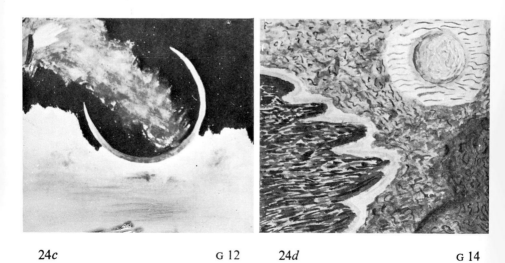

24*c*   G 12   24*d*   G 14

25a   G 14   25b   G 13

'*Mind-pictures*' MILHAM FORD, OXFORD (S)

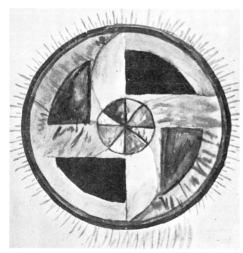

25c   **G 13**   25d   G 14

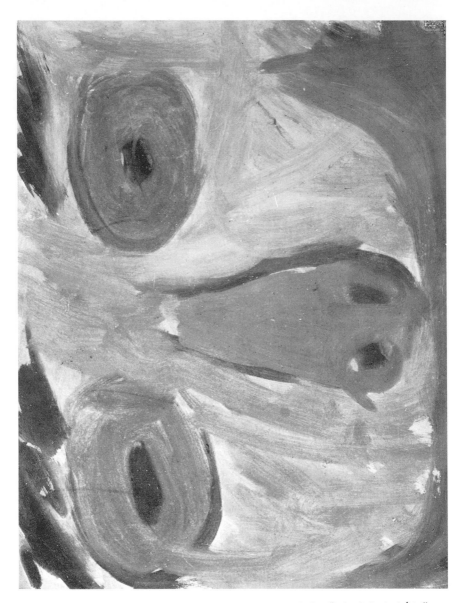

26 B 7   DOWNS SCHOOL,
COLWALL (s)

'Face'

Object and drawing space
completely fused—the ob-
ject not conceived as a
separate entity, with an environment. Introverted sensation type, with expres-
sionist (haptic) mode of
drawing. Compare Plate
37a by the same boy

27a G 13   'Earache'
DUNHURST (P)

Haptic over-emphasis of affected organ. The colouring is also expressionistic, the left half of the face being a sickly yellow, the right half an inflamed red

27b G 11   'Two Heads'
FRENSHAM HEIGHTS (S)

The expressionistic style of the introverted sensation type influenced by an intuitive awareness of structural form

28a B 10 'Samson'
ST JOHN'S JUNIOR,
RED LION SQUARE,
LONDON (E)

A perfect example of the expressionist style of the introverted sensation type. Note emphatic representation of the cheek. Reminiscent of the work of the French expressionist painter, Georges Rouault

28b B 10 'Samson'
ST JOHN'S JUNIOR,
RED LION SQUARE,
LONDON (E)

The same subject drawn by a boy of backward intellectual development. The same expressionist style. Samson is here carrying the Gates of Gaza on his shoulders, which is a more intelligent realization of the scene than

29a G 12
'The Flower Seller'
LADY MARGARET SCHOOL,
LONDON

Introverted feeling type (imaginative mode of expression) with expressionist features due to subsidiary tendencies of introverted sensation attitude

29b G 12
'Tom before he became a Water Baby'
SIR WM. PERKINS'S
SCHOOL, CHERTSEY (S)

Introverted sensation + introverted intuition = expressionist mode with structural form

30*a* B 8
'*Out for a Walk*' LEICESTER (E)
Extraverted attitude (sensation)=empathetic type of drawing

30*b* G 7
Self-portrait LEICESTER (E)
The same type. Compare Plate 50 for a more developed stage of the same style

31   B 13+   *'The Princess and the Swans'*   MILL HILL (S)

The strong feeling for rhythm suggests the extraverted intuitive type

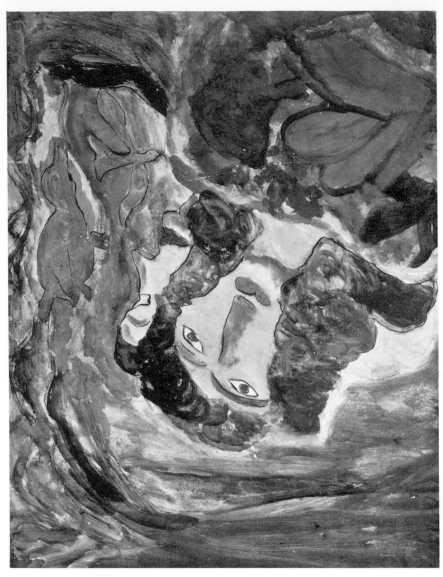

32 G 14
'*The Babes in the Wood*'
SIR WM. PERKINS'S SCHOOL,
CHERTSEY (S)

Treatment of a similar literary theme by a more introverted type
(imaginative=expressionist)

G 11   *'The Witches'*   HIGHBURY HILL (S)

ere the expressionist element tends to predominate over the imaginative. Probably introverted sensation type

34   G 11+   *'Girl at Window'*   HABERDASHERS' ASKE'S SCHOOL, ACTON

This drawing, with its extraordinarily poetic atmosphere, is probably an expression of
integration of all the mental functions of an introverted attitude. Haptic expression is sho
in the over-emphasized head and the undersized cat; imaginative expression in the associati
of images (girl, cat, tree and house); organic sensibility in the drawing of the tree and t
fluttering of the curtains; structural form in the general balance and spatial coherence of t
design. The colours show a restrained and harmonious control of purple, yellow, white a
black

35 G 14 +
'*Wild Horses*'
LANGFORD GROVE (S)

These two drawings show the persistence of the introverted attitude into the adolescent stage. The vigorous rendering of the action of the horses and the animation of the whole landscape suggests the introverted thinking type with an organic mode of expression, whereas the

second drawing, with its more summary treatment of detail and its strong contrasts, is more expressionist in style and suggests the introverted sensation type

36 B 14   *The Circus*
CHARTERHOUSE (S)

37a B 7   *'Four Trees'*   THE DOWNS SCHOOL, COLWALL (P)

37b B 9   *Landscape*   CLIFTON COLLEGE (S)

These two drawings illustrate the contrast between an extraverted sensation of landscape (*a*) and an introverted intuition of a similar subject (*b*), the first resulting in an empathetic style of painting, the second in a strong emphasis on structural form

38   **B 12**   'Concert'   BEDALES (S)   Introverted sensation type=expressionist style

39 B 14+   'The Avenue'   MILL HILL (S)

Extravert sensation type=empathetic style. (The butcher's boy, whose blue-striped smock makes such an effective contrast to the black and white snow-scene, was the boy's own addition to the set subject)

40 G 12   *'Bridling a Pony'*   THE HALL SCHOOL, WEYBRIDGE (S)

Extravert intuitive type=rhythmical pattern

41   G 16   *'Trying on Wellington Boots'*   THE HALL SCHOOL, WEYBRIDGE (S)
This strongly emphasized rhythmical pattern suggests the extraverted intuitive type

42 G 15   '*Snowballing*'   THE HALL SCHOOL, WEYBRIDGE (S)
Similar rhythmical pattern, with colour more harmonized (subsidiary tendency to extraverted sensation)

43a B 14 *Landscape* CHARTERHOUSE (S)

Reduction of the subject to structural form. Suggests introverted intuition type. Everything is built up in the same vertical plane—the plane of the picture-surface—a characteristic of certain types of primitive art

43b B 14 *'An Irish Valley'* CHARTERHOUSE (S)

By contrast, a landscape produced at the same school under the same conditions by a boy of the same age. Its expressionist style suggests an introverted sensation type

44 B 14 *Landscape* (oil) THE DOWNS SCHOOL (S)

Painted directly from nature, but with unconscious emphasis, subordination and re-adjustment. Structural form imposed on organic (introverted intuitive+thinking type). The boy is now a musician

45 G 16
'The Beach' LANGFORD GROVE (S)

Another landscape contrast (Pl. 45) is the decorative style characteristic of the extraverted feeling attitude

Pl. 46 shows structural form combined with organic style, which is the combination of attitudes (intuition + thought) which the academic tradition requires and which the average school of art tries to achieve

46 B 14
'The Farm'   BATH
SCHOOL OF ART

47　G 13　　'*Gypsies*'　　　　　　　WARRINGTON SECONDARY SCHOOL

Decorative style (? extraverted feeling type)

48   G 13   *Family Group*   WARRINGTON SECONDARY SCHOOL

This extremely sensitive drawing suggests an integrated feeling+sensation type with extravert attitude (empathetic+decorative)

49*a* B 15   *Drawing*   CRANBROOK (S)

Characteristic drawing of the introverted sensation type (with tetanoid features belonging to the physiology of this type— *cf.* p. 80)

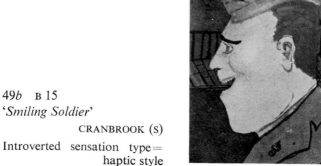

49*b* B 15
'*Smiling Soldier*'

         CRANBROOK (S)

Introverted sensation type =
         haptic style

50   G 14   *Portrait*   GIRLS' HIGH SCHOOL, WESTCLIFF (S)

Extraverted sensation type=empathetic style

51*a* B 14
Self-portrait (oil)
THE DOWNS SCHOOL,
COLWALL (S)

51*b* B 14
Self-portrait (oil)
THE DOWNS SCHOOL,
COLWALL (S)

These two portraits, done by boys of the same age under identical conditions, illustrate the contrast between the modes of expression of the introverted thinking type (*a*) with its subtle realization of the organic vitality of the subject (combined with introverted intuition of structural form) and expressionist technique of the introverted sensation type (*b*)

52   B 15   '*The Sea Lion*'   ILKLEY GRAMMAR SCHOOL (S)

Observation controlled by rhythmical pattern; extraverted intuitive type

53   G 12   *'The Sweep'*   HIGHBURY HILL HIGH SCHOOL (S)
Observation with empathetic tendency; extravert attitude (thinking+sensation)

54 G 14   '*Cat and Goldfish*'   SIR WM. PERKINS'S SCHOOL, CHERTSEY (S)

Dramatic (imaginative) reconstruction of an event, with emphasis on structural form: introverted feeling+intuition

55 G 14   '*A Vase of Imaginary Flowers*'   SIR WM. PERKINS'S SCHOOL, CHERTSEY (s)

Decorative, without much sense of form or rhythm; probably extravert feeling type (confirmed by the teacher's description of the child)

56*b* B 17
Flower Study
CHARTERHOUSE (S)
Contrasted modes of expression, produced under identical conditions. Both studies have a bold decorative intention, but whilst (*a*) is empathetic, (*b*) is wholly occupied with the two-dimensional pattern suggested by the subject (extraverted as compared with introverted treatment of the same subject)

57 *'Russian Peasants Working in the Fields'*   Margaret Power (14)

THE HALL SCHOOL, WEYBRIDGE

58

'*Ma-Ma, Da-Da, and Ba-Ba*'
Mary Major (5)
MAJOR SCHOOL,
WIGAN

59
'Girls Skipping'
Angela Lewsley
(5)

60
'Ginger and Sooty'
Jeffery Owen (6)

61

*'Partridge in a
Pear Tree'*
Janet Banks (12)
PARLIAMENT HILL
SCHOOL, LONDON

62
'The Cowboy'
Vivienne Innes (14)
LANGFORD GROVE
SCHOOL

EDUCATION THROUGH ART
HERBERT READ

63

'Margate'
Francis Thornicroft (16)
BEDALES SCHOOL

64

Landscape

Pat Parker (16)

DATE DUE

GAYLORD			PRINTED IN U.S.A.